COMPUTER
DESIGN
DEVELOPMENT
principal papers

COMPUTER
DESIGN
DEVELOPMENT
principal papers

edited by

EARL E. SWARTZLANDER, JR.
Systems Group of TRW, Inc.

HAYDEN BOOK COMPANY, INC.
Rochelle Park, New Jersey

To Joan

Library of Congress Cataloging in Publication Data

Main entry under title:

Computer design development.

   Includes index.
   1. Electronic digital computers--Addresses, essays,
lectures. I. Swartzlander, Earl E.
QA76.5.C612565   621.3819'58'2   75-30982
ISBN 0-8104-5988-4

1 2 3 4 5 6 7 8 9   PRINTING

76 77 78 79 80 81 82 83   YEAR

PREFACE

This book is a collection of many significant historical papers in the fields important to designers and users of digital computers and computer systems. The material is grouped into three somewhat overlapping areas: Logic design, arithmetic algorithms, and computer architecture.

The area of logic design includes papers on combinational logic synthesis, sequential machine design, hazard detection and elimination, and critical race-free design methods. The second part, which treats arithmetic algorithms, contains papers on high-speed arithmetic, various multiplication methods, the residue number system, and a detailed description of a high-performance floating-point processor. The final part on computer architecture is comprised of papers on computer structures, ranging from the classic von Neumann machine to array processors, and also includes papers on microprogramming and virtual memory.

This triad of topics was selected because of the editor's conviction that students should be exposed to computers in a progressive manner: starting with basic design concepts, leading into small subsystems which are implemented with the basic methods, and finally challenging the student with an introduction to complete computing systems. In view of the broad nature of each of these subject areas, and the vast amount of available material that might have been included, the editor selected a historical approach with primary emphasis on providing a balanced view of the development of the computer design field. In spite of the relative youth of the computer industry, there is much perspective to be gained from the study of historical papers that have been organized in a logical progression. Use of this collection in conjunction with any of the many available logic design or computer design texts will result in a thorough understanding of the key factors in the development of the modern digital computer.

This material is intended to be used as a supplemental text for undergraduate courses in logic design, or as a primary text for graduate level courses in computer design. It is suitable for short courses or seminars, and will also be useful to computer designers who wish to broaden their background and perspective on a self-study basis.

A secondary purpose in the preparation of this collection is to increase the accessability of these classic papers; many of the older papers are becoming very difficult to obtain. The editor hopes that the papers contained herein will serve to record the excellent work which has occurred in this vital field.

This book owes much to the help that I have received from many people, especially: Professor S. W. Maley, Professor H. C. Andrews, and Professor I. S. Reed. I appreciate the help of the staff of the Hughes

Aircraft Company Technical Library. Most importantly, I wish to express my thanks to the Hughes Doctoral Fellowship Program which gave me the opportunity to start this project.

I am happy to acknowledge many valuable conversations with friends and with my wife: these were of invaluable assistance to me. Thanks are also due to the typists who prepared the final copy, and to the Hayden Book Company for making the book possible.

Bel Air, Calif.   EARL E. SWARTZLANDER, JR.

CONTENTS

PART I. LOGIC DESIGN

PART II. ARITHMETIC ALGORITHMS

PART III. COMPUTER ARCHITECTURE

APPENDIX

COMPUTER
DESIGN
DEVELOPMENT
principal papers

PART I   LOGIC DESIGN

Before a computer or any of its major components can be designed, thorough knowledge of the techniques of logic design is required. Logic design involves two distinct types of networks; combinational networks which do not contain memory elements, and sequential networks which use memory elements to differentiate between various input sequences. Since sequential networks are combinations of memory elements and combinational feedback networks, combinational network design methods will be treated first.

A SYMBOLIC ANALYSIS OF RELAY AND SWITCHING CIRCUITS

CLAUDE E. SHANNON

The field of Boolean algebra was derived from concepts presented in 1847 by George Boole in his classic The Mathematical Analysis of Logic. Boolean algebra was enhanced considerably by many mathematicians, but it was not until after the publication of this paper that Boolean algebra gained the widespread acceptance of switching network designers. It is only fitting that this book begin with Shannon's classic work.

Shannon begins his paper with an introduction to the notion of describing the performance of a switching network in terms of the hindrance between input and output terminals. The hindrance X_{ab} of the two-terminal circuit a-b is defined as zero for a closed circuit and 1 for an open circuit. Shannon then develops an algebra for deriving the hindrance of complex networks and presents a number of theorems useful for synthesizing networks with specified hindrances. He concludes his paper with three examples.

The author has modified a portion of Section 4 to correct an error that appeared in the original paper. Although the paper is concerned exclusively with relay networks (for obvious reasons), the theorems and analytic procedures are useful for combinational network design, regardless of the final logic that will be used for implementation.

THE MAP METHOD FOR SYNTHESIS OF COMBINATIONAL LOGIC CIRCUITS

M. KARNAUGH

The map method presented in this paper facilitates visualization of combinational network operation, thus simplifying network synthesis. The basic procedure is similar to the Veitch chart minimization procedure except for the labeling of the map squares (Veitch used a binary count while Karnaugh uses a Gray code count which results in the placement of all squares for a given variable adjacent to each other.) After an introduction to the basic map method and its use for network synthesis, Karnaugh concludes by describing a simple three dimensional extension that easily accommodates up to six input variables.

MINIMIZATION OF BOOLEAN FUNCTIONS

E. J. McCLUSKEY

This paper describes the Quine-McCluskey procedure for the design of minimized logic networks. Two basic steps are required to design a minimum complexity network: (1) the prime implicants of the Boolean function are generated, and then (2) a minimal set of prime implicants is selected. The minimization criterion that McCluskey uses, i.e., minimum sum terms, may be varied to accommodate different implementation technologies. For example, with Large Scale Integration it may be best to minimize the number of terms containing more than e.g., four literals since large numbers of four input NAND gates may be readily available.

These three papers effectively summarize the theoretical material necessary for combinational circuit design and optimization; the remaining papers in this part deal with sequential network design.

A METHOD FOR SYNTHESIZING SEQUENTIAL CIRCUITS

GEORGE H. MEALY

Mealy introduced the model for a sequential network wherein the network's output and next state are functions of the input and current state. In addition to introducing this useful model, the paper describes earlier work by Huffman and Moore and gives pragmatic procedures for the synthesis of both synchronous and asynchronous machines. The basic design tool is the state or flow diagram; it clearly illustrates the effect of input changes on the internal state and the output of the network. Also it is easily manipulated to change the function of the machine or to observe the effects of abnormal input sequences, etc. The final state diagram is implemented directly with flip-flops (see also the paper in the Appendix, describing the first flip-flop) to store the machine state and combinational networks to generate the output and next state.

HAZARDS AND DELAYS IN ASYNCHRONOUS SEQUENTIAL SWITCHING CIRCUITS

S. H. UNGER

The penultimate paper of this part deals with the detection and elimination of hazards in asynchronous networks. A hazard occurs when a network generates spurious outputs in response to input changes. The problem is compounded for asynchronous networks since they may be forced into an undesired state by the spurious output. Unger defines hazards, develops theorems for detecting hazards in arbitrary networks, and concludes with detailed methods for eliminating the effect of hazards by adding at most one delay element to the feedback portion of the sequential network.

INTERNAL STATE ASSIGNMENTS FOR ASYNCHRONOUS SEQUENTIAL MACHINES

JAMES H. TRACEY

This paper is concerned with critical races in asynchronous sequential networks; a critical race exists when variations in the response-speed of the flip-flops comprising the network's memory affect the next state of the machine. Tracey presents procedures for assigning the internal state codes that eliminate critical races, although in some cases the race-free network will be more complex to implement. A minor typographical error in the original text has been corrected by the author.

The material contained in this part provides a sound introduction to the design methods generally used for both combinational and sequential networks. The major topics: Boolean algebra, Karnaugh maps, Quine-McCluskey reduction, Mealy machines, hazard elimination, and race prevention are all treated in detail. For additional information on some of the remaining problem areas in sequential machine design and use as well as a very complete (as of 1964) but somewhat cryptic bibliography, the editor suggests E. F. Moore's anthology.*

---

* E. F. Moore, <u>Sequential Machines: Selected Papers</u>, (Reading, Mass: Addison-Wesley Publishing Company, 1964.)

A SYMBOLIC ANALYSIS OF RELAY AND SWITCHING CIRCUITS

CLAUDE E. SHANNON

1. INTRODUCTION

In the control and protective circuits of complex electrical systems it is frequently necessary to make intricate interconnections of relay contacts and switches. Examples of these circuits occur in automatic telephone exchanges, industrial motor-control equipment, and in almost any circuits designed to perform complex operations automatically. In this paper a mathematical analysis of certain of the properties of such networks will be made. Particular attention will be given to the problem of network synthesis. Given certain characteristics, it is required to find a circuit incorporating these characteristics. The solution of this type of problem is not unique and methods of finding those particular circuits requiring the least number of relay contacts and switch blades will be studied. Methods will also be described for finding any number of circuits equivalent to a given circuit in all operating characteristics. It will be shown that several of the well-known theorems on impedance networks have roughly analogous theorems in relay circuits. Notable among these are the delta-wye and star-mesh transformations, and the duality theorem. The method of attack on these problems may be described briefly as follows: any circuit is represented by a set of equations, the terms of the equations corresponding to the various relays and switches in the circuit. A calculus is developed for manipulating these equations by simple mathematical processes, most of which are similar to ordinary algebraic algorisms. This calculus is shown to be exactly analogous to the calculus of propositions used in the symbolic study of logic. For the synthesis problem the desired characteristics are first written as a system of equations, and the equations are then manipulated into the form representing the simplest circuit. The circuit may then be immediately drawn from the equations. By this method it is always possible to find the simplest circuit containing only series and parallel connections, and in some cases the simplest circuit containing any type of connection.

Our notation is taken chiefly from symbolic logic. Of the many systems in common use we have chosen the one which seems simplest and most suggestive for our interpretation. Some of our phraseology, as node, mesh, delta, wye, etc., is borrowed from ordinary network theory for similar concepts in switching circuits.

2. SERIES-PARALLEL TWO-TERMINAL CIRCUITS

FUNDAMENTAL DEFINITIONS AND POSTULATES

We shall limit our treatment to circuits containing only relay contacts and switches, and therefore at any given time the circuit between any two terminals must be either open (infinite impedance) or closed (zero impedance). Let us associate a symbol X_{ab} or more

---

This paper is an abstract of a thesis presented at MIT for the degree of master of science. The author is indebted to Doctor F. L. Hitchcock, Doctor Vannevar Bush, and Doctor S. H. Caldwell, all of MIT, for helpful encouragement and criticism.

Reprinted with permission from the AIEE Transactions, Vol. 57, 1938, pp. 713-723, with corrections from the author.

simply X, with the terminals a and b. This variable, a function of time, will be called the hindrance of the two-terminal circuit a-b. The symbol 0 (zero) will be used to represent the hindrance of a closed circuit and the symbol 1 (unity) to represent the hindrance of an open circuit. Thus when the circuit a-b is open $X_{ab} = 1$ and when closed $X_{ab} = 0$. Two hindrances X_{ab} and X_{cd} will be said to be equal if whenever the circuit a-b is open, the circuit c-d is open, and whenever a-b is closed, c-d is closed. Now let the symbol + (plus) be defined to mean the series connection of the two-terminal circuits whose hindrances are added together. Thus $X_{ab} + X_{cd}$ is the hindrance of the circuit a-d when b and c are connected together. Similarly the product of two hindrances $X_{ab} \cdot X_{cd}$ or more briefly $X_{ab}X_{cd}$ will be defined to mean the hindrance of the circuit formed by connecting the circuits a-b and c-d in parallel. A relay contact or switch will be represented in a circuit by the symbol in Fig. 1, the letter being the corresponding hindrance function. Figure 2 shows the interpretation of the plus sign and Fig. 3 the multiplication sign. This

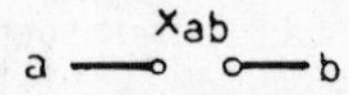

Fig. 1   Symbol for the Hindrance Function

Fig. 2   Interpretation of Addition

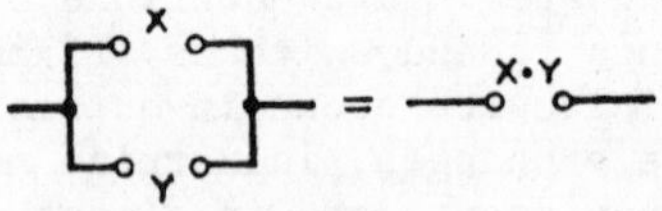

Fig. 3   Interpretation of Multiplication

choice of symbols makes the manipulation of hindrances very similar to ordinary numerical algebra.

It is evident that with the above definitions the following postulates will hold:

POSTULATES

1. a. $0 \cdot 0 = 0$
          A closed circuit in parallel with a closed circuit is a closed circuit.

    b. $1 + 1 = 1$
          An open circuit in series with an open circuit is an open circuit.

2. a. $1 + 0 = 0 + 1 = 1$
          An open circuit in series with a closed circuit in either order (i.e., whether the open circuit is to the right or left of the closed circuit) is an open circuit.

    b. $0 \cdot 1 = 1 \cdot 0 = 0$
          A closed circuit in parallel with an open circuit in either order is a closed circuit.

3. a. $0 + 0 = 0$
          A closed circuit in series with a closed circuit is a closed circuit.

    b. $1 \cdot 1 = 1$
          An open circuit in parallel with an open circuit is an open circuit.

4. At any given time either $X = 0$ or $X = 1$.

These are sufficient to develop all the theorems which will be used in connection with circuits containing only series and parallel connections. The postulates are arranged in pairs to emphasize a duality relationship between the operations of addition and multiplication and the quantities zero and one. Thus, if in any of the a postulates the zero's are replaced by one's and the multiplications by additions, and vice versa, the corresponding b postulate will result. This fact is of great importance. It gives each theorem a dual theorem, it being necessary to prove only one to establish both. The only one of these postulates which differs from ordinary algebra is 1b. However, this enables great simplifications in the manipulation of these symbols.

In this section a number of theorems governing the combination of hindrances will be given. Inasmuch as any of the theorems may be proved by a very simple process, the proofs will not be given except for an illustrative example. The method of proof is that of "perfect induction," i.e., the verification of the theorem for all possible cases. Since by postulate 4 each variable is limited to the values 0 and 1, this is a simple matter. Some of the theorems may be proved more elegantly by recourse to previous theorems, but the method of perfect induction is so universal that it is probably to be preferred.

$$X + Y = Y + X \tag{1a}$$
$$XY = YX \tag{1b}$$
$$X + (Y + Z) = (X + Y) + Z \tag{2a}$$
$$X(YZ) = (XY)Z \tag{2b}$$
$$X(Y + Z) = XY + XZ \tag{3a}$$
$$X + YZ = (X + Y)(X + Z) \tag{3b}$$
$$1 \cdot X = X \tag{4a}$$
$$0 + X = X \tag{4b}$$
$$1 + X = 1 \tag{5a}$$
$$0 \cdot X = 0 \tag{5b}$$

For example, to prove theorem 4a, note that X is either 0 or 1. If it is 0, the theorem follows from postulate 2b; if 1, it follows from postulate 3b. Theorem 4b now follows by the duality

principle, replacing the 1 by 0 and the · by +.

Due to the associative laws (2a and 2b) parentheses may be omitted in a sum or product of several terms without ambiguity. The Σ and Π symbols will be used as in ordinary algebra.

The distributive law (3a) makes it possible to "multiply out" products and to factor sums. The dual of this theorem (3b), however, is not true in numerical algebra.

We shall now define a new operation to be called negation. The negative of a hindrance X will be written X' and is defined as a variable which is equal to 1 when X equals 0 and equal to 0 when X equals 1. If X is the hindrance of the make contacts of a relay, then X' is the hindrance of the break contacts of the same relay. The definition of the negative of a hindrance gives the following theorems:

$$X + X' = 1 \tag{6a}$$
$$XX' = 0 \tag{6b}$$
$$0' = 1 \tag{7a}$$
$$1' = 0 \tag{7b}$$
$$(X')' = X \tag{8}$$

ANALOGUE WITH THE CALCULUS OF PROPOSITIONS

We are now in a position to demonstrate the equivalence of this calculus with certain elementary parts of the calculus of propositions. The algebra of logic[1-3] originated by George Boole, is a symbolic method of investigating logical relationships. The symbols of Boolean algebra admit of two logical interpretations. If interpreted in terms of classes, the variables are not limited to the two possible values 0 and 1. This interpretation is known as the algebra of classes. If, however, the terms are taken to represent propositions, we have the calculus of propositions in which variables are

---

1. For all numbered references, see list at end of paper.

Table 1.

Analog Between the Calculus of
Propositions and the Symbolic Relay Analysis

Symbol	Interpretation in Relay Circuits	Interpretation in the Calculus of Propositions
X	The circuit X	The proposition X
0	The circuit is closed	The proposition is false
1	The circuit is open	The proposition is true
X + Y	The series connection of circuits X Y	The proposition which is true if either X or Y is true
XY	The parallel connection of circuits X and Y	The proposition which is true if both X and Y are true
X'	The circuit which is open when X is closed and closed when X is open	The contradictory of proposition X
=	The circuits open and close simultaneously	Each proposition implies the other

limited to the values 0 and 1,[*] as are the hindrance functions above. Usually the two subjects are developed simultaneously from the same set of postulates, except for the addition in the case of the calculus of propositions of a postulate equivalent to postulate 4 above. E. V. Huntington[4] gives the following set of postulates for symbolic logic:

1. The class K contains at least two distinct elements.
2. If a and b are in the class K then $a + b$ is in the class K.
3. $a + b = b + a$.
4. $(a + b) + c = a + (b + c)$
5. $a + a = a$
6. $ab + ab' = a$ where ab is defined as $(a' + b')'$

If we let the class K be the class consisting of the two elements 0 and 1, then these postulates follow from those given in the first section. Also postulates 1, 2, and 3 given there can be deduced from Huntington's postulates. Adding 4 and restricting our discussion to the calculus of propositions, it is evident that a perfect analogy exists between the calculus for switching circuits and this branch of symbolic logic.[**] The two interpretations of the symbols are shown in Table 1.

Due to this analogy any theorem of the calculus of propositions is

---

[*] This refers only to the classical theory of the calculus of propositions. Recently some work has been done with logical systems in which propositions may have more than two "truth values".

[**] This analogy may also be seen from a slightly different viewpoint. Instead of associating X_{ab} directly with the circuit a-b let X_{ab} represent the proposition that the circuit a-b is open. Then all the symbols are directly interpreted as propositions and the operations of addition and multiplication will be seen to represent series and parallel connections.

also a true theorem if interpreted in terms of relay circuits. The remaining theorems in this section are taken directly from this field.

De Morgan's theorem:

$$(X + Y + Z \ldots)' = X' \cdot Y' \cdot Z' \ldots \qquad (9a)$$

$$(X \cdot Y \cdot Z \ldots)' = X' + Y' + Z' + \ldots \qquad (9b)$$

This theorem gives the negative of a sum or product in terms of the negatives of the summands or factors. It may be easily verified for two terms by substituting all possible values and then extended to any number n of variables by mathematical induction.

A function of certain variables $X_1, X_2 \ldots \ldots X_n$ is any expression formed from the variables with the operations of addition, multiplication and negation. The notation $f(X_1, X_2, \ldots \ldots X_n)$ will be used to represent a function. Thus we might have f (X, Y, Z) = XY + X' (Y' + Z'). In infinitesimal calculus it is shown that any function (providing it is continuous and all derivatives are continuous) may be expanded in a Taylor series. A somewhat similar expansion is possible in the calculus of propositions. To develop the series expansion of functions first note the following equations.

$$f(X_1, X_2, \ldots X_n) = X_1 \cdot f(1, X_2 \ldots X_n) + X_1' \cdot f(0, X_2 \ldots X_n) \qquad (10a)$$

$$f(X_1 \ldots X_n) = [f(0, X_2 \ldots X_n) + X_1] \cdot [f(1, X_2 \ldots X_n) + X_1'] \qquad (10b)$$

These reduce to identities if we let X_1 equal either 0 or 1. In these equations the function f is said to be expanded about X_1. The coefficients of X_1 and X_1 in 10a are functions of the (n − 1) variables $X_2 \ldots X_n$ and may thus be expanded about any of these variables in the same manner. The additive terms in 10b also may be expanded in this manner. Expanding about X_2 we have:

$$f(X_1 \ldots X_n) = X_1 X_2 f(1, 1, X_3 \ldots X_n) +$$
$$X_1 X_2' f(1, 0, X_3 \ldots X_n) +$$
$$X_1' X_2 f(0, 1, X_3 \ldots X_n) +$$
$$X_1' X_2' f(0, 0, X_3 \ldots X_n) \qquad (11a)$$

$$f(X_1 \ldots X_n) = [X_1 + X_2 + f(0, 0, X_3 \ldots X_n)] .$$
$$[X_1 + X_2' + f(0, 1, X_3 \ldots X_n)] .$$
$$[X_1' + X_2 + f(1, 0, X_3 \ldots X_n)] .$$
$$[X_1' + X_2' + f(1, 1, X_3 \ldots X_n)] \qquad (11b)$$

Continuing this process n times we will arrive at the complete series expansion having the form:

$$f(X_1 \ldots X_n) = f(1, 1, 1 \ldots 1) X_1 X_2 \ldots X_n + f(0, 1, 1 \ldots 1) X_1' X_2 \ldots X_n + \ldots + f(0, 0, 0 \ldots 0) X_1 X_2' \ldots X_n' \qquad (12a)$$

$$f(X_1 \ldots X_n) = [X_1 + X_2 + \ldots X_n + f(0, 0, 0 \ldots 0)] \cdot \ldots \cdot [X_1' + X_2' \ldots + X_n' + f(1, 1 \ldots 1)] \qquad (12b)$$

By 12a, f is equal to the sum of the products formed by permuting primes on the terms of $X_1 X_2 \ldots X_n$ in all possible ways and giving each product a coefficient equal to the value of the function when that product is 1. Similarly for 12b.

As an application of the series expansion it should be noted that if we wish to find a circuit representing any given function we can always expand the function by either 10a or 10b in such a way that any given variable appears at most twice, once as a make contact and once as a break contact. This is shown in Fig. 4. Similarly by 11 any other variable need appear no more than four times (two make and two break contacts), etc.

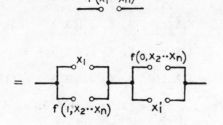

Fig. 4   Expansion About One
          Variable

A generalization of De Morgan's
theorem is represented symbolically in
the following equation:

$$f(X_1, X_2 \ldots X_n, +, \cdot)' =$$
$$f(X_1', X_2' \ldots X_n', \cdot, +) \qquad (13)$$

By this we mean that the negative of
any function may be obtained by replacing each variable by its negative and
interchanging the + and · symbols.
Explicit and implicit parentheses will,
of course, remain in the same places.
For example, the negative of $X + Y \cdot (Z + WX')$ will be $X'[Y' + Z'(W' + X)]$.
Some other theorems useful in
simplifying expressions are given below:

$$X = X + X = X + X + X = \text{etc.} \qquad (14a)$$

$$X = X \cdot X = X \cdot X \cdot X - \text{etc.} \qquad (14b)$$

$$X + XY = X \qquad (15a)$$

$$X(X + Y) = X \qquad (15b)$$

$$XY + X'Z = XY + X'Z + YZ \qquad (16a)$$

$$(X + Y)(X' + Z) =$$
$$(X + Y)(X' + Z)(Y + Z) \qquad (16b)$$

$$Xf(X, Y, Z, \ldots) = Xf(1, Y, Z, \ldots) \qquad (17a)$$

$$X + f(X, Y, Z, \ldots) = X + f(0, Y, Z, \ldots) \qquad (17b)$$

$$X'f(X, Y, Z, \ldots) = X'f(0, Y, Z, \ldots) \qquad (18a)$$

$$X' + f(X, Y, Z, \ldots) = X' + f(1, Y, Z, \ldots) \qquad (18b)$$

All of these theorems may be
proved by the method of perfect induction.

Any expression formed with the
operations of addition, multiplication,
and negation represents explicitly a
circuit containing only series and
parallel connections. Such a circuit
will be called a series-parallel circuit. Each letter in an expression of
this sort represents a make or break
relay contact, or a switch blade and
contact. To find the circuit requiring
the least number of contacts, it is
therefore necessary to manipulate the
expression into the form in which the
least number of letters appear. The
theorems given above are always sufficient to do this. A little practice
in the manipulation of these symbols is
all that is required. Fortunately most
of the theorems are exactly the same as
those of numerical algebra--the associative, commutative, and distributive
laws of algebra hold here. The writer
has found theorems 3, 6, 9, 14, 15,
16a, 17, and 18 to be especially useful
in the simplification of complex
expressions.

Frequently a function may be
written in several ways, each requiring
the same minimum number of elements.
In such a case the choice of circuit
may be arbitrarily from among these, or
from other considerations.

As an example of the simplification of expressions consider the circuit shown in Fig. 5. The hindrance
function X_{ab} for this circuit will be:

$$X_{ab} = W + W'(X + Y) + (X + Z) \cdot$$
$$(S + W' + Z) (Z' + Y + S'V)$$

$$= W + X + Y + (X + Z) \cdot$$

$$(S + 1 + Z) (Z' + Y + S'V)$$

$$= W + X + Y + Z \cdot (Z' + S'V)$$

These reductions were made with 17b using first W, then X and Y as the "X" of 17b. Now multiplying out:

$$X_{ab} = W + X + Y + ZZ' + ZS'V$$

$$= W + X + Y + ZS'V \quad .$$

The circuit corresponding to this expression is shown in Fig. 6. Note the large reduction in the number of elements.

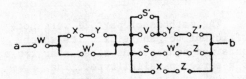

Fig. 5 Circuit to be Simplified

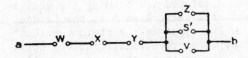

Fig. 6 Simplification of Fig. 5

It is convenient in drawing circuits to label a relay with the same letter as the hindrance of make contacts of the relay. Thus if a relay is connected to a source of voltage through a network whose hindrance function is X, the relay and any make contacts on it would be labeled X. Break contacts would be labeled X'. This assumes that the relay operates instantly and that the make contacts close and the break contacts open simultaneously. Cases in which there is a time delay will be treated later.

3. MULTITERMINAL AND NON-SERIES-PARALLEL CIRCUITS

EQUIVALENCE OF n-TERMINAL NETWORKS

The usual relay control circuit will take the form of Fig. 7, where X_1, X_2, ... X_n are relays or other devices controlled by the circuit and N is a network of relay contacts and switches. It is desirable to find transformations that may be applied to N which will keep the operation of all the relays X_1 ... X_n the same. So far we have only considered transformations which may be applied to a two-terminal network keeping the operation of one relay in series with this network the same. To this end we define equivalence of n-terminal networks as follows. Definition: Two n-terminal networks M and N will be said to be equivalent with respect to these n terminals if and only if $X_{jk} = Y_{jk}$; j, k = 1, 2, 3...n, where X_{jk} is the hindrance of N (considered a two-terminal network) between terminals j and k, and Y_{jk} is that for M between the corresponding terminals. Under this definition the equivalences of the preceding sections were with respect to two terminals.

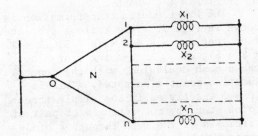

Fig. 7 General Constant-Voltage Relay Circuit

STAR-MESH AND DELTA-WYE TRANSFORMATIONS

As in ordinary network theory there exist star-to-mesh and delta-to-wye transformations. In impedance circuits these transformations, if they

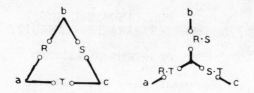

Fig. 8 Delta-Wye Transformation

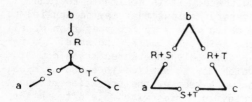

Fig. 9 Wye-Delta Transformation

exist, are unique. In hindrance networks the transformations always exist
and are not unique. Those given here
are the simplest in that they require
the least number of elements. The
delta-to-wye transformation is shown
in Fig. 8. These two networks are
equivalent with respect to the three
terminals a, b, and c, since by the
distributive law X_{ab} = R(S + T) = RS
+ RT and similarly for the other pairs
of terminals a-c and b-c.

The wye-to-delta transformation is
shown in Fig. 9. This follows from the
fact that X_{ab} = R + S = (R + S) (R + T
+ T + S), etc. An n-point star also
has a mesh equivalent with the central
junction point eliminated. This is
formed exactly as in the simple three-
point star, by connecting each pair of
terminals of the mesh through a hindrance which is the sum of the corresponding arms of the star. This may be
proved by mathematical induction. We
have shown it to be true for n = 3.
Now assuming it true for n - 1, we
shall prove it for n. Suppose we construct a mesh circuit from the given
n - point star according to this method.
Each corner of the mesh will be an
n - 1-point star and since we have
assumed the theorem true for n - 1 we
may replace the nth corner by its mesh

equivalent. If Y_{oj} was the hindrance
of the original star from the central
node 0 to the point j, then the reduced
mesh will have the hindrance (Y_{os} +
Y_{or})·(Y_{os} + Y_{on} + Y_{or} + Y_{on}) connecting
nodes r and s. But this reduces to
$Y_{os}Y_{or}$ which is the correct value,
since the original n-point star with
the nth arm deleted becomes an n - 1-
point star and by our assumption may
be replaced by a mesh having this
hindrance connecting nodes r and s.
Therefore the two networks are equivalent with respect to the first n - 1
terminals. By eliminating other nodes
than the nth, or by symmetry, the
equivalence with respect to all n terminals is demonstrated.

HINDRANCE FUNCTION OF A NON-SERIES-
PARALLEL NETWORK

The methods of part II were not
sufficient to handle circuits which
contained connections other than those
of a series-parallel type. The
"bridge" of Fig. 10, for example, is
a non-series-parallel network. These
networks will be treated by first reducing to an equivalent series-parallel circuit. Three methods have
been developed for finding the equivalent of a network such as the bridge.

The first is the obvious method
of applying the transformations until
the network is of the series-parallel
type and then writing the hindrance
function by inspection. This process
is exactly the same as is used in
simplifying the complex impedance
networks. To apply this to the circuit of Fig. 10, first we may eliminate

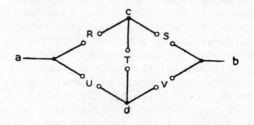

Fig. 10 Non-Series-Parallel Circuit

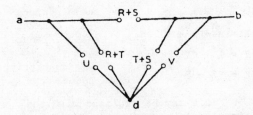

Fig. 11   Hindrance Function by
Means of Transformations

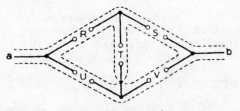

Fig. 12   Hindrance Function as a
Product of Sums

the node c, by applying the star-to-mesh transformation to the star a-c, b-c, d-c. This gives the network of Fig. 11. The hindrance function may be written down from inspection for this network.

$$X_{ab} = (R + S)[U(R + T) + V(T + S)]$$

This may be written:

$$X_{ab} = RU + SV + RTV + STU$$
$$= R(U + TV) + S(V + TU)$$

The second method of analysis is to draw all possible paths between the points under consideration through the network. These paths are drawn along the lines representing the component hindrance elements of the circuit. If any one of these paths has zero hindrance, the required function must be zero. Hence if the result is written as a product, the hindrance of each path will be a factor of this product. The required result may therefore be written as the product of the hindrances of all possible paths between the two points. Paths which touch the same point more than once need not be considered. In Fig. 12 this method is applied to the bridge. The paths are shown dotted. The function is therefore given by:

$$X_{ab} = (R + S)(U + V)(R + T + V) \cdot$$
$$(U + T + S)$$

$$= RU + SV + RTV + UTS$$

$$= R(U + TV) + S(V + TU)$$

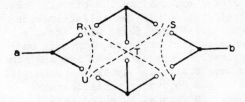

Fig. 13   Hindrance Function as a
Sum of Products

The same result is thus obtained as with the first method.

The third method is to draw all possible lines which would break the circuit between the points under consideration, making the lines go through the hindrances of the circuit. The result is written as a sum, each term corresponding to a certain line. These terms are the products of all the hindrances on the line. The justification of the method is similar to that for the second method. This method is applied to the bridge in Fig. 13.

This again gives for the hindrance of the network:

$$X_{ab} = RU + SV + RTV + STU$$
$$= R(U + TV) + S(V + TU)$$

The third method is usually the most convenient and rapid, for it gives the result directly as a sum. It seems much easier to handle sums than products due, no doubt, to the fact that in ordinary algebra we have the distributive law X(Y + Z) - XY + XZ, but not its dual X + YZ = (X + Y)(X + Z). It is, however, sometimes difficult to apply the third method to nonplanar

networks (networks which cannot be
drawn on a plane without crossing
lines) and in this case one of the
other two methods may be used.

SIMULTANEOUS EQUATIONS

In analyzing a given circuit it is
convenient to divide the various variables into two classes. Hindrance elements which are directly controlled by
a source external to the circuit under
consideration will be called independent variables. These will include
hand-operated switches, contacts on
external relays, etc. Relays and other
devices controlled by the network will
be called dependent variables. We
shall, in general, use the earlier
letters of the alphabet to represent
independent variables and the later
letters for dependent variables. In
Fig. 7 the dependent variables are X_1,
$X_2 \ldots X_n$. X_k will evidently be operated if and only if $X_{ok} = 0$, where X_{ok}
is the hindrance function of N between
terminals o and k. That is:

$$X_k = X_{ok} \qquad k = 1, 2, \ldots n$$

This is a system of equations which
completely define the operation of the
system. The right-hand members will
be known functions involving the various dependent and independent variables
and given the starting conditions and
the values of the independent variables
the dependent variables may be computed.

A transformation will now be described for reducing the number of elements required to realize a set of
simultaneous equations. This transformation keeps X_{ok} (k = 1, 2 ... n) in-
variant, but X_{jk} (j, k = 1, 2 ... n)
may be changed, so that the new network may not be equivalent in the
strict sense defined to the old one.
The operation of all the relays will
be the same, however. This simplification is only applicable if the X_{ok}
functions are written as sums and
certain terms are common to two or
more equations. For example suppose
the set of equations is as follows:

$$W = A + B + CW$$

$$X = A + B + WX$$

$$Y = A + CY$$

$$Z = EZ + F$$

This may be realized with the
circuit of Fig. 14, using only one A
element for the three places where A
occurs and only one B element for its
two appearances. The justification is
quite obvious. This may be indicated
symbolically by drawing a vertical line
after the terms common to the various
equations, as shown below.

$$
\begin{array}{lll}
W & = & \quad|\ B +\ |\ CW \\
X & = A +\ |\quad\ |\ WX \\
Y & = & \quad|\ CY \\
Z & = F +\ EZ
\end{array}
$$

It follows from the principle of
duality that if we had defined multiplication to represent series connection, and addition for parallel connection, exactly the same theorems of
manipulation would be obtained. There
were two reasons for choosing the definitions given. First, as has been
metnioned, it is easier to manipulate
sums than products and the transformation just described can only be
applied to sums (for constant-current
relay circuits this condition is exactly reversed), and second, this choice
makes the hindrance functions closely
analogous to impedances. Under the

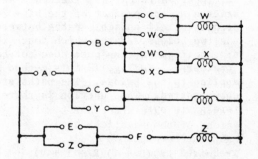

Fig. 14   Example of Reduction of
Simultaneous Equations

alternative definitions they would be more similar to admittances, which are less commonly used.

Sometimes the relation $XY' = 0$ obtains between two relays X and Y. This is true if Y can operate only if X is operated. This frequently occurs in what is known as a sequential system. In a circuit of this type the relays can only operate in a certain order or sequence, the operation of one relay in general "preparing" the circuit so that the next in order can operate. If X precedes Y in the sequence and both are constrained to remain operated until the sequence is finished then this condition will be fulfilled. In such a case the following equations hold and may sometimes be used for simplification of expressions. If $XY' = 0$, then

$$X'Y' = Y'$$
$$XY = X$$
$$X' + Y = 1$$
$$X' + Y' = X'$$
$$X + Y = Y$$

These may be proved by adding $XY' = 0$ to the left-hand member or multiplying it by $X' + Y = 1$, thus not changing the value. For example to prove the first one, add XY' to $X'Y'$ and factor.

SPECIAL TYPES OF RELAYS AND SWITCHES

In certain types of circuits it is necessary to preserve a definite sequential relation in the operation of the contacts of a relay. This is done with make-before-break (or continuity) and break-make (or transfer) contacts. In handling this type of circuit the simplest method seems to be to assume in setting up the equations that the make and break contacts operate simultaneously, and after all simplifications of the equations have been made and the resulting circuit drawn, the required type of contact sequence is found from inspection.

Relays having a time delay in operating or deoperating may be treated similarly or by shifting the time axis. Thus if a relay coil is connected to a battery through a hindrance X, and the relay has a delay of p seconds in operating and releasing, then the hindrance function of the contacts of the relay will also be X, but at a time p seconds later. This may be indicated by writing $X(t)$ for the hindrance in series with the relay, and $X(t - p)$ for that of the relay contacts.

There are many special types of relays and switches for particular purposes, such as the stepping switches and selector switches of various sorts, multiwinding relays, cross-bar switches, etc. The operation of all these types may be described with the words "or," "and," "if," "operated," and "not operated." This is a sufficient condition that they may be described in terms of hindrance functions with the operations of addition, multiplication, negation, and equality. Thus a two-winding relay might be so constructed that it is operated if the first or the second winding is operated (activated) and the first and the second windings are not operated. If the first winding is X and the second Y, the hindrance function of make contacts on the relay will then be $XY + X'Y'$. Usually, however, these special relays occur only at the end of a complex circuit and may be omitted entirely from the calculations to be added after the rest of the circuit is designed.

Sometimes a relay X is to operate when a circuit R closes and to remain closed independent of R until a circuit S opens. Such a circuit is known as a lock-in circuit. Its equation is:

$$X = RX + S$$

Replacing X by X' gives:

$$X' = RX' + S$$

or

$$X = (R' + X)S'$$

In this case X is opened when R closes and remains open until S opens.

4. SYNTHESIS OF NETWORKS

SOME GENERAL THEOREMS ON NETWORKS AND FUNCTIONS[*]

It has been shown that any function may be expanded in a series consisting of a sum of products, each product being of the form $X_1 X_2 \ldots X_n$ with some permutation of primes on the letters, and each product having the coefficient 0 or 1. Now since each of the n variables may or may not have a prime, there is a total of 2^n different products of this form. Similarly each product may have the coefficient 0 or the coefficient 1 so there are 2^{2^n} possible sums of this sort. Hence we have the theorem: The number of functions obtainable from n variables is 2^{2^n}.

Each of these sums will represent a different function, but some of the functions may actually involve less than n variables (that is, they are of such a form that for one or more of the n variables, say X_k, we have identically $f\big|_{xk=0} = f\big|_{xk=1}$ so that under no conditions does the value of the function depend on the value X_k). Thus for two variables, X and Y, among the 16 functions obtained will be X, Y, X', Y', 0, and 1 which do not involve both X and Y. To find the number of functions which actually involve all of the n variables we proceed as follows Let $\phi(n)$ be the number. Then by the theorem just given:

$$2^{2^n} = \sum_{k=0}^{n} \binom{n}{k} \phi(k)$$

where $\binom{n}{k} = n!/k!(n-k)!$ is the number of combinations of n things taken k at a time. That is, the total number of functions obtainable from n variables is equal to the sum of the numbers of those functions obtainable from each possible selection of variables from these n which actually in-

---

* This section has been revised by the author from the original 1938 paper, which contained an error.

volve all the variables in the selection. Solving for $\phi(n)$ gives:

$$\phi(n) = 2^{2^n} - \sum_{k=0}^{n-1} \binom{n}{k} \phi(k)$$

By substituting for $\phi(n-1)$ on the right the similar expression found by replacing n by n - 1 in this equation, then similarly substituting for $\phi(n-2)$ in the expression thus obtained, etc., an equation may be obtained involving only $\phi(n)$. This equation may then be simplified to the form:

$$\phi(n) = \sum_{k=0}^{n} \binom{n}{k} 2^{2^k} (-1)^{n-k}$$

As n increases this expression approaches its leading term 2^{2^n} asymptotically. The error in using only this term for n = 5 is less than 0.01 per cent.

An interesting function of two variables is the sum modulo two or disjunct of the variables. This function is written $X_1 \oplus X_2$ and is defined by the equation:

$$X_1 \oplus X_2 = X_1 X_2' + X_1' X_2$$

It is easy to show that the sum modulo two obeys the commutative, associative, and the distributive law with respect to multiplication, that is,

$$X_1 \oplus X_2 = X_2 \oplus X_1$$

$$(X_1 \oplus X_2) \oplus X_3 = X_1 \oplus (X_2 \oplus X_3)$$

$$X_1 (X_2 \oplus X_3) = X_1 X_2 \oplus X_1 X_3$$

Also:

$$(X_1 \oplus X_2)' = X_1 \oplus X_2' = X_1' \oplus X_2$$

$$X_1 \oplus 0 = X_1$$

$$X_1 \oplus 1 = X_1'$$

Since the sum modulo two obeys the associative law, we may omit parentheses in a sum of several terms without ambiguity. The sum modulo two of the n variables X_1, X_2 ... X_n will for convenience be written:

$$X_1 \oplus X_2 \oplus X_3 \cdots \oplus X_n = \overset{n}{\underset{k=1}{\Xi}} \; X_k$$

We shall now find an upper bound for the number of contacts required in realizing any switching functions of n variables.

Theorem: Any switching function of n variables $f(X_1, X_2, ..., X_n)$ can be realized in a series parallel circuit with not more than $(3 \cdot 2^{n-1}-2)$ elements (relay contacts).

This will be proved by mathematical induction. It is certainly true for n = 1 since the only possible functions of one variable are 0, 1, X and X' and these can all be realized with one contact or less. Now assume the theorem true for n - 1. Any function of n variables can be expanded:

$$f(X_1, X_2, ..., X_n) =$$
$$X_n f_1(X_1, X_2, ..., X_{n-1})$$
$$+ X_n' f_2(X_1, X_2, ..., X_{n-1}).$$

f_1 and f_2 are functions of n - 1 variables and by the inductive assumption require at most $3 \cdot 2^{n-2}-2$ contacts. The circuit of Fig. 4 (middle), corresponding to this expansion, then requires not more than

$$2(3 \cdot 2^{n-2}-2) + 2 = 3 \cdot 2^{n-1}-2$$

contacts. Thus the theorem is true for n, completing the proof.

DUAL NETWORKS

The negative of any network may be found by De Morgan's theorem, but the network must first be transformed into an equivalent series-parallel circuit

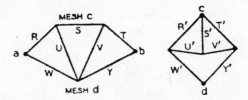

Fig. 15 (left) Planar Network for Illustration of Duality Theorem

Fig. 16 (right) Dual of Fig. 15

(unless it is already of this type). A theorem will be developed with which the negative of any planar two-terminal circuit may be found directly. As a corollary a method of finding a constant-current circuit equivalent to a given constant-voltage circuit and vice versa will be given.

Let N represent a planar network of hindrances, with the function X_{ab} between the terminals a and b which are on the outer edge of the network. For definiteness consider the network of Fig. 15 (here the hindrances are shown merely as lines).

Now let M represent the dual of N as found by the following process; for each contour or mesh of N assign a node or junction point of M. For each element of N, say X_k, separating the contours r and s there corresponds an element X_k connecting the nodes r and s of M. The area exterior to N is to be considered as two meshes, c and d, corresponding to nodes c and d of M. Thus the dual of Fig. 15 is the network of Fig. 16.

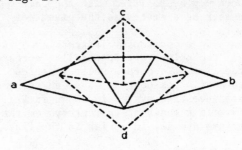

Fig. 17 Superposition of a Network and its Dual

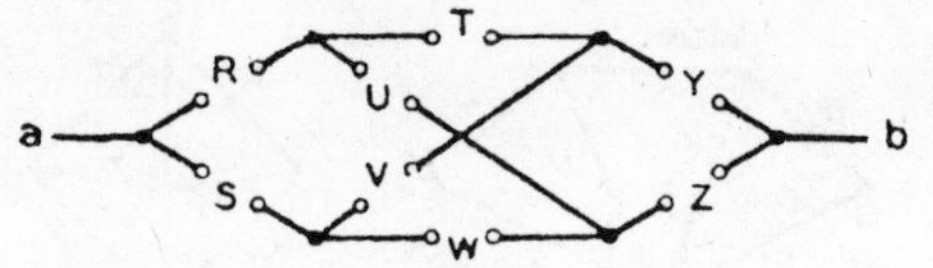

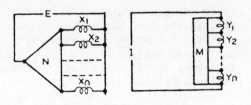

Fig. 18 Nonplanar Network

Fig. 19 (left) General Constant-
         Voltage Relay Circuit

Fig. 20 (right) General Constant-
         Current Relay Circuit

    Theorem: If M and N bear this du-
ality relationship, then $X_{ab} = X'_{cd}$.
To prove this, let the network M be
superimposed upon N, the nodes of M
within the corresponding meshes of N
and corresponding elements crossing.
For the network of Fig. 15, this is
shown in Fig. 17 with N solid and M
dotted. Incidentally, the easiest
method of finding the dual of a network (whether of this type or an
impedance network) is to draw the required network superimposed on the
given network. Now, if $X_{ab} = 0$, then
there must be some path from a to b
along the lines of N such that every
element on this path equals zero. But
this path represents a path across M
dividing the circuit from c to d along
which every element of M is one.
Hence $X_{cd} = 1$. On the other, if X_{ab}
= 1, there must be a path across N
(as in Fig. 13) with all elements one.
This corresponds to a path along the
elements of M from c to d with all
elements zero. Hence $X_{cd} = 0$, and it
follows that $X_{ab} = X'_{cd}$.
    It is evident from this theorem
that a negative for any planar network may be realized with the same
number of elements as the given network.†
    In a constant-voltage relay system
all the relays are in parallel across
the line. To open a relay a series
connection is opened. The general constant-voltage system is shown in Fig.
19. In a constant-current system the
relays are all in series in the line.

---

† This is not in general true if the
word "planar" is omitted. The nonplanar network X_{ab}, of Fig. 18, for
example, has no negative containing
only eight elements.

To de-operate a relay it is short-cir-
cuited. The general constant-current
circuit corresponding to Fig. 19 is
shown in Fig. 20. If the relay Y_k of
Fig. 20 is to be operated whenever the
relay X_k of Fig. 19 is operated and not
otherwise, then evidently the hindrance
in parallel with Y_k which short-cir-
cuits it must be the negative of the
hindrance in series with X_k which con-
nects it across the voltage source. If
this is true for all the relays, we
shall say that the constant-current and
constant-voltage systems are equivalent.
The above theorem may be used to find
equivalent circuits of this sort, for
if we make the networks N and M of
Figs. 19 and 20 duals in the sense described, with X_k and Y_k as corresponding elements, then the condition will
be satisfied. A simple example of
this is shown in Figs. 21 and 22.

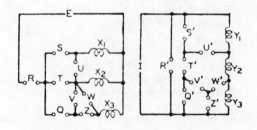

Fig. 21 (left) Simple Constant-
         Voltage System

Fig. 22 (right) Constant-Current
         System Equivalent to Fig. 21

SYNTHESIS OF THE GENERAL SYMMETRIC FUNCTION

It has been shown that any function represents explicitly a series-parallel circuit. The series-parallel realization may require more elements, however, than some other network representing the same function. In this section a method will be given for finding a circuit representing a certain type of function which in general is much more economical of elements than the best series-parallel circuit. This type of function is known as a symmetric function and appears frequently in relay circuits.

Definition: A function of the n variables X_1, X_2, ... X_n is said to be symmetric in these variables if any interchange of the variables leaves the function identically the same. Thus $XY + XZ + YZ$ is symmetric in the variables X, Y, and Z. Since any permutation of variables may be obtained by successive interchanges of two variables, a necessary and sufficient condition that a function be symmetric is that any interchange of two variables leaves the function unaltered.

By proper selection of the variables many apparently unsymmetric functions may be made symmetric. For example, $XY'Z + X'YZ + X'Y'Z'$ although not symmetric in X, Y, and Z is symmetric in X, Y, and Z'. It is also sometimes possible to write an unsymmetric function as a symmetric function multiplied by a simple term or added to a simple term. In such a case the symmetric part may be realized with the methods to be described, and the additional term supplied as a series or parallel connection.

The following theorem forms the basis of the method of design which has been developed.

Theorem: A necessary and sufficient condition that a function be symmetric is that it may be specified by stating a set of numbers a_1, a_2, ... a_k such that if exactly a_j (j = 1, 2, 3 ... k) of the variables are zero, then the function is zero and not otherwise. This follows easily

from the definition. The set of numbers a_1, a_2, ... a_k may be any set of numbers selected from the numbers 0 to n, inclusive, where n is the number of variables in the symmetric function. For convenience, they will be called the a-numbers of the function. The symmetric function $XY + XZ + YZ$ has the a-numbers 2 and 3, since the function is zero if just two of the variables are zero or if three are zero, but not if none or if one is zero. To find the a-numbers of a given symmetric function it is merely necessary to evaluate the function with 0, 1 ... n of the variables zero. Those numbers for which the result is zero are the a-numbers of the function.

Theorem: There are 2^{n+1} symmetric functions of n variables. This follows from the fact that there are n + 1 numbers, each of which may be taken or not in our selection of a-numbers. Two of the functions are trivial, however, namely, those in which all and none of the numbers are taken. These give the "functions" 0 and 1, respectively. The symmetric function of the n-variables X_1, X_2 ... X_n with the a-numbers a_1, a_2 ... a_k will be written $S_{a_1 a_2 ... a_k}$ $(X_1, X_2 ... X_n)$. Thus the example given would be $S_{2,3}(X, Y, Z)$. The circuit which has been developed for realizing the general symmetric function is based on the a-numbers of the function and we shall now assume that they are known.

Theorem: The sum of two given symmetric functions of the same set of variables, is a symmetric function of these variables having for a-numbers those numbers common to the two given functions. Thus $S_{1,2,3}(X_1 ... X_6) + S_{2,3,5}(X_1 ... X_6) = S_{2,3}(X_1 ... X_6)$.

Theorem: The product of two given symmetric functions of the same set of variables is a symmetric function of these variables with all the numbers appearing in either or both of the given functions for a-numbers. Thus $S_{1,2,3}(X_1 ... X_6) \cdot S_{2,3,5}(X_1 ... X_6) = S_{1,2,3,5}(X_1 ... X_6)$. To prove these theorems, note that a product is zero of either factor is zero, while a sum is zero only if both terms are zero.

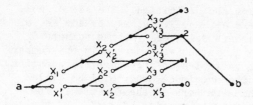

Fig. 23   Circuit for Realizing
         $S_2(X_1, X_2, X_3)$

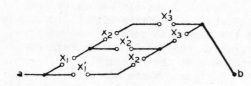

Fig. 24   Simplification of Fig. 23

Theorem: The negative of a symmetric function of n variables is a symmetric function of these variables having for a-numbers all the numbers from 0 to n, inclusive, which are not in the a-numbers of the given function. Thus $S_{2,3,5}(X_1 \cdots X_6) = S_{0,1,4,6}(X_1 \cdots X_6)$.

Before considering the synthesis of the general symmetric function $Sa_1, a_2 \cdots a_k (X_1, X_2 \cdots X_n)$ a simple example will be given. Suppose the function $S_2(X_1, X_2, X_3)$ is to be realized. This means that we must construct a circuit which will be closed

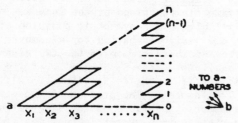

Fig. 25   Circuit for Realizing the General Symmetric Function
         $Sa_1, a_2 \cdots a_k (X_1, X_2 \cdots X_n)$

Each sloping element has the hindrance of the variable written below it, each horizontal element has the negative of this hindrance. This convention will be used on most symmetric-function drawings.

when any two of the variables X_1, X_2, X_3 are zero, but open if none, or one or three are zero. A circuit for this purpose is shown in Fig. 23. This circuit may be divided into three bays, one for each variable, and four levels marked 0, 1, 2, and 3 at the right. The terminal b is connected to the levels corresponding to the a-numbers of the required function, in this case to the level marked 2. The line coming in at first encounters a pair of hindrances X_1 and X_1'. If $X_1 = 0$, the line is switched up to the level marked 1, meaning that one of the variables is zero; if not it stays at the same level. Next we come to hindrances X_2 and X_2'. If $X_2 = 0$, the line is switched up a level; if not, it stays at the same level. X_3 has a similar effect. Finally reaching the right-hand set of terminals, the line has been switched up to a level equal to the total number variables which are zero. Since terminal b is connected to the level marked 2, the circuit a-b will be completed if and only if 2 of the variables are zero. If $S_{0,3}(X_1, X_2, X_3)$ had been desired, terminal b would be connected to both levels 0 and 3. In Fig. 23 certain of the elements are evidently superfluous. The circuit may be simplified to the form of Fig. 24.

For the general function exactly the same method is followed. Using the general circuit for n-variables of Fig. 25, the terminal b is connected to the levels corresponding to the a-numbers of the desired symmetric function. In Fig. 25 the hindrances are represented merely by lines, and the letters are omitted from the circuit, but the hindrance of each line may easily be seen by generalizing Fig. 23. After terminal b is connected, all superfluous elements may be deleted.

In certain cases it is possible to greatly simplify the circuit by shifting the levels down. Suppose the function $S_{0,3}, (X_1 \cdots X_6)$ is desired. Instead of continuing the circuit up to the sixth level back down to the zero level as shown in Fig. 26. The zero level then also becomes the third level and the sixth level. With terminal b connected to this level, we

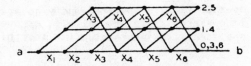

Fig. 26   Circuit for $S_{0, 3, 6}(X_1 \cdots X_6)$ Using the "Shifting Down" Process

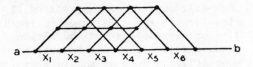

Fig. 27   Simplification of Fig. 26

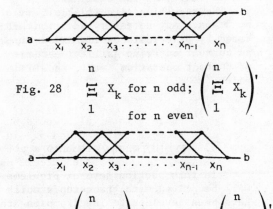

Fig. 28 $\displaystyle\mathop{\Xi}_{1}^{n} X_k$ for n odd; $\left(\displaystyle\mathop{\Xi}_{1}^{n} X_k\right)'$ for n even

Fig. 29 $\left(\displaystyle\mathop{\Xi}_{1}^{n} X_k\right)$ for n even; $\left(\displaystyle\mathop{\Xi}_{1}^{n} X_k\right)'$ for n odd

have realized the function with a great saving of elements. Eliminating unnecessary elements the circuit of Fig. 27 is obtained. This device is especially useful if the a-numbers form an arithmetic progression, although it can sometimes be applied in other cases.

The functions $\displaystyle\mathop{\Xi}_{1}^{n} X_k$ and $\left(\displaystyle\mathop{\Xi}_{1}^{n} X_k\right)'$ have very simple circuits when devel-

oped in this manner. It can be easily shown that if n is even, then $\displaystyle\mathop{\Xi}_{1}^{n} X_k$ is the symmetric function with all the even numbers for a-numbers, if n is odd it has all the odd numbers for a-numbers. The function $\left(\displaystyle\mathop{\Xi}_{1}^{n} X_k\right)'$ is, of course, just the opposite. Using the shifting-down process the circuits are as shown in Figs. 28 and 29. These circuits each require $4(n - 1)$ elements They will be recognized as the familiar circuit for controlling a light from n points, using $(n - 2)$ double-pole double-throw switches and two single-pole-double-throw switches. If at any one of the points the position of the switch is changed, the total number of variables which equal zero is changed by one, so that if the light is on, it will be turned off and if already off, it will be turned on.

More than one symmetric function of a certain set of variables may be realized with just one circuit of the form of Fig. 25, providing the different functions have no a-numbers in common. If there are common a-numbers the levels may be shifted down, or an extra relay may be added so that one circuit is still sufficient.

The general network of Fig. 25 contains $n(n + 1)$ elements. We will show that for any given selection of a-numbers, at least n of the elements will be superfluous. Each number from 1 to $n - 1$, inclusive, which is not in the set of a-numbers produces two unnecessary elements; 0 or n missing will produce one unnecessary element. However, if two of the a-numbers differ by only one, then two elements will be superfluous. If more than two of the a-numbers are adjacent, or if two or more adjacent numbers are missing, then more than one element apiece will be superfluous. It is evident then that the worst case will be that in which the a-numbers are all the odd numbers or all the even numbers from 0 to n. In each of these cases it is easily seen that n of the elements will be

superfluous. In these cases the shifting down process may be used if n > 2
so that the maximum of n^2 elements
will be needed only for the four particular functions X, X', X $\oplus$ Y, and
(X $\oplus$ Y)'.

EQUATIONS FROM GIVEN OPERATING CHARACTERISTICS

In general there is a certain set
of independent variables A, B, C ...
which may be switches, externally operated or protective relays. There is
also a set of dependent variables x,
y, z ... which represent relays, motors
or other devices to be controlled by
the circuit. It is required to find a
network which gives, for each possible
combination of values of the independent variables, the correct values for
all the dependent variables. The
following principles give the general
method of solution.

1. Additional dependent variables
must be introduced for each added phase
of operation of sequential system.
Thus if it is desired to construct a
system which operates in three steps,
two additional variables must be introduced to represent the beginning of the
last two steps. These additional variables may represent contacts on a
stepping switch or relays which lock
in sequentially. Similarly each required time delay will require a new
variable, representing a time delay
relay of some sort. Other forms of
relays which may be necessary will
usually be obvious from the nature of
the problem.
2. The hindrance equations for each
of the dependent variables should now
be written down. These functions may
involve any of the variables, dependent or independent, including the
variable whose function is being
determined (as, for example, in a lock-
in circuit). The conditions may be
either conditions for operation or for
nonoperation. Equations are written
from operating characteristics according to Table 2. To illustrate the use
of this table suppose a relay U is to

operate if x is operated and y or z
is operated and v or w or z is not
operated. The expression for A will
be:

$$U = x + yz + v'w'z'$$

Lock-in relay equations have already
been discussed. It does not, of
course, matter if the same conditions
are put in the expression more than
once--all superfluous material will
disappear in the final simplification.
3. The expressions for the various
dependent variables should next be
simplified as much as possible by
means of the theorems on manipulation
of these quantities. Just how much
this can be done depends somewhat on
the ingenuity of the designer.
4. The resulting circuit should now
be drawn. Any necessary additions dic-
tated by practical considerations such
as current-carrying ability, sequence
of contact operation, etc., should be
made.

5. ILLUSTRATIVE EXAMPLES

In this section several problems
will be solved with the methods which
have been developed. The examples are
intended more to illustrate the use of
the calculus in actual problems and to
show the versatility of relay and
switching circuits than to describe
practical devices.

It is possible to perform complex
mathematical operations by means of
relay circuits. Numbers may be represented by the positions of relays or
stepping switches, and interconnections
between sets of relays can be made to
represent various mathematical operations. In fact, any operation that
can be completely described in a finite
number of steps using the words "if,"
"or," "and," etc. (see Table 2), can
be done automatically with relays. The
last example is an illustration of a
mathematical operation accomplished
with relays.

Table 2.

Relation of Operating Characteristics and Equations *

Symbol	In Terms of Operation	In Terms of Nonoperation
X	The switch or relay X is operated	The switch or relay X is not operated
=	If	If
X'	The switch or relay X is not operated	The switch or relay X is operated
.	Or	And
+	And	Or
(- -)'	The circuit (- -) is not closed, or apply De Morgan's theorem	The circuit (- -) is closed, or apply De Morgan's theorem
X(t-p)	X has been operated for at least p seconds	X has been open for at least p seconds

If the dependent variable appears in its own defining function (as in a lock-in circuit) strict adherence to the above leads to confusing sentences. In such cases the following equivalents should be used.

X = RX + S   X is operated when R is closed (providing S is closed) and remains so independent of R until S opens

X = (R' + X)S'   X is opened when R is closed (providing S is closed) and remains so independent of R until S opens

A SELECTIVE CIRCUIT

A relay U is to operate when any one, any three or when all four of the relays w, x, y, and z are operated but not when none or two are operated.

The hindrance function for U will evidently be:

$$U = wxyz + w'x'yz + w'xy'z + w'xyz' + wx'y'z + wx'yz' + wxy'z'$$

Reducing to the simplest series-parallel form:

$$U = w[x(yz + y'z') + x'(y'z + yz')] + w'[x(y'z + yz') + x'yz]$$

This circuit is shown in Fig. 30. It requires 20 elements. However, using the symmetric-function method, we may write for U:

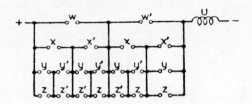

Fig. 30   Series-Parallel Realization
          of Selective Circuit

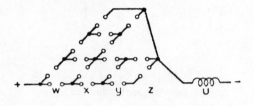

Fig. 31   Selective Circuit from
          Symmetric-Function Method

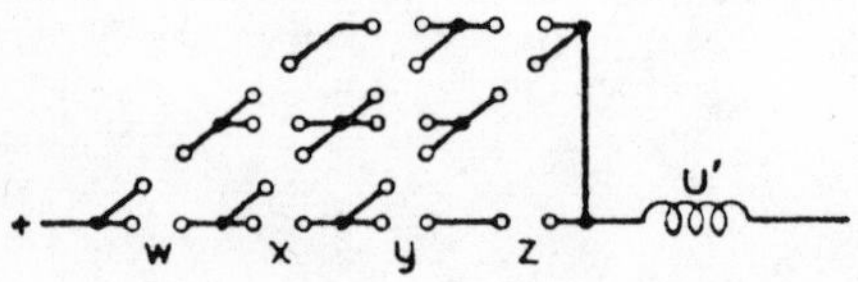

Fig. 32   Negative of Selective Circuit
          from Symmetric-Function Method

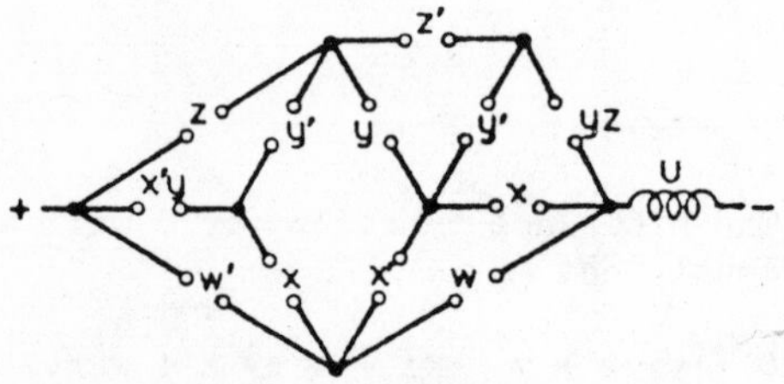

Fig. 33   Dual of Fig. 32

$$U = S_{1,3,4}(w,\ x,\ y,\ z)$$

This circuit (Fig. 31) contains only 15
elements. A still further reduction
may be made with the following device.
First write:

$$U' = S_{0,2}(w,\ x,\ y,\ z)$$

This has the circuit of Fig. 32. What
is required is the negative of this
function. This is a planar network
and we may apply the theorem of the
dual of network, thus obtaining the
circuits shown in Fig. 33. This contains 14 elements.

DESIGN OF AN ELECTRIC
COMBINATION LOCK

An electric lock is to be constructed with the following characteristics. There are to be five push-
button switches available on the front
of the lock. These will be labeled a,
b, c, d, e. To operate the lock the
buttons must be pressed in the following order: c, b, a, and c simultaneously, d. When operated in this
sequence the lock is to unlock, but if
any button is pressed incorrectly an
alarm U is to operate. To relock the
system a switch g must be operated.
To release the alarm once it has started a switch h must be operated.
This being a sequential system either
a stepping switch or additional sequential relays are required.   Using
sequential relays let them be denoted
by w, x, y and z corresponding, respectively, to the correct sequence of
operating the push buttons. An additional time-delay relay is also required due to the third step in the
operation. Obviously, even in correct
operation a and c cannot be pressed at
exactly the same time, but if only one
is pressed and held down the alarm
should operate. Therefore assume an
auxiliary time delay relay v which
will operate if either a or c alone is
pressed at the end of step 2 and held
down longer than time s the delay of
the relay.

When z has operated the lock un-
locks and at this point let all the
other relays drop out of the circuit.
The equations of the system may be
written down immediately:

$$w = cw + z' + U'$$
$$x = bx + w + z' + U'$$
$$y = (a + c)y + x + z' + U'$$

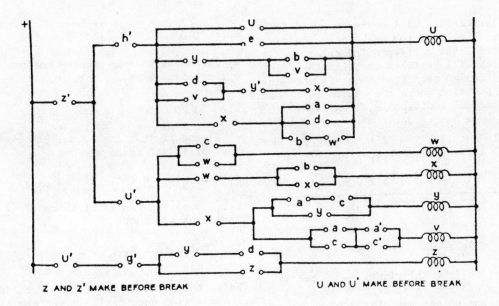

Fig. 34   Combination-Lock Circuit

$$z = z(d + y) + g' + U'$$

$$v = x + ac + a'c' + z' + U'$$

$$U = e(w' + abd)(w + x' + ad) \cdot$$

$$[x + y' + dv(t - s)] \cdot$$

$$[y + bv(t - s)]U + h' + z'$$

These expressions can be simplified considerably, first by combining the second and third factors in the first term of U, and then by factoring out the common terms of the several functions. The final simplified form is as below:

$$U = \begin{vmatrix} & h' + e[ad(b + w') + x'] \cdot \\ & (x + y' + dv)(y + vb)U \end{vmatrix}$$

$$w = z' + \begin{vmatrix} & cw \\ & bx + w \end{vmatrix}$$

$$x = z' + \begin{vmatrix} U' + & \\ & x + \end{vmatrix} \begin{vmatrix} (a + c)y \\ ac + a'c' \end{vmatrix}$$

$$v = g' + (y + d)z + U'$$

$$z = g' + (y + d)z + U'$$

This corresponds to the circuit of Fig. 34.

ELECTRIC ADDER TO THE BASE TWO

A circuit is to be designed that will automatically add two numbers, using only relays and switches. Although any numbering base could be used the circuit is greatly simplified by using the scale of two. Each digit is thus either 0 or 1; the number whose digits in order are a_k, a_{k-1}, a_{k-2}, $\cdots$ a_2, a_1, a_0 has the value

$$\sum_{j=0}^{k} a_j 2^j$$

Let the two numbers which are to be added be represented by a series of switches; a_k, a_{k-1}, $\cdots$ a_1, a_0 representing the various digits of one of the numbers and b_k, b_{k-1}, $\cdots$ b_1, b_0 the digits of the other number. The sum will be represented by the positions of a set of relays s_{k+1}, s_k, s_{k-1} $\cdots$ s_1, s_0. A number which is carried to the jth column from the (j-1)th column will be represented by a relay c_j. If the value of any digit is zero, the corresponding relay or switch will be taken to be in the position of zero hindrance; if one, in the position where the hindrance is one. The actual addition is shown below:

$$c_{k+1} \; c_k \qquad c_{j+1} c_j \qquad c_2 c_1 \quad \text{Carried numbers}$$
$$\phantom{c_{k+1}} a_k \text{---} a_{j+1} a_j \text{---} a_2 a_1 a_0 \quad \text{First number}$$
$$\phantom{c_{k+1}} b_k \qquad b_{j+1} b_j \qquad b_2 b_1 b_0 \quad \text{Second number}$$

$$c_{k+1} \; S_k \text{---} S_{j+1} S_j \text{---} S_2 S_1 S_0 \quad \text{Sum}$$
or
$$S_{k+1}$$

Starting from the right, s_0 is one if a_0 is one and b_0 is zero or if a_0 is zero and b_0 but not otherwise. Hence:

$$s_0 = a_0 b_0' + a_0' b_0 = a_0 \oplus b_0$$

c_1 is one if both a_0 and b_0 are one but not otherwise.

$$c_1 = a_0 \cdot b_0$$

s_j is one if just one of a_j, b_j, c_j is one, or if all three are one.

$$S_j = S_{1,3}(a_j, b_j, c_j) \quad j = 1, 2, \ldots k$$

c_{j+1} is one if two or if three of these variables are one.

$$c_{j+1} = S_{2,3}(a_j, b_j, c_j) \quad j = 1, 2, \ldots k$$

Using the method of symmetric functions and shifting down for s_j gives the circuits of Fig. 35. Eliminating superfluous elements we arrive at Fig. 36.

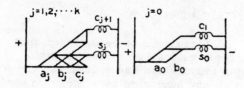

Fig. 35 Circuits for Electric Adder

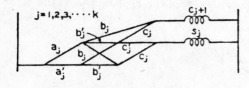

Fig. 36 Simplification of Fig. 35

REFERENCES

1. A complete bibliography of the literature of symbolic logic is given in the Journal of Symbolic Logic, vol. 1, number 4, December 1936. Those elementary parts of the theory that are useful in connection with relay circuits are well treated in the two following references.

2. Louis Cauturat, The Algebra of Logic, The Open Court Publishing Company.

3. A. N. Whitehead, Universal Algebra, University of Cambridge Press, Cambridge, vol. 1, book III, chapters I and II, pp. 35-82.

4. E. V. Huntington, Transactions of the American Mathematical Society, vol. 35, 1933, pp. 274-304. The postulates referred to are the fourth set, given on page 280.

THE MAP METHOD FOR SYNTHESIS OF
COMBINATIONAL LOGIC CIRCUITS

M. KARNAUGH

The search for simple abstract techniques to be applied to the design of switching systems is still, despite some recent advances, in its early stages. The problem in this area which has been attacked most energetically is that of the synthesis of efficient combinational, that is, non-sequential, logic circuits.

While this problem is closely related to the classical one of simplifying logical truth functions, there are some significant differences. To each logical truth function, or Boolean algebraic expression, there corresponds a combinational circuit which may be constructed from a given set of appropriate components. However, minimization of the number of appearances of algebraic variables does not necessarily lead to the most economical circuit. Indeed, the criteria of economy and simplicity may vary widely for different types of components. A general approach to circuit synthesis must therefore be highly flexible. What is perhaps most to be desired is a simple and rapid technique for generating a variety of near-minimal algebraic forms for the designer's inspection.

Boolean algebra,[1] or the calculus of propositions, is a basic tool for investigation of circuits constructed from 2-valued devices. Its direct application to synthesis problems is, nevertheless, not completely satisfactory. The designer employing Boolean algebra is in possession of a list of theorems which may be used in simplifying the expression before him; but he may not know which ones to try first, or to which terms to apply them. He is thus forced to consider a very large number of alternative procedures in all but the most trivial cases. It is clear that a method which provides more insight into the structure of each problem is to be preferred. Nevertheless, it will be convenient to describe other methods in terms of Boolean algebra. Whenever the term "algebra" is used in this paper, it will refer to Boolean algebra, where addition corresponds to the logical connective "or," while multiplication corresponds to "and."

The minimizing chart,[2] developed at the Harvard Computation Laboratory, represents a step in the desired direction. It makes possible the fairly rapid derivation of near-minimal 2-stage forms. By a 2-stage form is meant a sum of products of the elementary variables, or else a product of sums of the elementary variables. These expressions may then be further reduced by algebraic factoring. The chief drawback to this method lies in the necessity of writing, and perhaps erasing, on a chart that, for n variables, contains 2^{2n} entries. Thus, we must keep track of 1,024 entries for five variable problems and 4,096 entries for six variable problems.

E. W. Veitch[3] has suggested a method whereby results similar to those yielded by the minimizing chart can be obtained from an array containing only 2^n entries in a more rapid and elegant manner. The map method, which is explained in this paper, involves a reorganization of Veitch's charts, an extension to the use of 3-dimensional arrays, and some

Reprinted with permission from the AIEE Transactions-Communications and Electronics, Vol. 72, pt. I, Nov. 1953, pp. 593-599, with corrections from the author.

special techniques for diode and relay circuits.

MAPS

Let the active and inactive conditions of the inputs to a combinational circuit be designated by assigning the values 1 and 0 respectively to
the associated algebraic variables.
An assignment of a simultaneous set of
values to the n variables for a given
problem will be called an input condition. There are 2^n possible input
conditions.

For example, with only two variables, there are four input conditions.
They may be represented graphically by
the four squares in Fig. 1(A). Here,
the values of variables A and B have
simply been plotted along two perpendicular axes. It should be noted that
squares which are adjacent, either
horizontally or vertically, differ in
the value of only one of the variables.

If Fig. 1(A) is cut along its
horizontal midsection and the bottom
half is rotated into line with the
top, as in Fig. 1(B), then a representation of the input conditions for two
variables is obtained along a single
axis. Let us consider the squares at
opposite ends of the row to be adjacent, as if it were wrapped on a cyl-
inder. Then, as before, adjacent
squares differ in the value of only
one variable. Conversely, if two input conditions differ in the value
assigned to just one of the variables,
they are represented by adjacent
squares.

If one also makes use of the vertical axis, one can represent the input conditions for three variables as
in Fig. 2(A), and for four variables
as in Fig. 2(B). In the latter case,
opposite ends of each row or column
should be considered adjacent, as
though the figure were inscribed on a
torus.

The labels on the diagrams may be
simplified as shown in Fig. 3. The
rows or columns within a bracket are
those in which the designated variable

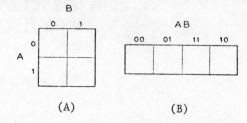

Fig. 1. Graphical Representation of
the Input Conditions for Two Variables.

(A) Along Two Axes
(B) Along a Single Axis

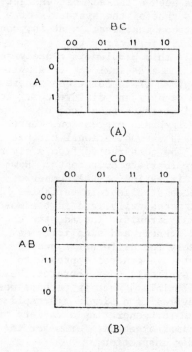

Fig. 2. Graphical Representations of
the Input Conditions for Three and for
Four Variables.

has the value 1, while it is 0 elsewhere.

A combinational circuit of the
type under consideration has a 2-
valued output which is a function of
the input condition. The synthesis
problem may be said to begin with the
specification of this functional de-

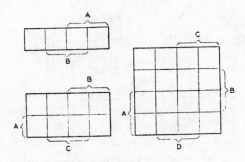

Fig. 3. Input Representations with
Simplified Labels.

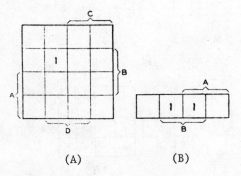

(A)   (B)

Fig. 4. Maps of Two Functions.

(A)   f=A'BC'D

(B)   f=A'B+AB=B(A'+A)=B

pendence. Such information may be
represented on a map as follows: Place
a 1 in each square which represents an
input condition for which the output
is to have the value 1. The other
squares may be imagined to contain
zeroes.

SYNTHESIS OF 2-STAGE FORMS

Consider the function mapped in
Fig. 4(A). Its algebraic realization
is the product A'BC'D, where the primes
indicate negation or complementaion,
for A'BC'D = 1 if, and only if, A = 0,
B = 1, C = 0, and D = 1.

Let us define a complete product
to be a product in which each of the
variables appears as one factor,

either primed or not. Then any function whose map contains a single 1
may be represented by a single complete product. Each factor is primed
if, and only if, it has the value 0 at
the square in question. Because each
square that contains a 1 gives rise to
a product, such squares will be called
p-squares.

If the map of a function contains
k p-squares, then the function may be
represented by the logical sum of the
corresponding k complete products,
each selected by this rule. This
form of representation is the complete
disjunctive normal form of the calculus of propositions. It is often the
starting point for algebraic simplification.

However, it is usually possible
to write down a more economical representation than a complete normal form
by direct inspection of the map. Consider the function whose map is shown
in Fig. 4(B). Its complete disjunctive normal form is AB + A'B. This is
easily reducible algebraically: AB +
A'B = B(A + A') = B. Now note that
the p-squares on the map are precisely
that set for which B = 1.

Let us define a subcube to be the
set of all squares on a map over which
certain of the variables have fixed
values. A subcube formed entirely of
p-squares will be called a p-subcube.

Each p-subcube may be regarded as
the map of a product formed according
to the rules:

1. The factors of the product are
those variables whose values are fixed
within the subcube.

2. A factor is primed if, and
only if, its value within the subcube
is 0.

Fig. 5 shows some typical p-
subcubes and the corresponding products.
Each p-subcube may be thought of as a
simply connected square or rectangular
group of p-squares, if it is recalled
that opposite ends of columns and
rows are adjacent.

If m variables are not fixed
in a given subcube, it is said to
be m-dimensional, and it contains
2^m squares. A single square is thus
a zero-dimensional subcube. Note

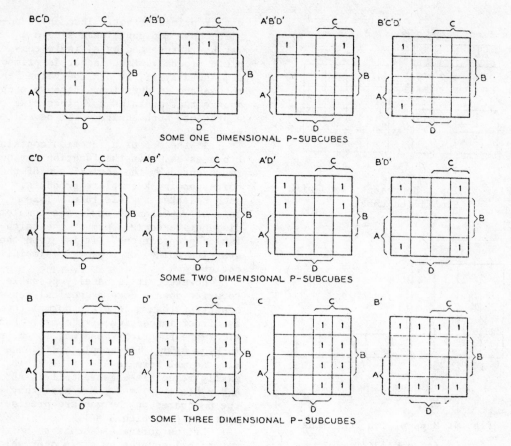

Fig. 5. A Number of Typical p-Subcubes and the Corresponding Algebraic Products.

that the larger p-subcubes correspond
to products having fewer factors,
since fewer variables are fixed in
them.

It is now easy to see how to
obtain economical 2-stage forms from
maps. The rules are:

1. Choose a set of p-subcubes
which includes every p-square at least
once. In general, it is desirable to
make the selected subcubes as large
and as few in number as possible.

2. Write down the sum of the products which correspond to the selected
p-subcubes. This gives the desired
expression.

As an example of this procedure,
we can, for the function mapped in
Fig. 6, make the selection

$$f = AC' + A'CD + BCD$$

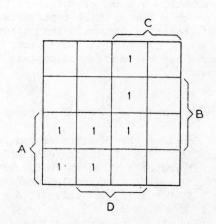

Fig. 6. Map of a Function.

An alternate procedure is possible that leads to a product of sums, that is, a conjunctive normal form instead of a sum of products. First, this procedure is used to obtain an expression for the negative of the function mapped. This is done by considering the empty squares to be the new p-squares. In the case of Fig. 6,

$$f' = A'C' + CD' + AB'C$$

The function desired, which is the negative of this, is now obtained by the simultaneous interchange of primes and non-primes, and of multiplication and addition signs.

Thus

$$f = (A + C)(C' + D)(A' + B + C')$$

Both of these procedures have been proposed by Veitch.[3]

MINIMAL 2-STAGE FORMS

In combinational diode circuits, there is usually one diode per input lead to every stage. For 2-stage circuits, this means one diode per appearance of each algebraic variable plus one diode per product, or per sum, of these variables. It is often a simple matter to minimize rigorously the number of diodes used in such a circuit.

Consider Fig. 7(A). The dotted lines correspond to the choice of p-subcubes.

$$f = B + AC$$

Now note that asterisks are placed in two of the p-squares, so chosen that no single p-subcube includes both of them. Hence at least two p-subcubes are required. Furthermore, the selected p-subcube containing each asterisk is of maximum possible dimensionality. Hence each of the corresponding products contains the minimum number of factors.

The same kind of proof must be carried out for the alternate proce-

dure, as illustrated in Fig. 7(B). Here we have

$$f' = A'B' + B'C'$$
$$f = (A + B)(B + C)$$

This is not as good, however, as the previous result, which we have now proved to be minimal in
1. Number of terms
2. Appearances of the variables
3. Diodes

This proof depends upon the fact that no one pair of asterisks lies in the same p-subcube. In some cases it may be be found that only k asterisks can be placed on a map in this manner, and yet more than k terms are required to represent the function. When this occurs, a proof that at least k + 1 terms are necessary can be carried through by contradiction. When the attempt to associate a p-subcube with each asterisk is made, it will be found impossible to include all p-squares in the k p-subcubes so selected.

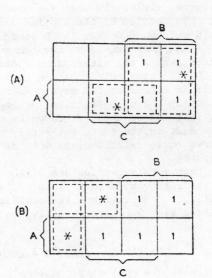

Fig. 7. Maps Used to Minimize a Diode Circuit.

FACTORING BY INSPECTION

When circuits are not restricted to the 2-stage variety, it is sometimes advantageous to reduce further the 2-stage forms by algebraic factoring. It is of some importance to show that factoring may also be carried out directly by inspection of a map.

For example, the function mapped in Fig. 8 is

$$f = A'B' + B'C = B'(A' + C)$$

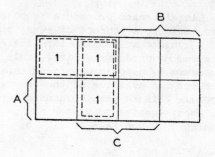

Fig. 8. Map of a Factorable Function.

Since both the chosen p-subcubes lie within subcube B, the presence of the common factor is established by inspection.

Occasionally, observation of the possibilities for factoring will determine the selection of subcubes and lead to a better circuit than would otherwise be obtained. In the case of Fig. 6, the choices

$$f = AC' + A'CD + BCD = AC' + CD(A' + B)$$
$$f = AC' + A'CD + ABD = A(C' + BD) + A'CD$$
$$\text{OR} \qquad = AC' + D(A'C + \mathbf{AB})$$

lead to equally good 2-stage forms; but the former yields the best factored form. Inspection of the map indicates that p-subcube BCD lies in CD along with A'CD, thus providing two common factors, while the alternative choice of ABD will give only a single common factor in either of two ways. When inspecting the map, it is not necessary to think of these subcubes by name as we must in the text, but merely to observe their relations, as sets of p-squares.

Even more extensive use of the set theoretic union (our +) and intersection (our ·) relations is possible. Consider Fig. 9. Algebraically, we get

$$f = A'B'C'D + A'B'CD' + ABC'D + ABCD'$$
$$= A'B'(C'D + CD') + AB(C'D + CD')$$
$$= (A'B' + AB)(C'D + CD')$$

But it can be seen directly that the

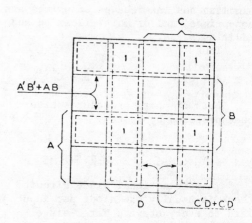

Fig. 9. Set Theoretic Interpretation of a Map.

four p-squares form the set which is the intersection of the union of A'B' and AB and the union of C'D and CD'. Thus $f = (A'B' + AB)(C'D + CD')$, as illustrated by the dotted lines.

"DON'T-CARE" CONDITIONS

Very often, the output of a circuit is subject to less rigid restriction than the assignment of a definite value, 0 or 1, for some input conditions. The simplest such case is that of no restriction at all. This may occur because the input conditions in question never are realized in practice, or because the output has no effect in those cases. We shall designate such don't-care conditions by placing the symbol d in the appropriate squares.

It is usually quite simple to make an economical assignment of values to the d-squares by inspection of a map. Since these are at the disposal of the designer, it is to his advantage to employ them so as to simplify the resulting circuit.

The best 2-stage form for the function in Fig. 10 is

$$f = AC' + BD$$

obtained by setting the two d's on the right equal to 0, and the other two equal to 1.

The rule for making such choices is as follows: Assign values to the d's which enlarge and combine the necessary p-subcubes as much as possible but do not make necessary the selection of any additional subcubes.

The ease with which don't-cares can be properly evaluated is one of the major advantages shared by the minimizing chart, Veitch chart, and map methods in varying degree.

DISJUNCTIVE COMBINATION IN RELAY NETS

The map method, inasmuch as it yields expressions in Boolean algebra, can be used to design 2-terminal, series-parallel relay contact networks, but not bridge-type 2-terminal networks. Hence, many 2-terminal contact networks designed by means of the map method will not be minimal in contacts or springs. This will be true, in particular, of the symmetric circuits.[4]

However, in the case of complicated, multioutput networks, the map method may be a very effective tool. Suppose that terminal i is a ground, to be connected through networks f_{ij} and f_{ik} to the output terminals j and k respectively. The specifications for f_{ij} and f_{ik}, which are networks on the contacts of relays A, B, C, D, are mapped in Fig. 11. If each net is synthesized separately, there results the circuit of Fig. 12(A). In Fig. 12(B),

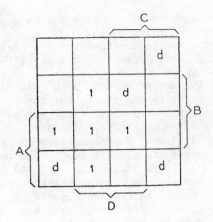

Fig. 10. Map of an Incompletely Specified Function.

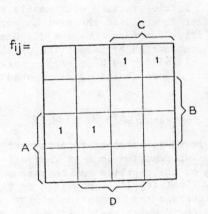

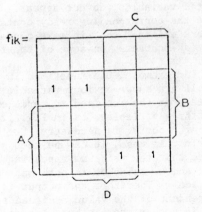

Fig. 11. A 2-Output Problem.

it is shown how, with a slight rear-
rangement, parts of the upper paths to
j and k can be combined, as can parts
of the lower paths. This results in
a saving of four contacts.

The second circuit is completely
equivalent to the first, for the
transfers on relay A prevent any sneak
paths between terminals j and k.
While disjunctive combinations of this
sort are certainly not new to the relay art,[5] this section is included to
show how they may easily be recognized
on maps, and hence how they play a
part in the selection of subcubes.

Note that the paths ABC' and
$A'BC'$, which give rise to one of the
combinations, differ by only a prime
on A. The corresponding subcubes in
Fig. 11 are seen to be related by a
simple displacement. The same is true
for the other pair of p-subcubes.

A little practice will enable the
designer to evaluate the various possibilities for factoring and disjunctive combination by inspection of the
maps. It will then be a simple task
to make a good choice of p-subcubes.

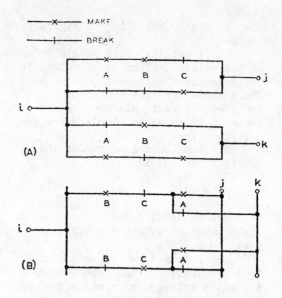

Fig. 12. Synthesis of a 2-Output Circuit.

(A) Two Separate Contact Networks.
(B) Networks Disjunctively Combined.

UNNECESSARY CONTACTS

It is of interest to note that for
any given function some of the variables or their primes may be unnecessary. That is, it is possible to find
an algebraic representation of the
function in which these variables, or
negated variables, do not appear.
Hence the corresponding relay contact
network will not contain make contacts,
or break-contacts, on some of the relays.

For example, the functions in
Fig. 11 are shown on four-variable maps,
but they may be realized in terms of
only three variables, as in Fig. 12.
Neither D nor D' is necessary.

In this case, it can be seen at a
glance that the patterns appearing in
the D and D' subcubes in both maps are
identical. Therefore the output is
independent of the value assigned to D.
This is a case wherein both the following rules hold:

1. A function may be represented
without the appearance of an unprimed
variable, say D if, and only if, to
each p-square in subcube D there
corresponds an adjacent p-square in
subcube D'.

2. A function may be represented
without the appearance of D' if, and
only if, to each p-square in subcube
D' there corresponds an adjacent p-
square in D.

ILLUSTRATIVE EXAMPLE:
A RELAY TRANSLATOR

Suppose it is desired to find a
relay contact network to translate
coded decimal digits from a 1-2-4-5
code to 2-out-of-5 code. The five outputs will operate the relays Z (zero),
0 (one), T (two), F (four), and S
(seven). The required translation properties are listed in Table 1. The un-
arithmetic representation for zero is
standard in the 2-out-of-5 code.

Table 1.

Specifications for a Coded Decimal
Digit Translator

Digit	1	2	4	5		Z	0	T	F	S
0	0	0	0	0		0	0	0	1	1
1	1	0	0	0		1	1	0	0	0
2	0	1	0	0		1	0	1	0	0
3	1	1	0	0		0	1	1	0	0
4	0	0	1	0		1	0	0	1	0
5	0	0	0	1		0	1	0	1	0
6	1	0	0	1		0	0	1	1	0
7	0	1	0	1		1	0	0	0	1
8	1	1	0	1		0	1	0	0	1
9	0	0	1	1		0	0	1	0	1

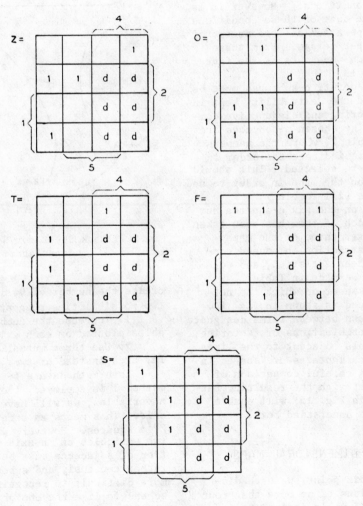

Fig. 13. A Translator Problem.

Table 2.

A List of Selected p-Subcubes

Z		T	S		O		F
(1) 45'		(2) 45	(10) 1'2'4'5'		(6) 12		(8) 12'5
(3) 12'5'		(4) 12'5	(12) 25		(7) 12'5'		(13) 45'
(5) 1'2		(11) 25'	(14) 45		(9) 1'2'4'5		(15) 1'2'4

The remaining six input conditions for the 1-2-4-5 relays are unused or don't-care conditions. However it is required that none of these conditions results in operation of zero or two of the five output relays. From these specifications, one obtains the five maps in Fig. 13.

At this point, p-subcubes must be selected, and the desirability kept in mind of factoring and disjunctive combinations. The chosen p-subcubes are listed in Table 2, where the numbers in parenthesis indicate the order in which they were selected. This should be followed on the maps in order to see how the terms will combine.

A check on the six d-squares now shows that each of them has been taken = 1 on at least three of the maps. Hence the restriction on unused conditions has been satisfied, and no changes need be made in Table 2.

The worksheet on which the network is planned is shown in Fig. 14. The lines drawn between terms designate disjunctive combinations or factoring; and the symbols adjacent to the lines indicate which contacts are shared in each case. A careful comparison of this worksheet with the resulting network, shown in Fig. 15, will enable the reader to understand both.

THREE-DIMENSIONAL MAPS

Up to this point, we have discussed functions of no more than four variables. If it is desired to in-

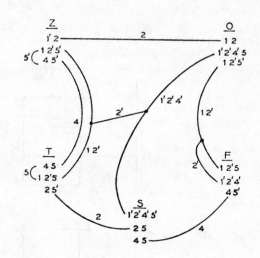

Fig. 14. Work Sheet for Synthesis of the Translator.

crease the number of variables on a map, two possibilities suggest themselves:

1. Increase the number of variables plotted on each axis.

2. Use three mutually perpendicular axes instead of two.

Both methods are feasible. If method 1 is employed, then for (even) n variables, we will have n/2 on each axis. This means an array of $2^{n/2}$ by $2^{n/2}$ squares. However, with more than two variables on an axis, the definition of adjacence must be extended rather tenuously and subcubes become more difficult to recognize. This scheme is like the one originally suggested by Veitch.[3]

We have chosen method 2, which allows a 50-per-cent increase in the number of variables without any extension of the rules. Thus, for six variables, the methods we have described still apply, but in three dimensions.

A suitable framework is shown in Fig. 16. It consists of four 6-inch square plexiglass sheets supported at 1-1/2 inch intervals by rods of the same material. The rods and sheets are glued together. The author has been told that the 3-dimensional tick-tacktoe boards sold at some toy shops under various names are satisfactory.

Each sheet is ruled at 1-1/2 inch intervals parallel to both pairs of edges. Thus we have a 4-by-4 array of squares on every sheet. The plexiglass framework enables us to do away with the writing and erasing which would be necessary when dealing with similar problems by other methods. In using it, we employ movable markers, such as 7/8-inch plastic roulette chips. The following scheme is suggested:

1. Mark all p-squares with white chips.

2. Mark all d-squares with black chips.

3. As subcubes are selected, mark each one with a set of distinctively colored chips.

Chips of eight or nine different colors are usually sufficient to make all the selected subcubes easily distinguishable. The corresponding products are then found by means of labels on the edges of the plastic cube.

One satisfactory labeling scheme is shown in Fig. 16. The two bottom planes are A, while the middle two are B. The variables C, D, E, and F are arranged on each plane as on the top, each letter serving to label two rows or columns. Opposite ends of any row, column, or vertical on the cube must be considered adjacent. Then every subcube may be thought of as a rectangular parallelpiped with edges 1, 2, or 4 units long. For multioutput problems, it is best to have a set of

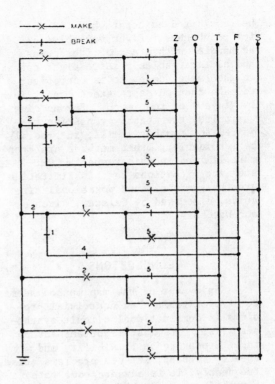

Fig. 15. The Finished Translator Network.

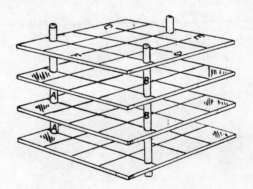

Fig. 16. The Cube: a 3-Dimensional Plastic Framework for Maps.

cubes, one per output.

The extension to seven variables is probably best accomplished by placing two cubes side by side. Corresponding squares in the two cubes must

be considered adjacent when looking
for p-subcubes. Eight variables can
be handled with a set of four cubes,
and nine variables require eight cubes.
In the latter case, it is convenient
to make then so as to stack easily into
two layers of four each. Beyond nine
variables, the mental gymnastics required for synthesis will, in general,
be formidable. Other methods are even
more limited in this respect. Out-
standing exceptions to this limitation
are the symmetric and positional circuits, discussed by Keister, Ritchie,
and Washburn.[4]

CONCLUSIONS

Employment of the map method seems
to be profitable when nontrivial problems in combinational circuit synthesis arise. Its most important advantages appear to be flexibility and
speed. Further, if such problems arise
frequently, it is advantageous to have
a method, such as this, which can be
learned and used effectively in a short
time by designers new to the field.

REFERENCES

1. W. Keister, A. E. Ritchie, and S. H.
Washburn, The Design of Switching
Circuits, New York, Van Nostrand, 1951,
Chapter 5.
2. Staff of the Harvard Computation
Laboratory, Synthesis of Electronic
Computing and Control Circuits,
Cambridge, Harvard University Press,
1951, Chapter 4.
3. E. W. Veitch, "A Chart Method for
Simplifying Truth and Functions,"
Proceedings, Association for Computing
Machinery, Pittsburgh, Pa., May 2, 3,
1952.
4. Reference 1, pp. 55-64.
5. Reference 1, pp. 295-297.

ACKNOWLEDGMENT

The author wishes to express his
indebtedness for many valuable sug-
gestions, help, and encouragement to
E. F. Moore, K. Goldschmidt, and W.
Keister, all of the Bell Telephone
Laboratories.

MINIMIZATION OF BOOLEAN FUNCTIONS

E. J. McCLUSKEY

1 INTRODUCTION

In designing switching circuits such as digital computers, telephone central offices, and digital machine tool controls, it is common practice to make use of Boolean algebra notation.[1,2,3,4] The performance of a single-output circuit is specified by means of a Boolean function of the input variables. This function, which is called the circuit transmission, is equal to 1 when an output is present and equals 0 when there is no output. A convenient means of specifying a transmission is a table of combinations such as that given in Table 1. This table lists, in the column under T, the output condition for each combination of input conditions. If there are some combinations of input conditions for which the output is not specified (perhaps because these combinations can never occur), d-entries are placed in the T-column of the corresponding rows of the table of combinations. The actual values (0 or 1) assigned to these rows are usually chosen so as to simplify the circuit which is designed to satisfy the requirements specified in the table of combinations.

This paper was derived from a thesis submitted to the Massachusetts Institute of Technology in partial fulfillment of the requirements for the degree of Doctor of Science on April 30, 1956. This research was supported in part by the Signal Corps; the Office of Scientific Research, Air Research and Development Command; and the Office of Naval Research.

For each row of the table of combinations a transmission can be written which equals "one" only when the variables have the values listed in that row of the table. These transmissions will be called elementary product terms (or more simply, p-terms) since any transmission can always be written as a sum of these p-terms. Table 1(b) lists the p-terms for Table 1(a). Note that every variable appears in each p-term. The p-term corresponding to a given row of a table of combinations is formed by priming any variables which have a "zero" entry in that row of the table and by leaving unprimed those variables which have "one" entries.

Table 1.

Circuit Specifications

	x_1	x_2	x_3	T	
0	0	0	0	0	$x_1'x_2'x_3'$
1	0	0	1	1	$x_1'x_2'x_3$
2	0	1	0	1	$x_1'x_2x_3'$
3	0	1	1	1	$x_1'x_2x_3$
4	1	0	0	1	$x_1x_2'x_3'$
5	1	0	1	1	$x_1x_2'x_3$
6	1	1	0	1	$x_1x_2x_3'$
7	1	1	1	0	$x_1x_2x_3$

A. Table of Combinations   B. p-terms

$$T = x_1'x_2'x_3 + x_1'x_2x_3' + x_1'x_2x_3 + x_1x_2'x_3'$$
$$+ x_1x_2'x_3 + x_1x_2x_3'$$

C. Canonical Expansion

37

It is possible to write an algebraic expression for the over-all circuit transmission directly from the table of combinations. This over-all transmission, T, is the sum of the p-terms corresponding to those rows of the table of combinations for which T is to have the value "one". See Table 1(c). Any transmission which is a sum of p-terms is called a canonical expansion.

The decimal numbers in the first column of Table 1(a) are the decimal equivalents of the binary numbers formed by the entries of the table of combinations. A concise method for specifying a transmission function is to list the decimal numbers of those rows of the table of combinations for which the function is to have the value one. Thus the function of Table 1 can be specified as $\Sigma(1, 2, 3, 4, 5, 6)$.

One of the most basic problems of switching circuit theory is that of writing a Boolean function in a simpler form than the canonical expansion. It is frequently possible to realize savings in equipment by writing a circuit transmission in simplified form. Methods for expressing a Boolean function in the "simplest" sum of products form were published by Karnaugh,[1] Aiken,[5] and Quine.[6] These methods have the common property that they all fail when the function to be simplified is reasonably complex. The following sections present a method for simplifying functions which can be applied to more complex functions than previous methods, is systematic, and can be easily programmed on a digital computer.

2 THE MINIMUM SUM

By use of the Boolean algebra theorem $x_1 x_2 + x_1' x_2 = x_2$ it is possible to obtain from the canonical expansion other equivalent sum functions: that is, other sum functions which correspond to the same table of combinations. These functions are still sums of products of variables but not all of the variables appear in each term. For

example, the transmission of Table 1, $T = x_1' x_2' x_3 + x_1' x_2 x_3' + x_1' x_2 x_3 + x_1 x_2' x_3' + x_1 x_2' x_3 + x_1 x_2 x_3' = (x_1' x_2' x_3 + x_1' x_2 x_3) + (x_1' x_2 x_3' + x_1 x_2 x_3') + (x_1 x_2' x_3' + x_1 x_2' x_3) = (x_1' x_2' x_3 + x_1 x_2' x_3) + (x_1' x_2 x_3' + x_1' x_2 x_3) + (x_1 x_2' x_3' + x_1 x_2' x_3)$ can be written as either $T = x_1' x_3 + x_2 x_3' + x_1 x_2'$ or $T = x_2' x_3 + x_1' x_2 + x_1 x_3'$.

A literal is defined as a variable with or without the associated prime (x_1, x_2' are literals). The sum functions which have the fewest terms of all equivalent sum functions will be called minimum sums unless these functions having fewest terms do not all involve the same number of literals. In such cases, only those functions which involve the fewest literals will be called minimum sums. For example, the function
$$T = \Sigma(7, 9, 10, 12, 13, 14, 15)$$
can be written as either
$T = x_4 x_2 x_1' + x_3 x_2 x_1 + x_4 x_2' x_1 + x_4 x_3 x_1'$
or as
$T = x_4 x_2 x_1' + x_3 x_2 x_1 + x_4 x_2' x_1 + x_4 x_3$
Only the second expression is a minimum sum since it involves 11 literals while the first expression involves 12 literals.

The minimum sum defined here is not necessarily the expression containing the fewest total literals, or the expression leading to the most economical two-stage diode logic circuit,[1] even though these three expressions are identical for many transmissions. The definition adopted here lends itself well to computation and results in a form which is useful in the design of contact networks. A method is presented in Section 9 for obtaining directly the expressions corresponding to the optimum two-stage diode logic circuit or the expressions containing fewest literals.

In principle it is possible to obtain a minimum sum for any given transmission by enumerating all possible equivalent sum functions then selecting those functions which have the fewest terms, and finally selecting from these the functions which contain the fewest literals. Since the number of equivalent sum functions may be quite large, this procedure is not generally practical. The following sections present a practical method for obtaining a minimum sum without resorting to an enumeration of all equivalent sum functions.

3 PRIME IMPLICANTS

When the theorem $x_1x_2 + x_1x_2' = x_1$ is used to replace by a single term, two p-terms, which correspond to rows i and j of a table of combinations, the resulting term will equal "one" when the variables have values corresponding to either row i or row j of the table. Similarly, when this theorem is used to replace, by a single term, a term which equals "one" for rows i and j and a term which equals "one" for rows k and m, the resulting term will equal "one" for rows i, j, k and m of the table of combinations. A method for obtaining a minimum sum by repeated application of this theorem $(x_1x_2' + x_1x_2 = x_1)$ was first presented by Quine.[6] In this method, the theorem is applied to all possible pairs of p-terms, then to all possible pairs of the terms obtained from the p-terms, and so on, until no further applications of the theorem are possible. It may be necessary to pair one term with several other terms in applying this theorem. In Example 3.2 the theorem is applied to the terms labeled 5 and 7 and also to the terms labeled 5 and 13. All terms paired with other terms in applying the theorem are then discarded. The remaining terms are called prime implicants.[6] Finally a minimum sum is formed as the sum of the fewest prime implicants which when taken together will equal "one" for all required rows of the table of combinations. The terms in the minimum sum will be called minimum sum terms or ms-terms.

EXAMPLE 3.1

$T = \Sigma(3, 7, 8, 9, 12, 13)$

Canonical Expansion:

$$T = x_1'x_2'x_3x_4 + x_1'x_2x_3x_4$$
$$\begin{bmatrix} 0\ 0\ 1\ 1 \\ 3 \end{bmatrix} \quad \begin{bmatrix} 0\ 1\ 1\ 1 \\ 7 \end{bmatrix}$$
$$+ x_1x_2'x_3'x_4' + x_1x_2'x_3'x_4$$
$$\begin{bmatrix} 1\ 0\ 0\ 0 \\ 8 \end{bmatrix} \quad \begin{bmatrix} 1\ 0\ 0\ 1 \\ 9 \end{bmatrix}$$
$$+ x_1x_2x_3'x_4' + x_1x_2x_3'x_4$$
$$\begin{bmatrix} 1\ 1\ 0\ 0 \\ 12 \end{bmatrix} \quad \begin{bmatrix} 1\ 1\ 0\ 1 \\ 13 \end{bmatrix}$$

The bracketed binary and decimal numbers below the sum terms indicate the rows of the table of combinations for which the corresponding term will equal "one." A binary character in which a dash appears represents the two binary numbers which are formed by replacing the dash by a "0" and then by a "1." Similarly a binary character in which two dashes appear represents the four binary numbers formed by replacing the dashes by "0" and "1" entries, etc.

$$x_1'x_2'x_3x_4 + x_1'x_2x_3x_4 = x_1'\ x_3x_4$$
$$\begin{bmatrix} 0\ 0\ 1\ 1 \\ 3 \end{bmatrix} \quad \begin{bmatrix} 0\ 1\ 1\ 1 \\ 7 \end{bmatrix} \quad \begin{bmatrix} 0\ -\ 1\ 1 \\ 3,\ 7 \end{bmatrix}$$

$$x_1x_2'x_3'x_4' + x_1x_2'x_3'x_4 = x_1x_2'x_3'$$
$$\begin{bmatrix} 1\ 0\ 0\ 0 \\ 8 \end{bmatrix} \quad \begin{bmatrix} 1\ 0\ 0\ 1 \\ 9 \end{bmatrix} \quad \begin{bmatrix} 1\ 0\ 0\ - \\ 8,\ 9 \end{bmatrix}$$

$$x_1x_2x_3'x_4' + x_1x_2x_3'x_4 = x_1x_2x_3'$$
$$\begin{bmatrix} 1\ 1\ 0\ 0 \\ 12 \end{bmatrix} \quad \begin{bmatrix} 1\ 1\ 0\ 1 \\ 13 \end{bmatrix} \quad \begin{bmatrix} 1\ 1\ 0\ - \\ 12,\ 13 \end{bmatrix}$$

$$x_1x_2'x_3' + x_1x_2x_3' = x_1\ x_3'$$
$$\begin{bmatrix} 1\ 0\ 0\ - \\ 8,\ 9 \end{bmatrix} \quad \begin{bmatrix} 1\ 1\ 0\ - \\ 12,\ 13 \end{bmatrix} \quad \begin{bmatrix} 1\ -\ 0\ - \\ 8,9,12,13 \end{bmatrix}$$

Prime Implicants:

$$x_1\ x_3', \qquad x_1'\ x_3x_4$$
$$\begin{bmatrix} 1\ -\ 0\ - \\ 8,9,12,13 \end{bmatrix} \quad \begin{bmatrix} 0\ -\ 1\ 1 \\ 3,\ 7 \end{bmatrix}$$

Minimum Sum:

$$T = x_1x_3' + x_1'x_3x_4$$

EXAMPLE 3.2

$T = \Sigma(5, 7, 12, 13)$

Canonical Expansion:

$$T = x_1'x_2x_3'x_4 + x_1'x_2x_3x_4$$
$$\begin{bmatrix} 0\ 1\ 0\ 1 \\ 5 \end{bmatrix} \quad \begin{bmatrix} 0\ 1\ 1\ 1 \\ 7 \end{bmatrix}$$

$$+ x_1x_2x_3'x_4' + x_1x_2x_3'x_4$$

$$\begin{bmatrix} 1 & 1 & 0 & 0 \\ & 12 & & \end{bmatrix} \quad \begin{bmatrix} 1 & 1 & 0 & 1 \\ & 13 & & \end{bmatrix}$$

$$x_1'x_2x_3'x_4 + x_1'x_2x_3x_4 = x_1'x_2\ x_4$$

$$\begin{bmatrix} 0 & 1 & 0 & 1 \\ & 5 & & \end{bmatrix} \quad \begin{bmatrix} 0 & 1 & 1 & 1 \\ & 7 & & \end{bmatrix} \quad \begin{bmatrix} 0 & 1 & - & 1 \\ & 5, & 7 & \end{bmatrix}$$

$$x_1'x_2x_3'x_4 + x_1x_2x_3'x_4 = x_2x_3'x_4$$

$$\begin{bmatrix} 0 & 1 & 0 & 1 \\ & 5 & & \end{bmatrix} \quad \begin{bmatrix} 1 & 1 & 0 & 1 \\ & 13 & & \end{bmatrix} \quad \begin{bmatrix} - & 1 & 0 & 1 \\ & 5, & 13 & \end{bmatrix}$$

$$x_1x_2x_3'x_4' + x_1x_2x_3'x_4 = x_1x_2x_3'$$

$$\begin{bmatrix} 1 & 1 & 0 & 0 \\ & 12 & & \end{bmatrix} \quad \begin{bmatrix} 1 & 1 & 0 & 1 \\ & 13 & & \end{bmatrix} \quad \begin{bmatrix} 1 & 1 & 0 & - \\ & 12, & 13 & \end{bmatrix}$$

Prime Implicants:

$$x_1'x_2\ x_4, \qquad x_2x_3'x_4, \quad x_1x_2x_3'$$

$$\begin{bmatrix} 0 & 1 & - & 1 \\ & 5, & 7 & \end{bmatrix} \quad \begin{bmatrix} - & 1 & 0 & 1 \\ & 5, & 13 & \end{bmatrix} \quad \begin{bmatrix} 1 & 1 & 0 & - \\ & 12, & 13 & \end{bmatrix}$$

Minimum Sum:

$$T = x_1'x_2x_4 + x_1x_2x_3'$$

Quine's method, as illustrated in Examples 3.1 and 3.2, becomes unwieldly for transmissions involving either many variables or many p-terms. This difficulty is overcome by simplifying the notation and making the procedure more systematic. The notation is simplified by discarding the expressions involving literals and using only the binary characters. This is permissible because the expressions in terms of literals can always be regained from the binary characters. The theorem being used to combine terms can be stated in terms of the binary characters as follows: If two binary characters are identical in all positions except one, and if neither character has a dash in the position in which they differ, then the two characters can be replaced by a single character which has a dash in the position in which the original characters differ and which is identical with the original characters in all other positions.

The first step in the revised method for determining prime implicants is to list in a column, such as that shown in Table 2(a),

the binary equivalents of the decimal numbers which specify the function. It is expedient to order these binary numbers so that any numbers which contain no 1's come first, followed by any numbers containing a single 1, etc. Lines should be drawn to divide the column into groups of binary numbers which contain a given number of 1's. The theorem stated above is applied to these binary numbers by comparing each number with all the numbers of the next lower group. Other pairs of numbers need not be considered since any two numbers which are not from adjacent groups must differ in more than one binary digit. For each number which has 1's wherever the number (from the next upper group) with which it is being compared has 1's, a new character is formed according to the theorem. A check mark is placed next to each number which is used in forming a new character. The new characters are placed in a separate column, such as Table 2(b), which is again divided into groups of characters which have the same number of 1's. The characters in this new column will each contain one dash.

After each number in the first column has been considered, a similar process is carried out for the characters of column two. Two characters from adjacent groups can be combined if they both have their dashes in the same position and if the character from the lower group has 1's wherever the upper character has 1's. If any combinations are possible the resulting characters are placed in a third column such as Table 2(c), and the Column II characters from which the new characters are formed are checked. All the characters in this third column will have two dashes. This procedure is repeated and new columns are formed, Table 2(d), until no further combinations are possible. The unchecked characters, which have not entered into any combi-

Table 2.

Determination of Prime Implicants for Transmission

$$T = \Sigma(0,\ 2,\ 4,\ 6,\ 7,\ 8,\ 10,\ 11,\ 12,\ 13,\ 14,\ 16,\ 18,\ 19,\ 29,\ 30)$$

(a) I

$x_5 x_4 x_3 x_2 x_1$

0	0 0 0 0 0 √
2	0 0 0 1 0 √
4	0 0 1 0 0 √
8	0 1 0 0 0 √
16	1 0 0 0 0 √
6	0 0 1 1 0 √
10	0 1 0 1 0 √
12	0 1 1 0 0 √
18	1 0 0 1 0 √
7	0 0 1 1 1 √
11	0 1 0 1 1 √
13	0 1 1 0 1 √
14	0 1 1 1 0 √
19	1 0 0 1 1 √
29	1 1 1 0 1 √
30	1 1 1 1 0 √

(b) II

$x_5 x_4 x_3 x_2 x_1$

0 2	0 0 0 - 0 √
0 4	0 0 - 0 0 √
0 8	0 - 0 0 0 √
0 16	- 0 0 0 0 √
2 6	0 0 - 1 0 √
2 10	0 - 0 1 0 √
2 18	- 0 0 1 0 √
4 6	0 0 1 - 0 √
4 12	0 - 1 0 0 √
8 10	0 1 0 - 0 √
8 12	0 1 - 0 0 √
16 18	1 0 0 - 0 √
6 7	0 0 1 1 -
6 14	0 - 1 1 0 √
10 11	0 1 0 1 -
10 14	0 1 - 1 0 √
12 13	0 1 1 0 -
12 14	0 1 1 - 0 √
18 19	1 0 0 1 -
13 29	- 1 1 0 1
14 30	- 1 1 1 0

(c) III

$x_5 x_4 x_3 x_2 x_1$

0 2 4 6	0 0 - - 0 √
0 2 8 10	0 - 0 - 0 √
0 2 16 18	- 0 0 - 0
0 4 8 12	0 - - 0 0 √
2 6 10 14	0 - - 1 0 √
4 6 12 14	0 - 1 - 0 √
8 10 12 14	0 1 - - 0 √

(d) IV

$x_5 x_4 x_3 x_2 x_1$

0 2 4 6 8 10 12 14	0 - - - 0

nations, represent the prime implicants.

Each binary character is labeled with the decimal equivalents of the binary numbers which it represents (see note in Example 3.1). These decimal numbers are arranged in increasing arithmetic order. For a character having one dash this corresponds to the order of its formation: When two binary numbers combine, the second number always contains all the 1's of the first number and one additional 1 so that the second number is always greater than the first. Characters having two dashes can be formed in two ways. For example, the character (0,2,4,6) can be formed either by combining (0,2) and (4,6) or by combining (0,4) and (2,6) as given in Table 3. Similarly, there are three ways in which a character having three dashes can be formed (in Table 2 the 0,2,4,6,8, 10,12,14 character can be formed from the 0,2,4,6, and 8,10,12,14 characters or the 0,2,8,10, and 4,6,12,14 characters or the 0,4,8,12 and 2,6,10,14 characters), four ways in which a character having four dashes can be

Table 3.

Example of the Two Ways of Forming a
Character Having Two Dashes

0	0 0 0 0	0 2	0 0 - 0	0 2 4 6	0 - - 0
		0 4	0 - 0 0	(0 4 2 6	0 - - 0)
2	0 0 1 0				
4	0 1 0 0	2 6	0 - 1 0		
		4 6	0 1 - 0		
6	0 1 1 0				

Table 4.

Prime Implicant Table for the Transmissi
of Table 2

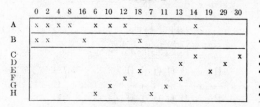

	0	2	4	8	16	6	10	12	18	7	11	13	14	19	29	30
A	x	x	x	x		x	x	x					x			
B	x	x				x		x								
C													x		x	
D												x				
E							x		x							
F									x	x						
G							x				x					
H							x					x				

formed, etc.

In general, any character can be formed by combining two characters whose labels form an increasing sequence of decimal numbers when placed together. It is possible to shorten the process of determining prime implicants by not considering the combination of any characters whose labels do not satisfy this requirement. For example, in Table 2(b) the possibility of combining the (0,4) character with either the (2,6), (2,10) or the (2,18) character need not be considered. If the process is so shortened, it is not sufficient to place check marks next to the two characters from which a new character is formed; each member of all pairs of characters which would produce the same new character when combined must also receive check marks. More simply, when a new character is formed a check mark is placed next to all characters whose labels contain only decimal numbers which occur in the label of the new character. In Table 2, when the (0,2,4,6) character is formed by combining the (0,2) and (4,6) characters, check marks must be placed next to the (0,4) and (2,6) characters as well as the (0,2) and (4,6) characters. If the process is not shortened as just described, the fact that a character can be formed in several ways can serve as a check on the accuracy of the process.

It is possible to carry out the entire process of determining the prime implicants solely in terms of the decimal labels without actually writing the binary characters. If two binary characters can be combined as described in this section, then the decimal label of one can be obtained from

the decimal label of the other character by adding some power of two (corresponding to the position in which the two characters differ) to each number in the character's label. For example, in Table 2 (b) the label of the (4,6)(0 0 1 - 0) character can be obtained by adding $4 = (2^2)$ to the numbers of the label of the (0,2)(0 0 0 - 0) character. By searching for decimal labels which differ by a power of two, instead of binary characters which differ in only one position, the prime implicants can be determined as described above without ever actually writing the binary characters.

4 PRIME IMPLICANT TABLES

The minimum sum is formed by picking the fewest prime implicants whose sum will equal one for all rows of the table to combinations for which the transmission is to equal one. In terms of the characters used in Section 3 this means that each number in the decimal specification of the function must appear in the label of at least one character which corresponds to a ms-term (term of the minimum sum).

The ms-terms are selected from the prime implicants by means of a prime implicant table,* Table 4. Each column of the prime implicant

* This table was first discussed by Quine.[6] However, no systematic procedure for obtaining a minimum sum from the prime implicant table was presented.

table corresponds to a row of
the table of combinations for which
the transmission is to have the
value one. The decimal number
at the top of each column specifies
the corresponding row of the table
of combinations. Thus the numbers
which appear at the tops of the
columns are the same as those which
specify the transmission. Each
row of the prime implicant table
represents a prime implicant.
If a prime implicant equals "one"
for a given row of the table of
combinations, a cross is placed at
the intersection of the corresponding
row and column of the prime implicant table. All other positions
are left blank. The table can be
written directly from the characters
obtained in Section 3 by identifying each row of the table with a
character and then placing a cross
in each column whose number appears
in the label of the character.

It is convenient to arrange the
rows in the order of the number
of crosses they contain, with those
rows containing the most crosses
at the top of the table. Also,
horizontal lines should be drawn
partitioning the table into groups
of rows which contain the same
number of crosses, Table 4. If,
in selecting the rows which are to
correspond to ms-terms, a choice
between two equally appropriate
rows is required, the row having
more crosses should be selected.
The row with more crosses has
fewer literals in the corresponding prime implicant. This choice
is more obvious when the table is
partitioned as suggested above.

A minimum sum is determined
from the prime implicant table by
selecting the fewest rows such that
each column has a cross in at least
one selected row. The selected
rows are called basis rows, and the
prime implicants corresponding
to the basis rows are the ms-terms.
If any column has only one entry,
the row in which this entry
occurs must be a basis row. There-

fore the first step in selecting
the basis rows is to place
an asterisk next to each row which
contains the sole entry of any
column (rows A,B,C,D,E,F,G,H, in
Table 4). A line is then drawn
through all rows marked with an
asterisk and through all columns
in which these rows have entries.
This is done because the requirement that these columns have entries
in at least one basis row is satisfied by selecting the rows marked
with an asterisk as basis rows.
When this is done for Table 4, all
columns are lined out and therefore the rows marked with asterisks
are the basis rows for this table.
Since no alternative choice of
basis rows is possible, there is
only one minimum sum for the transmission described in this table.

5 ROW COVERING

In general, after the appropriate rows have been marked with
asterisks and the corresponding
columns have been lined out,
there may remain some columns which
are not lined out; for example,
column 7 in Table 5(b). When this
happens, additional rows must be
selected and the columns in which
these rows have entries must be
lined out until all columns of the
table are lined out. For Table 5(b),
the selection of either row B or row
F as a basis row will cause column 7
to be lined out. However, row B
is the correct choice since it has
more crosses than row F. This is
an example of the situation which
was described earlier in connection
with the partitioning of prime implicant tables. Row B is marked
with two asterisks to indicate that
it is a basis row even though it
does not contain the sole entry of
any column.

The choice of basis rows to
supplement the single asterisk rows
becomes more complicated when several columns (such as columns 2,3,
and 6 in Table 6(a)) remain to be

Table 5.

Determination of the Minimum Sum for $T = \Sigma(0, 1, 2, 3, 7, 14, 15, 22, 23, 29, 31)$

(a) Determination of Prime Implicants

	$x_5 x_4 x_3 x_2 x_1$
0	0 0 0 0 0 $\checkmark$
1	0 0 0 0 1 $\checkmark$
2	0 0 0 1 0 $\checkmark$
3	0 0 0 1 1 $\checkmark$
7	0 0 1 1 1 $\checkmark$
14	0 1 1 1 0 $\checkmark$
22	1 0 1 1 0 $\checkmark$
15	0 1 1 1 1 $\checkmark$
23	1 0 1 1 1 $\checkmark$
29	1 1 1 0 1 $\checkmark$
31	1 1 1 1 1 $\checkmark$

		$x_5 x_4 x_3 x_2 x_1$
0	1	0 0 0 0 – $\checkmark$
0	2	0 0 0 – 0 $\checkmark$
1	3	0 0 0 – 1 $\checkmark$
2	3	0 0 0 1 – $\checkmark$
3	7	0 0 – 1 1
7	15	0 – 1 1 1 $\checkmark$
7	23	– 0 1 1 1 $\checkmark$
14	15	0 1 1 1 –
22	23	1 0 1 1 –
15	31	– 1 1 1 1 $\checkmark$
23	31	1 – 1 1 1 $\checkmark$
29	31	1 1 1 – 1

				$x_5 x_4 x_3 x_2 x_1$
0	1	2	3	0 0 0 – –
7	15	23	31	– – 1 1 1

(b) First Step in Selection of Basis Rows

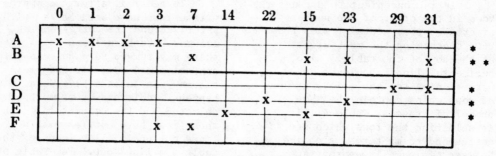

(c) Minimum Sum

$$T = \Sigma \left[(0, 1, 2, 3), (7, 15, 23, 31), (29, 31), (22, 23), (14, 15) \right]$$

$$T = x_5' x_4' x_3' + x_3 x_2 x_1 + x_5 x_4 x_3 x_1 + x_5 x_4' x_3 x_2 + x_5' x_4 x_3 x_2$$

lined out. The first step in choosing these supplementary basis rows is to determine whether any pairs of rows exist such that one row has crosses only in columns in which the other member of the pair has crosses. Crosses in lined-out columns are not considered. In Table 6(a), rows A and B and rows B and C are such pairs of rows since row B has crosses in columns 2, 3, and 6 and row A has a cross in column 6 and row C has crosses in columns 2 and 3. A convenient way to describe this situation is to say that row B covers rows A and C, and to write $B \supset A$, $B \supset C$. If row i is selected as a supplementary basis row and row i is covered by row j, which has the same total number of crosses as row i, then it is possible to choose row j as a basis row instead of row i since row j

Table 6.

Prime Implicant Tables for

$$T = \sum (0, 1, 2, 3, 6, 7, 14, 22, 30, 33, 62, 64, 71, 78, 86)$$

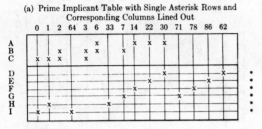

(a) Prime Implicant Table with Single Asterisk Rows and Corresponding Columns Lined Out

(b) Prime Implicant Table with Rows which are Covered by Other Rows Lined Out

6 PRIME IMPLICANT TABLES IN CYCLIC FORM

has a cross in each column in which row i has a cross.

The next step is to line out any rows which are covered by other rows in the same partition of the table, rows A and C in Table 6(a). If any column now contains only one cross which is not lined out, columns 2,3 and 6 in Table 6(b), two asterisks are placed next to the row in which this cross occurs, row B in Table 6(b), and this row and all columns in which this row has crosses are lined out. The process of drawing a line through any row which is covered by another row and selecting each row which contains the only cross in a column is continued until it terminates. Either all columns will be lined out, in which case the rows marked with one or two asterisks are the basis rows, or each column will contain more than one cross and no row will cover another row. The latter situation is discussed in the following section.

If the rows and columns of a table which are not lined out are such that every column has more than one cross and no row covers another row, as in Table 7(b), the table will be said to be in cyclic form, or, in short, to be cyclic. If any column has crosses in only two rows, at least one of these rows must be included in any set of basis rows. Therefore, the basis rows for a cyclic table can be discovered by first determining whether any column contains only two crosses, and if such a column exists, by then selecting as a trial basis row one of the rows in which the crosses of this column occur. If no column contains only two crosses, then a column which contains three crosses is selected, etc. All columns in which the trial basis row has crosses are lined out and the process of lining out rows which are covered by other rows and selecting each row which contains the only cross of some column is carried out as described above. Either all columns will be lined out or another cyclic table will result. Whenever a cyclic table occurs, another trial row must be selected. Eventually all columns will be lined out. However, there is no guarantee that the selected rows are actually basis rows. The possibility exists that a different choice of trial rows would have resulted in fewer selected rows. In general, it is necessary to carry out the procedure of selecting rows several times, choosing different trial rows each time, so that all possible combinations of trial rows are considered. The set of fewest selected rows is the actual set of basis rows.

Table 7 illustrates the process of determining basis rows for a cyclic prime implicant table. After rows G and J have been select-

Table 7.

Determination of Basis Rows for a Cyclic Prime Implicant Table

(a) Selection of Single Asterisk Rows

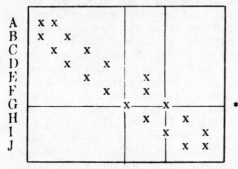

(b) Selection of Double Asterisk Rows

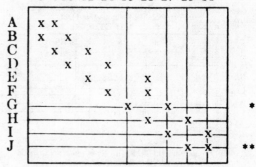

(c) Selection of Row 1 as a Trial Basis Row (Column 0)

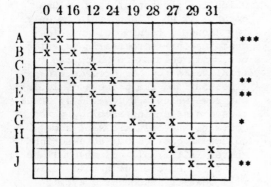

(d) Selection of Row 2 as a Trial Basis Row (Column 0)

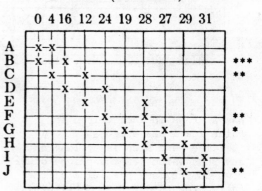

ed a cyclic table results, Table 7(b). Rows A and B are then chosen as a pair of trial basis rows since column 0 has crosses in only these two rows. The selection of row A leads to the selection of rows D and E as given in Table 7(c). Row A is marked with three asterisks to indicate that it is a trial basis row. Table 7(d) illustrates the fact that the selection of rows C and F is brought about by the selection of row B. Since both sets of selected rows have the same number of rows (5) they are both sets of basis rows. Each set of basis rows corresponds to a different minimum sum so that there are two minimum sums for this function.

Sometimes it is not necessary to determine all minimum sums for the transmission being considered. In such cases, it may be possible to shorten the process of determining basis rows. Since each column must have a cross in some basis row, the total number of crosses in all of the basis rows is equal to or greater than the number of columns. Therefore, the number of columns divided by the greatest number of crosses in any row (or the next highest integer if this ratio is not an integer) is equal to the fewest possible basis rows. For example, in Table 7 there are ten columns and two crosses in each row. Therefore, there must be at least 10 divided by 2 or 5 rows in any set of basis rows. The fact that there are only five rows selected in Table 7(c) guarantees that the selected rows are basis rows and therefore Table 7(d) is unnecessary if only one minimum sum is required. In general, the process of trying different combinations of trial rows can be stopped as soon as a set of selected rows which contains the fewest possible number of basis rows has been found (providing that it is not necessary to discover all minimum sums). It should be pointed out that more than the minimum number of basis rows may be required in some cases and in these cases all combinations of trail rows must be considered. A more accurate lower bound on the number of basis rows can be obtained by considering the number of rows which have the most crosses. For example, in Table 6 there are 15 columns and 4 crosses, at most, in any row. A lower bound of 4 (15/4=3 3/4) is a little too optimistic since there are only three rows which contain four crosses. A more realistic lower bound of 5 is obtained by noting that the rows which have 4 crosses can provide crosses in at most 12 columns and that at least two additional rows containing two crosses are necessary to provide crosses in the three remaining columns.

7 CYCLIC PRIME IMPLICANT TABLES AND GROUP INVARIANCE

It is not always necessary to resort to enumeration in order to determine all minimum sums for a cyclic prime implicant table. Often there is a simple relation among the various minimum sums for a transmission so that they can all be determined directly from any single minimum sum by simple interchanges of variables. The process of selecting basis rows for a cyclic table can be shortened by detecting beforehand that the minimum sums are so related.

An example of a transmission for which this is true is given in Table 8. If the variables x_1 and x_2 are interchanged, one of the minimum sums is changed into the other. In the prime implicant table the interchange of x_1 and x_2 leads to the interchange of columns 1 and 2, 5 and 6, 9 and 10, 13 and 14, and rows A and B, C and D, E and F, G and H. The transmission itself remains the same after the interchange.

In determining the basis rows for the prime implicant table, Table 8(d), either row G or row H can be chosen as a trial basis row. If row G is selected the i-set of basis rows will result and if row H is selected the ii-set of basis rows will result. It is unnecessary to carry out the procedure of determining both sets of basis rows. Once the i-set of basis rows is known, the ii-set can be determined directly by interchanging the x_1 and x_2 variables in the i-set. Thus no enumeration is necessary in order to determine all minimum sums.

In general, the procedure for a complex prime implicant table is to determine whether there are any pairs of variables which can be interchanged without effecting the transmission. If such pairs of variables exist, the corresponding interchanges of pairs of rows are determined. A trial basis row is then selected from a pair of rows which contain the only two crosses of a column and which are interchanged when the variables are permuted. After the set of basis rows has been determined, the other set of basis rows can be obtained by replacing each basis row by the row with which it is interchanged when variables are permuted. If any step of this procedure is not possible, it is necessary to resort to enumeration.

In the preceding discussion only simple interchanges of variables have been mentioned. Actually all

Table 8.

Determination of the Minimum Sums for T = Σ(0, 1, 2, 5, 6, 7, 9, 10, 11, 13, 14, 1$

(a)

	$x_4 x_3 x_2 x_1$
0	0 0 0 0 $\checkmark$
1	0 0 0 1 $\checkmark$
2	0 0 1 0 $\checkmark$
5	0 1 0 1 $\checkmark$
6	0 1 1 0 $\checkmark$
9	1 0 0 1 $\checkmark$
10	1 0 1 0 $\checkmark$
7	0 1 1 1 $\checkmark$
11	1 0 1 1 $\checkmark$
13	1 1 0 1 $\checkmark$
14	1 1 1 0 $\checkmark$
15	1 1 1 1 $\checkmark$

(b)

		$x_4 x_3 x_2 x_1$
0,	1	0 0 0 –
0,	2	0 0 – 0
1,	5	0 – 0 1 $\checkmark$
1,	9	– 0 0 1 $\checkmark$
2,	6	0 – 1 0 $\checkmark$
2,	10	– 0 1 0 $\checkmark$
5,	7	0 1 – 1 $\checkmark$
5,	13	– 1 0 1 $\checkmark$
6,	7	0 1 1 – $\checkmark$
6,	14	– 1 1 0 $\checkmark$
9,	11	1 0 – 1 $\checkmark$
9,	13	1 – 0 1 $\checkmark$
10,	11	1 0 1 – $\checkmark$
10,	14	1 – 1 0 $\checkmark$
7,	15	– 1 1 1 $\checkmark$
11,	15	1 – 1 1 $\checkmark$
13,	15	1 1 – 1 $\checkmark$
14,	15	1 1 1 – $\checkmark$

(c)

				$x_4 x_3 x_2 x_1$
1	5	9	13	– – 0 1
2	6	10	14	– – 1 0
5	7	13	15	– 1 – 1
6	7	14	15	– 1 1 –
9	11	13	15	1 – – 1
10	11	14	15	1 – 1 –

(d)

	0	1	2	5	6	9	10	7	11	13	14	15
A		x		x		x				x		
B				x		x		x			x	
C			x						x		x	x
D					x				x		x	x
E							x			x	x	x
F								x		x		x	x
G	x	x										
H	x		x									

(e)

(i) (0, 1) + (2, 6, 10, 14) + (5, 7, 13, 15) + (9, 11, 13, 15)

(ii) (0, 2) + (1, 5, 9, 13) + (6, 7, 14, 15) + (10, 11, 14, 15)

$$T_i = x_4'x_3'x_2' + x_2x_1' + x_3x_1 + x_4x_1$$

$$T_{ii} = x_4'x_3'x_1' + x_1x_2' + x_3x_2 + x_4x_2$$

possible permutations of the contact variables should be considered. It is also possible that priming variables or both priming and permuting them will leave the transmission unchanged. For example, if $T = x_4 x_3'x_2x_1' + x_4'x_3x_2'x_1$, priming all the variables leaves the function unchanged. Also, priming x_4 and x_3 and then interchanging x_4 and x_3 does not change the transmission. The general name for this property is group invariance. This was discussed by Shannon.[4] A method for determining

the group invariance for a specified
transmission is presented in "Detection
of Group Invariance or Total Symmetry
of a Boolean Function."[7]

8 AN APPROXIMATE SOLUTION FOR CYCLIC PRIME IMPLICANT TABLES

It has not been possible to
prove in general that the procedure
presented in this section will always
result in a minimum sum. However,
this procedure should be useful when
a reasonable approximation to a minimum sum is sufficient, or when it
is possible to devise a proof to show
that the procedure does lead to a
minimum sum for a specific transmission (such proofs were discussed in
Section 6). Since this procedure is
much simpler than enumeration, it
should generally be tested before resorting to enumeration.

The first step of the procedure
is to select from the prime implicant
table a set of rows such that (1) in
each column of the table there is a
cross from at least one of the selected rows and (2) none of the selected
rows can be discarded without destroy-
ing property (1). Any set of rows
having these properties will be called
a consistent row set. Each consistent
row set corresponds to a sum of products expression from which no product term can be eliminated directly
by any of the theorems of Boolean
Algebra. In perticular, the consistent
row sets having the fewest members
correspond to minimum sums. The first
step of the procedure to be described
here is to select a consistent row-
set. This is done by choosing one of
the columns, counting the total number
of crosses in each row which has a
cross in this column, and then selecting the row with the most crosses. If
there is more than one such row, the
topmost row is arbitrarily selected.
The selected row is marked with a
check. In Table 9, column 30 was
chosen and then row A was selected
since rows A and Z each have a cross
in column 30, but row A has 4 crosses

while row Z has only 2 crosses. The
selected row and each column in which
it has a cross is then lined out.
The process just described is repeated by selecting another column (which
is not lined out). Crosses in lined-
out columns are not counted in determining the total number of crosses in
a row. The procedure is repeated until
all columns are lined out.

The table is now rearranged so
that all of the selected rows are at
the top, and a line is drawn to
separate the selected rows from the
rest. Table 10 results from always
choosing the rightmost column in
Table 9. If any column contains
only one cross from a selected row,
the single selected-row cross is
circled. Any selected row which
does not have any of its crosses
circled can be discarded without
violating the requirement that each
column should have at least one
cross from a selected row. Rows
with no circled entries are discarded
(one by one, since removal of one
row may require more crosses to be
circled) until each selected row
contains at least one circled
cross. This completes the first
step. The selected rows now
correspond to a first approximation
to a minimum sum. A check should
be made to determine whether the
number of selected rows is equal
to the minimum number of basis
rows. In Table 10 there are at most
4 crosses per row and 26 columns
so that the minimum number of basis
rows is $[\,26/4\,] + 1 = 7$. Since the
number of selected rows is 9 there
is no guarantee that they correspond
to a minimum sum.

If such an approximation to
a minimum sum is not acceptable,
then further work is necessary in
order to reduce the number of
selected rows. For each of the
selected rows, a check is made of
whether any of the rows in the
lower part of the table (non-selected rows) have crosses in all
columns in which the selected
row has circled crosses. In Table 10

Table 9.

Table of Prime Implicants for Transmission

$T = \Sigma(0,\ 1,\ 2,\ 4,\ 5,\ 6,\ 7,\ 8,\ 9,\ 11,\ 13,\ 14,\ 15,\ 16,\ 18,\ 19,\ 20,\ 21,\ 23,\ 24,\ 25,\ 26,$
$27,\ 28,\ 29,\ 30)$

The selection of row A is shown

0 1 2 4 8 16 5 6 9 18 20 24 7 11 13 14 19 21 25 26 28 15 23 27 29 30

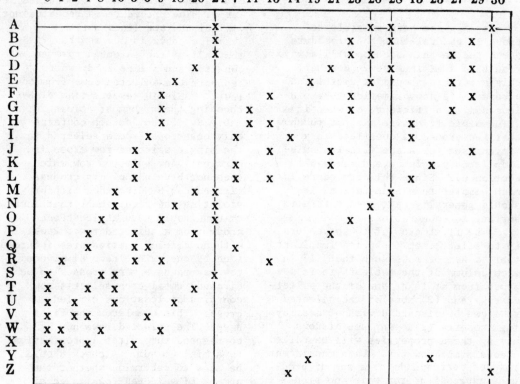

row E has a circled cross only in column 19; since row Y also has a cross in column 19 rows E and Y are labeled "a." Other pairs of rows which have the same relation are labeled with lower case letters, b,c,d,e in Table 10. It is possible to interchange pairs of rows which are labeled with the same lower case letter without violating the requirement that each column must contain a cross from at least one selected row. If a nonselected row is labeled with two lower case letters then it may be possible to replace two selected rows by this one non-selected row and thereby reduce the total number of selected rows (a check must be made that the two selected rows being removed do not contain the only two selected-row crosses in a column). In Table 10 no such interchange is possible.

Next a check should be made as to whether two of the labeled nonselected rows can be used to replace three selected rows, etc. In Table 10 rows Y(a) and J(b) can replace rows E(a), F(b) and K or rows Y(a) and P(d) can replace rows E(a), T(d) and K. The table which results from replacing rows E, F and K by rows Y and J is given in Table 11. The number of selected rows is now 8 which is still greater

Table 10.

Table 9 after Partitioning

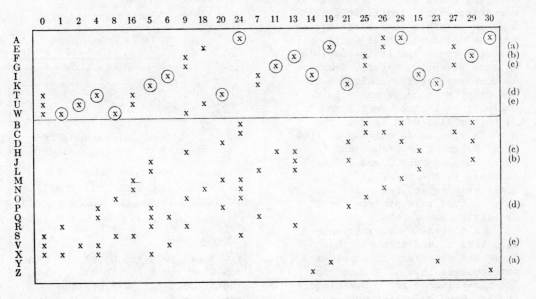

Table 11.

Table 10 with rows E, F, and K, Replaced by rows Y and J

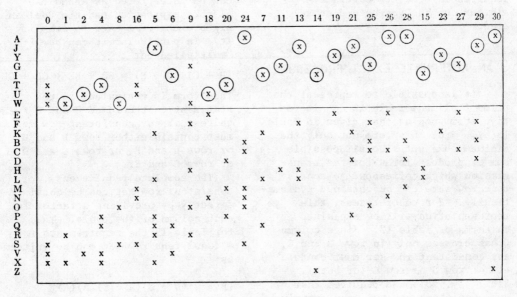

than 7, the minimum number possible. This table actually represents the minimum sum for this transmission even though this cannot be proved rigorously by the procedure being described.

If it is assumed that a minimum sum can always be obtained by exchanging pairs of selected and non-selected rows until it finally becomes possible to replace two or more selected rows by a single selected row, then it is possible to show directly that the Table 11 does represent a minimum sum. The only interchange possible in Table 11 is that of rows T and P. If this replacement is made then a table results in which only rows J and F can be interchanged. Interchanging rows J and F does not lead to the possibility of interchanging any new pairs of rows so that this process cannot be carried any further.

On the basis of experience with this method it seems that it is not necessary to consider interchanges involving more than one non-selected row. Such interchanges have only been necessary in order to obtain alternate minimum sums; however no proof for the fact that they are never required in order to obtain a minimum sum has yet been discovered.

9 AN ALTERNATE EXACT PROCEDURE

It is possible to represent the prime implicant table in an alternative form such as that given in Table 12(b). From this form not only the minimum sums but also all possible sum of product forms for the transmission which correspond to consistent row sets can be obtained systematically. For concreteness, this representation will be explained in terms of Table 12. Since column 0 has crosses only in rows B and C, any consistent row set must contain either row B or row C (or both). Similarly, column 3 requires that any consistent row set must contain either row D or row E (or both). When both columns 0 and 3 are considered they require that any consistent row set must contain either

Table 12.

Derivation of the Minimum Sums for the Transmission
$$T = \sum (0, 3, 4, 5, 6, 7, 8, 10, 11)$$

(a) Table of Prime Implicants

		0	3	4	5	6	7	8	10	11
$x_4'x_1$	A			x	x	x	x			
$x_4'x_2'x_1'$	B	x	x							
$x_3'x_2'x_1'$	C	x					x			
$x_4'x_2x_1$	D		x					x		
$x_3x_2x_1$	E		x							x
$x_4x_3'x_2$	F								x	x

(b) Boolean Representation of Table

$(B + C)(D + E)(A + B)(A)(A)(A + D)(C)(F)(E + F)$

(c) Consistent Row Sets

$(A, C, F, D), \quad (A, C, F, E)$

$T = x_4'x_3 + x_3'x_2'x_1' + x_4x_3'x_2 + x_4'x_2x_1$

$T = x_4'x_3 + x_3'x_2'x_1' + x_4x_3'x_2 + x_3'x_2x_1$

row B or row C (or both) and either row D or row E (or both). This requirement can be expressed symbolically as $(B + C)$ $(D + E)$ where addition stands for "or" (non-exclusive) and multiplication signifies "and." This expression can be interpreted as a Boolean Algebra expression and the Boolean Algebra theorems used to simplify it. In particular it can be "multiplied out":

$(B + C)$ $(D + E)$ = $BD + BE + CD + CE$

This form is equivalent to the statement that columns 0 and 3 require that any consistent row set must contain either rows B and D, or rows B and E, or rows C and D, or rows C and E.

The complete requirements for a consistent row set can be obtained directly by providing a factor for each column of the table. Thus for Table 12 the requirements for a consistent row set can be written as:

$(B + C)(D + E)(A + B)(A)(A)$

$(A + D)(C)(F)(E + F)$

By using the theorems that A (A + D)=A and A A = A, this can be simplified

Table 13.

Determination of the Minimum Sums for the Prime Implicant Table of Table 7 by
Means of the Boolean Representation

(a) Boolean Representation of the Prime Implicant Table of Table 7
(A+B)(A+C)(B+D)(C+E)(D+F)(G)(E+F+H)(G+I)(H+J)(I+J)

(b) The expression of (a) after multiplying out. (The terms in italics
correspond to minimum sums.)

$$ADEJG + ACDFJG + ACDHJG + ADEHIG + ACDHIG + ABEFJG$$
$$+ ABEFHIG + BCDEJG + BCDHJG + BCDHIG + BCFJG + BCFHIG$$

(c) Tree circuit equivalent of (b)

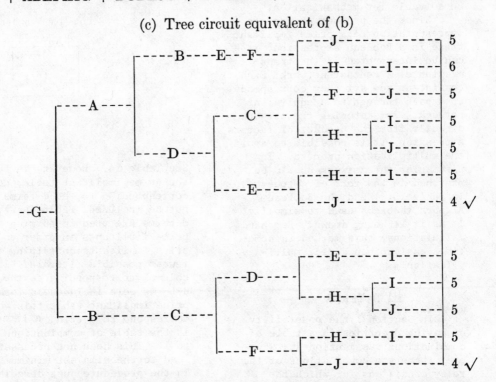

to ACF(D + E). Thus the two consistent row sets for this table are A,C,F,D and A,C,F,E and since they both contain the same number of rows, they both represent minimum sums. This is true only because rows D and E contain the same number of crosses. In general, each row should be assigned a weight $w = n - \log_2 k$, where n is the number of variables in the transmission being considered and k is the number of crosses in the row.* To select the

minimum sums, the sum of the weights of the rows should be calculated for each row set containing the fewest rows. The row sets having the smallest total weight correspond to minimum sums. If, instead of the minimum sum, the form leading to the two-stage diode-logic circuit requiring fewest diodes is desired, a slightly different procedure is appropriate. To each row set is assigned to total weight equal to the sum of the weights of the rows plus the number of rows in the set. The desired form then corresponds to the row set having the smallest total weight.

* $n-\log_2 k$ is the number of literals in the prime implicant corresponding to a row containing k crosses.

The procedure for an arbitrary table is analogous. A more complicated example is given in Table 13. In this example the additional theorem $(A + B)(A + C) = (A + BC)$ is useful. This example shows that for a general table the expressions described in this Section and the multiplication process can become very lengthy. However, this procedure is entirely systematic and may be suitable for mechanization.

Since the product of factors representation of a prime implicant table is a Boolean expression, it can be interpreted as the transmission of a contact network. Each consistent row set then corresponds to a path through this equivalent network. By sketching the network directly from the product of factors expression, it is possible to avoid the multiplication process. In particular the network should be sketched in the form of a tree, as in Table 13(c) and the Boolean Algebra theorems used to simplify it as it is being drawn. For hand calculations, this method is sometimes easier than direct multiplication.

10 D-TERMS

In Section 1 the possibility of having d-entries in a table of combinations was mentioned. Whenever there are combinations of the relay conditions for which the transmission is not specified, d-entries are placed in the T-column of the corresponding rows of the table of combinations. The actual values (0 or 1) of these d-entries are chosen so as to simplify the form of the transmission. This section will describe how to modify the method for obtaining a minimum sum when the table of combinations contains d-entries.

The p-terms which correspond to d-entries in the table of combinations will be called d-terms. These d-terms should be included in the list of p-terms which are used to form the prime implicants.

Table 14.

Determination of the Minimum Sum for the Transmission $T = \Sigma(5, 6, 13) + d(9, 14)$ Where 9 and 14 are the d-Terms

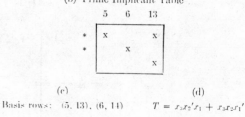

(a) Determination of Prime Implicants

	$x_4 x_3 x_2 x_1$			$x_4 x_3 x_2 x_1$
5	0 1 0 1 ✓		5 13	– 1 0 1
6	0 1 1 0 ✓		6 14	– 1 1 0
(d) 9	1 0 0 1 ✓		9 13	1 – 0 1
13	1 1 0 1 ✓			
(d) 14	1 1 1 0 ✓			

(b) Prime Implicant Table

	5	6	13
*	x		x
*		x	
			x

(c) Basis rows: (5, 13), (6, 14)

(d) $T = x_3 x_2' x_1 + x_3 x_2 x_1'$

See Table 14. However, in forming the prime implicant table, columns corresponding to the d-terms should not be included, Table 14(b). The d-terms are used in forming the prime implicants in order to obtain prime implicants containing the fewest possible literals. If columns corresponding to the d-terms were included in forming the prime implicant table this would correspond to setting all the d-entries in the table of combinations equal to 1. This does not necessarily lead to the simplest minimum sum. In the procedure just described, the d-entries will automatically be set equal to either 0 or 1 so as to produce the simplest minimum sum. For the transmission of Table 14 the 14 d-entry has been set equal to 1 and the 9 d-entry has been set equal to 0.

11 NONCANONICAL SPECIFICATIONS

A transmission is sometimes specified not by a table of combinations or a canonical expansion, but as a sum of product terms (not necessarily prime implicants). The method described in Section 3 is applicable to such a transmission

if the appropriate table of combinations (decimal specification)
is first obtained. However, it is
possible to modify the procedure
to make use of the fact that the
transmission is already partly
reduced. The first step is to
express the transmission in a
table of binary characters such
as Table 15(a). Then each
pair of characters is examined
to determine whether any different
character could have been formed
from the characters used in
forming the characters of the pair.
For example, in Table 15(a)
a (1) (00001) was used in
forming the (0,1) (0000-)
character and a (3)(00011) was
used in forming the (3,7)(00-11)
character. These can be combined
to form a new character (1,3)
(000-1). The new characters formed
by this process are listed in another
column such as Table 15(b). This
process is continued until no
new characters are formed.

In examining a pair of characters,
it is sufficient to determine
whether there is only one position
where one character has a one and
the other character has a zero.
If this is true a new character is
formed which has a dash in this
position and any other position
in which both characters have
dashes, and has a zero (one)
in any position in which either
character has a zero (one). In
Table 15(a) the (0,1) character
has a zero in the x_2-position
while the (3,7) character has a
one in the x_2-position. A new
character is formed (1,3) which
has a dash in the x_2-position.

This rule for constructing new
characters is actually a generalization of the rule used in Section 3
and corresponds to the theorem.

$$x_1 x_2 + x_1' x_3 = x_1 x_2 + x_1' x_3 + x_2 x_3.$$

Repeated application of this rule will
lead to the complete set of prime
implicants. As described in Section 3,

Table 15.

Determination of the Prime Implicants for
the Transmission of Table 14 Specified as
a Sum of Product Terms

(a) Specification		(b) Characters Derived from (a)	
$x_5 x_4 x_3 x_2 x_1$		$x_5 x_4 x_3 x_2 x_1$	
0 1	0 0 0 0 −	1 3	0 0 0 − 1
0 2	0 0 0 − 0	2 3	0 0 0 1 −
3 7	0 0 − 1 1	7 15	0 − 1 1 1
11 15	0 1 1 1 −	7 23	− 0 1 1 1
22 23	1 0 1 1 −	15 31	− 1 1 1 1
29 31	1 1 1 − 1	23 31	1 − 1 1 1

(c) Characters Derived from (a) and (b)	
$x_5 x_4 x_3 x_2 x_1$	
0 1 2 3	0 0 0 − −
7 15 23 31	− − 1 1 1

any character which has all of the numbers of its decimal label appearing
in the label of another character should
be checked. The unchecked characters
then represent the prime implicants.
The process described in this section
was discussed from a slightly different
point of view by Quine.[8]

12 SUMMARY AND CONCLUSIONS

In this paper a method has been
presented for writing any transmission
as a minimum sum. This method is
similar to that of Quine; however,
several significant improvements have
been made. The notation has been
simplified by using the symbols 0,1
and − instead of primed and unprimed
variables. While it is not completely new in itself, this notation
is especially appropriate for the
arrangement of terms used in determining the prime implicants.
Listing the terms in a column which
is partitioned so as to place terms
containing the same number of 1's
in the same partition reduces
materially the labor involved in
determining the prime implicants.
Such a list retains some of the
advantage of the arrangement of
squares in the Karnaugh Chart
without requiring a geometrical
representation of an n-dimen-
sional hypercube. Since the
procedure for determining the
prime implicants is completely
systematic it is capable of
being programmed on a digital

computer. The arrangement of
terms introduced here then results
in a considerable saving in both
time and storage space over previous methods, making it possible
to solve larger problems on a
given computer. It should be
pointed out that this procedure
can be programmed on a decimal
machine by using the decimal
labels instead of the binary characters introduced.

A method was presented for
choosing the minimum sum terms from
the list of prime implicants by
means of a table of prime implicants.
This is again similar to a method
presented by Quine. However, Quine
did not give any systematic procedure for handling cyclic prime
implicant tables; that is, tables
with more than one cross in each
column. In this paper a procedure
is given for obtaining a minimum
sum from a cyclic prime implicant
table. In general, this procedure
requires enumeration of several
possible minimum sums. If a transmission has any nontrivial group invariances it may be possible to
avoid enumeration or to reduce considerably the amount of enumeration
necessary. A method for doing this
is given.

The process of enumeration used
for selecting the terms of the minimum sum from a cyclic prime implicant
table is not completely satisfactory
since it can be quite lengthy. In
seeking a procedure which does not
require enumeration, the method involving the group invariances of a
transmission was discovered. This
method is an improvement over complete enumeration, but still has two
shortcomings. There are transmissions which have no nontrivial
group invariances but which give
rise to cyclic prime implicant
tables. For such transmissions
it is still necessary to resort to
enumeration. Other transmissions
which do possess nontrivial group
invariances still require enumeration after the invariances have been

used to simplify the process of selecting minimum sum terms. More
research is necessary to determine
some procedure which will not require
any enumeration for cyclic prime
implicant tables. Perhaps the concept of group invariance can be
generalized so as to apply to all
transmissions which result in cyclic
prime implicant tables.

13 ACKNOWLEDGEMENTS

The author wishes to acknowledge his indebtedness to Professor
S. H. Caldwell, Professor D. A.
Huffman, Professor W. K. Linvill,
and S. H. Unger with whom the
author had many stimulating discussions. Thanks are due also to
W. J. Cadden, C. Y. Lee, and G. H.
Mealy for their helpful comments
on the preparation of this paper.

14 REFERENCES

1. M. Karnaugh, "The Map Method
    for Synthesis of Combinational
    Logic Circuits Circuits,"A.I.E.E
    Trans. - Communications and Elec-
    tronics, vol. 72, Part I, pp. 593-
    598, 1953. (Reprinted in this
    part of this volume).

2. W. Keister, A. E. Ritchie, and
    S. Washburn, The Design of Switch-
    ing Circuits, Van Nostrand, New
    York, 1951.

3. C. E. Shannon, "A Symbolic Anal-
    ysis of Relay and Switching Cir-
    cuits," Trans. A.I.E.E. Vol. 57
    pp. 713-723, 1938. (Reprinted in
    this part of this volume).

4. C. E. Shannon, "The Synthesis of
    Two-Terminal Switching Circuits".
    Bell System Technical Journal,
    Vol. 28, pp. 59-98, 1949.

5. Staff of the Harvard Computa-
    tional Laboratory, Synthesis of
    Electronic Computing and Control
    Circuits, Harvard University
    Press, Cambridge, 1951.

6. W. V. Quine, "The Problem of
    Simplifying Truth Functions,"
    The American Mathematical Monthly,
    Vol. 59, pp. 521-531, October, 1952.

7. E. J. McCluskey, "Detection of
    Group Invariance or Total Symme-
    try of a Boolean Function," Bell

System Technical Journal, Vol.
35, pp. 1445-1453, 1956.

8. W. V. Quine, "A Way to Simplify
    Truth Functions," The American
    Mathematical Monthly, Vol. 62,
    pp. 627-631, November, 1955.

A METHOD FOR SYNTHESIZING SEQUENTIAL CIRCUITS

GEORGE H. MEALY

1. INTRODUCTION

1.1 FOREWARD

The designer of a sequential switching circuit - a circuit with storage or "memory" - faces a far more difficult problem than is faced by the designer of, say, a simple translating circuit. In the latter case, comparatively simple and straightforward methods of synthesis are known.[1] In the former case, the designer frequently does not even know how to begin to solve the problem. Only recently did D. A. Huffman develop a method which, at an early point in the design, gives rather explicit procedures for carrying the design through to completion.[2] The method relies for its success on a tabular method of presenting the circuit requirements. This table, called a flow chart, may be subjected to simple manipulations which remove redundancies in the verbal statement of the circuit requirements. When supplemented by somewhat more complicated procedures, the flow chart is reduced to a form which leads directly to a circuit having a minimal number of storage elements. This process will be called reduction in this paper, and direct manipulation of the flow chart will be called merging.

Independently, E. F. Moore investigated the abstract properties of sequential circuits.[3] In particular, Moore asked what can be said about a circuit when one knows nothing about it except what may be inferred by performing experiments involving only the input and output terminals of the circuit. A by-product of Moore's theory was a general method for reducing (if necessary) a circuit whose description is completely known.* This method is essentially the same as Huffman's methods, sans flow chart manipulation.

The situation, then, is the following: Once a flow chart, or some equivalent statement of circuit requirements, has been obtained, one may use Moore's procedure for reducing the circuit. Once the circuit has been completely reduced, the remainder of the synthesis procedure is fairly uncomplicated. On the other hand, one may use the merging process of Huffman on the flow table. Very often this will result in complete reduction; less often it will be necessary to use additional procedures equivalent to the Moore process. Merging, when it is possible, is easier to use than is the Moore procedure, hence one would like to find a method which is as simple as merging and at the same time results in complete reduction more often than does merging.

Huffman's method was originally developed in connection with relay circuits, although it is applicable in other instances. It does not, however, always work in its unmodified form when applied to switching circuitry of the type that is commonly used in the design of digital computers.[4,5] One then asks, how can Huffman's method be extended to cover such instances?

This paper offers one possible solution to both questions. After

Reprinted with permission from the Bell System Technical Journal, Vol. 34, Sept. 1955, pp. 1045-1079. Copyright 1955, American Telephone and Telegraph Company.

---

* We shall use the word "circuit" to refer both to physical circuits and to abstract representations of circuit requirements (such as flow charts). The latter of course, may correspond to many physical circuits.

describing an abstract model for sequential circuits, we develop Moore's method for reduction, as it applies to our model. We then develop a new method applicable to synchronous circuitry, which is commonly used in computer design. Finally, the method is extended to relay circuitry as an example of asynchronous circuitry. The relationship between our method and Huffman's method, as they are applied to this class of circuits, is then explained.

1.2 INTRODUCTORY REMARKS

It is very tempting at the outset to make the flat statement: There is no such thing as a synchronous circuit. This would be strictly true if we defined a synchronous circuit as one with the properites:

(S1) Any lead or device within the circuit may assume, at any instant of time. only one of two conditions, such as high or low voltage, pulse or no pulse.

(S2). The behavior of the circuit may be completely described by the consideration of conditions in the circuit at equally-spaced instants in time.*

Because it is quite clear that no physical circuit satisfies (S1) and (S2), such a blanket statement would be a quibble, for the engineer does recognize a certain class of circuits which he calls synchronous. The unfortunate fact is that the distinction between a synchronous and an asynchronous circuit is very hazy in many cases of actual engineering interest. Roughly, we may say that the more nearly a circuit satisfies (S1) and (S2), the more likely will an engineer be to identify it as a synchronous circuit.

As intuitive guides to the usual

_____

* Actually, these need not be equally-spaced. However, the instants considered must not depend on any property of any sequence of inputs presented to the circuit, such as the duration of a pulse.

properties of a synchronous circuit, these characteristics are offered:

1. There is a so-called clock which supplies timing pulses to the circuit.

2. Inputs and outputs are in the form of voltage or current pulses which occur synchronously with pulses from the clock.

3. The repetition rate of the clock pulses may be varied, within limits, without affecting the correct operation of the circuit, so long as input pulses remain synchronized with the clock.

Another assumption that is commonly made, although it does not bear on the distinction between synchronous and asynchronous circuits, should nevertheless be mentioned. If this assumption is made, then we may distinguish between combinational and sequential circuits.

D. Certain circuits contain no time delay - their input combinations in every case completely determine their output combinations.

We will be concerned mainly with a technology in which these assumptions are nearly satisfied - that of the type employed in Leiner et al.[4,5] In this technology, one uses AND gates (with or without inhibiting inputs), OR gates, delay lines, and amplifiers. For our purposes, we may ignore the need for amplifiers. The other basic circuits are as shown in Fig. 1. The properties of these circuit blocks

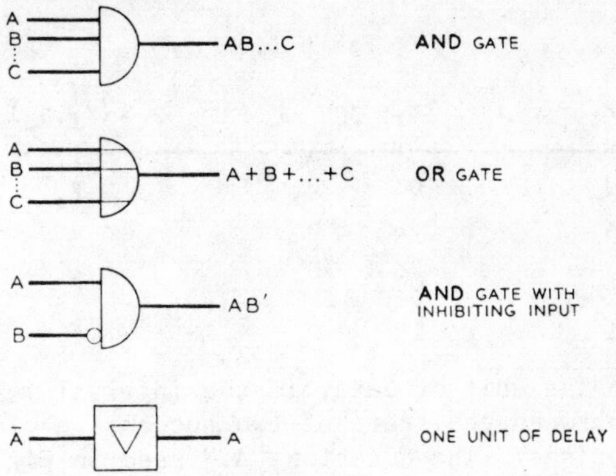

Fig. 1.

are defined by the algebraic expressions in the illustration.*

The familiar switching (or Boolean) algebra is used, where 0 stands for no pulse, 1 for pulse, + for OR, · for AND and ( )' for NOT. It is assumed that the reader is familiar with switching algebra and its use in practical design problems. We recall from switching algebra:

1. A switching function is any (finite) expression in switching algebra.

2. A minimal polynomial of n variables is any product of the form:

$$x_1^{a_1} x_2^{a_2} \cdots x_n^{a_n}$$

where

$$x_i^{a_i} = \begin{cases} x_i' & a_i = 0 \\ \\ x_i & a_i = 1 \end{cases}$$

3. We define

$$P_j = x_1^{a_1} x_2^{a_2} \cdots x_n^{a_n}$$

where j is the decimal form of $a_1 a_2 \cdots a_n$, considered as a binary number. For example, if n = 3, $P_0 = x_1' x_2' x_3'$, $P_1 = x_1' x_2' x_3$, etc.

4. Every switching function of n variables may be brought into a unique canonical form:

Table 1.

x_1	x_2	$f(x_1,x_2)$
0	0	f_0
0	1	f_1
1	0	f_2
1	1	f_3

* The unit of delay is the interval between the start of two successive clock pulses. The notation "$\overline{A}$," used in Fig. 1, will be explained in Section 2.1.

$$f(x_1,\ldots,x_n) = \sum_{i=0}^{2n-1} f_i P_i$$

where

$$f_i = f(a_1, a_2, \ldots, a_n)$$

5. Corresponding to each function is a truth-table which displays the value of the function for each set of arguments. For n = 2, the truth-table corresponding to the canonical form is found in Table 1. The correspondence between the truth-table and canonical form is one-to-one.

For further information about switching algebra see, for instance, Reference 9.

As an example, consider the function
$$f(x,y) = x' + y'$$

Its truth-table is Table 2, and, therefore, $f_0 = f_1 = f_2 = 1$ and $f_3 = 0$. The canonical form is

$$f(x,y) = x'y' + x'y + xy'$$

2. A MODEL FOR SEQUENTIAL CIRCUITS

2.1 THE MODEL

We begin by giving an abstract definition of a switching circuit:

A switching circuit is a circuit with a finite number of inputs, outputs, and (internal) states. Its present output combination and next state are determined uniquely by the present input combination and the present state. If the cir-

Table 2.

x	y	$f(x,y)$
0	0	1
0	1	1
1	0	1
1	1	0

cuit has one internal state, we call it a combinational circuit; otherwise, we call if a sequential circuit.

We have now to explain what we mean by this definition when we apply it to the technology introduced in Section 1. First, we assume a circuit has n binary-valued input variables, $x_1, x_2, \ldots, x_n$; m binary-valued output variables, $y_1, y_2, \ldots, y_m$; s binary-valued excitation variables, $\bar{q}_1, \bar{q}_2, \ldots, \bar{q}_s$; and s binary-valued state variables, $q_1, q_2, \ldots, q_s$, corresponding one-to-one with the excitation variables. In order to facilitate discussion, we note that a set of minimal polynomials may be associated with each set of variables. Specifically, corresponding to the input variables, we have the input combinations, X_j; associated with the output variables are the output combinations, Y_l; corresponding to the excitation variables are the next states, $\bar{Q}_k$; and with the state variables, we associate the present states, Q_i. For example, if n=m=s=3, we have:

$$X_4 = x_1 x_2' x_3'$$

$$Y_2 = y_1' y_2 y_3'$$

$$\bar{Q}_1 = \bar{q}_1' \bar{q}_2' \bar{q}_3$$

$$Q_7 = q_1 q_2 q_3$$

We will use this notation and terminology for convenience. Rather than stating that, at some time, $x_1 = 1$, $x_2 = 0$, and $x_3 = 0$, we will say that input combination X_4 (or its equivalent - input combination 100) is present. That is, $X_4 = 1$ and thus the inputs are, respectively, 1, 0, and 0.

Now, according to the definition given above, to each circuit we must be able to assign some set of equations relating the $\bar{q}_i$ and y_i to the x_i and q_i. These equations will have the general form:

$$\bar{Q}_k = \bar{Q}(Q_i, X_j)$$

$$Y_1 = Y(Q_i, X_j)$$

That is, k and 1 must be uniquely determined by i and j. Each circuit is associated with a truth-table with its columns headed (in order):

$$q_1, \ldots, q_s, \quad x_1, \ldots, x_n;$$

$$\bar{q}_1, \ldots, \bar{q}_s, \quad y_1, \ldots, y_m.$$

The number of circuits having n input, m output, and s internal variables is equal to

$$2^{(m+s)2^{(n+s)}}$$

since the truth table has $2^{(n+s)}$ rows and m + s columns which must be filled in with 0's and 1's.

The interpretation of this model is now fairly straightforward. We have assumed (S1), (S2), and (D) and know that, physically, the delay unit provides storage. We assign the $\bar{q}_i$, the excitation variables, to the inputs of delay lines, and we assign the q_j, the state variables, to delay line outputs. The present state of the circuit is the combination of conditions on the delay line outputs. The next state is the combination of conditions on the delay line inputs, since one time unit later this combination will be present on the outputs.

To make the discussion concrete, consider Fig. 2. The circuit equations

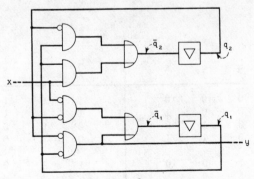

Fig. 2.

are:

$$\bar{q}_1 = q_1'q_2' + x'q_2'$$
$$\bar{q}_2 = q_1q_2' + xq_1$$
$$y = q_1'q_2'$$

From these equations, we write Table 3.

2.2 STATE DIAGRAMS

It is usually not clear from an examination of the circuit diagram or circuit equations just what a sequential circuit does. The truth-table is more helpful and tells the whole story if we put it in a different form, called a state diagram. In this diagram, circles will represent states. Each line of the truth-table will be represented by an arrow going from the present to the next state. A label on the arrow will give the corresponding input and output combination. The state diagram for the circuit discussed in Section 2.1 is given in Fig. 3.

The arrows in the state diagram correspond to changes of state of the associated circuit, and both the arrows and the changes of state are called transitions. A transition begins at a present state and ends at the next state. The transition is labeled X/Y. X is an input combination and Y is the corresponding output combination.

As an example, consider Table 4, which gives the sequences of states and outputs which correspond to each

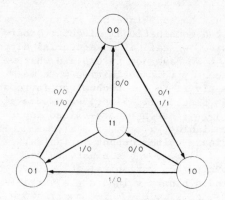

Fig. 3.

initial state of the circuit and the input sequence 100. Depending upon what state the circuit is started in the input sequence 100 produces three different output sequences. It is difficult and probably of little value to put into words exactly what this particular circuit does. However, given any initial state and any sequence of inputs, we can immediately tell what happens from the state diagram. (The truth table may be used for the same purpose, but less easily. It is far more difficult to determine circuit behavior by chasing signals around the circuit diagram.) The problem of circuit analysis is now completely solved. Given any circuit, we may immediately write its circuit equations. A truth-table is easily obtained from the equations. Given the truth-table or given the associated state diagram, we may determine exactly how the circuit behaves for any initial state and input sequence.

Table 3.

q_1	q_2	x	$\bar{q}_1$	$\bar{q}_2$	y
0	0	0	1	0	1
0	0	1	1	0	1
0	1	0	0	0	0
0	1	1	0	0	0
1	0	0	1	1	0
1	0	1	0	1	0
1	1	0	0	0	0
1	1	1	0	1	0

Table 4.

x	0	0	1	1	0	0	1	0	0	1	0	0
q_1	0	0	1	1	0	0	1	0	0	0	1	1
q_2	1	0	0	1	1	0	0	1	0	0	0	1
$\bar{q}_1$	0	1	1	0	0	1	0	0	1	1	1	0
$\bar{q}_2$	0	0	1	1	0	0	1	0	0	0	1	0
y	0	1	0	0	0	1	0	0	1	1	0	0

Conversely, once a state diagram or truth-table is found for a proposed circuit, the above steps may be traced backwards in order to arrive at a circuit diagram. The only problem here is designing combinational circuits economically. The really significant problem in sequential circuit synthesis is finding a suitable state diagram or truth-table. This problem, in turn, may be subdivided into two problems:

1. finding any state diagram or its equivalent which fulfills the circuit requirements and

2. reducing this to the state diagram which is to be used for the final part of the design process.

The next section of this paper develops Moore's method of reduction and is basic in justifying the methods developed in the succeeding sections.

3. CIRCUIT EQUIVALENCE

3.1 MOORE'S THEORY

The key to the synthesis of sequential circuits is the concept of circuit equivalence which was discovered independently by Huffman[2] and Moore[3] We are concerned mainly with the portions of Moore's theory which have direct application to synthesis; certain differences in treatment are necessary since Moore's model for sequential machines is different from ours. All of Moore's arguments carry over with only slight changes.

Roughly speaking, we call two circuits equivalent if we cannot tell them apart by performing experiments involving only their inputs and outputs. Once we have solved the first problem of synthesis by finding any state diagram which fulfills the circuit requirements it will usually be found that the state diagram has more states than are necessary to perform the assigned task. In such a case, we usually wish to simplify the circuit by removing redundant states in such a way that the final circuit is equivalent to the original one.

We must now make the concept of equivalence more precise. We define:

1. Two states, Q_i in circuit S and Q_j in circuit T, are called equivalent if, given S initially in state Q_i and T initially in state Q_j, there is no sequence of input combinations which, when presented to both S and T, will cause S and T to produce different sequences of output combinations.

2. Two circuits, S and T, are called equivalent if, corresponding to each state Q_i of S, there is at least one state Q_j of T such that Q_i is equivalent to Q_j; and corresponding to each state Q_j of T there is at least one state Q_k of S such that Q_j is equivalent to Q_k.

In (1), it should be noted that T may be a copy of S. Hence (1) is also a definition for equivalence between states in the same machine. Moore has shown that even if no two states in a given machine are equivalent, it is not always possible to find out what state the machine started in by some experiment. That is, there is not always a sequence of input combinations for each possible initial state of the circuit. The state diagram of Fig. 3 is the example used by Moore to prove this; state 11 may not be distinguished from state 10 by any experiment which begins with a 1, and state 01 may not be distinguished from state 11 by any experiment which begins with a 0.

If there are two states in a circuit which are equivalent, it should be possible to eliminate one of them. This will result in a circuit equivalent to the original circuit. This is indeed possible, and the process of reduction may be carried out in an essentially unique manner, as is stated by

Theorem 1. (Moore). Corresponding to each circuit, S, is a circuit T which has the properties: (1) T is equivalent to S, (2) T has a minimal number of states, (3)

no two states in T are equivalent,
and (4) T is unique, except for
circuits that result from T by
relabeling its states. T is
called the reduced form of S.

We shall state the procedure to
be followed in deriving T from S,
referring the reader to Reference 3
for a complete proof of Theorem 1.
First, divide the states of S into
sets such that (1) all states in
a given set are equivalent, (2) if
a state is in a given set then all
states equivalent to that state
are also in the same set, and (3)
no state is in two different sets.
These sets are called equivalence
sets or classes. Now, assign a
state of T to each equivalence set
of states. If there is a transition,
bearing the symbol X/Y, from a state
in one equivalence set of S to a
state in a different equivalence
set of S, insert a transition bearing
the same symbol X/Y between the
corresponding states in T. If there
is a transition between two states
in the same equivalence set of S,
insert a transition in T which begins
and ends at the corresponding state
of T. Do this for all transitions
in S.

We have not given as yet an
effective procedure for determining
the equivalence sets. This procedure
will be provided by the method of
proof of the next theorem. Before
stating the theorem, we state a
precise definition of what we
mean by "experiment." By an
experiment of length k, we mean
the process of presenting a circuit
which is in some specified initial
state with a sequence of k successive
input combinations. By the result
of an experiment, we mean the
sequence of output combinations
produced by the experiment. We say
that two states are indistinguishable
by any experiment of length k if
for all experiments of length k the
result does not depend on which
was the initial state. We may
now state

Theorem 2 (Moore). Given a
circuit S whose reduced form has
a total of p states, then for
any two states, Q_i and Q_j, in
S, Q_i is equivalent to Q_j if
and only if Q_i is not distinguishable from Q_j by any experiment of
length $(p - 1)$*

Proof: Consider all experiments
of length k. All states may be
divided into equivalence sets by
the rule: put two states in the same
equivalence set if and only if
they are indistinguishable by any
experiment of length k. For each k,
there is now defined a set of equivalence sets which we will call P_k.

Consider two states, a and b,
that are not equivalent but are
indistinguishable by any experiment
of length k. Since a and b are
not equivalent, there is an experiment of some minimum length, say n,
that will distinguish a from b.
Consider two states, $\bar{a}$ and $\bar{b}$,
that a and b are taken into by the
first $(n - k - 1)$ input combinations
of the experiment. $\bar{a}$ and $\bar{b}$ are
then distinguishable by an experiment
of length $(k + 1)$ but by no shorter
experiment.

We have now proved that P_k is
not already the set of equivalence
sets needed for the procedure of
Theorem 1 if and only if P_{k+1}
contains at least one more equivalence
set than P_k contains.

P_1 has at least two sets, for
otherwise no pairs of states would be
distinguishable, unless p = 1. If
k < p-1, then P_k has at least k+1
sets, by induction using the preceding
argument as the induction hypothesis.
Therefore, P_{p-1} has p sets and is the
set of equivalence classes we need for
construction of the reduced machine.

If Q_i and Q_j are not distinguishable by any experiment of length
(p-1), they are in the same set of
P_{p-1} and hence are equivalent. If Q_i
and Q_j are not equivalent, there is
some experiment of length (p-1), at
most, which will distinguish them.

---

* This theorem is a trivial extension
of Moore's result.

3.2 FIRST REDUCTION PROCESS

The above remarks give the complete story, as far as reduction is concerned. The first method of reduction is stated more explicitly by

Rule I: Separate the states into sets such that two states are in the same set if and only if no matter what input combination is given, both states produce the same output combination. Call these sets "$\bar{P}_1$." Given the set of sets $\bar{P}_k$, find if possible two states in the same set of $\bar{P}_k$ such that some input combination takes the two states into states which are in two distinct sets of $\bar{P}_k$. Put one of the former states, together with all states in the original set which go into the same set in $\bar{P}_k$, into a new set in $\bar{P}_{k+1}$ leaving the other sets in $\bar{P}_k$ fixed. If this is not possible, the process terminates. Now apply the process described following Theorem 1.*

As an example, consider the state diagram of Fig. 3. $\bar{P}_1$ is

$$(00) \ (01, 10, 11)$$

To get $\bar{P}_2$, consider the input 0. 01 and 11 go into 00 and 11 goes into 11. Therefore, we may let $\bar{P}_2$ be

$$(00) \ (10) \ (01, 11)$$

Finally, consider the input 1. 01 goes into 00 and 11 into 01. Therefore $\bar{P}_3$ is

$$(00) \ (01) \ (10) \ (11)$$

Schematically, we may represent this process as:

$\bar{P}_1$: (00) (01, 10, 11)   0

$\bar{P}_2$: (00) (01, 11) (10)   1

$\bar{P}_3$: (00) (01) (11) (10)

---

* This process is due to Moore,[3] except for slight details which concern the choice of model we have made.

This shows that the circuit is already in reduced form.

Note that the $\bar{P}_k$'s developed here are not the P_k's of the proof of Theorem 2. Actually, any two states of this circuit may be distinguished by an experiment of length 2 - the P_k's are:

P_1: (00) (01, 10, 11)

P_2: (00) (01) (10) (11)

The process of Rule I allows us to construct the equivalence sets one step at a time, and the order in which the states are considered does not matter. The result will be unique and must terminate after at most $(p-1)$ steps.

A restatement of Rule I will be given in Section 4.2 which will aply to truth-tables rather than to state diagrams.

As a more complete example, including the construction of a reduced machine, consider Fig.4(a). Apply Rule I, we get:

$\bar{P}_1$:   (0) (1,2,3,4)

$\bar{P}_2$:   (0) (2,4) (1,3)   1

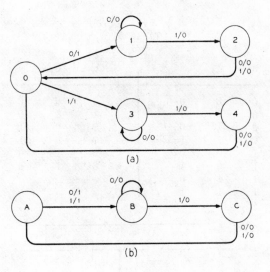

(a)

(b)

Fig. 4.

To construct the reduced circuit, assign state A in the new circuit to (0), B to (1,3), and C to (2,4_. The resulting circuit is shown as Fig. 4(b).

In order to develop a physical circuit, it is necessary to assign a binary code to the states. The assignment is more or less arbitrary for synchronous circuits, but will in general affect the number of circuit elements used. In this instance, we choose to make the assignment:

$$A \rightarrow 01$$
$$B \rightarrow 00$$
$$C \rightarrow 10$$

Rewriting the state diagram as a truth-table, we get Table 5. Two rows in the right half of the truth-table are blank, since state 11 does not appear in the state diagram. It is legitimate to fill these rows in in any way, and it is preferable to fill them in in a manner that results in simplification of the final circuit. Taking advantage of this fact, we may set:

$$\bar{q}_1 = q_1' q_2' x$$
$$\bar{q}_2 = q_1$$
$$y = q_2$$

The final circuit is shown in Fig 5. Fig. 6 shows the state diagram for the completed circuit. As it happens, state 11 is not equivalent to any other state.

This concludes the material on circuit equivalence. In the following section, we develop the method for synchronous circuits. As will be seen, an essential feature of the method is the use of truth-tables rather than state diagrams (which become unmanageable for circuits with more than a few variables) and a very much simplified form of Rule I which may be applied directly to truth-tables. Our program will be (1) to describe the kind of argument used in going from verbal circuit requirements to a truth-table; (2) to restate Rule I in a form (Rule II) which is adapted to synthesis and applies to truth-tables; (3) to develop Rule III, a generalized form of Huffman's merging process; (4) to discuss "don't care" situations, familiar to the reader from the study of combinational circuits; and (5) to give a summary of the method. A complete design example will be given in Section 5.5, following application of the method to asynchronous circuits.

Table 5.

q_1	q_2	x	$\bar{q}_1$	$\bar{q}_2$	y
0	0	0	0	0	0
0	0	1	1	0	0
0	1	0	0	0	1
0	1	1	0	0	1
1	0	0	0	1	0
1	0	1	0	1	0
1	1	0			
1	1	1			

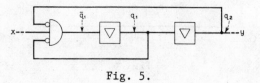

Fig. 5.

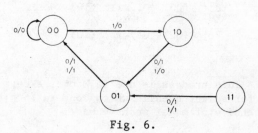

Fig. 6.

4. DEVELOPMENT OF THE METHOD FOR SYNCHRONOUS CIRCUITS

4.1 INTRODUCTORY REMARKS

As seen in the last section, the first problem in synthesis is finding some state diagram that will behave according to the circuit requirements. The state diagram need not be very efficient in the sense that it may have far more states than are actually needed, for the procedures developed in the last section give a straight-forward procedure for removing redundant states. Unfortunately, the initial step in the process relies heavily on the designer's ingenuity. However, we can outline procedures that are of some assistance in finding an initial state diagram.

The simplest case, and indeed the only wholly straightforward case, is that in which the circuit must always return to its initial state after it has received some fixed number of input combinations. Essentially, this case is simple because we may consider all pos-sible input sequences. We assign a new state any time anything happens, up to the last input. The last input then takes us back to the initial state. For instance, suppose that we want a circuit which receives sets of three binary digits in serial form and puts a pulse out on one of eight leads during the third digit to indicate the number that was received. The state diagram may immediately be written down, as shown in Fig. 7. Rather than write sets of 8 binary digits for the output symbols, we have designated the lead that should be energized, if any, and otherwise have written "0."

It is immediately clear that this is even a reduced machine - no two states are equivalent. This is an extreme case; usually there will be certain sequences of inputs which will never occur and/or certain sequences of inputs for

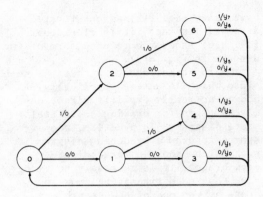

Fig. 7.

which (in Huffman's words) we do not care to specify the circuit action. More often, however, there will be patterns of successive input combinations that will produce the same circuit action. For instance, suppose that in a sequence of 4 inputs we wish to have a final output only if the input sequence is 1010 or 0101. Then we can draw a state diagram showing all sequences which is shown as Fig. 8(a). However, with a modest amount of ingenuity, we might

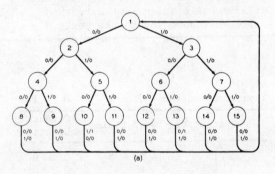

(a)

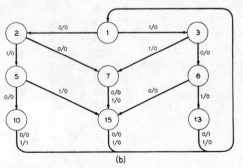

(b)

Fig. 8.

have drawn Fig. 8(b) as our first attempt. In fact, it is clear that Fig. 8(b) shows the reduced form of the diagram in Fig. 8(a).

On the other hand, if there is no state which is entered cyclically, as above, no really explicit directions may be given for drawing an initial state diagram. In practice, one starts to draw a branching diagram such as the above. To terminate each branch, it is necessary to recognize that each transition from the state at the end of the branch may terminate in some state which is already in the diagram. To the author's knowledge, no more specific directions for this are possible.

In practice, large state diagrams become very messy to draw. Where this is the case, it is better to revert to the truth-table, recast in a matrix form with states corresponding to rows and input combinations corresponding to columns. One of the most valuable features of this mode of presentation is that the truth-table may be used directly to perform a large part of the reduction process. To illustrate the truth-table in a simple case consider Table 6 which is the truth-table corresponding to the state diagram of Fig. 8(a). Of the two por-

tions of the table, the left hand one represents the next states and the right hand one gives the output combinations.

4.2 MODIFICATION OF THE FIRST REDUCTION PROCESS

At this point, we give an extension of Rule I which applies to truth-tables. It was noted above that Moore's theory assumes that each machine is completely specified, although the specification is not known to the experimenter. In our restatement of Rule I, we must allow for the possibility of blank entries in the truth-table. This provision amounts to calling two circuits equivalent if there is no evidence for believing that they are not equivalent.*

Rule II: Separate the rows of the truth-table into sets such that two rows are in the same set if and only if no corresponding entries in the right-hand portion of the rows are contradictory. (A blank entry is not considered to contradict any entry.) Call these sets "$\overline{P}_1$." Given the set of sets $\overline{P}_k$, find if possible two rows in the same set of $\overline{P}_k$ such that for some input combination the two rows have designations (next states) which are not blank and correspond to rows in different sets of $\overline{P}_k$. Put one of these rows into a new set in $\overline{P}_{k+1}$ together with all rows in the original set of $\overline{P}_k$ which go into the same set in $\overline{P}_k$ for the given row and input combination. Leave the other sets in $\overline{P}_k$ fixed in $\overline{P}_{k+1}$. If this is not possible, the process terminates. Now apply the truth-table analog of the process described following Theorem 1.

Except for the stipulations concerning blank entries, Rule II is merely a reworded form of Rule I.

4.3 SECOND REDUCTION PROCESS

Rule II, given above seems rather complicated. Although this complication is more apparent than real, one still wishes to find a reduction

Table 6.

Input Combination	0	1	0	1
Present State	Next State		Output Combination	
1	2	3	0	0
2	4	5	0	0
3	6	7	0	0
4	8	9	0	0
5	10	11	0	0
6	12	13	0	0
7	14	15	0	0
8	1	1	0	0
9	1	1	0	0
10	1	1	0	1
11	1	1	0	0
12	1	1	0	0
13	1	1	1	0
14	1	1	0	0
15	1	1	0	0

* This procedure is essentially that stated in Reference 2, pp. 183-185.

rule that has both the effect and the appearance of simplicity. Presumably, one must pay for this in one way or another - the surprising thing is that one is not required to pay too heavily. In point of fact the reduction rule given below, when applied to asynchronous circuits, is somewhat more powerful than Huffman's rule for merging.

We ask, then, what are the simplest circumstances in which a state may be eliminated by using Rule II? Is it possible to consider only pairs of states instead of considering larger sets of states? To answer these questions, consider any pair of rows that are in the same set of $\overline{P}_1$. That is, no corresponding entries in the right-hand portion of the rows may be contradictory. Now if in addition no corresponding entries in the left-hand portion of the rows are contradictory, then the two states have the same output combination for a given input combination and the next state is the same, or may be made to be the same by filling in a "don't care" entry, for any given input combination.* Therefore, the two states are equivalent. This means that we may eliminate one and keep the other. If we eliminate state A in favor of state B, then any appearance in the table of "A" must be changed to read "B."

We restate the above more formally as Rule III. This process is called merging, after Huffman, since we will see that it is a general form of his merging process.

Rule III: To merge state A with state B, change all appearances of "A" in the table to read "B" and copy the entries of row A into row B. Eliminate row A.

Rule III may be used whenever, after the "A's" have been changed to "B's," to each entry in row A corresponds either the same entry

_____
* Or the present state is also the next state in both cases.

in row B or a blank in row B.

As an example, consider Table 6. We see that states 8,9,11,12, and 14 may be merged with state 15. Then state 4 may be merged with state 7. The resulting table, Table 7 now corresponds to the state diagram of Fig. 8(b).†

Note that Rule III may not always give complete reduction. An example is Table 8, to which Rule III may not be applied. However, Rule II leads to the conclusion that states 2 and 3 are equivalent, as are states 1 and 4.

4.4 BLANK ENTRIES; UNIQUENESS OF REDUCTION

The provision for blank entries in Rules II and III corresponds to

Table 7.

Input Combination	0	1	0	1
Present State	Next State		Output Combination	
1	2	3	0	0
2	7	5	0	0
3	6	7	0	0
5	10	15	0	0
6	15	13	0	0
7	15	15	0	0
10	1	1	0	1
13	1	1	1	0
15	1	1	0	0

Table 8.

Input Combination	0	1	0	1
Present State	Next State		Output Combination	
1	1	2	0	0
2	3	1	0	1
3	2	4	0	1
4	4	3	0	0

_____
† The reader is urged to write out the intermediate truth-table derived by carrying out the mergers step by step.

"don't care" situations, which usually result from restrictions on the input sequences. The result of merging rows in different orders is not always unique. The reason for this is simple - when truth-tables have blanks, they may usually be filled in in different ways so as to result in circuits which are not equivalent. Since merging usually results in filling in blanks, different orders of merging may result in blanks being filled in differently. This situation is not in contradiction with Moore's theory; there it is assumed that the state diagram is completely specified at the outset.

As an example, consider Table 9(a). Here, there are four output leads. The designation of which lead is to be energized is given in the right portion of the table dash indicates that no lead is to be energized. Clearly, we may merge 8 and 9 with 7; 4 and 5 with 3; and 6 with 1. The result is shown in Table 9(b). A final merging of 7 with 3 and 2 with 1 leaves the table of Table 9(c). On the other hand, if we merge 2 with 1; 4 with 3; 6 with 5; and 8 and 9 with 7 we get Table 9(d) instead, and Rule II tells us that this is a completely reduced circuit.

We have, incidentally, demonstrated that reduction is not necessarily unique even if only Rule II is used, since Rule III is a restricted form of Rule II. Therefore, Theorem 1 is not necessarily valid unless the intitial truth-table has no blank entries. Again, this does not mean that the theorem as originally stated is false - it means only that we are applying it under conditions which are somewhat more general than those obtaining in Moore's theory. Actually, we are really considering sets of circuits in synthesis. Each circuit is described only partly by the initial truth table and the truth table is, in a mathematical sense, a kind of domain of definition for the circuits in the set considered. Within this domain all circuits in the set are identical while outside this domain the circuits are specified

Table 9(a).

Input Combination	00	01	11	10	00	01	11	10
Present State		Next State				Output Combination		
1	1	6		2	--	AA		AB
2			3	2			--	AB
3		4	3	5	DB		--	DA
4	1	4			--	DB		
5	1			5	--			DA
6		6	7		AA	--		
7		9	7	8	DB		--	DA
8	1			8	--			DA
9	1			9	--	DB		

Table 9(b).

Input Combination	00	01	11	10	00	01	11	10
Present State		Next State				Output Combination		
1	1	1	7	2	--	AA	--	AB
2			3	2			--	AB
3	1	3	3	3	--	DB	--	DA
7	1	7	7	7	--	DB	--	DA

Table 9(c).

Input Combination	00	01	11	10	00	01	11	10
Present State		Next State				Output Combination		
1	1	1	3	1	--	AA	--	AB
3	1	3	3	3	--	DB	--	DA

Table 9(d).

Input Combination	00	01	11	10	00	01	11	10
Present State		Next State				Output Combination		
1	1	5	3	1	--	AA	--	AB
3	1	3	3	5	--	DB	--	DA
5	1	5	7	5	--	AA	--	DA
7	1	7	7	7	--	DB	--	DA

only by "don't cares" and therefore
may differ. Moore's theory applies
to each individual circuit. We, on
the other hand, are applying it to
sets of circuits and must therefore
be prepared to find some differences
in detail.

4.5 SUMMARY OF METHOD

In general we start synthesis by
writing either (1) a state diagram
or (2) a truth-table, as outlined
in Section 4.1. Following this step,
we use Rule I supplemented by
stipulations concerning "don't cares"
or Rule III followed by Rule II to
achieve reduction. In case (1), the
state diagram must now be translated
into a truth-table. At this point
in the process binary coding must be
assigned to the states in order to
complete synthesis with two-valued
storage elements. Two remarks are
in order here:

1. The simplicity of the final
circuit will be affected by the
exact coding assigned as well as
by the truth-table finally chosen,
if reduction is not unique.

2. Using a minimum number of
storage elements is not always wise.
In practical situations, the choice
of components dictates one's criterion
for minimality, and this criterion
must ultimately be based on considerations of economy and reliability.
For instance, the present writer has
seen an example in which it was much
more economical to use seven, rather
than three, storage elements in
order to achieve eight states.
In fact one has doubts that complete
reduction, itself, is always
desirable.

5. THE METHOD APPLIED TO
ASYNCHRONOUS CIRCUITS

5.1 INTRODUCTORY REMARKS

In this section we carry out the
transition from synchronous to asynchronous circuitry. A more exhaustive treatment of the subject of

asynchronous circuitry is contained
in Huffman.[2]

We agree (1) that no clock will
be used and (2) that "1" in switching
algebra will correspond to a high
voltage or current, an energized
relay coil, or operated relay contacts. We must now pay careful
attention to circuit conditions
at every instant of time. One very
real difficulty arises since time
delays inherent in the "combinational" circuit elements may frequently
be of the same order of magnitude
as the time required to change the
state of a storage element. This
may mean that spurious inputs to
flip-flops may be produced by changes
of input combination solely because
of nonuniform delays in portions
of the "combinational" circuitry.
These difficulties will not be
considered further since little
can be said about them over and
above noting their existence.
Another problem – that of race
conditions (a definition of this
term will be given below) – can
be resolved by logical methods;
we shall treat this problem in
moderate detail.

5.2 INTERPRETATION OF THE MODEL

For the purpose of illustrating
the pertinent facts and methods
which relate to asynchronous circuits,
we use relay circuitry as being
typical of asynchronous circuitry.
Fig. 9 illustrates our conventions

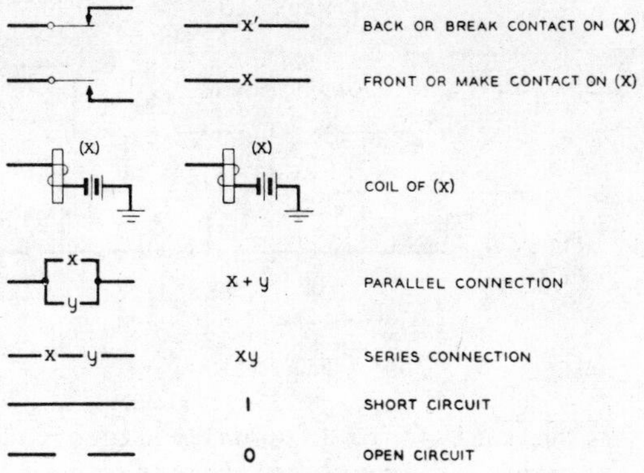

Fig. 9.

and notations.

Our interpretation of the abstract model for sequential circuits given in Section 2 must be changed somewhat. To be concrete, consider the circuit of Fig. 10. We think of this circuit as having two types of relays - to primary relays correspond input variables and to secondary relays correspond excitation and state variables. The general situation is shown in Fig. 11. The primary relays are controlled directly by the inputs; we shall use "x_i" to denote both the ith input and the contacts on relay (x_i). The secondary relays are controlled by contacts on any or all relays; they furnish the storage in the circuit. Considering relay (q_i), we shall say that $\bar{q}_i = 1$ whenever the coil of (q_i) is energized and that $q_i=1$ whenever $(\bar{q}_i)$ is fully operated. Note carefully the distinction between these two statements!

5.3 RACE CONDITIONS; CODING OF STATES

The meaning of "present state" is clear enough - it is determined by which secondary relays are operated. We shall

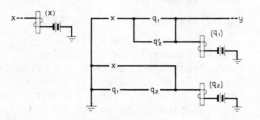

Fig. 10.

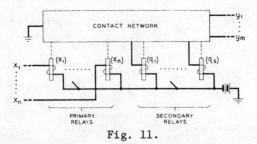

PRIMARY RELAYS　　SECONDARY RELAYS

Fig. 11.

---

* The time scale is usually distorted, sequence of events being more important than their duration.

Table 10.

q_1	q_2	x	$\bar{q}_1$	$\bar{q}_2$	y
0	0	0	0	0	0
0	0	1	1	1	1
0	1	0	0	0	0
0	1	1	0	1	0
1	0	0	0	0	0
1	0	1	1	1	1
1	1	0	0	1	0
1	1	1	1	1	1

say that the "next" state is determined by which secondary relays are energized. However, the "next" state may never be realized as a present state! We shall now reconsider the circuit of Fig. 10. On the basis of our previous agreement, we may draw a truth-table and state diagram. The truth-table is that given by Table 10, and the state diagram is shown in Fig. 12.

In order to study the action of asynchronous circuits, it is often convenient to make use of sequence diagrams.[6] These are essentially pictures of what happens in a circuit as a function of time;* a line opposite a relay or lead designation represents an operated relay or a grounded lead. For instance, assume that both relays in Fig. 10 are released, a ground is applied and then released later on, and moreover that (q_1) is faster in operating than $(q2)$. The corresponding sequence diagram is shown in Fig. 13(a). Clearly, in this case, the circuit does almost what one would expect from consideration of the state diagram, except that the circuit goes from state 00 to state 11 by way of state 10! The situ-

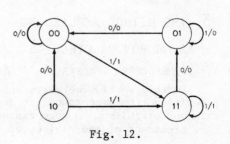

Fig. 12.

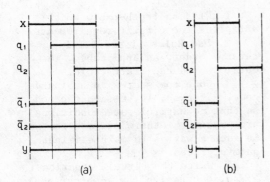

Fig. 13.

ation is quite different if (q_2) is faster in operating than (q_1), as shown by Fig. 13(b). In this case, although state 11 is the "next state," it is never reached, since (q_2) in operating breaks the operating path of (q_1). A situation such as this is called a race condition. Whether it is harmful or not depends on the circuit requirements.

We say that a race condition exists in a circuit for input combination X_i and present state Q_j if the next state Q_k is such that the binary forms of j and k disagree by more than one binary digit. For, if they do, more than one relay is attempting to change its state of operation, and differences in operate and/or release time may lead to differences in circuit behavior.

In order to avoid races, it is necessary and sufficient that any distinct state directly connected by a transition disagree in exactly one binary digit. We can always avoid races if we add enough extra states. On the other hand, if a race condition is not harmful, removing the race condition generally decreases circuit operating speed.

One further remark must be made: it is often very helpful to assume that only one input variable may change its value at any given instant and to arrange connecting circuits in a system so that this condition is satisfied. To appreciate why this might be the case, consider a system containing two interconnecting circuits. These circuits may be viewed together as a single, larger circuit. If the above condition on the interconnecting leads is not fulfilled, then race conditions may be present in the over-all circuit even though they are not present in either circuit considered by itself.

The usual state of affairs in an asynchronous circuit is this: upon a change of input combination, if the "next" state of the circuit is different from its present state, the states of the individual storage elements will change until a final state of the circuit is reached in which no further change of state is possible. Two remarks are in order here. First, we have already seen that in the presence of race conditions the final state, if any, may depend on operate and release times as well as on the truth-table for the circuit. Second, there may be no final state - this is the case for certain pulse-generating circuits.* Usually however, if the new input combination is maintained for a sufficiently long interval, a final state will be reached. Since in most cases of practical interest the time required to reach the final state is much less than the interval during which any given input combination is held, design effort is fixed on the final states, rather than any possible intermediate states.

For the above reasons, the formal part of synthesis - that part of synthesis which ends with writing out circuit equations - is both different and more difficult in the case of asynchronous circuitry. Although it is true that we need not consider the possibility of race conditions until that point in synthesis in which we assign binary coding to the states, it is not true that the same truth table may always be used for both a synchronous and an asynchronous realization of

_____

* See Reference 6, Chapter 18, for examples.

a given circuit. (That this is possible for the circuit of Table 9 is only accidental). The reason for this is tied in very closely with the fact that we speak of presence or absence of pulses in synschronous circuits but of quasi-steady-state conditions on leads in asynchronous circuits. A pulse on lead x_2. for instance, might be represented by X_2 in a synchronous circuit but as X_0 followed by X_2 followed by X_0 in an asynchronous circuit.

5.4 HUFFMAN'S METHOD

The purpose of this section is not to outline Huffman's method synthesis[2] but, rather, to support our claim made above that Rule III represents a slight generalization of Huffman's merging process. We shall assume familiarity with the contents of Reference 2.

The justification for this claim is immediate, if not already self-evident to the reader. Namely, suppose that an initial flow table is written down. By going immediately to the associated truth table, Huffman's rule for merging becomes the same as Rule III, except that Rule III allows somewhat more latitude for merging in that it is permissable to change the symbols corresponding to certain next states. In Huffman's method, it would be necessary to resort to equivalence arguments in such instances. We are considering here that the use of equivalence arguments is separate from the purely mechanical merging process, although there is evidence in Reference 2 that Huffman considers the use of such arguments to be a part of merging. Our point is that such arguments may be avoided in many cases if we work directly with the truth table and Rule III.

5.5 SUMMARY OF METHOD

We have now disposed of the basic principles of our method as applied to asynchronous circuits. The synthesis steps are:

1. Write a truth-table which satisfies the circuit requirements.
2. Use Rules II and III in reverse order, as applicable, to obtain a reduced truth-table.
3. Code the states in a binary code. If possible, assign the code so that no harmful race conditions are present. Otherwise, add states in such a way as to make eliminate harmful races.[2, 6]
4. Write the circuit equations.
5. Synthesize the combinational networks.

As our final example, we consider the following problem, taken from Reference 6 (Problem 8-9):

A rotating shaft carries a single grounded brush which makes contact with three stationary commutator segments arranged symmetrically around the shaft. A relay circuit is required which will indicate the direction of shaft rotation by lighting a lamp when the shaft is rotating in the clockwise direction. The shaft may reverse its direction at any time. Assume that the shaft is driven so that a brush contact closure is 0.25 second and that the open time between the brush leaving one segment and reaching another is 0.25 second. When the shaft changes direction, the output indication must change as quickly as possible, at most within 2 seconds.

Let the brush be grounded and the three segments be labelled "x_1," "x_2," and "x_3" respectively. For the output indication, let $y = 1$ when the shaft is rotating in the clockwise sense. Now, in order to write the initial truth-table, we may first consider what the circuit must do to keep track of the brush while it is rotating in only one direction. This situation is clearly taken care of by Table 11(a). All that remains is to enlarge the table to enable (say) the circuit to go from states 1-6 to states 7-12 when the direction is changed from clockwise to counter-clockwise. A usable strategy is this: as one segment, say x_1, is passed the circuit expects x_2 to come up next. If x_3 comes up before x_2, we

Table 11(a).

Input Combination	000	100	010	001	(All)
Present State		Next State			Output Combination
1	1	2			1
2	3	2			1
3	3		4		1
4	5		4		1
5	5			6	1
6	1			6	1
7	7			8	0
8	9			8	0
9	9		10		0
10	11		10		0
11	11	12			0
12	7	12			0

Table 11(b).

Input Combination	000	100	010	001	(All)
Present State		Next State			Output Combination
1	1	2	10		1
2	3	2			1
3	3		4	8	1
4	5		4		1
5	5	12		6	1
6	1			6	1
7	7		4	8	0
8	9			8	0
9	9	2	10		0
10	11		10		0
11	11	12		6	0
12	7	12			0

Table 11(c).

Input Combination	000	100	010	001	(All)
Present State		Next State			Output Combination
1	1	3	11	1	1
3	3	3	5	9	1
5	5	7	5	1	1
7	7	7	5	9	0
9	9	3	11	9	0
11	11	7	11	1	0

can cause the circuit to go to the counterclockwise state in which x_3 has occurred and x_2 is expected next. This has been done in Table 11(b).

With regard to the output note that it is sufficient to assign $y = 0$ to states 7 – 12 and $y = 1$ to state 1 – 6, regardless of input combination.

The possibilities for merging, (using Rule III), are obvious: merge 2 with 3,4 with 5,6 with 1,8 with 9,10 with 11, and 12 with 7. The result is Table 11(c). Now use Rule II to determine whether reduction is complete. Actually, literal use of Rule II is a waste of time, for we may use this argument:

$$\overline{P}_1: (1,3,5) \ (7,9,11)$$

By examining input combination 100, we split off both 5 and 9 from the sets above, arriving at:

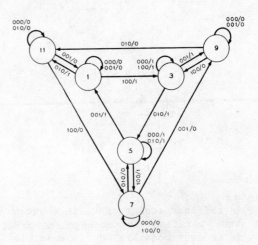

Fig. 14(a).

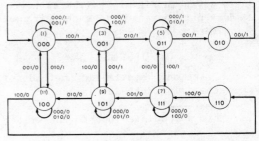

Fig. 14(b).

$\bar{P}_2$: (1,3) (5) (7,11) (9)

By examining input combination 010, we see that 1 and 3 (7 and 11) are distinguishable. Hence, the circuit is completely reduced.

We now have to code the states. To assist in this process, we draw the state diagram shown in Fig. 14(a). Since there are two triangles in the diagram, we cannot assign codes to avoid races, and therefore extra states must be added. One way to do this is to insert new states between 5 and 1 and between 11 and 7 in such a way that the circuit will treat the new states as transient states. This has been done and coding has been assigned in Fig. 14(b). The corresponding truth-table is shown as Table 12.

The circuit equations may be written as:

$$\bar{q}_1 = (q_2{'}q_3{'}x_2 + q_2q_3x_1 + q_2{'}q_3x_3 + q_1) \cdot$$

$$(q_2{'}q_3{'}x_3 + q_2{'}q_3x_1 + q_2q_3x_2){'}$$

$$\bar{q}_2 = (q_1{'}q_3x_2 + q_1q_3{'}x_1 + q_2) \cdot$$

$$(q_3{'}x_3 + q_1{'}x_3){'}$$

$$\bar{q}_3 = (q_1{'}q_2{'}x_1 + q_1q_2x_1 + q_3) \cdot$$

$$(q_1{'}q_2x_3 + q_1q_2{'}x_2){'}$$

In this particular case, if shunt-down operation[6] is not objectionable, it is even possible to dispense with primary relays.* A circuit that satisfies the stated conditions is given in Fig. 15. (The author does not guarantee that the circuit is minimal!)

6. DISCUSSION

Like any "systematic" method for synthesizing certain classes of

---

* This was pointed out to the writer by A. H. Budlong.

switching circuits, our method leaves much to be desired. First, the problem of synthesizing really large circuits has not been touched - one wonders whether it is really possible to do this with any method that relies on the use of a truth-table without making use of automatic design aids inasmuch as large truth-tables become unmanageable. Second,

Table 12.

Input Combination	000	100	010	001	(All)
Present State	Next State				Output Combination
000	000	001	100	000	1
001	001	001	011	101	1
011	011	111	011	010	1
010	d	d	d	000	1
100	100	110	100	000	0
101	101	001	100	101	0
111	111	111	011	101	0
110	d	111	d	d	0

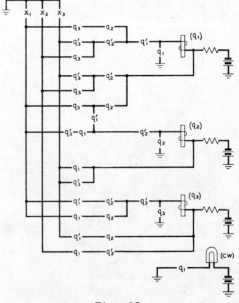

Fig. 15.

the first step of the process, as described in Section 4, has in no sense been eliminated - this is probably the step that asks the most of the designer's ingenuity and skill. Third, the process of coding the states may have a great effect on the final cost of the circuit - despite this, there are at present no rules for carrying out the coding in an optimal manner.

To compare our method with that of Huffman,[2] several pertinent comments may be made. First, our method applies equally well to synchronous and asynchronous circuit synthesis whereas Huffman's method was formulated specifically for asynchronous circuit synthesis. We hasten to add, however, that the basic concepts of Huffman's paper are valid in both cases. Such changes in detail as are required to adapt his method to synchronous circuit synthesis would almost certainly result in a method identical with the method of this paper. Second, for asynchronous circuits, the initial truth table we write down is different only in appearance from the initial flow table that we might have written - neither method offers any advantage in this respect. Third, the ease of using Huffman's merging rule as opposed to the use of Rule III must be weighed against the necessity of translating the final flow table into a truth table in order to develop circuit equations. Finally, the present method is more often successful (in principle, at least) in achieving complete reduction without the use of auxiliary equivalence arguments. Nevertheless, it is always advisable to use Rule II in order to test for complete reduction.

Finally, it should be pointed out that there are many cases where other, more intuitive, methods are more useful. Such methods for asynchronous circuit design are given in Reference 6.

In fact, the place of formal methods, such as that outlined in this paper, in the every day practice of synthesis is much smaller than might appear at first glance. It is probably fair to say that the theory furnishes, at present at least, only generalized methods of attack on synthesis together with a small handful of particularized tools for design. It is the author's belief that these methods are genuinely useful insofar as they aid in understanding the nature of sequential circuits and furnish a unified way of thinking about circuits during their design. It would be a mistake, however, to believe that they provide detailed design methods in the same sense in which such methods are available for electrical network synthesis. The engineer must make a judicious selection of his design tools and, most likely, must invent methods and diagrammatic devices which fit the particular problem at hand.

A few words should be said about the comparative originality of the author's treatment of this subject. The model proposed in Section 2 was suggested to the writer by the content of E. F. Moore, Reference 7, and, in the case of synchronous circuits, is almost identical with the discrete transducer of information theory.[8] Independently, S. H. Washburn proposed essentially the same model in an unpublished memorandum.

Our interpretation of the model for asynchronous circuits and consequences of that interpretation with relation to race conditions were independently treated by Huffman.[2] Our use of Rule III in the method owes much to Huffman's work.

7. ACKNOWLEDGEMENTS

The author gratefully acknowledges the constructive criticisms of many of his colleagues at Bell Telephone Laboratories, Inc. during the course of the work reported in this paper. He owes particular thanks to W. J. Cadden, E. F. Moore, and S. H. Washburn of Bell Telephone

Laboratories, Inc. and D. A. Huffman
of the Massachusetts Institute
of Technology for their participation
in many discussions, philosophical
and otherwise, which have greatly
aided the writer in clarifying
his thoughts on this subject and
which have resulted, it is hoped,
in a far better presentation than
would otherwise have been possible.

8. REFERENCES

1. M. Karnaugh, "The Map Method
    for Synthesis of Combinational
    Logic Circuits," AIEE Trans.
    Communications and Electronics,
    vol. 72, pp. 593-599, 1953.
    (Reprinted in this part of this
    volume.)
2. D. A. Huffman, "The Synthesis of
    Sequential Switching Circuits,"
    Journal of the Franklin Institute,
    vol. 257, pp. 161-190,275-303,
    March and April, 1954.
3. E. F. Moore, "Gedanken-Experiments
    on Sequential Machines," Automata
    Studies, ed. by C. E. Shannon
    and J. McCarthy, Princeton
    University press, 1956.
4. A. L. Leiner, W. A. Notz, J.L.Smith
    and A. Weinberger, "System Design
    of the SEAC and DYSEAC," IRE Trans.
    on Electronic Computers, vol.
    EC-3, pp. 8-22, June, 1954.
5. J. H. Felker, "Typical Block
    Diagrams for a Transistor Digital
    Computer," Trans AIEE, vol. 17-I,
    pp. 175-182, 1952.
6. W. Keister, A. E. Ritchie, and
    S. H. Washburn, The Design of
    Switching Circuits,   Van Nostrand,
    1951.
7. E. F. Moore, "A Simplified
    Universal Turing Machine," Associa-
    tion for Computing Machinery,
    Toronto Meeting, 1952.
8. C. E. Shannon, "A Mathematical
    Theory of Communication,"
    Bell System Technical Journal,
    vol. 27, pp.279-423,623-656,
    July and October, 1948.
9. E. C. Nelson, "An Algebraic Theory
    for Use in Digital Computer Design,"
    IRE Trans. on Electronic Computers,
    vol. EC-3, pp.12-21, September,1954
10. A. W. Burks and J. B. Wright,
    "Theory of Logical Nets," Proc.
    IRE. vol. 41, pp. 1357-1365, October,
    1953.
11. F. J. Murray "Mechanisms and
    Robots," Journal of the Assocation
    for Computing Machinery, vol. 2,
    pp. 61-82, April 1955.

HAZARDS AND DELAYS IN ASYNCHRONOUS SEQUENTIAL SWITCHING CIRCUITS

S. H. UNGER

1. INTRODUCTION

This paper is concerned with the class of sequential switching circuits which has been treated by Huffman, Caldwell, and others.[1-4] We shall not discuss clocked systems. The reader will be expected to be familiar with the essential ideas contained in these references, and so no effort will be made to review the material presented there.

Switching circuits can be physically realized with a wide variety of devices, ranging from electro-mechanical relays to transistors and cryotrons. The problems that we shall attack, and our results will not depend on the nature of the devices used. However, it will sometimes be convenient to think in terms of specific circuits, and in such cases we will refer to gate-type logic, which can be realized with diodes or transistors.

An inherent property of all physical systems is delay. Signals are never transmitted instantaneously, and devices never react in zero time, but nevertheless it is frequently possible to ignore relatively small (or sometimes even large) delays when analyzing or designing systems. In the case of sequential switching circuits, early studies took into account only certain first-order effects of delays. Other effects were generally swamped out by the deliberate insertion of delay elements at key points in the circuits. The large delays inherent in certain devices, such as relays, served, in a fortuitous manner, to prevent malfunctioning that might otherwise have been caused by delays due to second-order effects such as stray reactances. However, modern electronic components operate at such high speeds that the blanketing effect due to inherent delays may be lost, and the deliberate introduction of delay elements becomes necessary.

This may entail an added expense and, when great efforts are being made to develop faster components, it seems somewhat incongruous to have to put back some of the delay that was so painstakingly removed. It is therefore desirable to understand the nature of the troubles caused by unwanted delays. In particular it might often be important to know how to combat these troubles with a minimum amount of additional delay elements.

We shall demonstrate here that a certain class of sequential functions (which we shall specify precisely) can always be realized physically in a trouble-free manner without introducing delay elements. It will also be proved that circuits corresponding to all other functions will be subject to malfunctioning due to unwanted delays if no delay elements are specified in the design. Finally, a proof will be

This paper is based on an Sc. D. dissertation, Dept. Elec. Eng., M.I.T. Cambridge, Mass.; April, 1957. The work was performed at the Res. Lab. of Electronics, M.I.T., and was supported in part by the U.S. Army (Signal Corps), the U.S. Air Force (Office of Sci. Res., Air Res. and Dev. Command), and the U.S. Navy (Office of Naval Res.)

Reprinted with permission from the IRE Transactions on Circuit Theory, Vol. CT-6, March, 1959, pp. 12-25.

presented that any function can be
realized in a trouble-free manner by a
circuit containing just one delay
element. We shall also indicate some
simple techniques that might prove
useful in designing circuits with few
or no delay elements for functions
not so pathological to call for the
all-powerful methods used to prove
the theorems for the most general
cases.

In the next section we shall describe more precisely the kind of
functions and problems we are going
to study, and define a number of
concepts and terms which will be
employed in the main body of the
paper.

The material presented here is
based on a report by the author [5]
which deals somewhat more extensively
with some of the topics.

2. BASIC CONCEPTS AND TERMINOLOGY

A. SYSTEMS UNDER CONSIDERATION

Asynchronous, level-type sequential switching circuits are characterized by the fact that the signal
at each input terminal is at all times
in one of two distinct states-zero
or one-except for brief intervals
during which a transition from one
state to the other is occurring.
Such input changes may be made to
occur at any time, subject only
to the restriction that a minimum
time interval, determined by the
reaction times of the components, must
separate successive changes.

The discussion here will be restricted to sequential functions in
which no single input change is
required to produce more than one
change at any one output terminal.
In flow table terminology (which
will be presented shortly) this is
equivalent to saying that if an
uncircled j appears in any column of
the flow table, there must also be a
circled j in that same column and the
output states must be the same for
both total states.

Unless otherwise stated, it will
be assumed that only one input variable
at a time is permitted to change.

Table 1.

	$x_1 x_2$			
	00	01	11	10
1	①^{00}	2^{10}	①^{01}	4^{01}
2	1^{00}	②^{10}	②^{01}	3^{10}
3	4^{11}	③^{00}	1^{01}	③^{10}
4	④^{11}	3^{00}	2^{01}	④^{01}

B. FLOW TABLES

The terminal characteristics of
sequential switching circuits
(sequential functions) are described
by flow tables such as Table 1,
where the colums correspond to input
states, that is, states of the input
variables x_1 and x_2. The rows
represent internal states of the
system and the cells of the table
represent total states. Entries in
the centers of the cells indicate the
next internal state, which in the case
of circled entries is the same as
the present internal state. These are
the stable states. Output states
for each total state are specified
by the entries in the upper right
corners of the cells.

We shall often be focusing our
attention on the effects of changes
in a single input variable. In such
cases it will be convenient to refer
to the input state as being in column
L (left) or R(right) and total states
will be described as L3 or R5, meaning,
for example, the state corresponding
to the left-hand member of the pair
of columns under discussion and the
third row or the right column, fifth
row, respectively.

C. CIRCUIT MODELS AND FLOW MATRICES

The circuits that will be considered here will be in the form
shown in Fig. 1(a). All signals are
binary valued, and the box labeled
"combinational circuits" contains
no feedback paths. The elements in
the box are all of the type shown
in Fig. 1(b), that is, devices with

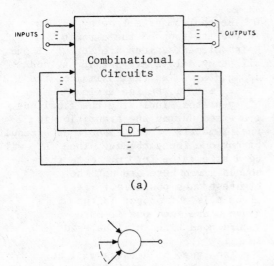

(a)

(b)

Fig. 1.

one output terminal whose signal is a combinational function of the signals at the one or more input terminals. The only other components allowed in our model are delay elements.

Those delays deliberately introduced by the designer are defined as delay elements and appear only in the external feedback branches of Fig. 1(a). It is assumed that every circuit lead, including those inside the box may contain a stray delay, defined as a delay not under the control of the designer.

Any sequential switching circuit composed of the type of elements mentioned here can be represented in the form of Fig. 1(a) (but not always uniquely).

The external feedback branches in Fig. 1(a) will be called "state-branches" and are defined as follows. A set of branches of a sequential circuit is a state-branch set (and its members are state-branches) if the set contains all delay elements in the circuit and if at least one member is included in every feedback loop. Such a set is obviously not generally unique. The

signal at the output end of each state-branch is defined as a state-variable and will be represented by y_i, for the ith state-branch. The y-state of a circuit at any given time is given by the set of values assumed by all of the state-variables of the circuit at that time. State-variable excitations are defined as the signals at the input ends of the state-branches and are represented by Y_i's. They may differ from the y_i's in cases where the branches contain delays.

The bridge between the flow table, describing the external characteristics of the circuit and the detailed circuit, is the flow matrix. Each row of the flow table (internal state) is associated with one or more y-states, defined as row-sets. The flow matrix of Table 2 illustrates such a row assignment for the flow table of Table 1. Each row set is comprised of two y-states. Given a flow matrix, a terminal description of the corresponding combinational circuit box can be obtained in the form of a Y-matrix. This is a table of combinations giving the Y_i values as functions of the y states and can be obtained directly from the flow matrix.[1,2] Table 3 is the Y matrix for Table 2.

D. HAZARDS

A circuit will be defined as proper if, for an $\varepsilon > 0$ there exists a δ such that if all stray delay

Table 2.

| | $x_1 x_2$ | | | | | | |
	00	01	11	10	y_1	y_2	y_3
1	①	2	①	4	0	0	0
					1	1	1
2	1	②	②	3	0	0	1
					1	1	0
3	4	③	1	③	0	1	1
					1	0	0
4	④	3	2	④	0	1	0
					1	0	1

Table 3.

00	01	11	10	y_1	y_2	y_3
$x_1 x_2$						
000	001	000	010	0	0	0
111	110	111	101	1	1	1
000	001	001	011	0	0	1
111	110	110	100	1	1	0
010	011	111	011	0	1	1
101	100	000	100	1	0	0
010	011	110	010	0	1	0
101	100	001	101	1	0	1

$$Y_1 Y_2 Y_3$$

values are less than ε and if all delay element values are greater than δ, then the circuit will operate in accordance with the given flow table, provided that successive input changes are separated by some minimum finite time interval m, which is a function of ε and the maximum delay element value. Roughly speaking, a circuit is proper if it operates in a consistent manner despite variations in all delay values, provided that a suitable margin is maintained between the values of stray delay and delay element magnitudes and provided that the circuit is allowed to settle down after each input change before the next input change is permitted to occur.

(The nature of the relationships among the various bounds for a proper circuit may be surmised from the following statements: A conservative value of δ would be the maximum time for a signal to propagate from any input terminal to any output terminal of the portion of the circuit labeled "combinational circuit" in the model of Fig. 1(a), assuming that a stray delay of magnitude ε is placed in every branch of the circuit. If β is the maximum delay element value in the circuit, then let

L_i be the sum of all delay values in the ith loop of the circuit when all delay element values are set at β and all stray delays are set at ε, and designate L as the maximum of the L_i's. Let T be the maximum number of y-states, including the final one, traversed during any transition in the Y-matrix of the circuit as a result of any one input change. Then LT will be a safe value for m. Note that the bounds given here are not the tightest ones possible.) If a circuit is not proper in the above sense then one or more hazard conditions will be said to exist.

Two types of hazards will be distinguished. A transient hazard is present if momentary false output terminals following certain changes in the input state. If it is possible for a circuit to enter the wrong internal state after certain input changes, then a steady-state hazard will be said to exist.

Transient hazards can exist in combinational circuits, but Huffman has shown that they can always be avoided by appropriate design techniques.[3] Henceforth we shall assume that all of the combinational functions which we must realize will be designed in a hazard-free manner. (This is possible in general only when just one input at a time is permitted to change.)

Another form in which a hazard can appear in a sequential circuit is a critical race condition.[1,2,4] This is a condition in a flow matrix where two or more state-variables become unstable simultaneously as a result of an input change and where the next stable state of the system depends on the order in which the unstable variables change. This source of hazards can be eliminated by design procedures described elsewhere[1,2,4] and will not be considered here.

Two types of delays will be defined. A pure delay is one which converts an input signal f(t) into an output f(t − D), where D is the value of the delay. An inertial delay defined only in terms of binary signals) behaves like a pure delay, except that input changes persisting for a time less than D, the delay magnitude, are ignored. Thus, rapid signal fluctuations are filtered out by such a device, which is somewhat analogous to a low-pass filter. While few if any physical devices behave exactly in accordance with either of the above descriptions, many real components closely approximate pure or inertial delays. Transmission lines and certain LC ladder networks resemble pure delays, whereas electromechanical relays behave like inertial delays. Stray delays, generally dominated by wiring reactances, possess important inertial characteristics and we shall assume that they are representable as inertial delays. This assumption will be used in the proof of the theorem of Section 4.

A typical hazard situation is depicted in the circuit of Fig. 2.

If we assume that the stray delays in the B_1 and B_2 branches are large compared to the delays in the other branches, then the circuit behavior will be correctly characterized by the flow matrix shown in Table 4. (In fact, one way of assuring proper operation is to insert delay elements in B_1 and B_2.)

Suppose now that a relatively large delay appears in the branch labeled H (how large will become clear during the subsequent

Table 4.

| | $x_1 x_2$ | | | | | |
	00	01	11	10	y_1	y_2
1	a ①⁰	2	①⁰	①⁰	0	0
2	c³	b ②⁰	②⁰	3	0	1
3	d ③¹	4	2	③¹	1	1
4	④¹	e ④¹	1	1	1	0

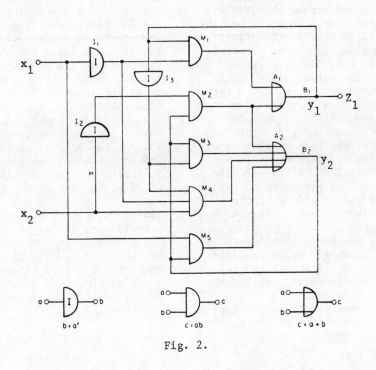

Fig. 2.

discussion). Then if, while the system is in the state labeled a in Table 4, x_2 is turned on (switched from zero to one) the next stable state will be in row 4 and not in row 2, as indicated in the flow matrix. This comes about as follows.

The switching of x_2 first changes to unity the output of the multiplier gate labeled M_4 in Fig. 2, and this switches on y_2, the output of A_2, which is connected to one input lead of M_2. The other input to this gate remains at unity since the delay in H prevents the x_2-change from having an immediate effect at this point. Therefore a one-signal appears at the output of M_2, penetrates through A_1, and turns on y_1. A feedback path through M_1 and A_1 now holds y_1 on independently of the output of M_2. A second effect of y_1 changing to unity is that a zero appears at the output of I_3, thus preventing anything but zeros from appearing at the outputs of M_3 and M_4. Now $y_1 = y_2 = 1$, and the system is in the state marked b in Table 4. But only the output of M_2 is holding y_2 on, and as soon as the effect of the original x_2-change penetrates I_2 and the delay in H, a zero appears at the output of M_2 causing the output of A_2 to go to zero, and the system is in row 4 as stated.

The possibility of such behavior could have been predicted from the structure of the flow matrix. When x_2 changes, y_2 becomes unstable and also switches. If the effects of the y_2-action penetrate to y_1 before the direct effect of the x_2-change (which is the case in our circuit), then as far as y_1 is concerned, the system state switches from a to c, where y_1 is unstable. This causes y_1 to switch to one and moves the internal state of the system to row 3 and, once this occurs, y_1 remains at unity value even after the effect of the x_2-change reaches it. Finally, since y_2 is

unstable in state b, it changes again and the system settles down in state e.

We shall see later that such behavior will always be possible in circuits realizing functions corresponding to flow matrices such as Table 4, unless delay elements are used.

3. FUNCTIONS REALIZABLE WITHOUT DELAY ELEMENTS

A. DEFINITIONS AND LEMMAS

Each definition and lemma in this section is numbered, and the first time the term or lemma is used in the main body of the text it will be italicized and the reference number will follow.

1. Definition-Essential Hazard: A sequential function contains an essential hazard if there exists a stable state S_0 and an input variable x such that, starting with the system in S_0 three consecutive changes in x bring the system to a state other than the one arrived at after the first change in x. The function corresponding to the matrix of Table 4 in the previous section has three essential hazards. One starts in state a with x_2 as the relevant input variable (and was discussed in the example). A second has its initial state labeled b, with x_2 as the input variable. Can you find the third?

2. Definition-Mod Sum: The mod sum of two positive integers a and b, written as $a \oplus b$ is the arithmetic sum of those powers of two appearing in the binary representation of a or of b, but not both. For example, $3 \oplus 7 = 4$ and $5 \oplus 3 = 6$. This operation is clearly associative and commutative, and $x \oplus x = 0$ for any x.

3. Definition-Hamming Row-Set: A y-state will be said to belong to the Hamming row set S_i if, and only if, the q's determined by the parity relations (involving modulo-two addition).

$$q_0 = y_1 \oplus y_3 \oplus y_5 \oplus y_7$$

$$q_1 = y_2 \oplus y_3 \oplus y_6 \oplus y_7$$

$$q_2 = y_4 \oplus y_5 \oplus y_6 \oplus y_7$$

correspond to the digits of the number i written in binary form, that is if $i = q_2 2^2 + q_1 2^1 + q_0 2^0$. For example, 0110111 belongs to S_5. These sets, which can be generated from any set of $2^n - 1$ binary variables, are related to Hamming error correcting codes,[6] and were first applied to sequential switching circuits by Huffman.[4] They have the property that, given any state in S_i, changing $y_{i \oplus j}$ converts the state to one belonging to S_j. For example, changing y_2 when the system is in state 0001101 (in set S_6) changes the state to 0101101 which is in S_4 $[6 \oplus 4 = 2]$. Transitions from any set to any other set thus require a change in only one variable. It will sometimes be convenient to refer to $y_{i,j}$ as the variable separating the states assigned to rows i and j. Where S_i and S_j are Hamming sets assigned to rows i and j, respectively,

$$y_{i,j} = y_{i \oplus j}.$$

4. <u>Definition-d-trio</u>: Three rows of a flow table r_1, r_2, and r_3 constitute a d-trio if, for some pair of input states L and R differing only in the value of one input variable, the next-state entries in L are r_1, r_3, and r_3 in rows r_1, r_2, and r_3, respectively, and the next-state entries in R are r_2 for all three rows. Part (d) of Table 6 in the next section depicts a d-trio (and a glance at this illustration will no doubt be more edifying than the tongue twisting definition given above.)

5. <u>Definition-d-Transition</u>: A d-transition is the activity occuring as a result of an input change from L and R with the system originally in row r_1 of a d-trio.

6. <u>Definition-Trap Row</u>: An auxiliary row added to a flow matrix to guard against malfunctioning during a particular d-transition. The row-set assigned to the trap row for each d-trio corresponds to the y-states other than those assigned to the d-trio which

might be seen during the d-transition due to the effects of stray delays. The next-state entries assigned to the trap rows assure proper termination of the d-transition.

7. <u>Lemma</u>: If a, b, and c are three integers no two of which are equal, then there is no integer d such that $2^d = 2^a \oplus 2^b \oplus 2^c$.

<u>Proof</u>: a. From the definition of $\oplus$ (see Section 3-A, 2) it is clear that $2^a \oplus 2^b \oplus 2^c = 2^a + 2^b + 2^c$ since each term in the sum is a unique power of two.

b. The sum $2^a + 2^b + 2^c$ can be written as a binary number with exactly three nonzero bits, one corresponding to each term.

c. If there existed an integer d such that $2^d = 2^a + 2^b + 2^c$, then the sum referred to in b) could also be written as a binary number with one nonzero bit corresponding to 2^d. But this is impossible since the binary form of any number is unique. Hence there cannot be any d such that $2^d = 2^a + 2^b + 2^c$. (Q.E.D.)

8. <u>Lemma</u>: If $a,b,c,a*,b*$, and $c*$ are positive integers with $a < b < c$ and $a* < b* < c*$, then $2^a \oplus 2^b \oplus 2^c = 2^{a*} \oplus 2^{b*} \oplus 2^{c*}$ implies that $a = a*$, $b = b*$, and $c = c*$.

<u>Proof</u>: First note that, from the definition of the $\oplus$ operation (Section 3-A, 2), $2^a + 2^b + 2^c = 2^{a*} + 2^{b*} + 2^{c*}$. If we write the sums on both sides of the equation in binary form we can see that each term corresponds to one binary digit, so that each term on one side must be matched by a term on the other side, and hence the exponents must be equal. (Q.E.D.)

B. THEOREM ON SEQUENTIAL FUNCTIONS WITHOUT ESSENTIAL HAZARDS

If a sequential function has no essential hazards (Section 3-A, 1) then it can always be realized by a circuit without delay elements, and this circuit will be free of steady-state hazards. Transient hazards may occur in some cases.

There will be two parts to the proof. First we shall describe a method for assigning row-sets to the rows of an augmented version of the flow table describing the function, and then we shall demonstrate that this assignment will result in proper operation without reliance on delay elements. (It is assumed that hazard-free combinational circuits will be used to realize the flow matrix.)

Let us assign the Hamming row-set (Section 3-A, 3) S_{2i} to row i (i = 1, 2, 3,...). For every d-trio (Section 3-A, 4) with rows a, b, and c form an auxiliary row of the flow matrix [called a trap row (Section 3-A, 6)] and assign to it the row-set S_t, where t = $2^a \oplus 2^b \oplus 2^c = 2^a + 2^b + 2^c$. [See definition in Section 3-A, 2 for meaning of $\oplus$ operation.] From our first lemma (Section 3-A, 7) we note that t cannot be expressed in the form 2^d (d an integer), so S_t could not have been assigned to any of the original rows of the table. Our second lemma (Section 3-A, 8) implies that every d-trio will have a trap row with a unique row-set assigned to it since $2^a \oplus 2^b \oplus 2^c = 2^{a*} \oplus 2^{b*} \oplus 2^{c*}$ implies a = a*, b = b*, and c = c*.

The entries in the trap rows of the matrix are filled as follows. For the input states in which the d-transitions (Section 3-A, 5) of the corresponding d-trios terminate we fill in numbers corresponding to the final states of the d-transitions. [That is the state labeled 2 in Table 6(d).] In the input column in which the d-transition starts, we insert a stable state in the corresponding trap row. All other trap row entries are arbitrary. Table 5-A shows a flow table with 4 d-transitions (labeled with arrows) and the row assignment is shown in Table 5-B. Rows 7-10 are the trap rows.

We will now show that, if row assignments are made as described above, then proper operation will be assured, without the need for delay elements. It will be necessary to enumerate all possible results of a sequence of three changes in one variable x, starting with the system in L1.

Part (a) of Table 6 illustrates the case where a change in x leads to a stable state in the same row as the initial state. If this is the case, then no other rows need be considered

since changes in x alone cannot lead to a new internal state. Now we consider those cases where the initial change in x leads to a stable state R2 in a new row. Starting with the system in R2, a change in x could lead to a stable state which is also in row 2, as is shown in part (b) of the diagram. Another possibility, depicted in part (c), is that the second x-change sends the system back into state L1. In both cases only rows 1 and 2 are relevant to the discussion, since there are no transitions possible out of this region during the sequence of x-changes that we are considering.

The third (and final) possible outcome of an x-change from state R2 is that a transition to state L3

Table 5.

A. Flow Table with 4 d-Trios

	$x_1 x_2$			
	00	01	11	10
1	① ⟶	2	6	①
2	3	②	② ⟶	1
3	③	2	③	4
4	④ ⟶	2	3	④
5	6	⑤	⑤ ⟶	4
6	⑥	5	⑥	1

B. Augmented Table Showing Row Assignment and Trap Rows

	$x_1 x_2$				
	00	01	11	10	
1	①	2	6	①	S_2
2	3	②	②	1	S_4
3	③	2	③	4	S_8
4	④	2	3	④	S_{16}
5	6	⑤	⑤	4	S_{32}
6	⑥	5	⑥	1	S_{64}
7	⑦	2	-	-	S_{14}
8	⑧	2	-	-	S_{28}
9	-	-	⑨	1	S_{70}
10	-	-	⑩	4	S_{56}

will occur. This contingency can be further subdivided into the three cases represented by parts (d), (e), and (f) of Table 6. With the system in state L3, switching x can produce a transition back to state R2, as shown in part (d). A second possibility is that shown in part (e), where both entries in row 3 are stable. Finally, as depicted in part (f), an x-change with the system in L3 might lead to a state R4 in a new row. Thus Table 6 shows all possible patterns possible in a flow table when activity is limited to allowing a single input variable to change three times.

Now, for each case shown in Table 6, examine the possible consequence of an x-change when the system is in state L1.

In case (a), none of the state-variables become unstable so that there is no change for malfunctioning.

In case (b) only $y_{1,2}$ (see latter part of Section 3, 3 for definition of $y_{i,j}$) changes and, regardless of the order in which the changes in x and $y_{1,2}$ are sensed by the other state-branches, none of them can become unstable since, in the region involved, there are no transitions involving state-variables other than $y_{1,2}$. However, a transient hazard exists unless the output state in L2 is the same as in either L1 or R2. This is because the output circuits might, due to stray delays, see the $y_{1,2}$ change before the x-change so that the output circuits might see the sequence of states as L1-L2-R2.

Again, in case (c), only $y_{1,2}$ can become unstable in the region under examination, so that no other state-branch can be affected. There is no opportunity for a transient hazard to occur since the output will change only after the output circuits recognize the x-change.

Case (d) is slighly more complicated, and it is this situation which forced us to introduce the trap rows. Refer to Table 7 which shows a d-trio and the associated trap row. After

Table 6.

A.	L	R		D.	L	R
1	①	①		1	①	2
				2	3	②
				3	③	2

B.	L	R		E.	L	R
1	①	2		1	①	2
2	②	②		2	3	②
				3	③	③

C.	L	R		F.	L	R
1	①	2		1	①	2
2	1	②		2	3	②
				3	③	4
				4	-	④

$y_{1,2}$ sees the x-change (the system starts in L1) it becomes unstable and changes. If $y_{2,3}$ recognizes the x-change before it sees the $y_{1,2}$ change then it will see the system in R2 and remain stable. No further activity will then be possible.

However, if stray delays cause $y_{2,3}$ to see the previous changes occur in reverse order then it will see the system in L2 and it will also change. At this point two y-variables, $y_{1,2}$ and $y_{2,3}$ have changed. Some other variable y_r might see these events occur in any of the following ways:

1. If it sees $y_{1,2}$ change first, it will see the system in row 2.

2. After recognizing both changes it would see the system in row 3.

Table 7.

	L	R	
1	①	2	S_2
2	3	②	S_4
3	③	2	S_8
4	④	2	S_{14}

3. If it sees $y_{2,3}$ change first, it will see the system in row 4, which is the trap row for this d-trio. This can be seen as follows. In our other notation $y_{2,3} = y_{12} (12 = 2^2 \oplus 2^3)$. Thus if this variable changes when the system is in row-set $S_2 1$ (the set assigned to row 1), the new state will be S_{14}, $(14 = 2^1 \oplus 2^2 \oplus 2^3)$. This is the state we assigned to the trap row of the d-trio consisting of rows 1, 2, and 3.

Before seeing either y-change, y_r, of course, sees the system in row 1. At any time it may see the x-change occur. Summing up, we see that y_r may see the system in any of the eight total states encompassed by input states L and R and internal states 1, 2, 3, and 4. But within this area of the flow table the only y-variables that ever become unstable are $y_{1,2}$ and $y_{2,3}$. Hence y_r will never change during the d-transition and the system remains in this region since changes in $y_{1,2}$ and $y_{2,3}$ cannot, as we have seen, take the system into any state other than the four we have been considering.

After $y_{1,2}$ changes at the start of the d-transition, it sees the system in column R, where its excitation is constant for all four rows so that it will not change again. As soon as $y_{2,3}$ sees the x-change, its excitation changes again, this time to correspond to its value in row 2. After this second change, it too will remain stable. Thus we see that shortly after the x-change propagates to all the y's, the system will inevitably come to rest in state R2, as specified by the flow table, and so there is no steady-state hazard for the d-transition.

A transient hazard does exist if the output state for L3 is different from the output states for both L1 and R2. This is because the output network might see the system in L2 or L3 during the course of the transition.

Cases (e) and (f) in Table 6 constitute essential hazards, which we have ruled out of our flow tables in the hypothesis of this theorem. Hence we have shown that all transi-

tions not involving essential hazards will be carried out successfully regardless of the delays involved, if the circuit is designed as we have indicated. This proves the theorem.

C. DISCUSSION

If a flow table contains neither essential hazards nor d-trios, then it can be realized without steady-state hazards by employing any row assignment having the property that any inter-row transition called for in the table will require a change in only one y-variable. The Hamming assignment discussed in this section is general enough to be applicable to all such cases, but, for many functions, simpler assignments can be found having the necessary property. If a d-trio is present, then there is an additional constraint on the design. During a d-transition, the input change and the y-change (in $y_{1,2}$) might be seen in reverse order by the y-variable that is unstable in L2 of Table 6 (d), and this latter variable ($y_{2,3}$) might also change. Since the changes in $y_{1,2}$ and $y_{2,3}$ might also be seen in reverse order by some other variable, it is necessary that the flow matrix entries in the states differing in the $y_{2,3}$-value from the state assigned to row 1 be such as to lead to the correct final state. Thus, once states have been assigned to certain rows, restrictions are placed on the use of other states. In our proof, we showed constructively that it is always possible to make a workable assignment, but in particular cases it is desirable and often possible to find more economical assignments.

4. FUNCTIONS REQUIRING DELAY ELEMENTS

A. THEOREM ON ESSENTIAL HAZARDS AND DELAYS

In this section we shall prove the following theorem: If a function contains an essential hazard, then any proper circuit realization of it must contain at least one delay element. Table 8 shows a portion of a flow table containing an essential hazard (υ can equal 3, but not 1 or 2). The proof will consist of a demonstration that it is always possible to choose the values of the stray delays in any circuit realizing the given function in such a manner that, for some y-state S_1 corresponding to row 1, if the circuit starts in state LS_1, a change in x will lead to state $R\upsilon$ (instead of R2, as specified in the flow table).

First it must be shown that if a proper circuit contains no delay elements then it is always possible to choose a set of state branches (generally not one of the minimum sets) such that the excitation circuits for the state branches contain no elements in common with one another. A circuit drawn in this form is shown in Fig. 3. (Output circuits have been omitted since they are not relevant to this discussion, and only one input is included). The boxes labeled d_{ij} represent stray inertial delays between the input of the y_i-circuit and the output of the jth statebranch.

Definition $-d_{ij}$ and d_{ix}: A change in y_i will be recognized at the Y_i terminal only after a time lapse of d_{ij} (provided that the change persists for at least this period.) Similarly, d_{iz} is the delay between the input x and Y_i.

Now let us see how an arbitrary, proper sequential network, such as the one in Fig. 4(a), can be redrawn in the form of a separate-excitation network. (Incidentially, the circuit shown is simply a random arrangement

of elements, doing nothing in partic- ular.) The method to be used will entail an increase in the number of state branches in the circuit.

First select some point in the network (other than a point connected directly to an input terminal or to a state-branch) such that signal variation at that point can affect more than one state-branch excitation (assuming that all feedback paths are interrupted by cutting all of the state-branches). Then label the branch terminating at this node as a new state-branch. Repeat this process until there are no such points remaining. Obviously this is a finite process since we start with a finite number of nodes and eliminate one at each step.

In Fig. 4(a) the signal at point A affects Y_1, Y_2, and Y_3, so that according to the above procedure a state-branch with a response that we will call y_4 is assumed to terminate

Table 8.

	x	
	L	R
1	①	2
2	3	②
3	③	υ
υ	–	ⓤ

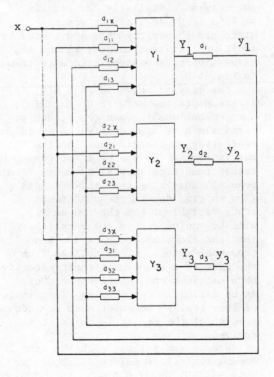

Fig. 3.

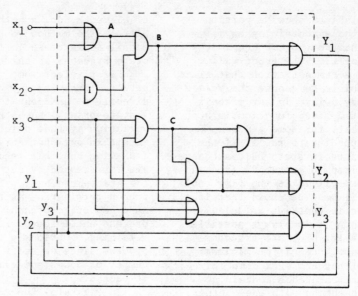

Fig. 4(a).

at A. The excitation circuit for y_4 is shown at the top of part (b) of the diagram. Similarly the signals at B and C each affect several state-branch excitations, and therefore additional state-branches, B5 and B6, respectively, are associated with them in Fig. 4(b).

The diagram shown in Fig. 4(b) is identical to the network of part (a); the connections between the Y_i and y_i terminals have been omitted to avoid cluttering up the diagram. A flow matrix derived on the basis of the transformed diagram will have, in general, more rows than the original flow matrix, due to the additional state-variables, but the two matrices will be equivalent in the sense that the same flow table can be derived from each matrix. This follows from the fact that the same circuit generated both matrices and, since the circuit is by definition proper, any description of its terminal behavior must be independent of the manner in which it is derived.

Now we can proceed with the proof. Assume that there exists a proper circuit without delay elements that realizes a function with an essential hazard

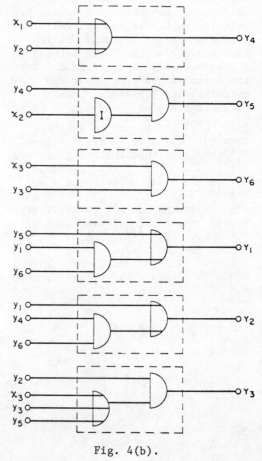

Fig. 4(b).

as shown in Table 8. Choose state-branches as previously described so that the excitation circuits for the various Y's are disjoint as in Fig. 4(b).

Since the circuit, by definition, must function correctly for any distribution of stray delays, let us first consider a distribution in which the delays in the state-branches (d_1, d_2, and d_3 in Fig. 3) are large compared with all other delays. Now suppose that the system is in some y-state S_1 corresponding to row 1 (all flow table references are to the segment of Table 8) and the input is switched from L to R. Then some state-variable excitation, say Y_1, changes. After a delay sufficient to allow all other Y's to see the x-change (remember the long delays in the state branches) y_1 changes. The new y-state may correspond to row 2 or it may lead to another y-change (occurring only after all Y's have seen the y_1-change). This process in general continues through a sequence of y-changes until eventually it terminates in some y-state S_2 corresponding to row 2. This must occur if the circuit realizes the given function.

In the course of the transition from S_1 to S_2 a given y-variable might change several times, and race conditions may occur in which several variables become unstable simultaneously.

In the latter case we shall assume that the values of the stray delays in the state-branches are such that if Y_a, Y_b, ..., Y_x change simultaneously, y_a will respond first, and the effects of its change will be seen at Y_b, Y_c,...,Y_x before the corresponding y's can change.

Let us describe this transition from L1 to R2 by a sequence indicating the order in which the variables change. Such a sequence, which will be defined as a C_{12}-sequence, is
$$xy_5y_2y_1y_2y_3y_2.$$

Similar sequences, C_{23} and $C_{3\upsilon}$ can be derived for transitions from R2 to L3 and from L3 to Rυ, respectively. Combining all three sequences

C_{12}, C_{23}, and $C_{3\upsilon}$, we obtain a C-sequence such as $xy_5y_2y_1y_2y_5y_3y_2$ $xy_5y_4xy_2y_3$. The following points concerning the C-sequence should be understood before we proceed:

1. If the kth term in the sequence is y_i and if, with the system initially in LS_1, all of the changes described by the first $k-1$ terms of the sequence occur and are seen by Y_i, then Y_i will change. Note that the behavior of Y_i depends only on what it sees, and if it sees the system in the indicated state it will change, regardless of the actual history of the situation and regardless of the stray delays. The C-sequence gives us information about the logical design of the circuit.

2. If the system starts in the indicated initial state and if all of the changes in the C-sequence occur, then the new state will be $R\upsilon$.

3. If a circuit properly realizes a flow table with a segment such as is shown in Table 8, then it must be possible to find at least one C-sequence. If several exist we arbitrarily choose one.

At this point it will be convenient to augment our notation slightly. Each y-variable appearing an odd number of times in the sequence will be starred. In addition, we shall relabel our y-variables so that the first y appearing in our sequence is called Y_1, and the other integers are assigned consecutively so that $i < j$ implies that the initial y_i precedes the initial y_j in the sequence. Thus the sequence $xy_5y_2y_1y_2y_5y_3y_2xy_5y_4xy_2y_3$ becomes $x*y_1*y_2y_3*y_2y_1*y_4y_2x*y_1*y_5*x*y_2y_4$. (The transformations 5→1, 2→2, 1→3, 3→4, 4→5 were made.)

Note that if the system starts in LS_1 and if all of the starred variables change any odd number of times and if the unstarred variables changes any even number of times, then the new state will be RS_υ.

Henceforth we drop our assumption concerning the distribution of stray delays which was used to derive the C-sequence and introduce a different distribution having the property that when the circuit starts in LS_1 and x is changed once, a different sequence of events will occur in which each starred y-variable changes once and each unstarred variable changes twice. Since this leads to RS_υ (corresponding to $R\upsilon$ in the flow table) instead of to a state assigned to $R2$ as specified by the flow table, it follows that, due to stray delays, the terminal behavior of the circuit may deviate from that specified by the flow table, which contradicts the assumption that the circuit is proper. The problem now is to find such a set of delays. Without loss of generality, we can set the state-branch delays (d_1, d_2, and d_3 in Fig. 3) equal to zero since their effects can be absorbed by the other delays. This simplifies our notation in that, for all i, $Y_i = y_i$, and so we need no longer use the Y_i's.

Assume that there are n different y-variables in the C-sequence, and that at time t = 0, the circuit state is changed from LS_1 to RS_1. Then the stray delays will be so chosen that at time t = i (the unit of time is arbitrary) y_i changes, for i = 1,2,...,n, and at t = n + i (again i ranges from 1 to n) y_i changes again if it is unstarred (in the C-sequence.) This brings about the result described in the previous paragraph.

Definition: N_{ji} is the number of y_i-appearances preceding the first y_i-appearance in the C-sequence.

Consider the following assignment of delay values:

1. If the initial y_i is preceded by an odd number of x's in the C-sequence (that is, if it is in C_{12} or $C_{3\upsilon}$) then let $d_{ix} = i$.

2. If the initial y_i is preceded by an even number of x's in the C-sequence (if it is in C_{23}) then let $d_{ix} = n + i$.

3. If N_{ji} is odd let $d_{ij} = i-j$. (Oddness of N_{ji} implies that i > j.)

4. If N_{ji} is even and if y_i is starred, let $d_{ij} = n + i - j$.

5. If N_{ji} is even and if y_i is not starred, let $d_{ij} > n$.

Now we shall explain how the delays specified above can cause the result described previously. Note first that starting with the system in LS, y_i will change if it sees the system in the state that precedes its initial appearance in the C-sequence. This will occur if it sees changes (always using LS_1 as the initial condition) in just those variables (including x) that appear an odd number of times prior to the first y_i in the sequence. We will now show that this happens for every i = 1,2,..., n, at t = i if the above delay assignment is used.

If x changes at t = 0, then y_1 will see the change and also switch at t = 1 due to (1). Assume that for i = 1, 2,...,k, y_k changes at t = k. Then at t = k + 1, (3-5) insure that y_{k+1} will see the changes in just those y_i's for which $N_{i(k+1)}$ is odd, and (1) and (2) insure that y_{k+1} will also see the x change at t = k if and only if an odd number of x-changes precedes the initial y_{k+1}. Hence by induction, we see that from t = 1 to t = n, the y_i's will changes, one by one, in sequence.

Observe next that if any y_i sees the system in RS_υ, it will switch to the value that it has in that state (since RS_υ is stable) or remain unchanged if it is already at that value. This will occur at t = n + i if at that time y_i sees changes in those starred variables that it did not see change at t = i, and if it sees a second change in each unstarred variable that it saw change at t = i.

At t = n + 1, (4) causes y_1 to see the changes in all starred variables that it did not see at t = 1. If y_p is any unstarred variable then, since N_{p1} is zero, (5) indicates that y_1 will not see

any change in y_p since the second
y_p-change will restore y_p to its
original value before y_1 sees any
change. This is due to the inertial
nature of the stray delays. Therefore y_1 will see the system in
RS_U and act accordingly (changing
if it is unstarred). Assume now
that all variables with indexes
$j < q$ have reacted correctly at
$t = n + j$. Then, at $t = n + q$, (4)
causes y_q to see those changes in
starred variables that it missed
at $t = q$, and (2) causes it to
see the x-change if it missed it at
$t = q$. If y_r is an unstarred
variable that y_q saw change at
$t = q_1$ then (3) insures that at
$t = n + qy_q$ will also see the second
change in y_r. Finally, if y_r is
an unstarred variable that y_q did
not see changes at $t = q_1$ then (5)
insures that it never will see that
change, since the second y_r-change
will have occurred before y_q saw
the first one. (Again the inertial
property of the stray delays is a
factor.) Thus, y_q will, at $t = n + q$,
see the system in RS_U, and also respond
correctly. By induction then, for
all $i = 1,2,...,n$, y_i will behave as
we have stated at $t = n + i$. At
$t = 2n$, the system will be stable
in RS_U. Thus the proposed delay
assignment has the desired (or perhaps
the word should be undersired) effect,
and the theorem is proved.

B. DISCUSSION AND SUMMARY

In the previous subsection it has
been demonstrated that a sequential
function with an essential hazard cannot be properly realized without the
use of delay elements. The proof
consisted of a procedure for dis-
tributing stray inertial delays among
the various branches of any circuit
purported to contradict the theorem.
With the indicated set of delays, the
circuit will then fail to operate
properly when the circuit starts in
a particular state of the x and
y-variables (LS_1) and a certain input
variable is switched.

Must the delay values be exactly

as specified in order for the indicated
malfunctioning to occur? If the answer
is yes, then it may be that the unfortunate combination of delay values
occurs with zero probability. This
is not the case, however, as small
variations in the delay values will
not change the nature of the circuit
action.

Suppose that, due to slightly
inaccurate d-values, the excitation
Y_i changes three times within the
interval from $t = i$ to $t = i + e$
(instead of once at $t = i$, as we
have specified), where e is small
compared to unity. Though this may
cause y_i to also change several
times (since we have not specified
delays in the state-branches) the
inertial nature of the delays that
appear between y_i and each excitation circuit will absorb the extra
two changes, and so subsequent operation will be unaffected, except
for slight deviations in timing,
which may in turn cause brief
false signal changes at a later time.
In general, if the errors in the
d-values are so small that even the
cumulative effects of a series of
errors will not add up to produce incorrect excitations lasting as long as
one time unit, then the system will
still operate so as to terminate in
state RS_U.

It should also be noted that there
may be many other troublesome sets
of delay values in addition to the
one proposed here.

If we can determine in advance
(possibly on the basis of estimates
arrived at by considering the number of
elements in the various paths) that the
stray delays will not be unfavorably
distributed, then delay elements
need not be employed.

Another conceivable way to
dispense with delay elements might
be to assign two sets of y-states,
designated as A and B, to each row
of the flow table. The system
would have two modes of operation,
one using only A-sets and the other
using only B-sets, and there would
be no way for a shift to occur

from one mode to the other during normal operation. The y-states would be chosen so that, for any set of stray delay values, the system would operate correctly in at least one of the modes. (Possibly more than two modes would be required.) We would then arrange matters so that when the system is first switched on, the initial internal state corresponds to the proper mode for the existing distribution of d's in the circuit. In other words, we thwart the demon who is adjusting the delays by letting him select the stray delay values on the assumption that the y-state corresponding to L1 (Table 8) is sometimes S_1, and then operating the system in a mode such that it never enters y-state S_1. Such a procedure will not work if the stray delays are liable to change after the system has been in operation for a while. In effect, this method resembles the one mentioned in the previous paragraph since a knowledge of the stray delay values is assumed, though in this case we might somehow make the system automatically ascertain and act upon the relevant data.

5. CIRCUITS WITH A MINIMUM NUMBER OF DELAY ELEMENTS

A. SUFFICIENCY OF A SINGLE DELAY ELEMENT

It has been shown in Sections III and IV that sequential functions without essential hazards can be properly realized without the use of delay elements, and that sequential functions with essential hazards cannot be realized properly without delay elements. In this subsection we shall prove the following theorem: Any sequential switching function can be realized with a proper circuit containing only one delay element (which can be pure or inertial). If simultaneous changes in several input variables are permitted then transient, but not steady-state hazards may occur in these circuits.

The proof of this theorem will be constructive in nature. An essential part of the construction is a circuit which we shall call a "delay box." This circuit has n inputs $Y_1, Y_2, \ldots, Y_n$ and, associated with each input Y_i, there is a single output y_i. In the steady-state condition, each y_i has the same value as the corresponding Y_i. The characteristic feature of the delay box is that if a single input signal Y_k changes, then after a delay D, the corresponding y_k also changes. In other words the delay box behaves as though an independent delay element (inertial as we shall see) linked each input-output pair, provided that sufficient time intervals separate consecutive input changes. We shall show that a single delay element (pure or inertial) is sufficient to construct a delay box with any number of inputs.

Such a circuit for three variables (it can be generalized to any number) is shown in Fig. 5. The elements denoted by circled plus signs are modulo-2 adders (the output is the modulo-2 sum of the inputs), the M's are majority elements (the output is unity if, and only if, at least two of the three inputs are ones) and the D is a pure or inertial delay element.

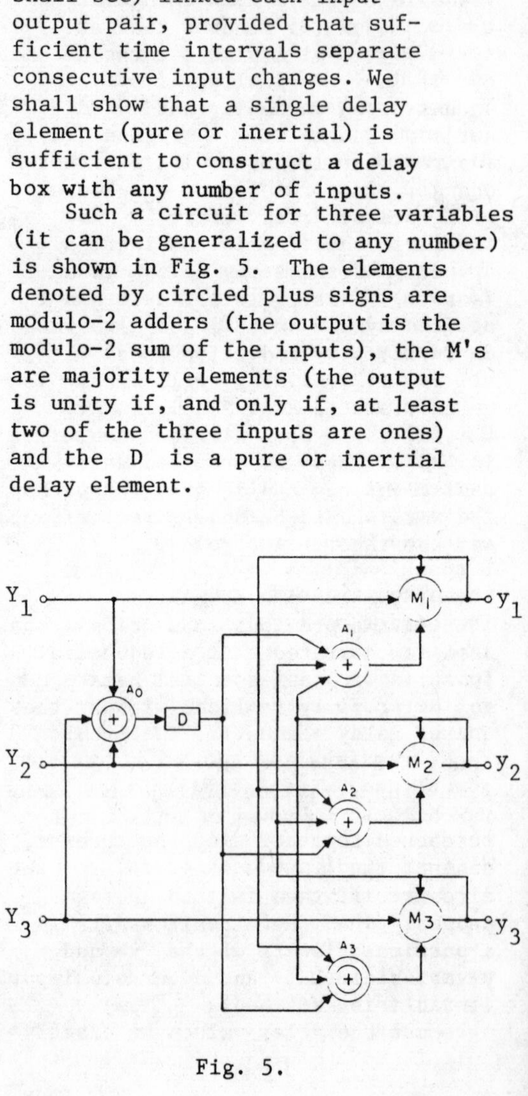

Fig. 5.

In order to see how this circuit works, let us focus our attention on the y_2 output-terminal. We can trace a path from Y_2 to y_2, which passes through adder A_0, the delay element, adder A_2, and the majority element M_2. In A_0, signals from all the other Y-terminals are added to the Y_2-signal, and in A_2, the resulting signal (delayed) is added to signals from all the y-terminals except y_2. If we assume that $Y_i = y_i$ for all i's except possibly for $i=2$, then, in the steady state, the output of A_2 should correspond to the input from Y_2 since all the other signals that were added to Y_2 cancel out in pairs ($Y_i \oplus y_i = 0$ if $Y_i = y_i$). Thus if we examine the inputs to M_2 we see that two of them are equal to Y_2 (one comes directly from the Y_2-terminal, and the other, just discussed, comes from A_2) so that y_2, the output of M_2, must equal Y_2 and, since y_2 is also the third input to M_2, all three inputs are the same. The same argument can be applied to each of the other Y_i-y_i-pairs, so that it follows that the circuit is stable with all y_i's equaling the corresponding Y_i's.

Suppose now that Y_2 is switched. One effect is to change one input to M_2, but this is not enough to switch y_2. The other effect is that the output of A_0 changes. Nothing else can happen until the output of D changes (after a delay) whereupon the output of each A_i switches. The effect of this is to change one input to each M_i. Since one input to M_2 (from Y_2) has already changed, y_2 thereupon switches. For all other values of i, the Y_i and y_i-inputs to M_i remain fixed so that no y_i other than y_2 can change. After y_2 changes, a second input (from y_2) to each A_i other than A_2 switches, so that the outputs of these A_i's are restored to their original values. The y_2-change is also transmitted to the third terminal of M_2, so that once again, for every i, all three inputs to M_i are in agreement. At this point the circuit is in an equilibrium state equivalent to the one which existed before Y_2 switched, and another input change can be applied.

Suppose that during some time interval (small compared to the delay magnitude) all of the Y-inputs to the delay box are subject to random variations provided only that at the end of the interval no more than one Y has undergone a net change. Assume first that none of the Y_i-values undergoes a net change. Then, if D is inertial, its output remains constant, and so none of the y's can switch. If D is a pure delay then its output will in general change several times (an even number). But by the time this occurs, all of the Y's will have resumed their original values, so that none of the y's can switch.

Next suppose that Y_k undergoes a net change (all other Y's changing an even number of times). If D is inertial then its output will change once, after a delay, and then y_k will change just once as though the transient fluctuations had not occurred. The D-output may switch several times if D is pure. But by the time these changes begin, only Y_k will show a change, so that only y_k can switch. The value of y_k will fluctuate in synchronism with the D-output and will then settle down to agree with the new Y_k-value.

Thus we see that the circuit of

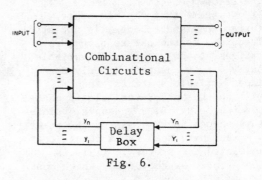

Fig. 6.

Fig. 5 does realize a delay box
while using only one delay
element, and it now remains to
show how this device can be
used to prove our theorem.

Consider a sequential circuit in
the form of Fig. 6 with a delay
box in cascade with the state-
branches and with the combinational circuit hazard-free.
A Hamming row-set (definition
Section 3-A, 3) is assigned to each
row of the flow table being
synthesized, so that any row-to-row
transition involves a change in
just one y-variable. We shall now
show that such a circuit will operate properly regardless of the
nature of the function.

With the circuit in some stable
state, let the input state be changed
by simultaneously switching one
or more x-variables. First consider
the case where the new state is also
stable. Then if just one x-variable
changes, there will be no changes at
all in any Y, and the Z's (system
outputs) will correctly assume their
new values without superfluous
changes. This follows from the
hazard-free nature of the combinational circuits. If several x's
change, then there may be some false
Z and Y-changes (an even number
for each variable) in addition to
any genuine Z-changes. As was
shown previously, the delay box will
prevent the false Y-changes from
appearing as its output terminals.
Thus there will be no further
activity. The possiblity of superfluous Z-changes constitutes a
transient hazard, as indicated in
the theorem statement.

Now assume that the new state
(after the input change) is not stable.
Then, due to the nature of our row
assignment, only one state-variable,
say y_k, must change. If only one
input-variable switches, then Y_k
will be the only Y-variable to change
after a delay D, y_k changes. Before
this change occurs, all of the other
Y's must have seen the x-change that
initiated the process. (This is
the purpose of the delay, which must

be sufficiently long to achieve this
result.) Hence the combinational
circuit is presented with a new
change (y_k) only after it has settled
down after the first change. Since
following the switching of y_k,
the system enters a stable state, there
will be no further activity. There
will be no transient hazards since
at no time was there a change in
more than one input to the combinational
circuit. If the input change involves
several variables, then again a
transient hazard exists. But the
delay box filters out all transient
false Y-changes, so that the only
change that appears at its output
is in y_k. (We previously noted that,
after a delay D, y_k may undergo an
even number of false changes before
assuming its final value. But,
since these changes occur at a time
when all outputs of the combinational
circuit are independent of y_k, this
"chatter" has no effect.) Thus
there is no steady-state hazard, and
our proof is complete.

It might be well to point out the
necessity for hazard-free combinational
circuits in the preceding construction.
At first glance they may seem unnecessary because the delay box behaves
somewhat like a set of inertial delays.
Suppose however, that the result of
an input change is to switch Y_1.
Then, after a delay, the output of
D (our discussion concerns Fig. 5)
changes, and y_1 switches. The
effect of the y_1-change is fed back
into the combinational circuit (here
we refer to Fig. 6) and the result
might be, for example, an even number
of Y_2-changes due to combinational
hazards. These Y_2-changes could
penetrate to y_2 without waiting for
D to react if the y_1-change has not
yet reached A_2 due to the effects
of stray delays. The y_2-change
might cause further activity and, in
general, the outcome will be uncertain.

B. AN ALTERNATIVE SINGLE-DELAY
   CIRCUIT MODEL

The number of state variables
that must be used in connection with
the preceding method grows linearly

with the number of rows of the flow table being realized. To be more precise, the number of state-variables needed for the most complex n-row flow table is $2^{S_0}-1$, where S_0 is the smallest integer such that $2^{S_0} \geq n$. In general, however, if we do not try to minimize the number of delay elements, then the number of state-variables necessary increases only logarithmically with the number of rows. With S_0 defined as above, the number of state-variables sufficient for the synthesis of any n-row table is $2S_0-1$.[4]

We shall now demonstrate a general method for a one-delay-element synthesis that calls for the use of $2S_0$ state-variables. This method is based on a $2S_0$-assignment presented by Huffman,[5] and an example of such an assignment for an 8-row flow table is shown in Table 9. The state-variables are y_a, y_{q1}, y_{q2}, y_b, y_{p1}, and y_{p2}, and the numbers in the matrix indicate the rows to which the y-states are assigned. For example, the 2-entry, labeled g in the diagram, tells us that for one of the y-states in the row-set corresponding to row 2, $y_a = y_b = 0$, $y_q = 0$, $y_{q1} = 1$, $y_{p1} = 0$ and $y_{p2} = 1$. Note that y_a^{q2} and y_b^{p2} designate the quadrant in which a given state lies,

and that within a quadrant the y_q-variables indicate the column and the y_p-variables indicate the row. To expand the number of row-sets we increase (by equal numbers) the number of y_p and y_q-variables, retaining the general form of Table 9.

Consider now a circuit of the form of Fig. 7, in which an arbitrary sequential function is realized using a $2S_0$-row assignment and a 2-variable delay box (of the type shown

Table 9.

$2S_0$ Assignment for an 8-Row Flow Table

y_a	y_{q1}	y_{q2}	y_b	0	0	0	0	1	1	1	1
			y_{p1}	0	0	1	1	0	0	1	1
			y_{p2}	0	1	1	0	0	1	1	0
0	0	0		1	1	1	1	1	2	3	4
0	0	1		2	2^g	2	2	1	2	3	4^h
0	1	1		3	3	3	3	1	2	3	4
0	1	0		4	4	4	4	1	2	3	4
1	0	0		5	6	7	8	5	5	5	5
1	0	1		5^f	6	7	8	6	6	6	6
1	1	1		5	6	7	8	7	7	7	7
1	1	0		5	6	7	8	8	8	8	8

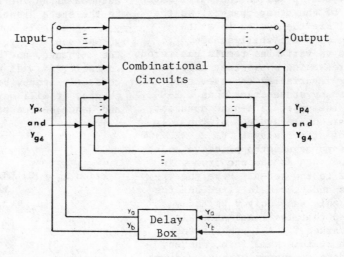

Fig. 7.

in Fig. 5) in the y_a and y_b state-branches. No delay elements appear anywhere else in the circuit, and all combinational networks are hazard-free.

Suppose that the system is stable in the y-state corresponding to the member of row-set-2, labeled g in Table 9, and that following an x-change the new state is to be in row 4. For the original input state and all y states in row-set-2, all y-variables should be stable. For the new input state, a transition from g to h (in row-set-4) will occur if, in all those members of row-set-2 that lie in the upper left-hand quadrant of Table 9, the Y-excitations correspond to the coordinates of $h(Y_a=0, Y_b=1, Y_{q1}=0, Y_{q2}=1, Y_{p1}=1, Y_{p2}=0)$. This means that the y_q-variables remain stable, some of the y_p-variables (in this case both of them) become unstable and switch, and y_b becomes unstable and eventually changes (after a delay). Due to the action of the delay box, all of the y_p-changes will have occured and will have been seen by all variables before y_b switches. The y_q-variables are certain to remain stable throughout the process since, no matter in what order they see the x-change and the y_p-changes occur, they will still see the system in one of the two-states (where they are stable), and by the time they see y_b switch they will have seen all of the other changes, so that they will see the system in state h, where the y_q's are still stable. Since the y_q-variables remain unaltered, similar reasoning shows that none of the other y-variables can ever see the system in any state other than a 2-state in the upper left-hand quadrant, or in state h, regardless of the effects of stray delays.

The same argument applies to a transition such as the one from g in row-set-2 to row-set-5. Here the y_q-variables and y_b remain fixed and the y_p's (in this case only y_{p2}) and y_a change, so that the final state is the one marked f. All other transitions are of this same form, whereby moves in one dimension with a quadrant via y_p or y_q-changes are followed by a hop to an adjacent quadrant via a y_a or y_b-change. A delay box can be shared by y_a and y_b since in no case do both of these variables have to change during the same transition.

We have not been able to devise a general one-delay-element synthesis procedure requiring only $2S_0 - 1$ state-variables, but it remains to be proved that one does not exist.

C. MISCELLANEOUS TECHNIQUES

In the two preceding subsections we described procedures whereby any sequential function could be realized by a circuit containing just one delay element. There are many situations, however, which can be handled by less cumbersome methods that do not require special row assignments which may complicate the logic. A few ideas and examples pertinent to such techniques will be presented here.

First let us see how trouble can be avoided when a single essential hazard exists, as in the flow-matrix section shown in Table 10. (The arrow indicates the hazardous transition.) If a delay element is associated with y_2, then no trouble can occur since, by the time y_2 responds to the x change, y_1 will already have seen x switch and hence will remain stable.

Proper operation can also be assumed if an inertial delay is placed in the state branch corresponding to y_1. If this is done, then even though y_1 may see the y_2-change before the x-change, and hence become unstable, it will not respond incorrectly since, before it can change, it will have seen the x-change and hence become stable again.

Table 10.

Section of a Flow Table with an Essential Hazard

	0	1	y_1	y_2
1	①	2	0	0
2	3	②	0	1
3	③	③	1	1

If a row assignment requiring only a single variable change for any row-to-row transition is used and if one of the two methods used above is employed wherever an essential hazard occurs, then proper operation will result. In many cases where several essential hazards are present, it is possible to make the row assignments in such a manner that the same y-variable is involved in more than one hazardous transition, so that a single delay-element serves a multiple purpose.

An interesting example of a situation in which such economy can be achieved is depicted in Table 11, a flow matrix for a 4-state binary counter. Every transition involves an essential hazard, and in each case y_3 corresponds to either y_1 or y_2 in the example previously discussed (Table 10). Thus if an inertial delay element is associated with y_3, then proper operation will always result.

Consider, for instance, the effect of an x-change when the system is initially in state 0-3 (column 0 and row 3). Following the x-change, y_3 becomes unstable but, due to the delay, does not change until the other y-variables (particularly y_1) have seen the x-change. Thus no trouble will occur during this action. If the system is initially in state 1-4 then an x-change will be followed by a y_1-change, and it is possible for y_3 to see the latter change occur first. This means that y_3 temporarily sees the system in state 1-4 and therefore becomes unstable. But, due to the inertial delay, y_3 will not respond to the false signal, and once again malfunctioning will be averted. This method can be applied to counters with any number of states, one inertial delay element always being sufficient.

6. CONCLUSIONS

The results described in this paper may be summarized:

1. Sequential functions free of essential hazards (definition, Section 3-A, 1) can always be realized with circuits having no delay elements and operating without steady-state hazards (but sometimes with transient hazards).

2. One delay element is necessary and sufficient for the proper realization of any function with one or more essential hazards.

In general, one can minimize the number of delay elements in a synthesis only at the expense of increasing the number of other components used. This increase may be substantial in some cases. However, there are other instances in which minimum-delay circuits are little or no more complex than circuits designed without regard for the number of delay elements required.

The question of what type of element should be minimized is of course dependent on considerations closely linked to the nature of the physical components to be used.

ACKNOWLEDGEMENT

Thanks are due to D. A. Huffman of M.I.T. who suggested the basic problem considered here and who, in his role as thesis supervisor, supplied valuable encouragement to the author.

Table 11.

Flow Matrix for 4-State Binary Counter

	x		y_1	y_2	y_3
	0	1			
1	①	2	0	0	0
2	3	②	0	0	1
3	③	4	0	1	1
4	5	④	0	1	0
5	⑤	6	1	1	0
6	7	⑥	1	1	1
7	⑦	8	1	0	1
8	1	⑧	1	0	0

REFERENCES

1. D.A. Huffman, "The Synthesis of Sequential Switching Circuits," Journal of the Franklin Institute," Vol. 257, pp. 161-190, 275-303, March and April, 1954.

2. S.H. Caldwell, Switching Circuits and Logical Design, McGraw-Hill Book Company, Inc., New York, 1958.

3. D.A. Huffman, "Design of Hazard-Free Switching Circuits," Journal of the Association for Computing Machinery, Vol. 4, pp. 47-62, January, 1957.

4. D.A. Huffman, "A Study of the Memory Requirements of Sequential Switching Circuits," Res. Lab. of Electronics, M.I.T., Cambridge, Mass., Tech. Rep. No. 293, March, 1955.

5. S.H. Unger, "A Study of Asynchronous Sequential Switching Circuits," Res. Lab. of Electronics, M.I.T., Cambridge, Mass., Tech. Rep. No. 320, April, 1957.

6. R.W. Hamming, "Error Detecting and Error Correcting Codes," Bell Systems Technical Journal, Vol., 29, pp. 147-160, April, 1950.

INTERNAL STATE ASSIGNMENTS FOR ASYNCHRONOUS SEQUENTIAL MACHINES

JAMES H. TRACEY

INTRODUCTION

Sequential switching circuits are normally categorized as being either synchronous or asynchronous. In synchronous circuits, clock pulses synchronize the operations of the circuit while in asynchronous circuits, it is usually assumed that no such clocking is available. A desirable feature of asynchronous design is that the resulting circuit may take full advantage of basic device speed since the circuit does not have to wait for the arrival of clock pulses before effecting a transition. However, the absence of clock pulses introduces the problem of insuring that the circuit functions according to specifications independent of variations in transmission delays of signals within the circuit. This important problem in the design of asynchronous sequential switching circuits is the topic of this paper.

A commonly used method for describing the terminal characteristics of a sequential circuit is a flow table[1] (see Fig. 1). Each column of the flow table represents an input state and each row represents an internal state. Entries of the table represent the "next" internal state of the circuit. For example, if machine A is presently in state b and an input I_1 is present, the internal state will change from b to c. No further changes in internal state will occur as long as I_1 is present. The total circuit state, defined by input I_1 and internal state c, is called stable and is denoted as such by a circled 5. With each stable state is associated an output state; output state 2 is associated with stable state 5 in machine A. If the input is now changed from I_1 to I_2, the circuit will undergo a transition from unstable 8 to stable 8 and the output will remain in state 2.

An important step in the synthesis procedure is the binary coding of the internal states. It is the construction of this code, called the state assignment, that must be made in such a fashion that the circuit will function according to flow table specifications independent of variations in transmission delays within the circuit. This paper develops systematic methods for the construction of internal state codes for a class of asynchronous circuits subject to the above constraint. The class of asynchronous circuits considered here is described by flow tables where each unstable leads directly to a stable state. Excluded are flow tables with cyclic or oscillatory internal state action.

Codes constructed from algorithms developed in this paper have the property that all internal transitions are completed in a minimum amount of time.

Reprinted with permission from the IEEE Transactions on Electronic Computers, Vol. EC-15, August 1966, pp. 551-560, with corrections from the author.

Inputs

		I_1	I_2	I_3	I_4
	a	①/1	2	3	4
Internal	b	5	②/1	⑥/1	⑦/2
States	c	⑤/2	8	6	④/2
	d	1	⑧/2	③/1	7

Fig. 1. Sequential Machine A.

Another property of these codes is that a single internal state is assigned to each row of the flow table. Liu[7] has treated this class of assignments, and this paper is an extension of his work.

THE INTERNAL STATE
ASSIGNMENT PROBLEM

A close examination will now be made of the internal state assignment problem and the constraints under which the assignment must be made. First it will be convenient to list some definitions.

Definition 1: When the binary code of the next internal state differs from the code of the present state in none of the bit positions, the circuit is stable.

Definition 2: When the binary code of the next internal state differs from the code of the present state in exactly one bit position, the circuit is said to be in transition from the present internal state to the next internal state.

Definition 3: When the binary code of the next internal state differs from the code of the present state in two or more bit positions, the circuit is said to be racing from the present internal state to the next internal state.

Definition 4: If a race condition exists and there is a possibility that unequal transmission delays may cause the circuit to reach stable state other than the one intended, the race is called critical; all other races are non-critical.

Definition 5: A direct transition from internal state S_i to S_j, written $[S_i, S_j]$, is a transition whereby all internal state variables that are to undergo a change to state are simultaneously excited.

Definition 6: A direct transition $[S_i, S_j]$ races critically with the direct transition $[S_k, S_\ell]$ if the possibility exists that unequal transmission delays may cause these two transitions to share a common internal state.

Definition 7: In a minimum transition time internal state assignment, all transitions are direct.

Quite obviously, critical races should be avoided in the design of asynchronous sequential switching circuits.

Three internal state assignments for machine A are shown in Figure 2. Assignment 1 is unsatisfactory because the transition from unstable 5 to stable 5 under input I_1 in machine A is a critical race. The desired transition is from internal state b to internal state c. Unequal transmission delays may cause internal state variable y_2 to change state before y_1. The next internal state would then be 0 0, the code for state a. But internal state a under input I_1 is stable state 1 and no further internal state changes will take place. Therefore, the transition in this case is from internal state b to internal state a instead of from b to c as specified.

Assignment 2 illustrates a situation where two direct transitions race critically with each other. Consider the pair of direct transitions under input I_2, a to b and c to d. In the transition from state a to state b, unequal delays may cause the circuit to be momentarily in internal state 0 0 0 1. Since both of these transitions do not end in the same stable state, unequal delays may cause false operation of the circuit. In this case, the transition from a to b is said to race critically with the transition c to d.

		1	2				3		
		y_1 y_2	y_1	y_2	y_3	y_4	y_1	y_2	y_3
	a	0 0	0	0	0	0	0	0	0
	b	0 1	0	0	1	1	0	1	1
State	c	1 0	0	1	0	1	1	1	0
	d	1 1	1	0	0	1	1	0	1

Fig. 2. Three Secondary Assignments for Machine A.

Assignment 2 can be a satisfactory assignment if one does not insist that all transitions be direct. The transition from a to b, for example, could be accomplished by first effecting a transition to internal state 0 0 1 0 and then to state 0 0 1 1. The transition from c to d would also involve a multiple transition. The first transition would be to internal state 1 1 0 1 and then to 1 0 0 1. If a unit of time, T, is defined as the average time required to change the state of an internal state variable, the transition from state c to state d requires a total time 2T. As a result, the circuit may accept input information at a rate no greater than 1/2T. Therefore, although Assignment 2 need not contain any critical races, all transitions cannot be made directly, and Assignment 2 cannot be classified as a minimum transition time assignment.

Assignment 3 is an example of a minimum transition time assignment. All transitions between internal states may be specified as direct transitions and all take place in approximately time T. The remainder of this paper consists of the development of systematic methods for the construction of codes with the characteristics of Assignment 3 for machine A.

PARTITION THEORY APPLIED TO MINIMUM TRANSITION TIME ASSIGNMENTS

A useful tool in the determination of minimum transition time assignments is the theory of partitions. At this point it is appropriate to introduce some important definitions and a theorem which relate partition theory to minimum transition time assignments.

Definition 8: A partition π on a set S is a collection of subsets of S such that their pairwise intersection is the null set. The disjoint subsets are called the blocks of π. If the set union of these subsets is S, the partition is completely specified; otherwise, the partition is incompletely specified. Elements of S that do

not appear in π are called unspecified or optional elements with respect to that partition.

In Assignment 3 for machine A, y_1 induces the partition $\pi_1 = \{\overline{a, b}; \overline{c, d}\}$. The blocks of π_1 are $\overline{a, b}$ and $\overline{c, d}$. The assignment is said to consist of the collection of partitions π_1, π_2, and π_3 induced by y_1, y_2, and y_3, respectively. Clearly, in the coding of a two-block partition, it is immaterial which block is coded with a 0 and which is coded with a 1. Similarly, the order in which the partitions appear is unimportant. The Hamming distance between all code points of the assignment is unchanged by complementation or permutation of the internal state variables. Henceforth, essentially different assignments will mean assignments different to within complementation and permutation of the internal state variables.

Definition 9: A flow table with the characteristic that each unstable state leads directly to a stable state is called a normal flow table.

Theorem 1: A row assignment allotting one y-state per row can be used for direct transition realization of normal flow tables without critical races if, and only if, for every transition $[S_i, S_j]$

    a. if $[S_m, S_n]$ is another transition in the same column, then at least one y-variable partitions the pair $\{S_i, S_j\}$ and pair $\{S_m, S_n\}$ into separate blocks and

    b. if S_k is a stable state in the same column then at least one y-variable partitions the pair $\{S_i, S_j\}$ and the state S_k into separate blocks and

    c. for $i \neq j$, S_i and S_j are in separate blocks of at least one y-variable partition.

Proof: a. There are eight different ways to partition the four states S_i, S_j, S_m, and S_n into partitions of two blocks or less. These are listed as follows:

$$\pi_1 = \{\overline{S_i, S_j, S_m, S_n}\}$$
$$\pi_2 = \{\overline{S_i}; \overline{S_j, S_m, S_n}\}$$

$$\pi_3 = \{\overline{S_i, S_j, S_m}; \overline{S_n}\}$$
$$\pi_4 = \{\overline{S_i, S_j, S_n}; \overline{S_m}\}$$
$$\pi_5 = \{\overline{S_i, S_m, S_n}; \overline{S_j}\}$$
$$\pi_6 = \{\overline{S_i, S_j}; \overline{S_m, S_n}\}$$
$$\pi_7 = \{\overline{S_i, S_m}; \overline{S_j, S_n}\}$$
$$\pi_8 = \{\overline{S_i, S_n}; \overline{S_j, S_m}\}$$

	y_1	y_2	y_3	y_4	y_5	y_6	y_7	y_8
S_i	0	0	0	0	0	0	0	0
S_j	0	1	1	0	0	0	1	1
S_m	0	1	0	1	0	1	0	1
S_n	0	1	0	0	1	1	1	0

The intermediate states involved in the direct transition $[S_i, S_j]$ are now $0\ 0\ -\ -\ 0\ 0\ 0\ -\ -$ and those involved in the direct transition $[S_m, S_n]$ are $0\ 1\ 0\ -\ -\ 1\ -\ -$. It is clear that none of those states associated with the $[S_i, S_j]$ transition are the same as those associated with the $[S_m, S_n]$ transition. The sufficiency part of the proof is based on the definition of a direct transition. Consider an assignment including y_6. Variable y_6 is 0 for both S_i and S_j. In a direct transition, all internal state variables that must change state in the transition are excited at the beginning of the transition. Variable y_6 is to be 0 at the beginning and end of the transition $[S_i, S_j]$, will therefore never be excited to 1, and cannot share any of the states entered by the direct transition $[S_m, S_n]$.

b. The proof of Part b is very similar to the proof of Part a. There are only four different ways to partition the three states S_i, S_j, and S_k into partitions of two blocks or less. These are listed as follows:

Only partitions of two blocks or less are considered since each partition is to be coded by a single binary variable. Note that π_6 is the only partition that meets the requirements of Part a of the theorem. An assignment will be constructed such that the y-variables induce all the given π-partitions with the exception of π_6. This assignment will be shown to contain a critical race. Let y_1 induce the partition π_1, y_2 induce the partition π_2, etc. The following state assignment results:

	y_1	y_2	y_3	y_4	y_5	y_7	y_8
S_i	0	0	0	0	0	0	0
S_j	0	1	1	0	0	1	1
S_m	0	1	0	1	0	0	1
S_n	0	1	0	0	1	1	0

Unequal transmission delay could cause the direct transition $[S_i, S_j]$ to momentarily assume any of the internal states $0\ -\ -\ 0\ 0\ -\ -$, where the dashes represent all combinations of 1's and 0's. Unequal transmission delay could cause the direct transition $[S_m, S_n]$ to momentarily assume any of the internal states $0\ 1\ 0\ -\ -\ -\ -$. Observe that the transitions $[S_i, S_j]$ and $[S_m, S_n]$ could share any of the internal states $0\ 1\ 0\ 0\ 0\ -\ -$ while the transitions are being effected. Therefore, according to definition 6, these transitions race critically with each other.

Now if the assignment is expanded to include y_6, which induces the partition π_6, the following assignment results:

$$\pi_1 = \{\overline{S_i, S_j, S_k}\}$$
$$\pi_2 = \{\overline{S_i}; \overline{S_j, S_k}\}$$
$$\pi_3 = \{\overline{S_i, S_j}; \overline{S_k}\}$$
$$\pi_4 = \{\overline{S_i, S_k}; \overline{S_j}\}$$

In this case, π_3 is the only π-partition that meets the conditions of Part b of the theorem. First an assignment is constructed without y_3 to induce the partition π_3.

	y_1	y_2	y_4
S_i	0	0	0
S_j	0	1	1
S_k	0	1	0

A direct transition $[S_i, S_j]$ could momentarily assume any of the internal states 0 - -, where again the dashes represent all combinations of 1's and 0's. It is clear, then, that this transition could assume the state 0 1 0, which is the stable state S_k. Therefore, according to definition 4, the transition $[S_i, S_j]$ is a critical race. With the assignment expanded to include y_3 and its induced partition π_3, the following assignment results:

	y_1	y_2	y_3	y_4
S_i	0	0	0	0
S_j	0	1	0	1
S_k	0	1	1	0

Now the direct transition $[S_i, S_j]$ may momentarily assume any of the states 0 - 0 -, none of which are stable state S_k, and therefore the race is noncritical. It is sufficient to include y_3 since in the direct transition $[S_i, S_j]$, y_3 will never be excited to 1 and therefore cannot enter state S_k.

c. The condition of Part c must be included. It can easily be shown by example that an assignment meeting the conditions of Part a and Part b does not necessarily distinguish all the internal states from one another.

Definition 10: Partition π_2 is less than or equal to π_1, ($\pi_2 \leq \pi_1$), where π_1 and π_2 may be incompletely specified, if and only if all elements specified in π_2 are also specified in π_1 and each block of π_2 appears in a unique block of π_1.

Definition 11: Let $[S_p, S_q]$ and $[S_r, S_s]$ be transitions in the same column of a flow table and let S_t be a stable state also in the same column. The collection of all two-block partitions $\{S_p, S_q; S_r S_s\}$ and $\{S_p, S_q; S_t\}$ of a flow table comprise the partition list of that flow table.

Definition 12: The two-block partitions τ_1, τ_2, ..., τ_p induced by the internal state variables y_1, y_2, ..., y_p in a minimum transition time assignment are called the set of τ-partitions of that assignment.

It follows from Theorem 1 that an internal state assignment for a normal flow table is a minimum transition time assignment free of critical races if and only if each partition of the partition list is $\leq$ some τ_i. This will be illustrated with sequential machine B shown in Fig. 3. The outputs are not shown.

The partition list for machine B is as follows:

$$\pi_1 = \{a, d; \overline{b, c}\}$$
$$\pi_2 = \{a, d; \overline{c, e}\}$$
$$\pi_3 = \{a; \overline{b, e}\}$$
$$\pi_4 = \{a; \overline{c, d}\}$$
$$\pi_5 = \{a, d; \overline{c, e}\}$$
$$\pi_6 = \{b, d; \overline{c, e}\}$$
$$\pi_7 = \{a, b; \overline{c, d}\}$$
$$\pi_8 = \{a, b; \overline{e}\}$$
$$\pi_9 = \{c, d; \overline{e}\}$$
$$\pi_{10} = \{b, e; \overline{c, d}\}$$

As previously stated, a set of τ-partitions must be found such that each partition from the partition list is

	I_1	I_2	I_3	I_4
a	①	②	8	4
b	5	③	8	④
c	⑤	7	9	⑥
d	1	⑦	⑧	6
e	5	3	⑨	⑩

Fig. 3. Machine B.

$\leq$ at least one τ-partition. In this paper, optimum assignments will be those assignments with the least number of y-variables. Therefore, an effort will be made to construct a minimum number of τ-partitions for the flow table. Consider the following set of τ-partitions for machine B:

$$\tau_1 = \{\overline{a, b, d}; \overline{c, e}\}$$
$$\tau_2 = \{\overline{a, be}; \overline{cd}\}$$
$$\tau_3 = \{\overline{a, e}; \overline{b, c, d}\}$$

Clearly, partitions π_2, π_5, π_6, and π_8 are $\leq \tau_1$, π_4, π_7, and π_9 are $\leq \tau_2$ and π_1 and π_3 are $\leq \tau_3$. If y_1, y_2, and y_3 are used to code τ_1, τ_2, and τ_3, respectively, the following assignment results for machine B.

	y_1	y_2	y_3
a -	0	0	0
b -	0	0	1
c -	1	1	1
d -	0	1	0
e -	1	0	1

It can easily be verified that with this assignment all internal transitions in machine B can be specified as direct transitions without the introduction of any critical races.

A set of τ-partitions for the previous example were just given without any mention of how they were developed. The remaining portion of this paper concerns itself with the development of systematic methods for the construction of these τ-partitions. Three such methods will be presented. The first of these, called Assignment Method 1, is described in the next section.

ASSIGNMENT METHOD 1

Assignment Method 1 is a systematic method for determining the set of τ-partitions from the partition list of the flow table. Incompletely speci-

fied machine C (Fig. 4) will be used to illustrate and explain the procedure.

The partition list for machine C is as follows:

$$\pi_1 = \{\overline{a, b}; \overline{c, f}\} \quad \pi_6 = \{\overline{a, d}; \overline{b, c}\}$$
$$\pi_2 = \{\overline{a, e}; \overline{c, f}\} \quad \pi_7 = \{\overline{a, d}; \overline{c, e}\}$$
$$\pi_3 = \{\overline{a, c}; \overline{d, e}\} \quad \pi_8 = \{\overline{a, c}; \overline{b, d}\}$$
$$\pi_4 = \{\overline{a, c}; \overline{b, f}\} \quad \pi_9 = \{\overline{a, c}; \overline{e, f}\}$$
$$\pi_5 = \{\overline{b, f}; \overline{d, e}\} \quad \pi_{10} = \{\overline{b, d}; \overline{e, f}\}$$

The unspecified entries in the flow table are ignored during the construction of the partition list. As a result, the possibility exists that in the construction of an assignment meeting the conditions of Theorem 1, an unspecified location may be entered during a specified transition. Such locations, then, do not remain unspecified. This causes no particular problem. Unspecified next-state entries can always be filled in uniqely since the conditions of Theorem 1 permit, at most, one transition to pass through a given internal state.

The problem is to reduce this partition list to a smallest set of τ-partitions. One could begin, for example, by constructing a two-block partition $\pi_A = \{\overline{a, b, e}; \overline{c, f}\}$. Since π_1 and π_2 are $\leq \pi_A$, π_1 and π_2 could be replaced by π_A and the partition list would contain only 9 partitions instead of 10. Similarly, one could then replace π_3 and π_4 with the partition $\pi_B = \{\overline{a, c}; \overline{b, d, e, f}\}$. When the point is reached where it is no longer

	I_1	I_2	I_3	I_4
a	①	4	7	10
b	1	5	8	⑪
c	2	④	⑧	⑩
d	-	⑥	⑦	11
e	1	6	8	⑫
f	②	⑤	-	12

Fig. 4. Machine C.

possible to replace a pair of partitions with a single partition, the resulting partitions could be called the set of τ-partitions. Every partition in the original partition list would be $\leq$ at least one of these τ-partitions. The obvious difficulty with this approach is that there are many different sets of τ-partitions for a given partition list and it is not clear how to proceed so as to obtain a smallest set.

If the partition list is converted to a Boolean matrix, the reduction of the partition list can be shown to be similar to the problem of encoding incompletely specified Boolean matrices treated by Dolotta and McCluskey.[3] The Boolean matrix for the partition list of machine C is shown in Fig. 5.

In Fig. 5, the internal states identify the columns of the matrix and the two-block partitions from the partition list identify the rows. The partitions are shown in abbreviated notation; they are numbered according to their respective π subscript and a space separates the blocks of each partition. Each row of the matrix consists of a binary code of the blocks of the respective two-block partition. The first row of Fig. 5 is identified by the partition {a, b; c, f}. Arbitrarily, the elements of the first block are coded with a 0 and the elements of the second block are coded with a 1. The remaining elements in the first row are unspecified (-). As stated previously, it is immaterial whether the first or second block of a two-block partition is coded with a 0, and therefore any or all of the rows of the matrix may be complemented without altering the problem description.

Some applicable definitions regarding the reduction of incompletely specified Boolean matrices will be given, with appropriate modifications, from Dolotta and McCluskey's paper.

Definition 13: Two rows of a Boolean matrix, R_i and R_j, have an intersection of R_i and R_j, written $R_i \cdot R_j$, if and only if R_i and R_j agree wherever both R_i and R_j are specified. The intersection is defined as a row which agrees with both R_i, and R_j wher-

ever either is specified and contains optional entries everywhere else.

Definition 14: Row R_i is said to include row R_j if and only if R_j agrees with R_i wherever R_i is specified.

Definition 15: Row R_i is said to cover row R_j if and only if R_j includes R_i or R_j includes the complement of R_i. The complement of R_i is designated by $\bar{R}_i$.

At this point, the problem has been transformed into one of finding a reduced Boolean matrix to cover the matrix derived from the partition list. Each row of the original matrix must be covered by at least one row of the reduced matrix. The rows of this reduced matrix are then interpreted as a set of coded two-block τ-partitions. Clearly, one assignment which makes use of these resulting τ-partitions is simply the columns of the reduced matrix. The number of rows in the reduced matrix is identical to the number of state variables in the assignment. Therefore, an assignment utilizing a minimum number of state variables is an assignment developed from a minimum row Boolean matrix that covers the original partition list matrix.

One way to reduce the partition list matrix would be to replace pairwise intersectable rows with their intersection and continue this process until there were no further reductions.

			a	b	c	d	e	f
1	ab	cf	0	0	1	-	-	1
2	ae	cf	0	-	1	-	0	1
3	ac	de	0	-	0	1	1	-
4	ac	bf	0	1	0	-	-	1
5	bf	de	-	0	-	1	1	0
6	ad	bc	0	1	1	0	-	-
7	ad	ce	0	-	1	0	1	-
8	ac	bd	0	1	0	1	-	-
9	ac	ef	0	-	0	-	1	1
10	bd	ef	-	0	-	0	1	1

Fig. 5. Boolean Matrix for Machine C

If this procedure is carried out for the matrix in Fig. 5, one might begin by replacing rows 1 and 2 with their intersection, which is 0 0 1 – 0 1. Rows 3 and 4 have an intersection 0 1 0 1 1 1. Row 6 and the complement of row 5 have an intersection 0 1 1 0 0 1. Rows 7 and 10 have an intersection 0 0 1 0 1 1 and rows 8 and 9 have an intersection 0 1 0 1 1 1. The intersection of rows 3 and 4 is identical to the intersection of rows 8 and 9 so it follows that the row 0 1 0 1 1 1 covers rows 3, 4, 8 and 9. The reduced matrix is shown in Fig. 6.

The columns of the reduced matrix in Fig. 6 are codes for the corresponding row of the flow table. Hence, row a would be assigned y-state 0 0 0 0, row b the state 0 1 1 0, row c the state 1 0 1 1, etc. The optional entry in the reduced matrix may be read as a 1 or 0. In either case, the resulting assignment is a minimum transition time assignment with no critical races. If internal state d is assigned the code 0 1 0 0, then the unspecified entry under input state I_1 must be filled in with a 1. Internal state f under input I_3 remains unspecified. On the other hand, if state d is assigned the code 1 1 0 0, both unspecified entries remain unspecified.

The assignment shown in the reduced matrix of Fig. 6 takes four y-variables, one y-variable for each row of the matrix. However, notice that the reduced matrix of Fig. 7 also covers the partition list matrix but yields a state assignment with only three y-variables. An obvious problem,

then, in the reduction of a large matrix is that if it is done by replacing pairs of rows with their intersections, it is nearly impossible to tell how to proceed so as to obtain an optimum reduction.

MATRIX REDUCTION ALGORITHM 1

One method of constructing a minimum row reduced matrix is to show all possible row intersections for the partition list matrix and then from this list determine a minimum number of these intersections to cover the entire matrix. It will be more convenient to designate the intersecting rows than to actually show the intersections, hence definition 16.

Definition 16: If a set of rows, R_i, R_j, ..., R_p, have an intersection, they are called intersectable and designated as such by (i, j, ..., p). If R_i, $\overline{R_j}$, ..., R_p are intersectable, the intersectable is designated by (i, $\overline{j}$, ..., p). An intersectable may be enlarged by adding an element q if and only if q has an intersection with every element of the set. An intersectable which cannot be added to is called a maximal intersectable.

The first step of this reduction algorithm is the construction of a list of all pairwise intersectables. For every pair of rows R_i and R_j one should check R_i and R_j, and R_i and $\overline{R_j}$ as possible intersectables. This is necessary since any of the intersections $R_i \cdot R_j$, $R_i \cdot \overline{R_j}$, $\overline{R_i} \cdot R_j$, $\overline{R_i} \cdot \overline{R_j}$ cover rows R_i and R_j. The pairwise intersectables for machine C are as follows:

	a	b	c	d	e	f
(1,2)	0	0	1	–	0	1
(3,4,8,9)	0	1	0	1	1	1
($\overline{5}$,6)	0	1	1	0	0	1
(7,10)	0	0	1	0	1	1

Fig. 6. A Reduced Boolean Matrix for Machine C

	a	b	c	d	e	f
(1,7,10)	0	0	1	0	1	1
(2,$\overline{5}$,6)	0	1	1	0	0	1
(3,4,8,9)	0	1	0	1	1	1

Fig. 7. Minimum Row Reduced Boolean Matrix for Machine C

(1,<u>2</u>) (1,7) (1,10)   (6,7)
(2,<u>5</u>) (2,6)   (7,10)
(3,4) (3,5) (3,8) (3,9)   (8,9) (8,<u>10</u>)
(<u>4</u>,5) (4,8) (4,9)   (9,10)
(<u>5</u>,6)

The second step of this matrix reduction algorithm consists of enlarging
these pairwise interselectables in
accordance with definition 16. For example, from the intersectables (1,7),
(1,10) and (7,10), one may construct a
new intersectable (1,7,10). The intersection of rows 1,7 and 10, 0 0 1 0 1 1,
covers each of these rows. The
intersectable (1,7,10) is a maximal
intersectable since no element can be
added to it. In like fashion, all
pair-wise intersectables are enlarged
to maximal intersectables, intersectables which are a proper subset of
other intersectables are discarded, and
one is left with a set of maximal intersectables. The maximal intersectables
for machine C are as follows:

A (1,2)   D (3,4,8,9)   G (6,<u>7</u>)
B (1,<u>7</u>,10)   E (3,5)   H (8,<u>10</u>)
C (2,<u>5</u>,6)   F (4,5)   J (9,10)

Each of the maximal intersectables have an intersection that covers
the rows of the partition list matrix
identified by the elements of the
corresponding intersectable. For example, maximal intersectable (2,<u>5</u>,6)
has an intersection 0 1 1 1 0 1 which
covers row 2, 5, and 6 of the partition
list matrix. The complement intersection, 1 0 0 0 1 0, also covers rows 2,
5, and 6. Therefore, there is no need
to distinguish between the intersectables (2,<u>5</u>,6) and (<u>2</u>,5,<u>6</u>).

The next step is to select a minimum number of maximal intersectables
such that each row of the partition
list matrix is covered by one intersectable. This entails the solution
of a covering problem of the type one
encounters in solving a prime implicant
table in the Quine-McCluskey procedure
for the simplification of Boolean
expressions. A large body of literature
exists on the treatment of this problem.
See, for example, Petrick's report[5] or

the more recent paper and references by
Gimpel[2]. One may determine by inspection that the maximal intersectable B,
C, and D cover all rows of the partition list matrix. Alternately, one may
use a procedure similar to Petrick's
method of obtaining an algebraic solution of prime implicant tables. This
involves writing a product-of-sums
Boolean expression that logically states
all possible ways of covering the rows
of the partition matrix with the maximal intersectables. The Boolean expression is converted to sum-of-products
form and the term containing the fewest
literals describes a least number of
maximal intersectables that covers all
rows of the original matrix.

To construct the Boolean expression
it is noted that intersectable A or B,
written logically as A + B, may be used
to cover row 1, the factor A + C describes the covering of row 2, etc.
The complete product of sums expression
is

$$(A + B) \ (A + C) \ (D + E) \ (D + F)$$
$$(C + E + F) \ (C + G) \cdot (B + G)$$
$$(D + H) \ (D + J) \ (B + H + J)$$

The equivalent sum of products
expression is

BCD + ABDFG + ADFGH + ADFGJ + ACDGH

   + ACDGJ + ABDEG + ADEGH + ADEGJ

   + BCEFHJ + ADFGHJ.

The selection of intersectables B, C,
and D as a minimum set is substantiated.
The corresponding reduced matrix was
shown previously in Fig. 7.   The
columns of the reduced matrix may be
taken as the codes for the internal
states.

The algorithm just discussed for
the reduction of the partition list
matrix to a minimum row matrix and minimum set of τ-partitions is called
Matrix Reduction Algorithm 1. The
steps of the algorithm are summarized
as follows.

1. Examine all pairs of rows of
the partition list matrix and list

those pairs that are intersectable.

2. From the list of pair-wise intersectables, determine all maximal intersectables. The mechanics of this step are nearly identical to those for finding maximal compatibles in the simplification of state tables. See, for example, the paper by Unger and Paull[4].

3. Determine a least number of maximal intersectables that will cover all the rows of the original matrix. This may be done by inspection, or systematically as follows:

   a. letter each maximal intersectable for identification,

   b. write a Boolean product of sums expression that logically states how the entire matrix may be covered,

   c. convert the Boolean expression to sum of products form,

   d. a term from the Boolean expression containing the fewest literals describes a least number of maximal intersectables that covers all rows of the original matrix.

4. The maximal intersectables selected in step 3 each describe an intersection row of the reduced matrix. Furthermore, each intersection represents one partition to be used in the state assignment.

A serious disadvantage of the algorithm just described is that it becomes quite lengthy for moderate increases in flow table size. Determination of the maximal intersectables by hand computation becomes tedious for matrices with more than 15 rows. Algebraic determination of a minimum covering set of intersectables is difficult when there are more than 10 maximal intersectables. It is advantageous, therefore, to develop an algorithm that is easier to apply for large matrices even though it cannot be guaranteed to always yield an optimum reduction. Such an algorithm, called Matrix Reduction Algorithm 2, will be discussed. Algorithm 2 is based on the assumption that for many Boolean matrices, an optimum or near optimum reduction may be obtained by constructing an intersect-

able that covers a large number of rows, removing the covered rows from the matrix, constructing an intersectable that covers a large number of the remaining rows, removing them from the matrix, etc., until all rows of the original matrix are covered. The algorithm will be stated and illustrated with an example. Then an attempt will be made to show some of the reasoning behind the steps.

MATRIX REDUCTION ALGORITHM 2

1. Select a column of the Boolean matrix with the largest number of specified entires and identify it with the letter A. If several columns have the same largest number of specified entries, arbitrarily select one of them.

2. Complement appropriate rows of the matrix so that all specified entries in the column selected in step 1 agree.

3. Identify those rows that are not specified under the column selected in step 1 with the letter B.

4. Examine each column not identified with an A and determine the difference between the number of 1's and 0's in each of these columns. Ignore for this count, those rows identified with a B or C.

5. Select the column from step 4 that has the largest difference magnitude. Set that column to a 1 or 0, whichever was larger, and identify the column with an A. If several columns have the same largest difference, arbitrarily select one of them.

6. Examine those rows not identified with a B or C. If a row does not agree with the setting of the column in step 5, identify that row with a C.

7. Consider those rows identified with a B and specified under the column selected in step 5. Remove the B identification from these rows and complement them, if necessary, so that they will agree with the selected column setting in step 5.

8. Go back to step 4 unless all columns are identified with an A. If all columns are identified with an A, go to step 9.

9. All rows not identified with a C have an intersection. This intersection represents one of the partitions to be used in the assignment. Determine this intersection and remove the covered rows from the matrix. Remove all identifiers from the remaining matrix and go back to step 1. The algorithm is ended when there are no rows remaining in the matrix.

To illustrate this algorithm, consider again the matrix in Fig. 5. The steps of the illustration are numbered to correspond to the steps of the algorithm.

1. Columns a and c have eight specified entries each. Select column a and identify it with an A.
2. No rows need to be complemented.
3. Identify rows 5 and 10 with a B.
4. Counts of 1's and 0's must be made for columns b through f. In column f, for example, there is a count of zero 0's and four 1's.
5. Column f has the largest count difference. Set column f to a 1 and identify it with an A.
6. No rows need to be identified with a C.
7. Remove the B identification from rows 5 and 10. Complement row 5.
8. Return to step 4.
4. Counts of 1's and 0's must be made for columns b, c, d, e.
5. Columns b, d, and e have a count difference of 2. Arbitrarily select column b and set it to a 1.
6. Identify rows 1 and 10 with a C.
7. No rows are identified with a B.
8. Return to step 4.

The process is continued until all columns are identified with an A and step 9 is entered. At this point all rows are identified with a C except rows 3, 4, 8, and 9. Rows 3, 4, 8, and 9 have an intersection described by the partition $\tau_1 = \{a, c; b, d, e, f\}$. So that the reader may

follow, in case of a tie in steps 1 or 5, the left-most column was selected. Now rows 3, 4, 8, and 9 are removed from the matrix, all identifications are removed, and the process is repeated. The reader may easily verify that the resulting partitions are those appearing in the state assignment given previously for machine B.

Some of the reasoning behind the steps of the algorithm will be discussed. The algorithm's purpose is to determine an intersection or partition that will cover a maximum or near maximum number of rows in the partition list matrix. After such an intersection is found, the covered rows are discarded and a subset of the original matrix is considered. In Algorithm 2 this intersection is arrived at by determining, one by one, the setting of each individual column so that a maximum number of rows are covered. Since the intent is to determine the column settings on a step by step basis, the outcome will be greatly dependent upon which column one starts with. Hence, in step 1 the column is selected that will bring a maximum number of rows into consideration at the beginning of the algorithm. One would suspect also, that the outcome depends on the order in which one determines the setting of each column. Therefore, in steps 4 and 5 the column is chosen which is most strongly associated with the already chosen columns and at the same time requires that a relatively few number of rows be excluded from further consideration.

The limitations of the algorithm are:

1. The algorithm does not always produce an intersection covering a maximum number of rows in a matrix.
2. There exist matrices where none of the members of the minimum set of covering partitions cover a maximum number of rows in the matrix. It has been the author's experience that in spite of these limitations, a true minimum set of covering partitions can be found in most cases. Important advantages of this algorithm are that the algorithm is very systematic, pro-

grammable on a computer and capable of handling relatively large matrices. Matrices of up to 60 rows have been reduced by hand computation using Matrix Reduction Algorithm 2.

The minimum transition time state assignment method discussed in this section, called Assignment Method 1, consists of the following steps.

1. Convert the merged flow table to a partition list.
2. Convert the partition list to a Boolean matrix.
3. Reduce the matrix by Matrix Reduction Algorithm 1 or 2.
4. Let the reduced matrix define the state assignment.

ASSIGNMENT METHOD 2

Assignment Method 1, even with the approximate Matrix Reduction Algorithm 2, may become quite long for flow tables with more than about four columns and ten rows. A shorter method, Assignment Method 2, will be developed even though it may be less efficient in terms of y-variables.

Definition 17: A k-set exists in a single column of a flow table and consists of all k-1 unstable entries leading to the same stable state, together with that stable state.

Theorem 2: A direct transition in k-set k_q does not race critically with a direct transition in k-set k_r if an assignment has been made such that at least one y-variable partitions the elements of k_q and the elements of k_r into separate blocks.

Proof: All internal state transitions following a change in input state are confined to a single k-set. Therefore internal states S_i and S_j of Theorem 1 must be elements of a k-set, which will be labeled k_q. Internal states S_m and S_n are elements of another k-set, k_r. If a y-variable, y_p, exists in the assignment and partitions k_q and k_r into separate blocks, then this same y-variable partitions the pairs $\{S_i, S_j\}$ and $\{S_m, S_n\}$ into separate blocks and the conditions of Theorem 1 are met.

Assignment Method 2 consists of constructing a partition list from the k-sets of a flow table instead of from the transition pairs. Consider again machine B in Fig. 3. By partitioning pairs of k-sets in each column, one constructs the following partition list for machine B:

$$\pi_1 = \{a, d; \overline{b, c, e}\}$$
$$\pi_2 = \{a; \overline{b, e}\}$$
$$\pi_3 = \{a; \overline{c, d}\}$$
$$\pi_4 = \{b, e; \overline{c, d}\}$$
$$\pi_5 = \{a, b, d; \overline{c, e}\}$$
$$\pi_6 = \{a, b; \overline{c, d}\}$$
$$\pi_8 = \{c, d; \overline{e}\}$$

Clearly, $\pi_2 \leq \pi_1$, $\pi_3 \leq \pi_6$, $\pi_7 \leq \pi_5$, and $\pi_8 \leq \pi_4$. Therefore, π_2, π_3, π_7, and π_8 may be removed from the partition list. If the remaining four π partitions are converted to matrix form, it is clear that no further reduction in the number of partitions is possible. The resulting assignment for machine B is the then

	y_1	y_2	y_3	y_4
a	0	–	0	0
b	1	0	0	0
c	1	1	1	1
d	0	1	0	1
e	1	0	1	–

Note that the assignment is not completely specified, but is free of critical races regardless of how the optional entries are filled in. This assignment is not minimum, however; Assignment Method 1 produces an assignment with only three y-variables.

The advantage of Assignment Method 2 is that it often results in a shorter partition list and is therefore easier to apply. The method represents a considerable saving in time and effort for flow tables with large k-sets. Obviously, if all k-sets contain no more than two states, Method 2 degenerates to Method 1.

ASSIGNMENT METHOD 3

An even greater saving in time and effort results if the state assignment is constructed from the column partitions of a flow table. This method will be called Assignment Method 3.

Definition 18: A column partition is a partition constructed from a single column of a flow table with each k-set of the column appearing as a separate block. A column partition may be either completely or incompletely specified.

Theorem 3: A state assignment constructed from the set of column partitions of a flow table contains no critical races, even if all transitions are direct.

Proof: Consider a column of a flow table to contain n k-sets. These n k-sets can be distinguished with N_0 two-block partitions where N_0 is the smallest integer such that $N_0 \geq \log_2 n$. For each pair of k-sets, k_q and k_r, one of these two-block partitions must contain k_q and k_r in separate blocks. Therefore, all the conditions of Theorem 2 are met and there are no critical races in the column. A state assignment constructed from all the column partitions contains no critical races in any column of the flow table.

Before the column partitions are coded to give the assignment, those column partitions equal to or less than some other partition should be discarded. Assignment Method 3 will be illustrated with an example taken from page 530 of Caldwell[6]. His flow table will be labeled here as machine D and is shown in Fig. 8.

The column partitions are

$$\pi_1 = \{\overline{\ell, f}; \ \overline{b, \ell}; \ \overline{c, e, g}; \ \overline{d, h, m}\}$$

$$\pi_2 = \{\overline{a, c}; \ \overline{b, d, f}; \ \overline{e, j}; \ \overline{g, h, k}\}$$

$$\pi_3 = \{\overline{a, f, j}; \ \overline{b, k, \ell}; \ \overline{e, g}; \ \overline{h, m}\}$$

$$\pi_4 = \{\overline{a, c, \ell}; \ \overline{b, d}; \ \overline{e, j, m}; \ \overline{h, k}\}$$

All the column partitions for machine D are incompletely specified. By inspection, π_1 and π_3 are less than the completely specified partition $\tau_1 = \overline{\{a, f, j; \ b, k, \ell; \ c, e, g; \ d, h, m\}}$ and π_2 and π_4 are less than the completely specified partition $\tau_2 = \overline{\{a, c, \ell; \ b, d; \ e, j, m; \ h, k\}}$. The coding of τ_1 and τ_2 produces a minimum transition time assignment for machine D. Two y-variables are needed to distinguish the blocks of τ_1 and two more are needed to distinguish the blocks of τ_2. Caldwell also shows an assignment with four y-variables but it was arrived at with considerably more effort than here.

Although Assignment Method 3 was very efficient for machine D, this is not always the case. For machine C, for example, Assignment Method 3 produces an assignment with five or six y-variables, depending on how the blocks of the column partitions are coded. Assignment Method 2 produces an assignment with five variables, but Assignment Method 1 has been shown to give an assignment with only three variables.

Assignment Method 3 is similar to a method given by Liu[7]. In his paper, Liu also presents an upper bound assignment method. He has shown that any 2^m-row flow table can always be

	I_1	I_2	I_3	I_4
a	①	⑤	11	15
b	②	7	12	⑬
c	③	5	–	15
d	④	7	–	13
e	3	⑥	⑨	16
f	1	⑦	11	–
g	3	⑧	9	–
h	4	8	⑩	⑭
j	–	6	⑪	16
k	–	8	⑫	14
l	2	–	12	⑮
m	4	–	10	⑯

Fig. 8. Machine D.

coded with $2^m - 1$ internal state variables to yield a minimum transition time assignment. Huffman[8] has also developed a general minimum transition time assignment method that uses $2^m - 1$ variables to code a 2^m-row flow table. One should be aware of this upper bound on the required number of internal state variables when using the assignment methods of this paper.

CONCLUSIONS

It is well known that as flow tables increase in number of rows, the number of essentially different internal state assignments that exist grows at a fantastic rate. Because of this, it seems to be the case that as one tries to achieve a minimum code for larger and larger flow tables, the amount of effort required increases tremendously. It is a characteristic of the assignment methods of this paper that those methods easy to apply often require more than the necessary number of variables, while those that minimize the number of variables tend to become quite long for large flow tables.

Three methods were presented for obtaining minimum transition time assignments. Mention was also made of the upper bound assignment methods of Liu and Huffman. A good procedure to use in obtaining an assignment is to consider Liu and Huffman's method as an upper bound on the number of variables for Assignment Methods 1, 2, and 3. Similarly, Method 3 can be considered to yield an upper bound on the number of variables for Methods 1 and 2, and Method 2 can be considered to yield an upper bound on the number of variables for Method 1. For most flow tables, Method 2 is easier to apply than Method 1 and Method 3 is easier to apply than Method 2. Liu and Huffman's upper bound assignment is easiest of all to apply because it can be made completely independent of the flow table structure. Note that all assignment methods work equally well for completely or incompletely specified machines.

ACKNOWLEDGMENT

The author wishes to thank Prof. R. M. Stewart, Jr., for advice and encouragement during the writing of this doctoral dissertation on which this paper is based. He also acknowledges the very careful reading and useful comments furnished by one of the reviewers.

REFERENCES

1. D. A. Huffman, "The synthesis of sequential switching circuits," J. Franklin Inst., vol. 257, pp. 151-190, 275-303, March and April 1954.
2. J. F. Gimpel, "A reduction technique for prime implicant tables," IEEE Trans. on Electronic Computers, vol. EC-14, pp. 535-541, August 1965.
3. T. A. Dolotta and E. J. McCluskey, "Encoding of incompletely specified Boolean matrices," Proc. Western Joint Computer Conf., vol. 18, pp. 231-238, 1960.
4. M. C. Paull and S. H. Unger, "Minimizing the number of states in incompletely specified sequential switching functions," IRE Trans. on Electronic Computers, vol. EC-8, pp. 356-367, September 1959.
5. S. R. Petrick, "A direct determination of the irredundant forms of a Boolean function from the set of prime implicants," Air Force Cambridge Research Center, Cambridge, Mass., Techn. Rept. AFCRC-TR-56-110, 1956.
6. S. H. Caldwell, Switching circuits and logical design, New York, Wiley, 1958.
7. C. N. Liu, "A state variable assignment method for asynchronous sequential switching circuits," J. ACM, vol. 10, pp. 209-216, 1963.
8. D. A. Huffman, "A Study of the memory requirements of sequential switching circuits," Research Lab. of Electronics, Mass. Inst. Techn., Cambridge, Techn. Rept. 293, 1955.

PART II   ARITHMETIC ALGORITHMS

In direct contrast to the rather general papers of Part I, the five papers of this part deal with specific arithmetic systems. These papers are implementation oriented, showing systems which are realized with the methods described previously. Although all but the final paper of this part describe systems for fixed point arithmetic, the modifications to adapt such a unit to floating point operation can be accomplished directly.

HIGH-SPEED ARITHMETIC IN BINARY COMPUTERS

O. L. MacSORLEY

This paper provides a thorough introduction to the design of computer arithmetic units. Much emphasis is given to the speed-complexity tradeoffs which must be considered when an arithmetic unit is developed. An appendix is included which was written after the original paper was published; the reader with little previous exposure to computer arithmetic will probably find the added explanation useful.

This paper contains an excellent explanation of the carry lookahead adder and the carry save multiplication scheme, both of which have been widely used. Integrated circuits are available which facilitate implementation of moderately fast arithmetic processors by these methods. These are fixed time procedures (e.g., addition always takes the same amount of time regardless of the operands). MacSorley also describes variable time algorithms such as completion recognition adders and variable shift length multipliers which may be faster on the average for a given complexity.

Also included is a fine discussion of methods for speeding the traditionally slow process of division. The practical value of these techniques depends on the percentage of divisions comprising the job mix of the arithmetic unit. Obviously unless a reasonable amount of division is contemplated, there is little to be gained from developing a fast divider. The division problem is also discussed at length in the final paper of this part.

A SIGNED BINARY MULTIPLICATION TECHNIQUE

ANDREW D. BOOTH

Slow multiplication was one of the most obvious faults of the earliest computers; Booth discovered an efficient method for two's complement multiplication that overcame the need for correction steps when either operand was negative. This multiplication scheme is still enjoying wide usage because of its simplicity and efficiency; indeed, parallel multipliers have recently been developed along similar lines.

The basic algorithm is similar to the "pencil and paper" shift and add algorithm except that more than one multiplier bit is inspected at each iteration. In addition to avoiding correction steps for negative operands, this method shifts across strings of ones and zeros, which is advantageous if shifting is faster than addition or subtraction.

Although the algorithm is presented as a time iteratative scheme, clearly it can be implemented with iterated hardware to produce a very fast two's complement multiplier.

SOME SCHEMES FOR PARALLEL MULTIPLIERS

L. DADDA

For arithmetic units that perform substantial amounts of multiplication (e.g., "scientific" computers), the speed advantage of a parallel multiplier may be sufficient to justify its cost. Dadda describes a number of efficient empirical procedures for the design of maximum speed multipliers. The basic concept of a parallel multiplier is to reduce the number of rows in the partial product bit matrix by means of parallel counters.

These multipliers achieve extremely high speed only by resorting to relativly high circuit complexity: the complexity problem becomes much more acute as the word size increases, since the complexity is roughly proportional to the square of the word size. Dadda also considers ways to implement parallel counters. His treatment is oriented toward implementation with threshold gates and serves to indicate some of the quasi digital (i.e., using both analog and digital methods) techniques which may become more significant in the future.

Current trends indicate that parallel multipliers are a viable method to increase the speed of a computer without greatly increasing its overall complexity. It is to be expected that parallel arithmetic will become more popular as Large Scale Integrated circuit implementation reduces the cost of realizing complex logical networks.

Some errors in the original have been corrected in this reprint with the author's permission.

THE RESIDUE NUMBER SYSTEM

HARVEY L. GARNER

The attraction of residue arithmetic lies in speed and simplicity of addition, subtraction, and multiplication in residue systems. This paper introduces the residue number system, describes its use for special purpose arithmetic processors, and presents methods for conversion between residue and conventional weighted number systems (and vice-versa).

Since arithmetic operations on residues do not generate carries between the residues, a separate small arithmetic unit can be provided for each residue, thus permitting very fast processing. Problems arise whenever division, magnitude comparison, or sign detection is required, so the residue system has not been widely used. Residue arithmetic can be very useful for specialized processing (e.g., correlation computation, solution of systems of linear equations, and matrix inversion).

THE IBM SYSTEM/360 MODEL 91: FLOATING POINT EXECUTION UNIT

S. F. ANDERSON, J. G. EARLE, R. E. GOLDSCHMIDT, AND D. M. POWERS

This paper gives a detailed description of the design of a complete floating point arithmetic unit for a high performance computer. The paper describes the additional difficulty in implementing a floating point system.

The paper begins with an introduction to floating point number systems, and a brief description of general methods to increase the speed of an arithmetic unit. In the detailed description which follows it is shown that pipelining is an effective method for speeding the operation of an adder. The speed advantage of a pipelined system is achieved at a relatively small increase in complexity, since the only added circuitry consists of storage platforms implemented with simple latches. The shift unit which is used to prenormalize addition operands is also described. Then the tradeoffs implicit in the

design of a fast multiplier are
considered. The resulting multiplier is somewhat slower but also
less complex than a parallel multiplier. As in the adder pipelining is used to greatly increase
throughput without significantly
increasing the complexity. Finally
a division scheme based on multiplicative iteration is described
in detail. A similar procedure
is considered (and discarded) in

the first paper of Part III; certainly the availability of fast
multipliers was the major factor
in selecting this algorithm.

The arithmetic unit is un-
questionably the most important
sub-system of a scientific computer; with this introduction to
arithmetic units it is appropriate
to focus attention on the overall
system design of general purpose
computers.

HIGH-SPEED ARITHMETIC IN BINARY COMPUTERS

O. L. MacSORLEY

INTRODUCTION

The purpose of this report is to describe various methods of increasing the speed of performing the basic arithmetic operations in such a manner that one method may be readily compared with another, both as to relative operating efficiency and relative equipment cost. It is divided into three parts: Adders, Multiplication, and Division.

ADDERS

As it is generally recognized that most of the time required by adders is due to carry propagation time, this section deals with methods of reducing this time, together with their efficiency and relative costs. It considers adders both from the standpoint of reducing the length of the carry path when using a fixed-time adder and of recognizing the completion of an addition to take advantage of the short length of an average carry. Circuits shown are in terms of basic logic blocks, and use the transit time of a logical block as a unit to permit the application of conclusions to various types of circuits.

MULTIPLICATION

In multiplication, if one addition is performed for each one in the multiplier, the average multiplication would require half as many additions as there are bits in the mul-

tiplier. This can be improved considerably by the use of both addition and subtraction of the multiplicand. The rules for determining when to add and subtract are developed, and the method of determining the number of operations to expect from the bit grouping is explained. This results in a variable number of add cycles for fixed-length multipliers. For some applications a fixed number of cycles is preferable. To accommodate this requirement, rules are developed for handling two- and three-bit multiplier groupings.

Multiplication, which involves repeated additions in which the selection of the various addends is not affected by a previous sum, offers the possibility of improved speed by the use of carry-save adders. Conditions under which such improvements will be realized are investigated, and methods that may be used to reduce the amount of equipment required are described.

DIVISION

Working from the premise that a division should require no more additions than would be required if the resulting quotient were used as the multiplier in a multiplication, the development of such a method is traced through several stages. Then another and still faster method is also described. Methods of evaluating the speeds of these various methods are developed in such a manner as also to permit evaluation of the effects of variation in maximum shifter size.

GENERAL

For the purpose of illustrating

Reprinted with permission from the Proceedings of the IRE, Vol.49, January, 1961, pp. 67-91, with an added section (The Appendix).

points in the use of these various arithmetical methods which may affect their application to computers, several typical systems circuits are shown, and the use of these is assumed in the numerical examples included. The following is a brief description of the circuits that are assumed available and a definition of terms that will be used.

DC rather than pulse-type logic is assumed. Registers, or data storage devices, are assumed to be separate from the adder. The use of a separate shifter rather than a shifting register is assumed. Most registers used are "latch-registers"; this means a register capable of being set from data lines, which are in turn controlled by the output of the same register upon the application of a latch-control signal. A gate is a group of two input AND circuits, each having one of its two inputs connected to a common line, and the other input to a data input line. A shifter is a device for transferring all bits in a register a specified number of positions left or right. The term "addition" will be used to include both addition and subtraction, and the same adder will be used for both. Subtraction will always be performed by the use of the two's complement of the number to be subtracted from the other. This will be obtained by inverting all bits in the number and also forcing an additional one into the carry position of the low order bit position of the adder when performing the addition.

Logical circuits are shown with inputs on the left and outputs on the right. The bottom output position represents the logical function described in the box, while the top output position represents its inverse. The logical symbols used within the boxes are AND (&), INCLUSIVE OR (V), and EXCLUSIVE OR ($\forall$). When the word OR is used alone, it means INCLUSIVE OR.

Unless otherwise specified, arithmetic used in examples is assumed to be binary floating point, although the methods described are not limited in their use to this type of arithmetic. When a number is described as normalized, it means that the fraction has been shifted in the register until the high order one in the fraction is located just to the right of the binary point, and the exponent has been adjusted accordingly. Thus a normalized fraction will always have a value less than one and equal to or greater than one-half. In the examples, exponent handling is implied but not described in detail.

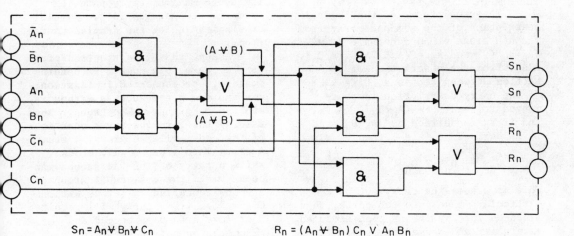

$$S_n = A_n \forall B_n \forall C_n \qquad\qquad R_n = (A_n \forall B_n) C_n \ V \ A_n B_n$$

Fig. 1. Full Adder, One Stage

BINARY ADDERS

BINARY ADDERS, FIXED TIME

The basic binary adder is comparatively simple and quite well known. It is also comparatively slow. Fig. 1 shows one version of one stage of such an adder.

In the discussion of adders, the lowest order bit or adder position will be designated as 1. The two multi-bit numbers being added together will be designated as A and B, with individual bits being A_1, A_2, B_1, etc. The third input will be C. Outputs will be S (sum), R(carry), and T (transmit).

The conventional ripple-carry adder consists of a number of stages like that shown in Fig. 1, connected in series, with R output of one stage being the C input of the next. The time required to perform an addition in such an adder is the time required for a carry originating in the first stage to ripple through all intervening stages to the S or R output of the final stage. Using the transit time of a logical block as a unit of time, this amounts to two levels to generate the carry in the first stage, plus two levels per stage for transit through each intervening stage, plus two levels to form the sum in the final stage, which gives a total of two times the number of stages.

The usual forms of the logical description of the sum and carry from the nth stage of an adder are $S_n = (A_n \vee B_n \vee C_n)$ and $R_n = (A_n B_n \vee A_n C_n \vee B_n C_n)$. Also, from the description of connection between sections, $C_n = R_{n-1}$. If the carry description is rearranged to read $R_n = (A_n \vee B_n)C_n \vee A_n B_n$, and if T_n is defined as $(A_n \vee B_n)$ and D_n is defined as $(A_n B_n)$, then

$$R_n = D_n \vee T_n C_n .$$

This separates the carry out of a particular stage into two parts, that produced internally and that produced externally and passed through. The former is called a generated carry

and the latter is called a propagated carry. From this the description of the carry into any stage may be expanded as follows:

$$C_n = R_{n-1}$$

$$C_n = D_{n-1} \vee T_{n-1} R_{n-2}$$

$$C_n = D_{n-1} \vee T_{n-1} D_{n-2} \vee T_{n-1} T_{n-2} R_{n-3}$$

$$C_n = D_{n-1} \vee T_{n-1} D_{n-2} \vee T_{n-1} T_{n-2} D_{n-3}$$
$$\vee T_{n-1} T_{n-2} T_{n-3} R_{n-4} .$$

This can be continued as far as is desired.

Fig. 2 illustrates the application of this principle to a section of a carry propagate adder to increase its speed of operation. By allowing n to have successive values starting with one and omitting all terms containing a resulting negative subscript, it may be seen that each stage of the adder will require one OR stage with n inputs and n AND circuits having one through n inputs, where n is the position number of the particular stage under consideration.

It is obvious that circuit limitations will put an upper limit on the number of stages of an adder that can be connected together in this manner. However, within this limit the maximum carry path between any two stages is two levels, or six levels for the complete addition.

Assume that five stages represent a reasonable number of adder stages to be connected in this manner and designate such an arrangement as a "group." The group containing the five low-order positions of the adder will.be group 1, etc. A carry into group n will be C_{gn}, while a carry out of the group will be R_{gn}. If these five-bit groups are now connected in series with $C_{gn} = R_{g(n-1)}$, a carry will require four levels to be produced and reach the output of the first group, two levels to go through

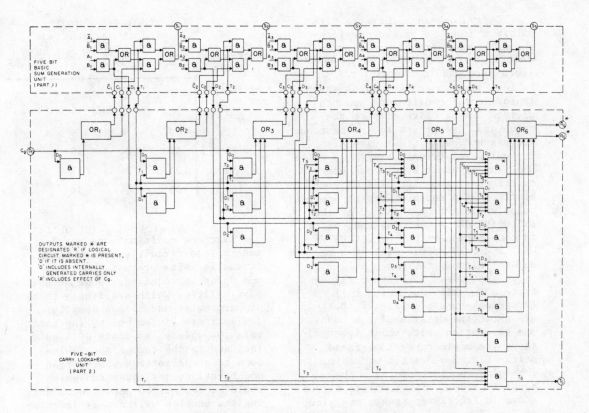

Fig. 2. Five-Bit Adder Group With Full Carry Look-Ahead

each intermediate group, and four levels to reach and be assimilated into the sum in the final group. Thus, for five-bit groups, the maximum carry path length would be $4+(2n/5)$ as compared to $2n$ for a straight ripple-carry adder. For a 50-bit adder this would give 24 levels as compared to 100.

Since each five-bit group may be considered as one stage in a radix-32 adder, a transmit signal may be generated to take a carry across the group. This will be designated as T_{gn}, and will be defined as $T_g = T_1 T_2 T_3 T_4 T_5$, where the numbers 1, 2, etc., refer to positions within the group rather than within the adder. At the same time D_{gn}, which includes only carries originating within the group, may replace R_{gn}, which includes the effect of C_{gn}, whenever a higher level of look-ahead than the

one under consideration is being used with it. The use of R_{gn} where D_{gn} is called for will not produce an error, but will add unnecessary components.

This process may be continued by designating five groups as a section and then using carry speed-up circuits between the sections. Carries into a section will be C_{sn}, and carries out of a section will be D_{sn}. (If the third level of carry look-ahead is not used, R_{sn} must be used in place of D_{sn}.) The maximum path length for a carry to be generated within a section and reach the output D_{sn} is six levels. The maximum path length for a carry appearing at the input to a section as C_{sn} to affect the sum is also six levels. The maximum path length for a carry originating within a section to affect a sum within the same section is ten levels.

Carry look-ahead between bits within a group is called one look-ahead, between groups within a section is called level two, and between sections is called level three. Table 1 gives a comparison of speed improvement for different amounts of look-ahead. Five bits to the group and five groups to the section are assumed. The time units are logical level transit times.

The transmit signal has been described as the EXCLUSIVE OR combination of A and B. Correct operation will also be obtained if the INCLUSIVE OR is used instead, of or in combination with, the EXCLUSIVE OR. The only effect will be a redundant signal at times.

Figs. 2 and 3 together illustrate a 100-bit adder with full carry look-ahead. In Fig. 2 (part 1) are shown the details of the basic sum generation unit, while (part 2) shows the basic carry look-ahead unit. Fig. 3 shows the method of combining the parts to give the complete adder. The complete circuit shown in Fig. 2 represents one group in Fig. 3.

Table 1.

Look-Ahead Levels	0	1	1&2	1,2,&3
Adder Bits				
5	10	6	–	–
10	20	8	–	–
25	50	14	10	–
50	100	24	12	–
100	200	44	16	14

Various modifications may be made to the circuit shown in Fig. 3 if smaller size or less than maximum speed is required. Some of the possibilities which are likely to be of particular use to the computer designer are listed below, and their relative speeds and costs will be included in the comparison table. Some minor variations which these modifications may cause and which would be obvious to anyone considering the problem will not be described in detail. Comparisons will be

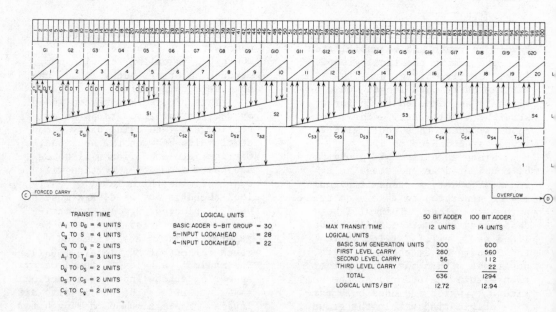

TRANSIT TIME		LOGICAL UNITS			50 BIT ADDER	100 BIT ADDER
A_1 TO D_G = 4 UNITS		BASIC ADDER 5-BIT GROUP = 30		MAX TRANSIT TIME	12 UNITS	14 UNITS
C_g TO S = 4 UNITS		5-INPUT LOOKAHEAD = 28		LOGICAL UNITS		
C_g TO D_g = 2 UNITS		4-INPUT LOOKAHEAD = 22		BASIC SUM GENERATION UNITS	300	600
A_1 TO T_g = 3 UNITS				FIRST LEVEL CARRY	280	560
D_g TO D_S = 2 UNITS				SECOND LEVEL CARRY	56	112
D_S TO C_S = 2 UNITS				THIRD LEVEL CARRY	0	22
C_S TO C_g = 2 UNITS				TOTAL	636	1294
				LOGICAL UNITS/BIT	12.72	12.94

Fig. 3. Carry-Propagate Adder With Full Carry Look-Ahead

made on the basis of 50-bit and 100-bit adders.

1. Eliminate the look-ahead within groups, but retain it between groups and between sections.
2. Retain the look-ahead within groups, but use ripple carry between groups.
3. Use the very elementary carry speed-up circuit used with the completion recognition adder (Fig. 4). This can be used with any adder, will give almost a four-to-one increase in speed over that of a full ripple-carry adder of 100 bits for only about 2.5 percent increase in equipment. It provides a carry bypass circuit within rather than around the group. Its principal merit is the high percentage improvement per unit increase in cost.

Table 2 summarizes the comparative costs and speeds for five different adder versions for 50-bit and 100-bit adders. The 50-bit ripple-carry adder is used as a reference for cost comparison. The types being compared are (1) full ripple carry, (2) full carry look-ahead, (3) ripple carry within five-bit groups, look-ahead between groups, (4) look-ahead within five-bit groups, ripple carry between groups, (5) carry bypass within five-bit groups, ripple carry between groups.

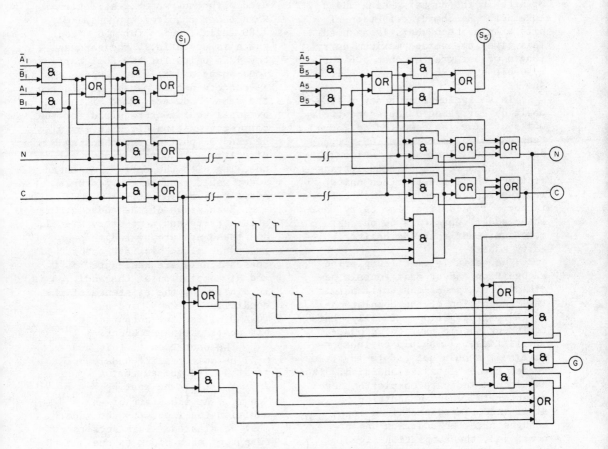

Fig. 4. Completion Recognition Adder

Table 2.

Adder Type	50 Bit Adder			100 Bit Adder		
	Logical Units	Comparative Cost	Time	Logical Units	Comparative Cost	Time
1	400	100.0	100	800	200.0	200
2	636	159.0	12	1294	323.4	14
3	466	116.5	24	954	238.4	26
4	580	145.0	24	1160	290.0	44
5	410	102.5	36	820	205.0	52

BINARY ADDERS, VARIABLE TIME

It can be shown that for a large number of binary additions the average length of the longest carry of each addition will not be greater than $\log_2 N$, where N is the number of bits in the numbers being added together. Random distribution of bits within the numbers is assumed. This gives an average maximum carry length of not greater than 5.6 for a 50-bit sum or 6.6 for a 100-bit sum.

In a ripple-carry adder a six-position carry would represent twelve units of time, as compared to fourteen units maximum for a 100-bit adder with full look-ahead. Also, the twelve units represent actual transit time, while the fourteen units represent predicted time with safety factor. In addition, the carry look-ahead adder represents 60 percent more equipment than the basic ripple-carry adder.

The variable time (completion recognition) adder must contain additional equipment that will permit the recognition of the completion of carry propagation. Ideally, this equipment should have three characteristics. It should be inexpensive. It should not add to the time needed to complete the addition. It should not indicate completion, even momentarily, when an addition is still incomplete, and if an input changes after an addition has been completed, the completion signal should immediately go off and remain off until the new result is completed.

Fig. 4 illustrates one version of a completion recognition adder. While it does not meet all of the requirements of an ideal unit, it does appear to be reliable when used with the proper restrictions. This adder requires approximately 1280 logical units for 100 bits, which is essentially the same as the 1294 units for the full carry look-ahead adder. Thus, where cost is concerned they may be considered the same. However, part of the additional equipment required for the carry-recognition circuits may also be used as part of the checking circuitry. To obtain equivalent checking with the carry look-ahead adder would require considerable additional equipment.

Each stage of the adder generates a carry and a no-carry signal, and these are propagated through the adder along separate paths. If these signals are designated as C and N, completion of the addition is recognized by the existence of the condition [(C OR N) and not (C AND N)] at the output of every bit position in the adder.

The operation of this adder will be more readily understood if it is recognized that $C_n = A_n B_n \lor T_n C_{n-1}$ and that $N_n = \overline{A}_n \overline{B}_n \lor T_n N_{n-1}$. At the start of an addition the inputs to the adder must be cleared. This sets the N output of each block to one and the C output to zero. The desired in-

puts are then entered, which changes
the N outputs to zero for those
positions which have a one in
either or both inputs. This turns
off the completion signal. The C
output is changed to one for those
positions having an input of 11 and
the T signal is changed to one for
those positions having 01 or 10.
The latter positions have zero on
both the C and N lines. Signals
will then ripple down either the
C or N lines from positions having
either 00 or 11 inputs until all
positions have either the C or the
N output energized, at which time
a completion signal will be generated. To prevent false indications
of completion, the two inputs must
enter the adder simultaneously;
once the operation has started,
no changes may be made in the inputs,
and both inputs must be changed to
zero before the next addition may be
performed. An alternative to this
is to force ones into all input
positions by using an additional
input to the OR circuits that are
usually present at the input to
adders. The restriction here would
be that the correct inputs are present at the input to the OR circuits
at the time the forcing inputs are
turned off.

No general statement can be
made as to whether fixed-time or
variable-time adders are better. ·
The use of a completion recognition
adder offers many attractions to
the systems designer, particularly
if his circuits have a large spread
between average and maximum transit
time. On the other hand, the
limitations on data handling required to prevent ambiguities in
the control signals may nullify
some or all of the theoretical
advantages. The best choice can
only be made by a careful consideration of all the factors involved
for the particular application.

BINARY MULTIPLICATION

MULTIPLICATION USING VARIABLE LENGTH SHIFT

Multiplication in a computer is
usually performed by repetitive addition. For constant circuit and adder
speeds, the time required to perform
a multiplication is proportional to
the number of additions required.
The slowest way would be to go through
one add cycle for each bit of the
multiplier. Substituting shift
cycles for add cycles when the multiplier bit is a zero can reduce this
time; supplying the ability to shift
across more than one position at a
time when there are several zeros
in a group can reduce the time still
further. Assuming random distribution with equal numbers of ones
and zeros in the multiplier, this
should result in a 50 percent reduction in time. This is as much
improvement as is obvious from
normal methods of performing multiplication.

Further improvements may be
secured by taking advantage of some
of the properties of the binary system. The rules for handling multiplication to obtain this improvement will be developed.

A binary integer may be written
in the following form:

$$A_n 2^n + A_{n-1} 2^{n-1} + A_{n-2} 2^{n-2} + \ldots$$
$$+ A_2 2^2 + A_1 2^1 + A_0 2^0 .$$

The actual number, as written,
consists of the characteristics only
and would be written $A_n A_{n-1} A_{n-2} \cdots$
$A_2 A_1 A_0$, where each A would have a
value of either one or zero. If
such a number contained the coefficients ...011111111110..., this
part of the number would have the
value $2^{n-1} + 2^{n-2} + \ldots + 2^{n-x}$,
where n is the position number of
the highest order one in the group

for which the lowest order position in the number is designated zero, and x is the number of successive ones in the group. The numerical value of this last expression may also be obtained from the expression 2^n-2^{n-x}, where n and x have the same values as before. For example, in the binary number 0111100, n is 6 and x is 4. The decimal equivalent of the number is given by $2^5+2^4+2^3+2^2$ = 32+16+8+4 = 60. It is also given 2^6-2^2 = 64-4 = 60. Thus for any string of ones in a multiplier, the necessity for one addition for each bit can be replaced by one addition and one subtraction for each group. The only additional equipment required is a means of complementing the multiplicand to permit subtracting and, of course, some additional control equipment. To illustrate this a typical multiplier is shown below with the required operations indicated. Each group of ones is underlined.

<u>1111</u>0000<u>111</u>0<u>111</u>0<u>1</u>0<u>1</u>000<u>101</u>

+   -   +   -+   -+-+-   +-+-

Additional improvement may be obtained by using the fact that $+2^n-2^{n-1}$ = $+2^{n-1}$ and -2^n+2^{n-1} = -2^{n-1}. This is illustrated by applying it to the above example. The original results are given first, with the operations to be combined underlined.

1111000011101110101000101

+   -   +   <u>-+</u>   <u>-+-+-</u>   <u>+-+-</u>

+   -   +   -   - --   + +

+   -   +   <u>-+</u>   <u>-+-+-</u>   <u>+-+-</u>

+   -   +   -   - + +   + +

Two different arrangements are shown. Both will give the correct result, and the number of cycles required is the same. The first is that obtained by

starting at the high order end, and the second by starting at the low order end.

For a given multiplier, the number of additions that will be required may be computed as follows. Define a group of ones as a series of bits containing no more than a single zero between any pair of ones within the series, containing at least one pair of adjacent ones, and starting and ending with a one. Then the number of add cycles is equal to the following: Two times the number of groups, plus the number of zeros contained within groups, plus the number of ones not contained within groups. This may be illustrated with the previous example.

1111000011101110101000101

There are two groups. The first group contains no zeros, the second contains three. There are two ones not contained in any groups. This gives (2x2)+3+2 = 9, which is the number of operations that was obtained. Within the limitation of using only multiples of the multiplicand that can be obtained directly by shifting and using only one of these at a time, it is believed that this represents the least number of additions with which a binary multiplication can be performed.

The rules for performing a multiplication may now be given. It is assumed that the multiplier and partial product will always be shifted the same amount and at the same time. The multiplier is shifted in relation to the decoder, and the partial product with relation to the multiplicand. Operation is assumed starting at the low-order end of the multiplier, which means that shifting is to the right. If the lowest-order bit of the multiplier is one, it is treated as though it had been approached by shifting across zeros.

1. When shifting across zeros (from low order end of multiplier), stop at the first one.

a. If this one is fol-
   lowed immediately by
   a zero, add the multi-
   plicand, then shift
   across all following
   zeros.

b. If this one is fol-
   lowed immediately by a
   second one, subtract
   the multiplicand, then
   shift across all fol-
   lowing ones.

2. When shifting across ones
   (from low order end of multiplier), stop at the first
   zero.

   a. If this zero is fol-
      lowed immediately by
      a one, subtract the
      multiplicand, then shift
      across all following
      ones.

   b. If this zero is fol-
      lowed immediately by a
      second zero, add the
      multiplicand, then
      shift across all
      following zeros.

A shift counter or some equivalent device must be provided to
keep track of the number of shifts
and to recognize the completion of
the multiplication.

If the high-order bit of the
multiplier is a one and is approached by shifting across ones, that
shift will be to the first zero beyond the end of the multiplier, and
that zero along with the bit in the
next higher order position of the
register will be decoded to determine whether to add or subtract.
For this reason, if the multiplier
is initially located in the part of
the register in which the product is
to be developed, it should be so
placed that there will be at least
two blank positions between the
locations of the low-order bit of
the partial product and the high-
order bit of the multiplier. Otherwise the low-order bit of the product will be decoded as part of the
multiplier. An alternative to this
is for the fact that the shift

counter indicates the end of the
multiplication to force the last
operation to be an addition.

It should be noted that whenever the shifting is across groups
of ones the partial product will be
in complement form, which means that
the shifter must contain provision
for inserting ones in all high
order positions that would normally
be left blank by the shifting.

If the multiplication is performed starting from the high-order
end of the multiplier, the partial
product will always be in true form,
but any operation may result in a
carry traveling the full length of
the partial product. The shifting
rules are a little more complicated
as may be seen below.

1. When shifting across
   zeros (from high-order
   end of multiplier)

   a. If the first one fol-
      lowing the zeros is
      followed immediately
      by a second one, stop
      shifting at the last
      zero and add the
      multiplicand, then shift
      across following ones.

   b. If the first one fol-
      lowing the zeros is fol-
      lowed immediately by a
      zero, stop shifting at
      the first one and add
      the multiplicand, then
      shift across following
      zeros.

2. When shifting across ones
   (from high-order end of multiplier)

   a. If the first zero fol-
      lowing the ones is fol-
      lowed immediately by a
      second zero, stop
      shifting at the last
      one and subtract the
      multiplicand; then
      shift across the fol-
      lowing zeros.

   b. If the first zero fol-
      lowing the ones is fol-

lowed immediately by a
one, stop shifting at
first zero and subtract
the multiplicand, then
shift across the fol-
lowing ones.

The high-order one of the multiplier is treated as though there
were at least two zeros immediately
preceding it.

As was previously stated, these
two methods of decoding the multiplier will yield the same number of
add cycles. This number is dependent on the number and distribution
of ones within the multiplier. If
random distribution is assumed, it
can be shown that the average shift
for each addition will be 3.0 bit
positions when using an infinite
shifter, or 2.9 bit positions for a
shifter having a limit of six.

MULTIPLICATION USING UNIFORM SHIFTS

For some applications a method
of multiplication which uses shifts
of uniform size and permits pre-
dicting the number of cycles that
will be required from the size of
the multiplier is preferable to a
method that requires varying sizes
of shifts. The most important use
of this method is in the application of carry-save adders to multiplication, although it can also be
used for other applications. The
use of carry-save adders will be
discussed in a later section.

Two methods will be described.
The first requires shifting the
multiplier and partial product in
steps of two, the second in steps
of three. Both methods require the
ability to shift position of entry
of the multiplicand into the adder
in relation to its normal position.
The latter is designated as the
one-times-multiplicand position
and used as a reference position
in all descriptions. This small
shifter will be the length of the
multiplicand rather than of the
partial product. Both methods
may be used starting from either
end of the multiplier, but because

of the reduced requirements on the
size of the adder, are usually used
starting from the low-order end.
The latter will be assumed for any
operating descriptions, but for
easier explanation the rules of
operation will be developed assuming
a start from the high-order end.

UNIFORM SHIFTS OF TWO

Assume the multiplier is divided into two-bit groups, an extra
zero being added to the high-order
end, if necesary, to produce an even
number of bits. Only one addition
or subtraction will be made for
each group, and, using the position
of the low-order bit in the group
as a reference, this addition or
subtraction will consist of either
two times or four times the multiplicand. These multiples may be
obtained by shifting the position
of entry of the multiplicand into
the adder one or two positions left
from the reference position. The
last cycle of the multiplication
may require special handling. Rules
for this will be considered after
the general rules have been developed.

The general rule is that, following any addition or subtraction,
the resulting partial product will be
either correct or larger than it
should be by any amount equal to one
times the multiplicand. Thus, if
the high-order pair of bits of the
multiplier is 00 or 10, the multiplicand would be multiplied by zero
or two and added, which gives a correct partial product. If the high-
order pair of bits is 01 or 11, the
multiplicand is multiplied by two
or four, not one or three, and
added. This gives a partial product that is larger than it should
be, and the next add cycle must
correct for this.

Following the addition the partial product is shifted left two
positions. This multiplies it by
four, which means that it is now
larger than it should be by four
times the multiplicand. This may be

corrected during the next addition by subtracting the difference between four and the desired multiplicand multiple.

Thus, if a pair ends in zero, the resulting partial product will be correct and the following operation will be an addition. If a pair ends in a one, the resulting partial product will be too large, and the following operation will be a subtraction.

It can now be seen that the operation to be performed for any pair of bits of the multiplier may be determined by examining that pair of bits plus the low-order bit of the next higher-order pair. If the bit of the higher-order pair is a zero, an addition will result; if it is a one, a subtraction will result. If the low-order bit of a pair is considered to have a value of one and the high-order bit a value of two, then the multiple called for by a pair is the numerical value of the pair if that value is even and one greater if it is odd. If the operation is an addition, this multiple of the multiplicand is used. If the operation is a subtraction (the low-order bit of the next higher-order pair a one), this value is combined with minus four to determine the correct multiple to use. The result will be zero or negative, with a negative result meaning subtract instead of add. Table 3 summarizes these results.

Table 3.

Multiplier	Operation
0 - 0 0	+ 0
0 - 0 1	+ 2
0 - 1 0	+ 2
0 - 1 1	+ 4
1 - 0 0	-4+0 = -4
1 - 0 1	-4+2 = -2
1 - 1 0	-4+2 = -2
1 - 1 1	-4+4 = -0

It is obvious from the method of decoding described that the multiplier may be scanned in either direction. When starting from the high-order end, the partial product will always be in true form, but starting from the low-order end will result in a complement partial-product part of the time. This means that the main shifter must be designed to handle the shifting of complement numbers.

The possibility that the low-order bit of the multiplier will be a one presents a special problem. For operations starting at the high-order end of the multiplier this may be handled in either of two ways. One requires an additional cycle only when the lower-order bit is a one, and consists of adding the complement of one-times the multiplicand following a zero shift after the completion of the last regular operation. The other method adds an additional add cycle to every multiplication by always treating the multiplier as though it had two additional low-order zeros. The two extra zeros which this introduces into the product are then ignored.

When operating from the low-order end of the multiplier this problem may be handled more easily. On the first cycle there is no previous partial product. Therefore zeros are being entered into one side of the adder. If the low-order bit of the multiplier is a one, enter the complement of one times the multiplicand into the adder by way of the input usually used for the partial product. At the same time, the multiple of the multiplicand selected by decoding the first pair of bits of the multiplier is entered at the other adder input. This does not require any additional cycles.

UNIFORM SHIFTS OF THREE

This method of handling three bits of the multiplier at a time requires being able to obtain two,

four, six, or eight times the multiplicand. One times may also be
required to handle the condition of
a one in the low-order bit position
of the multiplier. One, two, four,
and eight times can all be obtained
by proper positioning of the multiplicand, but the six times must
be generated in some manner. This
can be done by adding one times the
multiplicand to two times the multiplicand, shifting the result one
position, and storing it in a register.

The development of the decoding
rules for this method follows the
same basic requirements already
described for handling two-bit
groups. This is evident from Table
4 and will not be repeated.

There are some general facts
that apply to both the two-shift and
the three-shift methods of multiplication.

1. The choice of true or com-
    plement entry of the multi-

plicand into the adder is
dependent only on the condition of the low-order bit
of the next higher-order
group of the multiplier.
2. Special provision must be
    made for the condition of a
    one in the low-order bit
    position of the multiplier.
    Procedure is the same for
    both methods.
3. Whenever complement inputs
    are used for multiplicand
    multiples, there must also
    be provision for entering a
    low-order one into the ad-
    der to change the one's
    complement to a two's com-
    plement. This includes the
    complement of one times the
    multiplicand used because of
    low-order multiplier one.
    This can result in a design
    problem, since odd numbers
    in the two low-order groups
    of the multiplier may call
    for the entry of two addi-
    tional ones into the low-
    order position of the ad-
    der, making a total of four
    entries. A solution to
    this is to decode the low-
    order group of the mul-
    tiplier to call for the
    desired multiple, or one
    less instead of one more.
    Then the true value of one
    times the multiplicand can
    be used in the partial
    product position on the
    first cycle when the mul-
    tiplier has a low-order
    one. This may be done
    very easily, on the first
    cycle only, by forcing the
    low-order bit of the group
    to enter the decoder as a
    zero, but using actual
    value to determine whether
    or not to add one times
    the multiplicand. The
    justification for this may
    be seen from either table.
    This modification of the
    decoding will not work for
    any cycle except the first,

Table 4

Multiplier	Operation
0 - 0 0 0	+ 0
0 - 0 0 1	+ 2
0 - 0 1 0	+ 2
0 - 0 1 1	+ 4
0 - 1 0 0	+ 4
0 - 1 0 1	+ 6
0 - 1 1 0	+ 6
0 - 1 1 1	+ 8
1 - 0 0 0	-8+0 = -8
1 - 0 0 1	-8+2 = -6
1 - 0 1 0	-8+2 = -6
1 - 0 1 1	-8+4 = -4
1 - 1 0 0	-8+4 = -4
1 - 1 0 1	-8+6 = -2
1 - 1 1 0	-8+6 = -2
1 - 1 1 1	-8+8 = -0

and only when operating from the low-order end of the multiplier.

To permit a comparison, the illustrative multiplier used previously to show decoding for the variable-shift method will be shown below for variable shift, two-position shifts, and three-position shifts.

All decoding shown is based on starting at the low-order end of the multiplier. Multiplier groupings are indicated in (2) and (3). The use of multiples of four in (2) and of eight in (3) places the effective location of the operation under the low-order bit of the next higher group. An underline under a pair of operations in (3) indicates the use of the previously prepared three-times multiple. The (+) following the multiple figure for the low-order group indicates that one times the multiplicand is also used in the partial product entry position. The decoding for this particular group is assumed modified as previously described.

```
 0  0  1  1  1  1  0  0  0  0  1  1  1  0  1  1  1  0  1  0  1  0  0  0  1  0  1 (1)
    +           -              +              -           -        +        +              +        +

    +2    -0        -2  +0    +2    -0        -2    -0        -2        -2        -4        +2        -4 +
 0'  0  1'  1  1'  1  0'  0  0'  0  1'  1  1'  0  1'  1  1'  0  1'  0  1'  0  0'  0  1'  0  1'(2)
    +           -              +              -              -     -        +  -        +

    +2              -0        -8              +4              -2              -2              +6              -8              +4 +
 '0  0  1'  1  1  1'  0  0  0'  0  1'  1  1'  1  0  1'  1  1  0'  1  0  1'  0  0  0'  1  0  1'(3)
    +           -              +              -              -     + + -              +        +
```

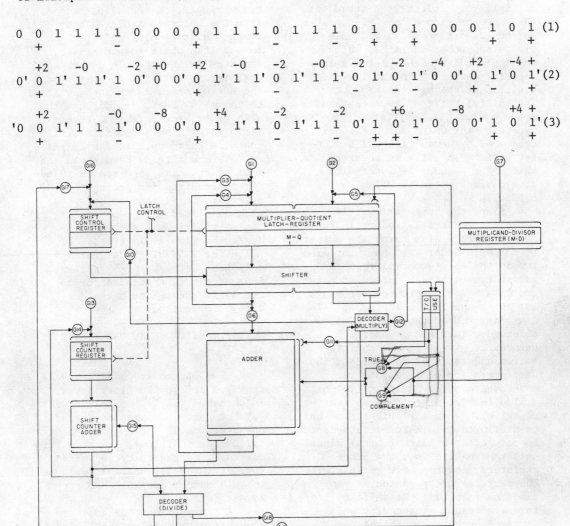

Fig. 5. Computer Arithmetic System

VARIABLE SHIFT MULTIPLICATION CIRCUIT

Fig. 5 shows a brief outline of a system capable of performing multiplication in the manner just described. At the start of the operation the multiplier is entered in the right half of the MQ register, the multiplicand into the MD register, one more than the multiplier size into the shift counter register, and two into the shift control register, and also the "use" trigger is set OFF. (It is assumed that the multiplier is initially entered into the same position of the MQ register as the low-order end of a double precision number would be, which would place its high-order bit immediately adjacent to the low-order position of the partial product. The initial shift of two separates these by two bit positions, the necessity for which was previously described. The initial shift counter register setting is adjusted for this. The decoder is located to give correct operation with this offset.)

Since the "use" trigger is OFF and the partial-product in the MQ register is also zero, the output of the main adder will be zero. The two in the shift-control register causes two to be subtracted from the contents of the shift counter register in the shift counter adder. The low-order end of the shifted multiplier goes into the decoder and is decoded to give the next shift required and to determine whether the next operation will be add-true, add-complement, or neither (if shift called for is larger than shifter can give). When sufficient time has been allowed for these operations to be completed, a latch control signal sets the results into the proper registers, and the next cycle starts. These cycles are repeated as many times as required, the shift called for as a result of decoding being compared each time with the contents of the shift counter register

to determine when sufficient cycles have been taken.

To determine the time required for a cycle, three data paths must be considered and the longest used. They all include time to power the latch control signal and set information into the proper trigger, plus any safety factor that must be allowed because of variation in transit times. One path is from the MQ register, through the shifter to the decoder, through the decoder to the shift control register or to the multiplicand true-complement control trigger. A second path is from the shift control register or the shift counter register through the shift counter adder, and back to the shift counter register. The third path is from the MQ register, through the shifter to the main adder, and through the main adder back to the MQ register. It will be assumed initially that the third path is the longest.

It has already been shown that most of the time required in an adder is required for propagation of carries, and various methods have been described for reducing this. The most efficient of these reduced the time to 12 transit time units for a 50-bit adder for a component increase of 59 percent. Four of the 12 units are due to the basic adder, and 8 are due to carry propagation.

MULTIPLICATION USING CARRY-SAVE ADDERS

When successive additions are required before the final answer is obtained, it is possible to delay the carry propagation beyond one stage until the completion of all of the additions, and then let one carry-propagate cycle suffice for all the additions. Adders used in this manner are called carry-save adders.

A carry-save adder consists of a number of stages, each similar to the full adder shown in Fig. 1. It differs from the ripple-carry adder in that the carry (R) output is not connected directly to the next-higher-order stage of the same adder, but goes to an intermediate register or other device in the same manner as the sum (S) output. Thus a carry-save adder has three inputs which, as far as use is concerned, may be considered identical, and two outputs which are not identical and must be treated in different manners.

The procedure for adding several binary numbers by using a carry-save adder would be as follows. Designate the inputs for the nth bit as A_n, B_n, and C_n, and the outputs for the same bit as S_n and R_n, where S_n is the sum output and R_n is the carry output. In the first cycle enter three of the input numbers into A, B, and C. In the second cycle enter the S and R obtained from the previous cycle into A and B and the fourth input number into C. In this operation S_n goes into A_n but R_n goes into B_{n+1}, where B_{n+1} is in the next-higher-order bit position than B_n. This is in accordance with the customary rule for addition that a carry resulting from adding one column of figures is added into the next higher-order column. The third cycle is the same as the second, etc. This is continued until all of the input numbers have been entered into the adder.

Carry propagation may be performed in either of two ways. Since each add cycle advances all carries one position, add cycles as already described may be continued with zeros being entered into the third input each time until the R outputs of all stages become zero. The alternative is to enter S and R into a carry-propagate adder and allow time for one cycle through it. This carry-propagate adder may be completely separate from the carry-save unit, or it may be a combined unit with a control line for selecting either carry-save or carry-propagate operation.

Before carry-save adders can be used in the multiplication loop, it is necessary to know the answers to these questions: (1) How should they be used? (2) How much additional equipment is required? (3) How much time will be saved? Assume that the circuit shown in Fig. 5 is modified by changing the adder to a CP/CS adder which is so designed that the ability to operate as either a carry-save or carry-propagate adder does not cause it to be any slower when operating in the carry-propagate mode than is a comparable adder without this feature. Such an adder can be constructed at an additional component cost of about 50 percent of the number of components in the corresponding ripple-carry adder. Also, since the partial product will now become a partial sum and a partial carry, and since the latch-register and shifter presently shown can only handle one of them, a duplicate latch-register and shifter must be provided for the other.

Figuring in necessary gates and mixing circuits, and allowing the equivalent of four levels for rise time, skew, and uncertainties in the latch driver power circuits, the data path loop contains fourteen levels besides those in the adder. Also, for the system shown in Fig. 5, no speed advantage is gained by making the main adder faster than the path through the decoder and shift-counter-adder. The latter will be in the neighborhood of eleven levels, seven for the adder and four for the complete decoder. Eleven levels, however, can be obtained at considerably less cost in equipment with the carry-propagate adder with full look-ahead. From this it may be concluded that there would be very little, if any, time gain and considerable additional expense if the adder in Fig. 5 were changed to a CP/CS adder with the necessary associated changes.

The above does not mean that faster multiplication cannot be obtained through the use of carry-save adders. It merely indicates that the particular method of applying it would not produce the desired result.

In Fig. 5 the high-speed main adder represents probably about half of the equipment in the complete data path. Figuring the adder as twelve, and the remainder of the path as fourteen, the total loop path is the equivalent of 26 logical levels. If a carry-save adder were connected in series with the present adder, then the total path length would be fourteen plus twelve plus four, or thirty; however, two additions could be performed in each cycle, which would halve the number of cycles. This is, of course, an oversimplified description of the method and its results, but its proper application will permit

profitable use of carry-save adders in multiplication.

When two or more adders are operated in series in the performance of multiplication, an attempt to have a variable shifter ahead of each of them will result in a more complicated decoder, longer path length, and considerable additional equipment. For this reason, a fixed shift type of operation, such as one of those already described, is more desirable than the variable-shift methods. The comparative merits of and requirements for two- and three-bit shifts have already been described, together with the decoding rules for each. The application of carry-save adders will be described in terms of the two-bit shift. Necessary variations in using the three-bit shift will be readily apparent from the previous description.

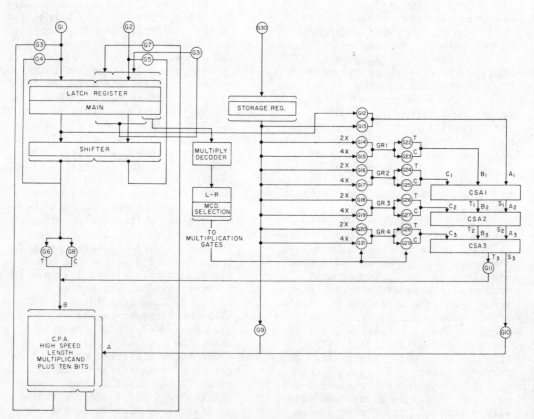

Fig. 6. High-Speed Multiplication System

Fig. 6 illustrates a system that will handle eight bits of the multiplier at a time. It shows three carry-wave adders operating in series, with the two outputs of the last of these going to a carry-propagate adder. One of the three inputs to CSA 1 is the partial product from the previous cycle. The other two are multiples of the multiplicand determined by decoding two groups of multiplier bits. Two of the three inputs of CSA 2 are required for the two outputs of CSA 1, leaving one for a multiple of the multiplicand obtained by decoding the third group of the multiplier. In a similar manner, CSA 3 provides an input for a fourth multiple. The two outputs of CSA 3 go to the inputs of the carry-propagate adder, and the single output of the CPA goes to the main latch-register as the partial product for the next cycle. The modification of the decoding of the first group for the first cycle is used as was described, so that the true value of one times the multiplier can be used when the low order bit of the multiplier is a one. Entry for this is shown as G13.

The details of one cycle of the multiplication of two 16-bit binary numbers are illustrated in Fig. 7. During the first add cycle a 16-bit number is being multiplied by an 8-bit number. This may give a true result not exceeding 24 bits in length. Therefore a one in position 25 will indicate a complement partial product. One times the multiplicand, when required, goes into positions 1-16 of the A input of CSA 1. Decoding of the low-order group of the multiplier calls for zero, two or four times the multiplicand to be entered at the B input of CSA 1. This multiple is referenced to position 1 of the adder, which means that two times the multiplicand would go to positions 2-17, while if four times were called for, it would go to positions 3-18. All other positions of this adder input get zeros if the input is true, and ones if it is complement.

Since the low-order bit of group 2 of the multiplier is two positions to the left of the corresponding bit of group 1, the reference position for determining entry into the adder is also two positions to the left of

Fig. 7. First Cycle of Multiplication Example Using Carry-Save Adders

that for group 1, that is, position 3 instead of position 1. This means that a two times multiple for group 2 will go into positions 3-19, while a four times multiple will go into positions 4-20. Again, unused positions get zeros for true and ones for complement.

For CSA 2 the A_2 input is the sum outputs (S_1) from CSA 1 carried down in the same columns. The B_2 input is the carry outputs (R_1) of CSA 1, each shifted one column left, which leaves column 1 for the complement forced carry input for group 2. The C_2 input is obtained from decoding group 3, and is referenced to column 5.

For CSA 3 the A_3 input is the sum output of CSA 2 brought straight down, and the B_2 input is the carry output of CSA 2 shifted one position left, which leaves column 1 of B_3 for the complement forced carry entry due to group 3. The C_3 input is obtained by decoding group 4, and is referenced to column 7. The sum outputs of this adder go into the corresponding columns of one of the inputs of the carry-propagate adder, while the carry outputs go into the carry-propagate adder shifted one position left. This leaves one entry in column 1 available for the forced carry input associated with group 4. The forced carry associated with group 1 can also be entered into the carry-propagate adder by way of the carry input circuit of position one. Rather than use a special adder connection, this can be done by entering an input into both sides of position zero when the carry input is desired.

For all of the adders, carry outputs from column 25 that would normally go into column 26 of the next following adder are ignored and lost, as it would serve no useful purpose to retain them. Column 25 supplies the required information as to whether the partial product is in true or complement form.

Fig. 7 assumes that each carry-save adder has a length equal to the length of the partial product devel-

oped in each cycle. Means for reducing each of these to approximately the length of the multiplicand will be described following a summary of the operating sequence. The sequence is essentially the same for either version.

Step 1. Enter the multiplier to the right half of the MQ register and the multiplicand into the MD register. Set the shifter to shift the right half of the MQ register eight positions to the right, keeping it at this setting throughout the multiply operation. Clear the multiplicand selection register. Set the first-cycle trigger to cause proper treatment of the low-order bit of the multiplier.

Step 2. Energize the latch-control signal. This sets decoder results into the multiplicand selection register that controls the gates into the carry-save adders, shifts the multiplier right eight positions to discard the low-order eight bits and bring the next group of bits into the decoder, and sets the output of the CPA adder (zero in this case) into the MQ register.

Step 3. Energize the latch-control signal (after sufficient time has elapsed for the data to have passed through all of the adders). This sets the results of decoding the second set of eight bits of the multiplier into the multiplicand selection register, shifts the multiplier eight positions right, and enters the data from adder output positions 1-25 into positions 9-33 of the MQ register. The low-order eight bits of this partial product are in their final form. These are in positions 9-16 of the register. Therefore, on this cycle, the entire adder group is effectively shifted eight positions, which means that data from register positions 17-33 will go to the A_1 input of CSA 1 positions 1-17. Since position 33 contains a zero if the partial product is true and a one if it is complement, input positions 18-25 of A_1 will be set to agree with the input to position 17.

Step 4. Energize the latch-control signal. This sets the decoder output into the multiplicand selection register (has no meaning since multiplier was shifted out of register by Step 3, but no advantage is gained by suppressing it), shifts the partial product that was in positions 9-16 of the MQ register into positions 1-8, and enters the remainder of the product from the carry-propagate adder into positions 9-33. Note that the data that was in positions 17-33 is replaced, and not shifted elsewhere. This completes the multiplication.

COMPONENT REDUCTION WITH CARRY-SAVE ADDERS

A carry-save adder takes in three signals and gives out two. If the number of inputs is reduced to two, the number of outputs still remains at two. Therefore, when two or more carry-save adders are used in series, any bit positions which always have zeros for one of the three inputs may be omitted. This eliminates two outputs from the omitted adders, thus vacating inputs to two positions farther down the adder chain. The two inputs that would have gone to the omitted adder positions can then go to these two positions. An input may be moved from any one place in the chain of adders to any other place as long as it is always kept in the same column.

When the two's complement of a binary number is desired, the one's complement is obtained, and then a one is added to this in the column of the lowest order bit. The column into which the one is entered may vary from this if the column selected is the same as, or of a lower order than, the column containing the lowest-order one in the true value of the number, and also if the zeros to the right of the selected column are not inverted when forming the one's complement of the number.

The application of these two principles will permit the elimination of a number of low-order positions from the adders shown in Fig. 7. This is illustrated in Fig. 8.

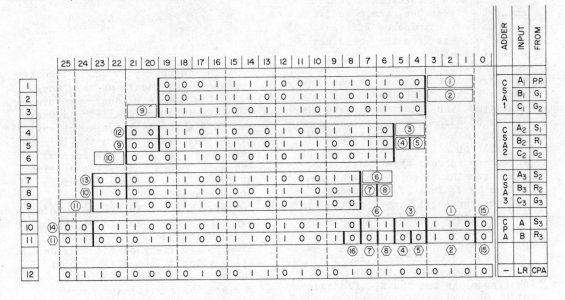

Fig. 8. Modified High-Speed Multiplication Adder System

Since the input C_1 never needs to have anything except zeros in positions 1, 2, and 3, and since nothing needs to be added into these columns in any other adder, the inputs for these columns that would normally go to A_1 and B_1 may be shifted down to the CPA inputs and all carry-save adder positions for these columns eliminated. The forced-carry input for group 1 remains the two CPA inputs in column zero. In Fig. 8, terminations for the adders are indicated by double vertical lines. Positions outside these terminations are designated by numbers in circles, and the position to which these are transferred is designated by the same number in a hexagon.

The three inputs for CSA 2 are the sun and carry from CSA 1 and the multiple obtained by decoding group 3. The lowest-order column required by the latter is six, which means that the inputs to columns 4 and 5 may be transferred. It should be noted that with the group 2 multiple ending at column 4, the forced carry for this was moved to column 4 of B_2, and is now being transferred to the same column of CPA input B. CSA 3 is then treated in a similar manner. Altogether, these modifications have eliminated fifteen adder positons from the low-order ends of the adders.

The modification of the high-order end of the adders is based on the fact that, since the inputs are staggered, the adders will have a number of high-order positions containing either a string of ones or a string of zeros. When two of the three inputs meet this condition, these two inputs may always be replaced by a single input, which reduces the total number of required inputs to two. As has already been shown, when this condition exists, these stages of the adder may be eliminated, and the pair of inputs moved down to the next adder in the chain. The operation of this is illustrated below

for the various combinations that may occur:

Two Complement Inputs

1	1	1	1	'	1	*	X	X	X	X	A_1
1	1	1	1	'	1	*	X	X	X	X	B_1
D	E	F	G	'	H		X	X	X	X	C_1
1	1	1	1	'	S		S	S	S	S	A_2
D	E	F	G	'	R		R	R	R	R	B_2

One Complement Input

1	1	1	1	'	1	*	X	X	X	X	A_1
0	0	0	0	'	0	*	X	X	X	X	B_1
D	E	F	G	'	H		X	X	X	X	C_1
$\overline{H}$	$\overline{H}$	$\overline{H}$	$\overline{H}$	'	S		S	S	S	S	A_2
D	E	F	G	'	R		R	R	R	R	B_2

No Complement Input

0	0	0	0	'	0	*	X	X	X	X	A_1
0	0	0	0	'	0	*	X	X	X	X	B_1
D	E	F	G	'	H		X	X	X	X	C_1
0	0	0	0	'	S		S	S	S	S	A_2
D	E	F	G	'	R		R	R	R	R	B_2

The three inputs shown together represent the inputs as they would be if the complete adder were used. The asterisks in two of the inputs indicate that there are never any high-order true bits to the left of this point for these two inputs. The apostrophes indicate the point at which it is desired to terminate the adder shown with three inputs. The two inputs below are two of the three inputs of the next following adder. For columns to the right of the termination point of the first adder, the inputs to the following adder are the sum (S) and carry (R) outputs of the adder above. To the left of the termination of adder 1, the B_2 input of adder 2 becomes what would have been the C_1 input of adder 1 for the same columns. Note that the carry output of the highest-order column of adder 1 after it is terminated does not go into the next higher order of column B_2, as this position is occupied by G from C_1. The corresponding A_2 inputs to adder 2 are the same for all bit positions to the left of the termination point of adder 1, and are determined from the three inputs to the highest order column of the terminated adder 1.

Fig. 8 illustrates the effect of applying this method to the adders of Fig. 7. In CSA 1, input A_1 is determined by its true or complement condition starting with column 17, B_1 with column 19, and C_1 with column 21. It is therefore possible to terminate this adder with position 19, and move the normal C_1 inputs for columns 20 and 21 to the corresponding columns of C_2.

The normal full adder used for each position of the CSA contains the following logic:

$$S = (A \veebar B) \veebar C , \qquad (4)$$

$$R = (A \veebar B) C \vee AB, \qquad (5)$$

For the high-order column of the terminated adder, in this case column 19, this is modified to the following:

$$S = (A \veebar B) \veebar C, \qquad (6)$$

$$D = (A \veebar B)\overline{C} \vee AB . \qquad (7)$$

In (4), (5), and (6), the terms A, B, and C may be applied to any of the three inputs to the adder. This is not true in (7), where the terms A and B refer to the two inputs determined by the fact that they are in true or complement form, while C refers to the data input. D describes the input that goes to all higher-order positions of the next adder, and for that adder it may be

treated as are those positions whose input is determined by knowledge of whether the input is true or complement.

By continuing with this procedure, CSA 2 may be terminated at position 21, the position 21 circuit being modified as described above; and CSA 3 may be terminated with column 23, the position 23 circuit also being modified.

The three carry-save adders as originally described in Fig. 7 required a total of 75 individual full adders. The same adders with the modifications described require 45 full adder units plus three modified units, a saving of 27 units.

For the operation described, the length of the carry-propagate adder had to exceed the length of the multiplicand by two more than the length of the section of the multiplier handled during each cycle. If this additional length is not required for other operations, and if the main part of the adder uses fully carry look-ahead, the reduced path length for the low-order bits in the carry-save adders resulting from the modifications made to save components permits the use of a ripple-carry adder for most of the extension to increase the length of the main adder without causing any loss in speed.

From the information given, the modifications required to permit the use of three-bit multiplier groups instead of two-bit groups are obvious. The question of how many carry-save adders to connect in series is a matter of economics to be decided for a particular application. The example given was intended merely to help describe the general method, and many modifications of it to suit special conditions will be readily apparent.

BINARY DIVISION

There are several methods, of varying complexity and speed, by which division may be performed in

a computer. The implementing of a
particular method will vary between
computers because of differences in
circuits and machine organization.
It is the intent here to discuss
primarily basic methods, and to
illustrate these methods, when required for clarity, with a particular type of machine organization.
The characteristics of this type
were described in the Introduction.

The time required to perform a
division is proportional to the
number of additions required to complete it, and the methods that will
be described for increasing speed
will be primarily concerned with the
reduction of the required number of
additions. These methods will all
use a variable length shift, and
the number of additions required for
any particular example will be dependent on bit distribution.

For all methods of division it
will be assumed that prior to the
start of the actual division the
divisor is so positioned in the
divisor register that it has a one
in the highest-order position of the
register. It will also be assumed
that the divisor and dividend are
binary fractions with the binary
point located just to the left of
the high-order position. Thus the
divisor will always have a numerical value less than one, but equal
to or greater than, one-half. These
assumptions do not limit the application of the principles of operation to be described, and they
simplify the description.

Since all of the methods to be
described involve variable shifts,
it will always be assumed that a
shift counter of some type is included, that this counter is set
initially with the number of quotient bits to be developed, and that
any shift-determining circuits include means for comparing the shift
called for against the number still
allowed by the shift counter and
then acting on this information
according to the rules that will be
developed for the particular method.

In all descriptions the term

dividend will be used to mean both
the initial and partial dividend
while the term remainder will
mean the final remainder after
the quotient is completely developed.

Fig. 5, which was used in the
description of multiplication, will
also be used as the basic circuit
for describing division. Any modifications required by a particular
method will be described. All
operations start by setting the
dividend into the MQ register, the
divisor into the MD register (including normalization of the divisor if
it is not already in this condition),
and the quotient length into the
shift counter (which is assumed to
count down). The high-order bit
position of the dividend (with a
shifter setting of zero) and the
high-order bit position of the
divisor enter the same column of
the adder unless stated otherwise.
Dividend shifting is to the left,
which clears the right end of the
MQ register as the operation
proceeds. The quotient is developed at the right end of the MQ
register and shifted along with
the dividend. The dividend decoder is assumed to be on the high-
order end of the adder output,
which means that the initial
operation always starts with a
forced zero shift, following which
the decoder takes control of the
shifting.

Some additional general rules
that apply to all methods, particularly those that deal with starting and terminating a division, will
be discussed following the detailed
descriptions of the several methods.

DIVISION USING SINGLE ADDER, ONE-
TIMES DIVISOR, AND SHIFTING ACROSS
ZEROS AND ONES

Assume a dividend in true from.
Since the high-order bit of the
divisor is required to be a one, if
the high-order bit of the dividend
is a zero, the divisor is obviously
larger than the dividend which will

result in a zero quotient bit. A
zero may therefore be placed in the
quotient, and the dividend and quotient each shifted left one position before any addition is performed. If there are n leading
zeros, and the decoder can recognize them, n positions may be
shifted across in one operation, a
zero also being inserted in the
quotient for each position shifted.

With the dividend true and the
high-order bit a one, an addition
must be performed to determine
whether or not the dividend is larger than the divisor. If the result is complement, the dividend
was smaller than the divisor, and
a zero is entered in the quotient.
In either case, the result of the
addition replaces that part of the
previous dividend in the MQ register that was used in the addition.
If the result of the addition was a
complement number, this will now
make the entire new dividend a complement number, even though part of
it did not go through the adder.

Shifting the dividend one position left is equivalent to dividing
the divisor by two with respect to
the original dividend. For a true
dividend with a high-order one, if
one times the divisor results in a
zero in that position of the quotient (divisor larger than dividend),
then one-half of the divisor (next
shift positon) will always result in
a one in the following bit position
of the quotient. (Dividend is equal
to or greater than one-half, while
one-half of divisor must be less
than one-half.) If, after the first
addition, the dividend had been returned to its original value, then,
using the first addition as a point
of reference, the second addition
would have given a tree result (indicating the one in the quotient)
with a value equal to the original
dividend minus one-half the divisor.
If, instead of returning to the
original dividend, shifting, and
adding complement, the complement
result of the previous addition had
been retained and shifted, and the

true value of the divisor added to
it, the result would have been
(original dividend minus divisor)
plus (one-half divisor). This
would also be a true final result
having the same value as was obtained by the previous method.

Assume that a partial division
has been performed yielding a partial quotient of 01111 and a corresponding partial dividend. This result could have been obtained by any
of the following series of operations:

dividend $+(-1/2-1/4-1/8-1/16)$ divisor,

dividend $+(-1.0+1/2-1/4-1/8-1/16)$
$$\text{divisor,}$$

dividend $+(-1.0+1/4-1/8-1/16)$ divisor,

dividend $+(-1.0+1/8-1/16)$ divisor,

dividend $+(-1.0+1/16)$ divisor

These are all equal to dividend minus
15/16 divisor. From this it may be
stated that if a complement result
is obtained under the condition that
it is known that the next succeeding
quotient bit is a one, then as many
positions of the dividend may be
shifted across, a one being entered
in the quotient for each position
shifted across, as is known will
still result in a true dividend
following the addition.

Since the high-order position
of the divisor, in its true form,
always contains a one, a true result will always be obtained if the
high-order bit position of the
complement dividend contains a one.
This justifies shifting across all
except the last one in a string of
high-order ones in a complement
dividend, together with the entering of a one in the quotient for
each position shifted across. It
is also known that if an addition
is performed without shifting across
the final one, a true dividend will
always be obtained together with
another one in the quotient. If the
complement result had been shifted
one position farther, the new
dividend obtained would be the same

following the addition of the true divisor as would have been obtained following a one-position shift of the true dividend and the addition of the complement of the divisor. Thus, it is evident that with either true or complement dividends it is only necessary to perform an addition when it is not evident what the quotient bit should be. From this the following operating rules may be stated.

1. When the dividend is true, shift across any leading zeros, entering a zero in the low-order end of the quotient for each position shifted across except the last; then add the complement of the divisor.

    a. If the result is true, enter a one in the low-order position of the quotient, then shift across.

    b. If the result is complement, enter zero in the low-order position of quoteint, then shift across ones.

2. When the dividend is complement, shift across any leading ones, entering a one in the low-order end of the quotient for each position shifted across except the last; then add the true divisor.

    a. If the result is true, enter a one in the low-order position of the quotient; then shift across zeros.

    b. If the result is complement, enter a zero in the low-order position of the quotient; then shift across ones.

If the decoder calls for a larger shift than can be obtained from the shifter in one operation, use the maximum shift available and suppress both the true and complement entry

of the divisor to the adder. This will pass the high-order part of the shifted dividend through the adder with zero added to it so that is is available to the decoder. If the dividend is complement, the output of the adder following this will be complement, which would normally result in the setting of a zero in the low-order position of the quotient However, this is in the middle of a shift across ones, not an addition to determine the proper quotient bit following a shift, and the dividend only goes through the adder because of the necessity of making it available to the decoder. Therefore, in this case, the low-order bit of the quotient following the shift must be set to agree with the bits being shifted across. The same control that suppresses the entry of the divisor into the adder can also control this.

Some special rules are required to terminate the division and to insure that the final remainder will be in true form. These are listed below.

1. Dividend true, shift called for by decoder larger than allowed by shift counter. Treat in same manner as when shift called for is greater than capacity of shifter. Make shift allowed by shift counter, suppress entry of divisor into adder, set low-order bit of quotient to agree with bits being shifted across. This will complete the division.

2. Dividend true, shift called for by decoder equal to that allowed by shift counter. Treat in the normal manner. If resulting adder output is in true form, division is complete with its entry into the register. If the resulting adder output is in complement form, one additional cycle is required

to get remainder into true
form. See 4. below.

3. Dividend complement, shift
called for by decoder equal
to or greater than that allowed by shift counter register.
Use allowed shift and proceed
in normal manner. If the
resulting remainder is in true
form, division is complete.
If the resulting remainder is
in complement form, the resulting quotient is complete,
but one additional cycle is
required to get remainder into
true form. See 4. below. The
latter condition can only
occur when the shift called
for and the shift counter
register are equal.

4. Dividend complement, shift
counter register is zero.
Take zero shift, add the
true value of the divisor,
suppress entry from adder
output into low-order bit
position of quotient as the
bit there is already correct
(zero) and the true output
of the adder would change it
to a one.

If the following binary division
is performed according to these rules,
it will require fourteen add cycles to
complete the operation:

If a quotient contains a string
of zeros followed by a string of
ones, it is possible to shift
across the ones only if the addition
made after the shift across the zeros
resulted in a complement dividend.
If the result was a true dividend,
then it is necessary to make a separate addition for each one in the
string. This means that in some
instances better results would have
been obtained if the addition had been
performed one position sooner than
the position resulting from following the shift rules. This condition
is most likely to occur with a small
divisor, as a small divisor is less
likely to produce a change in the
sign of the dividend than a large
divisor.

When a quotient contains two
strings of ones separated by a single
zero, more efficient operation will be
obtained if it is always treated as
one string of ones with an inter-
ruption. This may be seen by comparing the fourth and fifth operations of the previous divide example with the fourth operation of
the potential divide system obtained
by an inversion of the multiplication rules and shown for comparison. In this case, it is desired
that the addition at the end of the
first group of ones produce a com-

$$011,100,011,011,001,001,010,110$$
$$110,110\ \overline{\smash{)}\ 10,111,111,110,111,001,111,000,100,100}$$

To compare this with the inverse
operations required for multiplication,
the quotient is shown below with the
various additions and subtractions
used shown above the corresponding bit
positions, and the corresponding
operation as determined from the
multiplication rules shown below.

plement result which will supply the
single zero for the quotient and
leave the remainder in complement
form for shifting across ones again;
the inverse applies if the quotient
is two strings of zeros separated by
a single one. To obtain this condition, it is sometimes necessary to

```
  -       +       -   +   -   +       -     - +  - + -      + 0  [14]
  0 1 1, 1 0 0, 0 1 1, 0 1 1, 0 0 1, 0 0 1, 0 1 0, 1 1 0
  -       +       -       +   +       -     -      - -      + 0  [11]
```

DIVISION USING DOUBLE ADDER AND ONE-
HALF, ONE, AND TWO TIMES DIVISOR

perform the addition one position
later than the position given by

the shift rules. However, if this extra length shift is taken at other times it may produce incorrect results. The failure to obtain optimum operations under these conditions is most likely to occur when the divisor is large because a large divisor has a great probability of producing a change in the sign of the dividend.

It has been shown that the efficiency of the division operation may be improved if, on certain occasions, the addition following a shift could be made with the divisor one position to the left of the normal position, and on other occasions one position to the right of the normal position. By normal position is meant that position reached by shifting across all leading ones for a complement divisor or across all leading zeros for a true dividend. The divisor used in the normal position is designated as one times divisor, left of normal position as two times divisor,

and right of normal position as one-half times divisor.

One method of obtaining this improvement is by double addition. It requires that the main adder be slightly longer than twice the length of the divisor, or that there be two adders available. The procedure is to perform two additions simultaneously and then use the result that produces the largest shift. If a double-length adder is available, the two additions may be performed in it as long as there is at least one position with no inputs to it between the two operations. One addition will always be performed with the divisor located, with reference to the dividend, as called for by the shift decoder. The other addition will be performed using twice the divisor if the two high-order bits of the divisor in its true form are 10 (value of divisor less than three-fourths), and one-half the divisor if the two high-order bits are 11 (value of divisor equal to or greater than three-

DIVISOR TRUE		01111	01110	01101	01100	01011	01010	01001	01000	00111	00110	00101	00100	00011	00010	00001	00000	DIVIDEND COMPLEMENT
		0	1	2	3	4	5	6	7	8	9	10	11	12	13	14	15	
11111	15	01110	01101	01100	01011	01010	01001	01000	00111	00110	00101	00100	00011	00010	00001	00000	11111	15
11110	14	01101	01100	01011	01010	01001	01000	00111	00110	00101	00100	00011	00010	00001	00000	11111	11110	14
11101	13	01100	01011	01010	01001	01000	00111	00110	00101	00100	00011	00010	00001	00000	11111	11110	11101	13
11100	12	01011	01010	01001	01000	00111	00110	00101	00100	00011	00010	00001	00000	11111	11110	11101	11100	12
11011	11	01010	01001	01000	00111	00110	00101	00100	00011	00010	00001	00000	11111	11110	11101	11100	11011	11
11010	10	01001	01000	00111	00110	00101	00100	00011	00010	00001	00000	11111	11110	11101	11100	11011	11010	10
11001	9	01000	00111	00110	00101	00100	00011	00010	00001	00000	11111	11110	11101	11100	11011	11010	11001	9
11000	8	00111	00110	00101	00100	00011	00010	00001	00000	11111	11110	11101	11100	11011	11010	11001	11000	8
10111	7	00110	00101	00100	00011	000,10	00001	00000	11111	11110	11101	11100	11011	11010	11001	11000	10111	7
10110	6	00101	00100	00011	00010	00001	00000	11111	11110	11101	11100	11011	11010	11001	11000	10111	10110	6
10101	5	00100	00011	00010	00001	00000	11111	11110	11101	11100	11011	11010	11001	11000	10111	10110	10101	5
10100	4	00011	00010	00001	00000	11111	11110	11101	11100	11011	11010	11001	11000	10111	10110	10101	10100	4
10011	3	00010	00001	00000	11111	11110	11101	11100	11011	11010	11001	11000	10111	10110	10101	10100	10011	3
10010	2	00001	00000	11111	11110	11101	11100	11011	11010	11001	11000	10111	10110	10101	10100	10011	10010	2
10001	1	00000	11111	11110	11101	11100	11011	11010	11001	11000	10111	10110	10101	10100	10011	10010	10001	1
10000	0	11111	11110	11101	11100	11011	11010	11001	11000	10111	10110	10101	10100	10011	10010	10001	10000	0
		0	1	2	3	4	5	6	7	8	9	10	11	12	13	14	15	

Fig. 9. Division Table, Divisor True, Dividend Complement, Using One Times Divisor

fourths). Thus a small divisor uses the larger multiple, while a large divisor uses the smaller multiple for the auxiliary addition.

The circuitry required is similar to that of Fig. 5 except that the adder size is increased, gates are added to enter the dividend into the other half of the adder also, and to select two times or half times the divisor for entry there, the decoder is increased to decode and compare the two results, and a gate is added to permit a choice of the two outputs.

Although the two additions may be performed in two parts of one adder, the two parts will be called adder A and adder B. Adder A will correspond to the adder described in the previous method, while adder B will be the alternate adder. The output of adder B will be used only if its use results in a greater shift than would result from using adder A. If the shifts called for by the two adder outputs are the same, the adder A results will be used.

If the previously described example were performed using this method, the resulting operations would be exactly the same as those obtained by using the inverse of the multiplication rules. The rules for quotient development and division termination are very similar to those for the system using a single length adder, and will be developed when it is described.

Fig. 9 is a table showing all possible results that can be obtained for a five-bit true divisor and complement dividend under the restrictions that a true divisor always has a high-order one and a complement dividend is always used following shifting across all leading ones, which means that it will always have a high-order zero. A corresponding table can be prepared for comple-

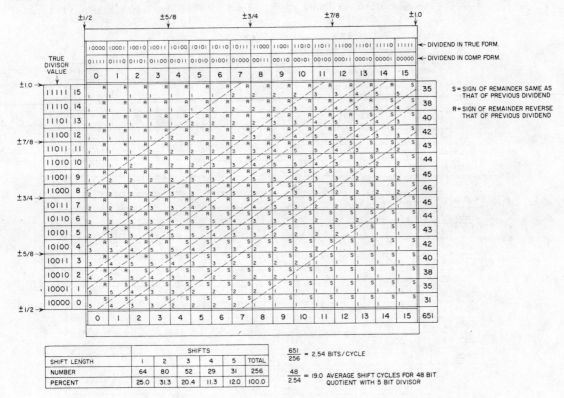

Fig. 10. Division Table Using One Times Divisor with Five-Bit Divisor

ment divisor and true dividend. If this is done and the two are compared, it will be found that for the same position the result on one table will be the exact inverse of that on the other table. For example, at column 3, row 10, of Fig. 9 the result is 00110, while the corresponding position of the other table would be 11001. The number of positions to be shifted is the same in both cases. The information of primary interest to be obtained from these tables is the number of shifts, which is shown in Fig. 10.

From this table it is apparent that points of maximum shift lie along the diagonal representing equal values for divisor and dividend. Also, if random distribution of divisor bits between problems and dividend bits between and within problems is assumed, then the average shift per cycle will be 651/256 = 2.54 for a five-bit divisor used

with a shifter capable of handling shifts of five or less. (It can be shown that the distribution of bits within a dividend does not remain completely random as the division progresses. However, the variations will not be sufficiently great to invalidate the results of the comparisons of efficiencies of different methods of division based on the assumption of complete randomness.)

Fig. 11 shows a table of shifts that may be obtained when using one-half times the divisor or two times the divisor. Both are shown on the same table, half of the table being used for each. These results apply both for dividend complement with divisor true and for dividend true with divisor complement. On this and the preceding figure, the pattern of shifts along any row should be noted, as each row contains a section of the pattern. The pattern goes both ways from the line of maximum shifts, and

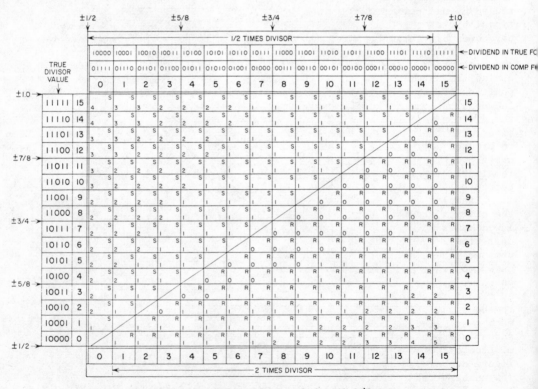

Fig. 11. Division Tables Using 2.0 and 1/2 Times Divisor

is one "5", one "4", two "3's", four "2's", eight "1's", and all that follow "0". Any selection system used must not permit the selection of zero shift during normal operation, as this will result in an error in the problem.

When one-half or two times the divisor is used, the dividend is positioned in the same manner as if one times the divisor were to be used; then the divisor is entered into the adder shifted one position to the left or right of where it would have been for one times. The columns of the output of the adder that are examined to determine the next shift are the same ones that would have been examined had one times the divisor been used. When preparing the table and using one-half times the divisor, the low-order bit of the divisor is lost as a result of the right shift. This would not be the case in an actual operation, as the adder would have been extended by one position and an additional bit of the dividend would have been brought into the adder. When two times the divisor is used, the high-order bit of the original divisor is entered into the overflow position of the adder, but for all the combinations for which two times the divisor would be used, this combines with the complement dividend to produce a true divisor with no overflow. Therefore this five-bit remainder used for the chart is correct.

Examples of the use of one times the divisor are shown in Table 5, followed by examples of one times and one-half times. The examples on the left use one times, while the top right uses two times and the bottom right one-half times. The part of the result that is used in the figures is to the right of the binary point in each case. The part to the left is shown indirectly by the indication of true or complement result. The figure numbers column numbers and row numbers refer to the table locations of the examples. The underlin-

Table 5.

Figs. 9 & 10	Fig. 11	
11·00010	11·00010	Column 13
00·10001	01·00010	Row 1
11·<u>10011</u>	00·<u>00100</u>	
11·01110	11·01110	Column 1
00·11101	00·01110	Row 13
00·<u>01011</u>	11·<u>1110</u>0	

ed part of the result indicates the amount of shift that would result in each case.

Fig. 12 is obtained by replacing all of the positions calling for a shift of one on Fig. 10 with the shift called for on the corresponding position of Fig. 11. The three sections are shown separated by heavy stepped lines. The circled numbers represent shifts that are the same on both figures. This represents the optimum combination that can be obtained when using one-half, one, and two times the divisor, and gives an average of 2.82 bits per cycle.

The heavy line between rows 7 and 8 represents the division that was made between the use of half times and two times divisor in the double adder method. As may be seen, the optimum use for each multiple is within this division, which means that the double-adder method of division will give the same results as are obtained from optimum use of these particular divisor multiples. An alternate selection rule which may be used with the double-adder method for these particular multiples is: If the output of the alternate adder does not call for a shift of two or more, use the output of the adder having the one times divisor input. This avoids the need for any compare circuits, and also gives correct results.

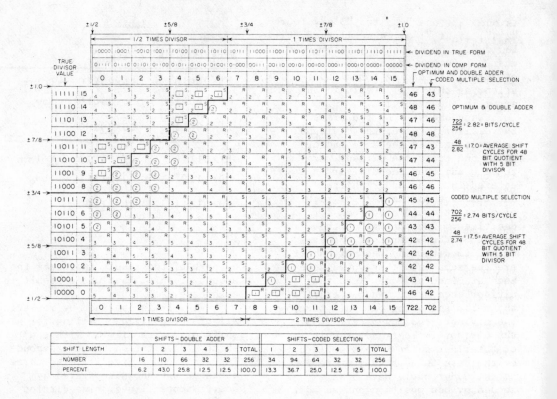

Fig. 12. Division Table Using 2.0, 1.0, 1/2 Times Divisor with Optimum Coding

DIVISION USING SINGLE ADDER WITH HALF, ONE AND TWO TIMES DIVISOR

If only a single length adder is available, the use of the three divisor multiples to improve efficiency is still possible, although the improvement may be somewhat less. In this case the selection must be made by examining, or decoding, the high-order bits of the divisor and dividend before each operation to determine what multiple to use. The degree of improvement will be dependent on the number of bits included, as will the complexity of the decoding system and the time required by it. The selection must be sufficiently accurate that it will never call for a multiple that will result in a zero shift. The dashed lines in Fig. 12 that outline rectangles in the upper left and lower right corners indicate what may be ex-

pected from very simple decoding. This is based on the following rules: (1) If the high-order bits of the divisor are 111 and the high-order bits of the dividend are either 011 or 100, use the half times divisor multiple. (2) If the high-order bits of the divisor are 100 and the high-order bits of the dividend are either 000 or 111, use the two times divisor multiple. (3) If neigher of these conditions exist, use the one times divisor multiple. This gives an average of 2.74 bits shifted per cycle as compared with 2.82 for the double adder.

QUOTIENT DEVELOPMENT AND TERMINATION WHEN USING 1/2, 1.0, and 2.0 MULTIPLES

When these multiples are used, an additional low-order register position is required. Designate the two low-order positions of this register as X and Y, where X is the position that is normally set by whether the output of the adder is true or complement when one times the divisor is used. Position Y is the next lower-order position in the register.

When the half times divisor is used, it is in the same position with respect to the dividend that the one times divisor would have been had the previous shift been one greater. Therefore the quotient bit determined by the output of the adder when the half times divisor is used must be placed where it will enter the quotient adjacent to position X, which is position Y. The quotient bit placed in position X must be the same that would have been placed there had one times the divisor been used and will always be the same as the bits shifted across during the preceding shift.

The bit placed in position Y as a result of the use of the half times divisor is a correct quotient bit. In the event that its generation is followed by a shift of one, the information that the half times divisor was used must be stored so that on the next add cycle position X can be set from data that was in position Y instead of from the condition of the adder output.

It should be noted that when the remainder from the use of the half times divisor multiple is decoded to give the number of bits to shift across, the number will always be one greater than would have been obtained had the previous shift been one greater followed by the use of one times the divisor, which puts the end of the shift at the same place in either case.

Whenever the one times divisor is used, position Y is set to agree with the bits that will be shifted across on the next shift. It enters into all shifting operations except shifts of one. It may be shifted across position X, but never into it (except for the special condition described above).

The two times multiple will be selected only when the one times multiple, if used, would not cause a reversal in dividend sign, but the use of the two times multiple will cause a reversal. Therefore, if the original dividend was true, X is set to a one; if it was complement, X is set to a zero. Y is set to agree with the bits that are to be shifted across as determined by the output of the adder using the two times multiple. This bit is not preserved in the event of a one-position shift.

The above information is summarized in Table 6.

To terminate a division, follow the rules previously given, with the added restriction that if the shift called for is equal to the contents of the shift counter register, the choice of the divisor multiple is limited to the one times multiple.

DIVISION USING DIVISOR MULTIPLES OF THREE-FOURTHS, ONE AND THREE-HALVES

It was previously stated that the largest shifts occurred along the diagonal of equal values of divisor and dividend. Fig. 11 shows that such diagonals for the half times or two times multiples would each intersect the rectangle at one corner only, the half times going through the corner at which the divisor has a value of 1.0 and the dividend 0.5, and the two times going through the corner at which the divisor has a value

Table 6.

Original Dividend	Multiple Selected	X	Y	Y Definite
True	Half Times	0	1	Yes
True	Two Times	1	1	No
Complement	Half Times	1	0	Yes
Complement	Two Times	0	0	No

of 0.5 and dividend 1.0. A multiple which would have its high points within the area so that the high values on both sides would be available should give a greater improvement in efficiency. To be of practical use, it should also be easy to generate. Such a multiple is three-halves times the divisor, which can be generated in one addition cycle by adding one times the divisor to one-half times the divisor. Three-fourths times the divisor can then be generated from this sum by shifting.

Fig. 13 shows a shift table obtained when using three-fourths and three-halves divisor multiples with five-bit divisors and five-bit dividends. The line of maximum shifts varies somewhat from the theoretical line because of the limits in size and the effects of truncating the three-fourths times multiple of five bits. Without

these limits, the line of maximum shifts for the three-fourths times divisor multiple would go between the points of divisor equal to 2/3 dividend equal to 1/2 and divisor equal to 1.0 dividend equal to 3/4; for the three-halves times divisor multiple, the line would go between the points of divisor equal to 1/2 dividend equal to 3/4 and divisor equal to 2/3 dividend equal to 1.0.

Fig. 14 shows a combination of Figs. 10 and 13 give the optimum arrangement when using the 3/4, 1.0, 3/2 multiples. The heavy stepped lines show the separation between the areas of the use of the three multiples. The circled numbers represent shifts that are the same in the two adjacent areas. The separation line could go on either side of these positions without changing the result. The heavy horizontal line at divisor equals three-fourths represents the separation between

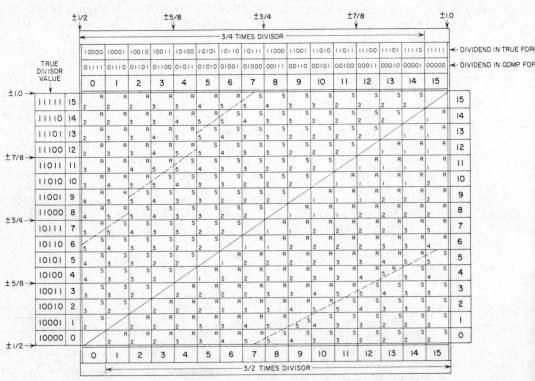

Fig. 13. Division Tables Using 3/2 and 3/4 Times Divisor

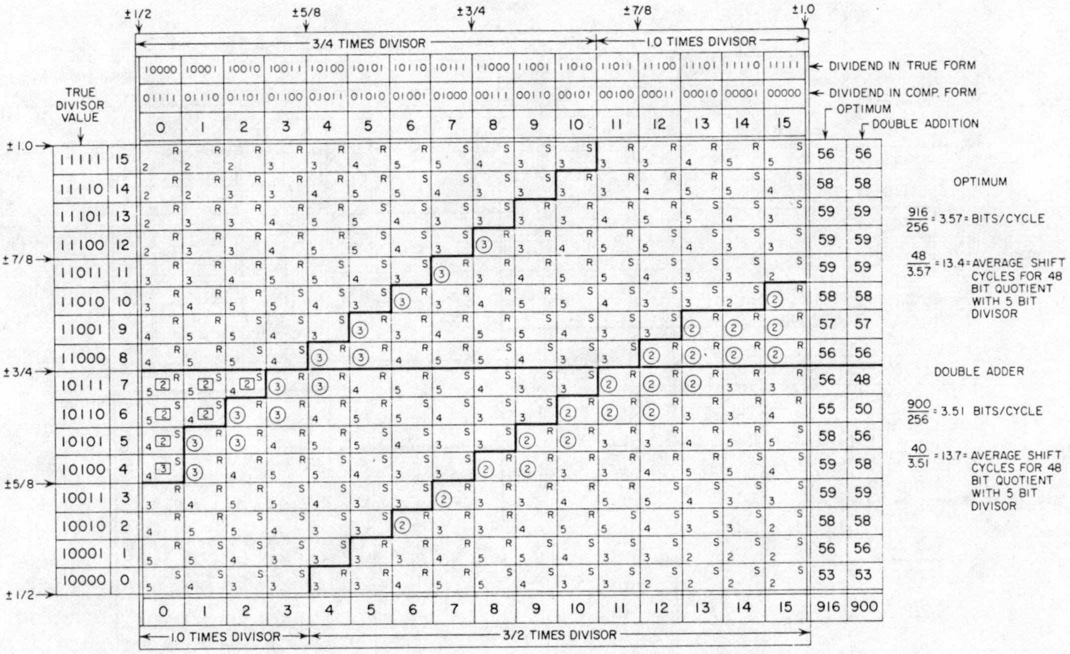

Fig. 14. Division Table Using 3/2, 1.0, 3/4 Times Divisor with Optimum Coding

SHIFT LENGTH	SHIFTS - OPTIMUM						SHIFTS – DOUBLE ADDER					
	1	2	3	4	5	TOTAL	1	2	3	4	5	TOTAL
NUMBER	0	37	96	61	62	256	0	43	97	57	59	256
PERCENT	0.0	14.5	37.5	23.8	24.2	100.0	0.0	16.8	37.9	22.3	23.0	100.0

the inputs to the alternate adder when these multiples are used in the double adder method, and the numbers in squares in the seven positions below this line indicate the shifts these positions would have as part of the one times area, instead of the three-fourths times area. The optimum arrangement here for the five-bit divisor indicates an average of 3.57 bits per cycle, while the use of these multiples in the double adder method gives 3.51 bits per cycle.

Fig. 15 shows a coding arrangement for multiple selection that gives the same results as are obtained from the double adder method. A simpler coding method, which uses the three-fourths times multiple when the high-order bits of the divisor are 11 and the high-order bits of the dividend are either 10 or 01, and uses the three-halves multiple when the high-order divisor bits are 10 and the high-order bits of the dividend are either 11 or 00, will give an average of 3.37 bits per cycle based on a similar table (not shown).

The use of the three-fourths, one, and three-halves divisor multiples requires an additional register position (Z) because the three-fourths multiple produces two advance quotient bits, three definite bits in all. These go into positions X, Y, and Z. The three-halves multiple produces two definite quotient bits in positions X and Y, and a tentative bit in position Z. The one-times multiple produces one definite quotient bit in position X and two tentative bits in positions Y and Z.

If the division example previously described were performed using the double-adder method with

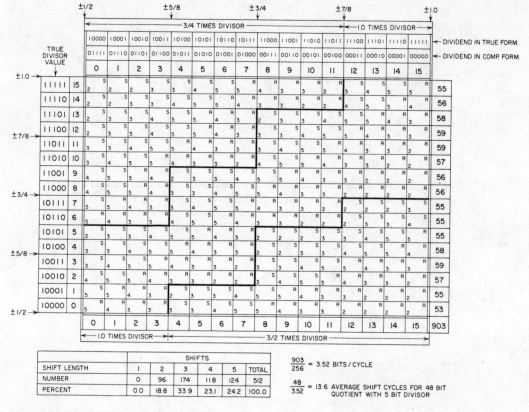

Fig. 15. Division Table Using 3/2, 1.0, 3/4 Times Divisor with Four-Way by Sixteen Way Coding

three-fourths, one, and three-halves divisor multiples, the number of operating cycles would be reduced from eleven to nine. One cycle would have to be added to this to allow for the generation of the three-halves times multiple of the divisor.

Fig. 16 illustrates graphically the various conditions that may occur when using the 3/4, 1.0, 3/2 divisor multiples. It shows an initial true dividend with complement divisor multiples only, but the inverse can easily be found from this by reversing all directions and interchanging zeros and ones in the quotient bit columns.

In example 1 the initial dividend is between 1 1/2 and 2 times the divisor. Selection here would choose the use of the 3/2 divisor multiple which would give two def-

inite quotient bits and one tentative (indicated by a circle). The 1.0 times multiple could be used, though it would be less efficient. It would give one definite quotient bit and two tentative bits. In this case the first tentative bit would be incorrect, and would be changed on the next cycle. The 3/4 multiple would not be selected for use with this initial condition.

In example 2 the initial dividend is greater than one times the divisor but less than one-and-a-half times the divisor. Either the 3/2 or 1.0 divisor multiple may be selected here, but not the 3/4 multiple as it would be less efficient than the 1.0 times multiple. Here again the 3/2 multiple gives two definite quotient bits and the 1.0 times multiple gives one.

Example 3 has a dividend less

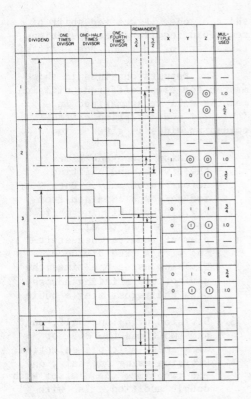

Fig. 16. Quotient Development Using
3/4, 1.0, 3/2 Times Divisor

than one times the divisor but
greater than 3/4 times. It may
use either of these multiples, but
not the 3/2 multiple. The 3/4
multiple gives three definite quotient bits, while the 1.0 multiple
gives one definite and two tentative.

In example 4 the dividend has
a value between 1/2 and 3/4 the
divisor. This condition will always result in the choice of the
3/4 divisor multiple, though the
1.0 times will give correct results.

Example 5 shows a dividend
having a value less than half the
divisor. This condition could only
arise as a result of an incorrect
previous cycle as it would require
a true dividend with a leading zero
following the shift.

The use of the 3/4 multiple
will never result in a following
shift of only one. If it results
in a shift of two, the fact that the

3/4 multiple was used must be remembered into the next cycle, and the
entry into position X must be made
from position Z instead of from data
obtained in that cycle from the adder result. Similar precautions
must be taken when using the 3/2
multiple to protect data from position Y in the event of a one-position
shift.

Division termination procedure
is the same as was previously described, with the additional requirement that the 3/2 multiple must not
be used if the shift counter register
agrees with the shift called for, and
the 3/4 multiple must not be used if
the shift counter register agrees with
or is one greater than the shift
called for by the decoder. In either
case, the one-times multiple should be
substituted.

COMPARATIVE EVALUATION OF VARIOUS
METHODS OF DIVISION

The effectiveness of several
methods of performing division has
been compared on the basis of five-
bit divisors. These results need
to be modified to show the effect
of larger divisors. A simple method
of doing this which will yield a
close approximation to the desired
result may be developed from a study
of the pattern of shift amount variations in Fig. 10. From this it can
be predicted that if a six-bit chart
is constructed, it will show the
same percentage of total operations
for shifts of 1, 2, 3, and 4 positions. The present shift of 5,
which actually represents five
or greater, would split approximately evenly into five, and six
or greater. The six or greater
could then be split approximately
evenly in six, and seven or greater.
The accuracy of this even division
increases as the number of positions
in the square increases.

In a computer the need for
large shifts occurs so infrequently
that it is usually not considered
practical to include a shifter
capable of making, in one shift
cycle, all shifts that may be re-

quired. Once the data has been expanded to include the possibility of long shifts, the effect of this of performance must be considered.

To permit easier expansion, the data for the five-bit divisor was transferred to a basis of 1000 operations rather than 256, the 1000 operations being obtained by using the percentage figures from the various tables with the decimal moved one position right. In each case the expansion was extended to include all shifts that would occur at least one-tenth of one percent of the time. The remaining shifts, amounting to one-tenth of one percent, were all assigned to the next shift length. All numbers of shifts were adjusted to be whole numbers. The average total positions shifted across for 1000 shifts was then obtained by multiplying each shift number by its frequency of occurrence, then adding these products together. This number divided by 1000 gave the average bits shifted across per cycle with no limitation on the shifter size.

Limiting the range of the Shifter leaves the number of bits shifted across the same as for the operation with no limit, but it increases the number of shift cycles required to get across them. If a limit of four is assumed, a desired shift of five will require two operations, one shift of four and one

shift of one. A desired shift of ten would require three operations, two shifts of four and one shift of two.

The results obtained in this manner for eight different division methods will be summarized in Table 7. A description of the column headings is given below.

1. Division using one times the divisor and shifting across zeros only. Data for this was obtained from Fig. 10 by assigning shift values of one to all complement results when starting with a true dividend.
2. Division using one times the divisor and shifting across ones and zeros, single addition.
3. Division using one-half, one, and two times the divisor with coded multiple selection.
4. Division using one-half, one, and two times the divisor with double addition, also with optimum selection.
5. Division using three-fourths, one, and three-halves times the divisor with simple (two by two) coding.
6. Division using three-fourths, one, and three-halves times the divisor with complex (four by eight) coding.
7. Division using three-fourths, one, and three-halves times

Table 7.

Average Bits Shifted Across Per Shift Cycle

Shifter Limit	1	2	3	4	5	6	7	8
None	1.86	2.66	2.86	2.94	3.59	3.77	3.75	3.82
8	1.85	2.64	2.84	2.92	3.54	3.72	3.69	3.76
6	1.83	2.54	2.78	2.86	3.40	3.55	3.54	3.60
4	1.76	2.39	2.53	2.61	2.98	3.07	3.08	3.03
5*	1.80	2.54	2.74	2.82	3.37	3.58	3.51	3.58

* Five Bit Divisor

the divisor with double addition.

8. Division using three-fourths, one, and three-halves times the divisor with optimum selection.

These figures are believed to represent an accurate comparison of the efficiencies of the different methods of division that have been described. The absolute accuracy is subject to the limitations previously explained.

APPENDIX

Readers who do not already have a fairly extensive background in computer binary arithmetic may find that some of the assumed facts in the main text are not obvious. This appendix will attempt to remedy this by covering some of these items in more detail.

THE FULL ADDER

The full adder, one version of which is illustrated in Fig. 1, may be described by the following table. From Table 8 it may be seen that, with the application of the rules of Boolean algebra, the Sum and Carry outputs may be described by any of the following equations.

$$S = (A \bar{B} \bar{C}) \vee (\bar{A} B \bar{C}) \vee (\bar{A} \bar{B} C) \vee (A B C)$$

$$S = (A \bar{B} \vee \bar{A} B) \bar{C} \vee (\bar{A} \bar{B} \vee A B) C$$

$$S = (A \veebar B) \veebar C$$

$$R = (A B \bar{C}) \vee (A \bar{B} C) \vee (\bar{A} B C) \vee (A B C)$$

$$R = (A \veebar B) C \vee (A B)$$

$$R = (A B) \vee (A C) \vee (B C)$$

Assume that an N-position adder is made by connecting N full adders of the type shown in Fig. 1 in series with the R output of each stage connected to the C input of the next higher order stage. In such an ad-

der, if one input number were all ones, and the other number were a single one in the lowest order position, a carry would be generated in the first position, then go through each position in turn, producing a change in each position it passed through, until it finally reached the Nth position. Such an addition would require 2N logical transit times to complete. Usually, however, carries will be generated at several points within the adder simultaneously, and each generation point will be the start of a ripple path. Each ripple path will continue until it reaches a stage with a zero zero input (which will not pass a carry) or a one one (which was the starting point of another ripple path). The required time to complete the addition will then be determined by the longest ripple path within the adder for that particular pair of input numbers. This can be shown, assuming random distribution within the numbers being added, to have an average value of less than seven for a hundred-bit adder. If means are available to recognize when all carry rippling is completed, this represents a considerable time reduction over the time required for a full-length ripple carry.

Table 8.

Input	Output	Sum	Carry	Not Sum	Not Carry
A B C	S R	S	R	$\bar{S}$	$\bar{R}$
0 0 0	0 0			$\bar{A} \bar{B} \bar{C}$	$\bar{A} \bar{B} \bar{C}$
1 0 0	1 0	$A \bar{B} \bar{C}$			$A \bar{B} \bar{C}$
0 1 0	1 0	$\bar{A} B \bar{C}$			$\bar{A} B \bar{C}$
1 1 0	0 1		$A B \bar{C}$	$A B \bar{C}$	
0 1 1	1 0	$\bar{A} B C$			$\bar{A} B C$
1 0 1	0 1		$A \bar{B} C$	$A \bar{B} C$	
0 1 1	0 1		$\bar{A} B C$	$\bar{A} B C$	
1 1 1	1 1	A B C	A B C		

COMPLETION RECOGNITION ADDERS

It was stated in the description of the operation of a completion recognition adder that to prevent false indications of completion the two inputs must enter the adder simultaneously; once the operation has started no changes may be made in the inputs; and both inputs must be changed to all zeros or all ones before the next addition may be performed. The reason for this may be seen from the following examples. Assume that the addition shown on the left is performed; then, without first clearing the adder, the input is changed as shown to give the resulting sum. In the first example

```
0 1 1 0 0 1 1 0 0 1 1 0   A
0 0 0 1 1 0 0 1 1 0 0 0   B
0 1 1 1 1 1 1 1 1 1 1 0   S

0 1 1 0 0 1 1 0 0 1 1 0   A
0 0 0 1 1 0 0 1 1 0 1 0   B
1 0 0 0 0 0 0 0 0 0 0 0   S
```

a no-carry signal generated in position one ripples down through positions two through ten into position eleven. There are transmit signals generated in positions two through eleven inclusive and a new no-carry signal originated in position twelve. Since the second example involves a change in position two only, other transmit signals are not disturbed, and the no-carry lines of the various stages do not change simultaneously. The change from On to Off, however, ripples from one stage to the next in the same manner that the change from On to Off did in the first example. Simultaneously with the termination of the no-carry signal from position two, a carry signal is generated and started along the carry line. Thus the two changes are moving from one stage to the next simultaneously, one going On at the same time the other goes Off. This could result in the completion signal not going Off at all, even though the sum is in the process of being changed. Changing the inputs to all zeros or all ones causes all of the transmit signals to go Off, which means that there are no ripple groups to go Off in sequence when the next number is entered. Obviously, making a change in either of the inputs after an addition has started would be the same as going from one completed addition to the next without clearing in between. The term clear means making the inputs to the adder either all zeros or all ones.

MULTIPLICATION

It was stated earlier that an average shift of three bits may be expected when using the variable shift method of multiplication described. The basis for this statement is shown below. Table 9 shows the eight possible combinations of the next four bits following a shift across zeros. From Table 9 it may be seen that fifty percent of the following shifts are across zeros and fifty percent across ones. These in turn split into two groups each, one of which contains known numbers of shifts, while the other calls for a known minimum plus a number to be determined from additional bits. Tables 10 and 11 describe the breakdown of the two incomplete groups. Table 10 refers to the group

Table 9.

(1)	0 0 - 1 1 1 1	3+
(2)	0 0 - 1 1 1 0	3+
(3)	0 0 - 1 1 0 1	3
(4)	0 0 - 1 1 0 0	2
(5)	0 0 - 1 0 1 1	1
(6)	0 0 - 1 0 1 0	2
(7)	0 0 - 1 0 0 1	2+
(8)	0 0 - 1 0 0 0	2+

Shift	(1)	(2)	(3)	(2+)	(3+)
Fraction	1/8	1/4	1/8	1/4	1/4

Table 10.

(1 - 1)	0 0 - 1 1 1 - 1 1 1	(3+)	2+
(1 - 2)	0 0 - 1 1 1 - 1 1 0	(3+)	2+
(1 - 3)	0 0 - 1 1 1 - 1 0 1	(3+)	2
(1 - 4)	0 0 - 1 1 1 - 1 0 0	(3+)	1
(2 - 5)	0 0 - 1 1 1 - 0 1 1	(3+)	1
(2 - 6)	0 0 - 1 1 1 - 0 1 0	(3+)	1
(2 - 7)	0 0 - 1 1 1 - 0 0 1	(3+)	0
(2 - 8)	0 0 - 1 1 1 - 0 0 0	(3+)	0

	(0)	(1)	(2)	(2+)
Additional Shift				
Fraction	1/4	3/8	1/8	1/4

Table 11.

(7 - 1)	0 0 - 1 0 0 - 1 1 1	(2+)	0
(7 - 2)	0 0 - 1 0 0 - 1 1 0	(2+)	0
(7 - 3)	0 0 - 1 0 0 - 1 0 1	(2+)	1
(7 - 4)	0 0 - 1 0 0 - 1 0 0	(2+)	1
(8 - 5)	0 0 - 1 0 0 - 0 1 1	(2+)	1
(8 - 6)	0 0 - 1 0 0 - 0 1 0	(2+)	2
(8 - 7)	0 0 - 1 0 0 - 0 0 1	(2+)	2+
(8 - 8)	0 0 - 1 0 0 - 0 0 0	(2+)	2+

	(0)	(1)	(2)	(2+)
Additional Shift				
Fraction	1/4	3/8	1/8	1/4

shifting across ones, while Table 11 refers to the group shifting across zeros. The additional shift fractions are seen to be the same for both groups.

From Tables 9-11, Table 12 can be made that will give the fraction of the total number of shifts made that should have each shift value for random bit distribution. The one-position shift is taken from the first table, and is one-eighth of the total shifts. The two-position shift is determined by a combination of two figures. From Table 9 it is known that one-quarter of the shifts will be two-position and another quarter will be two or more (2+). From Table 11 it can be seen that one-quarter of the latter are plus zero, which means that the total having a shift of two will be one-quarter plus one-quarter of one-quarter, or five-sixteenths. The three position shift is composed of one-eighth from Table 9, (1/4 x 3/8) from (2 + 1) and (1/4 x 1/4) from (3 + 0). The four-position shift requires a double extension of the table for its third term. It is composed of (1/4 x 1/8) from (2 + 2), (1/4 x 3/8) from (3 + 1), and (1/4 x 1/4 x 1/4) from (2 + 2 + 0). This procedure may be continued indefinitely, but an examination of the sums at the right of the last table indicates a uniform progression that makes this unnecessary. Instead, the following rule may be used.

Table 12.

Shift										
1								1/8	=	1/8
2					1/4	+	(1/4 x 1/4)		=	5/16
3		1/8	+	(1/4 x 3/8)	+	(1/4 x 1/4)			=	9/32
4	(1/4 x 1/8)	+	(1/4 x 3/8)	+	(1/16 x 1/4)				=	9/64
5	(1/4 x 1/8)	+	(1/16 x 3/8)	+	(1/16 x 1/4)				=	9/128
6	(1/16 x 1/8)	+	(1/16 x 3/8)	+	(1/64 x 1/4)				=	9/256
7	(1/16 x 1/8)	+	(1/64 x 3/8)	+	(1/64 x 1/4)				=	9/512
8	(1/64 x 1/8)	+	(1/64 x 3/8)	+	(1/256 x 1/4)				=	9/1024
9	(1/64 x 1/8)	+	(1/256 x 3/8)	+	(1/256 x 1/4)				=	9/2048
10	(1/256 x 1/8)	+	(1/256 x 3/8)	+	(1/1024 x 1/4)				=	9/4096

Then operating with multipliers having random bit distribution, the average shift distribution will be as follows: 1/8 will be shifts of one, 5/16 will be shifts of two. This leaves 9/16 which will be shifts of three or greater. Of these, half will be three-shift, half of the remainder will be four-shift, half of the remainder following that will be five-shift, etc.

This rule was developed on the assumption of starting by shifting across zeros. An initial assumption of shifting across ones would duplicate these results, giving exactly the same ratios. This must be true since the only difference in the rules for handling ones and zeros is that the locations of the words one and zero interchanged.

To determine the average shift, start with an assumed number of shifts, apply the preceding rule to determine the distribution among the various shift amounts, multiply the number of times each shift amount occurs by that shift amount, then add these products to determine the total number of positions shifted across. Divide the total number of shifts into the total number of positions shifted across to determine the average shift. It will be necessary to have one group which will include all shifts greater than some particular amount and assume some average value for these. This procedure is illustrated in Table 13. A total of 4096 shifts is assumed. All shifts of one through twelve are determined, and

the remainder are grouped as greater than twelve. This gives an average shift of three (12,288/4096) bits per shift cycle, based on the assumption that the shifter can supply any shift called for in one cycle. Usually this is not the case, and the figure must be modified accordingly. For example, if the maximum shift available is four, a desired shift of six would be obtained by one shift of four and one of two, while a desired shift of thirteen would be three shifts of four followed by one of one. To correct for this, leave the number of bits shifted across the same, but increase the number of shifts required in the following manner. Divide the table into groups, each group having a size equal to the maximum allowable shift. Keep the number of shifts

Table 13.

Shifts	Number of Shifts	Number of Bits
1	512	512
2	1280	2560
3	1152	3456
4	576	2304
5	288	1440
6	144	864
7	72	504
8	36	288
9	18	162
10	9	90
11	4.5	49.5
12	2.25	27
12+	2.25	31.5
Totals	4096	12288

Table 14.

Group 1	512	+	1280	+	1152	+	576	=	3520	3520
Group 2	288	+	144	+	72	+	36	=	540	1080
Group 3	18	+	9	+	4.5	+	2.25	=	33.75	101.25
Group 4	2.25							=	2.25	9
Sum										4710.25

in the first group as it is, double
the number in the second group,
triple the number in the third group,
etc. Add these results together,
then divide the sum into the total
number of bits to get the average
shift. For example, assume a maximum
shift of four. (See Table 14.) This
gives an average shift of $(12,288/4,710.25) = 2.60$ bits. A maximum
shift of five gives $(12,288/4378) = 2.81$, while a maximum shift of six
gives $(12,288/4242.25) = 2.90$.
There is an additional slight adjust-
ment due to the fact that the multiplier has a finite length which is
not included.

MULTIPLICATION USING CARRY-SAVE ADDERS

Fig. 17 illustrates two versions
of a combined carry-save carry-propagate adder. Each position has two
carry input connections, one for use
under carry-save conditions and the
other for use under carry-propagate
conditions. Carry look-ahead circuits
can be used with the carry-propagate
input.

Fig. 18 illustrates the modifications required in the system when
using three-bit multiplier groups.
Fig. 19 shows the use of storage
registers on the outputs of the last
carry-save adder. This costs an
additional carry-save adder and two
additional registers, but will give
some increase in speed. The part of
the partial product that is completed
goes through the carry-propagate
adder each cycle from the two registers,
but the remainder of the partial
product goes directly back to the

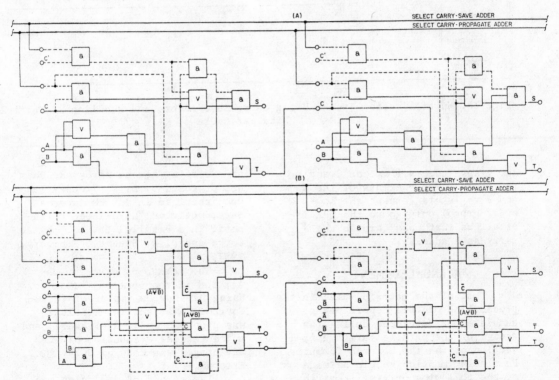

Fig. 17. Carry-Save/Carry-Propagate Adders. Two Versions of Combined Carry-Save/Carry-Propagate Adders Are Shown. Dotted Lines Are Additional Connections Required to Allow Choice. Additional Circuits do not Increase the Carry Path When in the CPA Mode. Carry Path may be Same as Sum Path in CSA Mode. Separate Carry Input Positions are Provided for the Two Modes, but the Same Carry Output Terminal (T) is Used for Both.

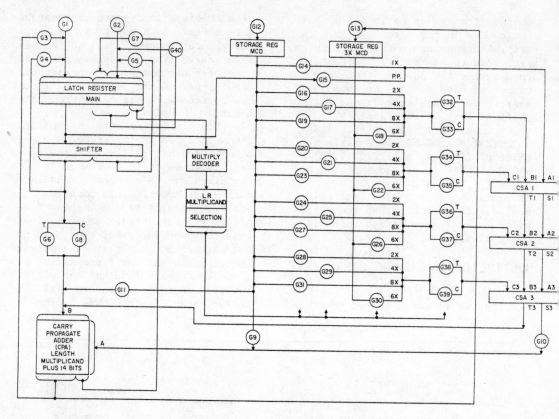

Fig. 18. Multiplication System Using Carry-Save Adders and Handling 12 Multiplier
Bits per Cycle

carry-save adders from the S and R
registers. The contents of the S
and R registers (except the low-
order group) only go to the CPA
after the last pass through the
carry-save adders.

ACKNOWLEDGMENT

Most of the material used in the
preparation of this report was accumulated or developed during the
design of the parallel arithmetic
section of the IBM Stretch Computer.
Particular mention should be made
of the following original contributions.

The method of division described in the section "Division Using Single Adder, One-Times Divisor,

and Shifting Across Zeros and Ones"
was proposed by D. W. Sweeney, and
was described in an IBM internal
paper entitled "High-Speed Arithmetic in a Parallel Device," by J.
Cocke and D. W. Sweeney, February,
1957.

The method of division described in the section "Division
Using Divisor Multiples of Three-
Fourths, One, and Three-Halves"
was proposed by J. R. Stewart, and
a theoretical evaluation of its
advantages was made by C. V.
Frieman.

The method of modifying the
high-order end of the adders described in the section "Component
Reduction with Carry-Save Adders"
was proposed by F. R. Bielawa.

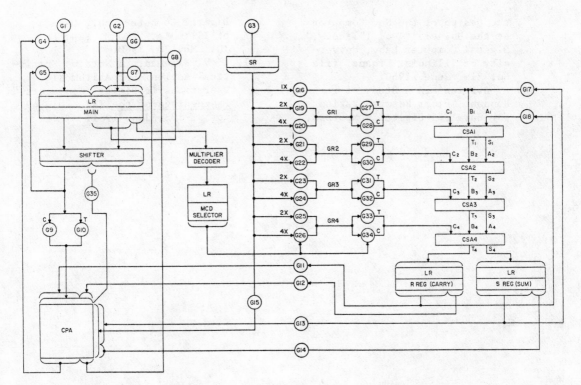

Fig. 19. Multiplication System Using Carry-Save Adders and Sum and Carry Registers

BIBLIOGRAPHY

1. A. W. Burks, H. Goldstine, and J. von Neumann, "Preliminary Discussion of the Logical Design of an Electronic Computing Instrument," The Institute for Advanced Study, Princeton, N.J., 1947. (Reprinted in Part 3 of this volume.)

2. A. L. Leiner, J. L. Smith, and A. Weinberger, "System Design of Digital Computer at the National Bureau of Standards," Natl. Bur. of Standards, Circular 591, February, 1958.

3. B. Gilchrist, J. H. Pomerene, and S. Y. Wong, "Fast-Carry Logic for Digital Computers," IRE Trans. on Electronic Computers, vol. EC-4, pp. 133-136, December, 1955.

4. M. Lehman, "High-speed Digital Multiplication," IRE Trans. on Electronic Computers, Vol. EC-6, pp. 204-205, September, 1957.

5. J. E. Robertson, "A New Class of Digital Division Methods," IRE Trans. on Electronic Computers, vol. EC-7, pp. 218-222, September, 1958.

6. E. Block, "The Engineering Design of the Stretch Computer," Proc. EJCC, Boston, Mass,, pp. 48-58, December 1-3, 1959.

7. S. J. Campbell and G. H. Rosser, Jr., "An Analysis of Carry Transmission in Computer Addition," 13th Natl. Meeting of the ACM, Univ. of Illinois, Urbana, June 11-13, 1958.

8. V. S. Burtsey, "Accelerating Multiplication and Division Operations in High-Speed Digital Computers," Exact Mechanics and Computing Technique, Acad. Sci. USSR, Moscow, 1958.

9. J. E. Robertson, "Theory of Computer Arithmetic Employed in

the Design of the New Computer
at the University of Illinois,"
Digital Computer Lab., University of Illinois, Urbana, file
No. 319, June, 1960.

10. A. Avizienis, "A Study of redundant Number Representation
for Parallel Digital Computers,"
Digital Computer Lab., Univ.
of Illinois, Urbana, Rep. No.
101, May 20, 1960.

11. C. V. Frieman, "A Note on Statistical Analysis of Arithmetic
Operations in Digital Computers,"
Proceedings of the IRE, Vol. 49,
pp. 91-103, Jan. 1961.

A SIGNED BINARY MULTIPLICATION TECHNIQUE

ANDREW D. BOOTH

In the design of automatic computing machines it is necessary to have available some means of multiplying together two numbers whose signs are not necessarily positive. This, of course, is completely trivial when the process is to be performed by a human operator since a large number of processes exist. However, few of these seem to be suitable for mechanization with the types of circuit currently available on account of the complexity of the discrimination required for their execution, and the problem is to find a procedure which can be engineered with the minimum of equipment. Several ways of accomplishing this have been used to date, all more or less unsatisfactory, for example:

1. the machine may use numbers in the form (sign) (absolute value of number), in which case, although multiplication (and division) are particularly simple, the much more frequent operation of subtraction needs special circuitry;

2. negative numbers may be represented in complementary form mod 2^p

when it is necessary either first to convert them to positive form, multiply, and then to correct the resulting product to its signed value by means of a special sub-routine; or to apply appropriate corrections to the product, obtained in the usual way, by neglecting the fact that the numbers may be non-positive. The nature of these corrections is seen from the following discussion.

Reprinted from the Quarterly Journal of Mechanics and Applied Mathematics, Vol. 4, pt. 2, 1951, pp. 236-240, by permission of The Clarendon Press, Oxford.

Assume that the machine in question (this is the case in the machines under construction in this and many other laboratories) deals with negative numbers by taking their complement mod 2, then:

$$+m \equiv m$$
$$-m \equiv 2-m.$$

Whence if two numbers m and r are to be multiplied, the machine will generate the following results:

$$+m \times +r = +mr, \qquad (a)$$
$$-m \times +r = 2r-mr, \qquad (b)$$
$$+m \times -r = 2m-mr, \qquad (c)$$
$$-m \times -r = 4-2m-2r+mr. \qquad (d)$$

Thus, in order to correct (b), (c), and (d), it is necessary to apply the following process:

1. if m is negative, subtract 2r from the product obtained in the normal manner;

2. if r is negative, subtract 2m from the product obtained in the normal manner;

and application of both of these corrections also gives correct results in case (d), since if m and r are negative subtraction is in effect addition and since operations are all mod 2 the added 4 is in any case ignored by the machine.

It is evident that the application of this correction process involves examination, by the machine, of the signs of both m and r and this, in turn, requires for the efficient engineering of the sequence the storage of the signs of m and r in auxiliary circuits[1].

Such correction operations as envisaged above are highly undesirable, and it is natural to inquire whether any process exists whereby multiplication can be performed in a uniform manner without the necessity of any special devices to examine the signs of the interacting numbers. That this was a reasonable quest was rendered probable by the development, by Burks, Goldstein, and von Neumann[2], of the so-called 'non-restoring' process for the division of signed binary numbers, and a somewhat complicated process for multiplication had in fact been suggested previously by Rey and Spencer[3].

An extremely simple process (both mathematically and technically) has now been evolved and forms the subject of this note; it was suggested by the standard 'shortcutting' method of multiplication used on desk machines operating in decimal scale. Thus, to multiply by 057737 (i.e., + 57737) on a desk calculating machine using the shortcutting method, the operator effectively multiplies by $1\ \bar{4}\ \bar{2}\ \bar{3}\ 4\ \bar{3}$. Similarly to multiply by the number 977563 (i.e., -22437) the operator effectively multiplies by $1\ 0\ \bar{2}\ \bar{2}\ 4\ \bar{4}\ 3$. The corresponding process for binary numbers gives for multiplication by the positive numbers $0\ 1\ \bar{1}\ 1\ 0\ 1\ 1$, multiplication by $1\ 0\ 0\ \bar{1}\ 1\ 0\ \bar{1}$. The process is precisely this, provided the multiplication starts with the least significant digit, and may be described as follows:

To multiply two numbers m and r together, examine the nth digit (m_n) of m,

1. If $m_n = 0$, $m_{n+1} = 0$, multiply the existing sum of partial products by 2^{-1}, i.e., shift one place to the right.
2. If $m_n = 0$, $m_{n+1} = 1$, add r into the existing sum of partial products and multiply by 2^{-1}, i.e., shift one place to the right.
3. If $m_n = 1$, $m_{n+1} = 0$, subtract r from existing sum of partial products and multiply by 2^{-1}, i.e., shift one place to right.
4. If $m_n = 1$, $m_{n+1} = 1$, multiply the sum of partial products by 2^{-1}, i.e., shift one place to

the right.
5. Do not multiply by 2^{-1} at m_0 in the above processes.

Note that if m is given to n digits, at the start of the process it is assumed that $m_{n+1} = 0$.

In proving this process it will be assumed that operations are (mod 2). Thus

$$m \equiv m_0 \cdot m_1 m_2 \ldots m_n$$

$$\equiv m_0 \cdot 2^0 + 2^{-1} m_1 + 2^{-2} m_2 \ldots + 2^{-n} m_n \ldots + 2^{-N} m_N$$

$$(m_n = 0, 1).$$

Now consider the multiplication of r by the number $0.0\ldots01_n00\ldots0$, i.e., by 2^{-n}. It is seen that the process (1)-(5) gives, for the product:

$$-r \times 2^{-n} + r \times 2^{-n+1},$$

i.e., $r \times 2^{-n}(2 - 1) = 2^{-n}r,$

which is the correct result whatever the sign of r since the multiplication by 2^{-n} is achieved by successive right-shift operations.

Thus, up to m_0, the following results will be obtained in the complete multiplication by m:

(+m) x r is correct for all signs of r,

(-m) x r = (1-m)r = r-mr for all signs of r.

At stage m_0, however, the quantity $m_0 \cdot r (m_0 = 0, 1)$ is subtracted from these results, giving:

(+m) x r-0 x r = +mr for all signs of r,

(-m) x r-1 x r = (1-m)r-r = -mr for all signs of r.

Whence the process outlined gives the correct product for m x r (mod 2) whatever the signs of m and r.

In conclusion an example of the application of the procedure to each possible combination of signs will render the process clear.

(1) $m = 0 \cdot 101 \; (+ \frac{5}{8})$ $r = 0 \cdot 110 \; (+ \frac{3}{4})$

$m_3 = 1 \; (m_4 = 0)$	subtract r		$1 \cdot 010$
	shift right		$1 \cdot 101,0$
$m_2 = 0, \; m_3 = 1$	add r	$1 \cdot 1010$	
		$0 \cdot 110$	
		$\overline{0 \cdot 0110}$	
	shift right		$0 \cdot 001,10$
$m_1 = 1, \; m_2 = 0$	subtract r	$0 \cdot 00110$	
		$1 \cdot 010$	
		$\overline{1 \cdot 01110}$	
	shift right		$1 \cdot 101,110$
$m_0 = 0, \; m_1 = 1$	add r	$1 \cdot 101,110$	
		$0 \cdot 110$	
		$\overline{0 \cdot 011,110}$ (mod 2)	
	no shift		$0 \cdot 011,110 \; (= + \frac{15}{32})$

(2) $m = 1 \cdot 011 \; (- \frac{5}{8})$ $r = 0 \cdot 110 \; (+ \frac{3}{4})$

$m_3 = 1 \; (m_4 = 0)$	subtract r	$1 \cdot 010$	
	shift right		$1 \cdot 101,0$
$m_2 = 1, \; m_3 = 1$	shift right		$1 \cdot 110,10$
$m_1 = 0, \; m_2 = 1$	add r	$1 \cdot 110,10$	
		$0 \cdot 110$	
		$\overline{0 \cdot 100,10}$	
	shift right		$0 \cdot 010,010$
$m_0 = 1, \; m_1 = 0$	subtract r	$0 \cdot 010,010$	
		$1 \cdot 010$	
		$\overline{1 \cdot 100,010}$	
	no shift		$1 \cdot 100,010 \; (= - \frac{15}{32})$

(3) $m = 0 \cdot 101 \; (+ \frac{5}{8})$ $r = 1 \cdot 010 \; (- \frac{3}{4})$

$m_3 = 1 \; (m_4 = 0)$	subtract r	$0 \cdot 110$	
	shift right		$0 \cdot 011,0$
$m_2 = 0, \; m_3 = 1$	add r	$0 \cdot 011,0$	
		$1 \cdot 010$	
		$\overline{1 \cdot 101,0}$	
	shift right		$1 \cdot 110,10$
$m_1 = 1, \; m_2 = 0$	subtract r	$1 \cdot 110,10$	
		$0 \cdot 110$	
		$\overline{0 \cdot 100,10}$	
	shift right		$0 \cdot 010,010$
$m_0 = 0, \; m_1 = 1$	add r	$0 \cdot 010,010$	
		$1 \cdot 010$	
		$\overline{1 \cdot 100,010}$	
	no shift		$1 \cdot 100,010 \; (= - \frac{15}{32})$

(4) $m = 1 \cdot 011 \; (- \frac{5}{8})$ $r = 1 \cdot 010 \; (- \frac{3}{4})$

$m_3 = 1 \; (m_4 = 0)$	subtract r	$0 \cdot 110$	
	shift right		$0 \cdot 011,0$
$m_2 = 1, \; m_3 = 1$	shift right		$0 \cdot 001,10$

$$m_1 = 0, \; m_2 = 1 \qquad \text{add } r$$

$$
\begin{array}{l}
0\cdot001,10 \\
\underline{1\cdot010} \\
1\cdot011,10
\end{array}
$$

shift right $1\cdot101,110$

$$m_0 = 1, \; m_1 = 0 \qquad \text{subtract } r$$

$$
\begin{array}{l}
1\cdot101,110 \\
\underline{0\cdot110} \\
0\cdot011,110
\end{array}
$$

no shift $0\cdot011,110 \; (+ \frac{15}{32})$

REFERENCES

1. A. D. Booth and K. H. V. Britten, <u>General Considerations in the Design of an Electronic Computer</u>, Princeton, 1947.

2. A. Burks, H. Goldstine, and J. von Neumann, "Preliminary Discussion of the Logical Design of an Electronic Computing Instrument," The Institute for Advanced Study, Princeton, 1947, (Reprinted in Part 3 of this volume.)

3. T. J. Rey and R. E. Spencer, <u>Sign Correction in Modulus Convention</u>, Cambridge Conference Report, 1950.

SOME SCHEMES FOR PARALLEL MULTIPLIERS

L. DADDA

1. INTRODUCTION

The realization of a parallel multiplier for digital computers has been considered in a recent paper by C. S. Wallace[1] who proposed a tree of pseudo-adders (i.e., adders without carry propagation) producing two numbers, whose sum equals the product. This sum can be obtained by applying the two numbers to a carry-propagating adder.

The purpose of this note is to present some schemes for parallel multipliers, based on a different principle and having some advantages over the one by Wallace. Also some of the proposed schemes will obtain two numbers whose sum equals the product.

2. THE MULTIPLIER SCHEME, BASED ON PARALLEL COUNTERS

The new schemes are based on the use of logical blocks that we will call "parallel (n,m) counters": these are combinational networks with m outputs and n ($\leq 2^m$) inputs. The m outputs considered as a binary number, codify the number of "ones" present at the inputs. In a subsequent paragraph some implementations of such parallel counters will be illustrated.

Consider now the process of multiplication of two binary numbers, each composed of n bit, as been based on obtaining the sum of v summands.

This paper has been presented at the "Colloque sur l'Algebre de Boole," Grenoble, 11-17, January, 1965.

Reprinted with permission from Alta Frequenza, Vol. 34, May, 1965, pp. 349-356, with a correction from the author.

These summands are obtained, in the simplest schemes, by shifting left the multiplicand by 1, 2, 3, (n-1) places, and multiplying it by the corresponding bits of the multiplier. In this case, v = n.

As it is well known, the number of summands can be made less than n by using some simple multiples of the multiplicand, on the basis of two or more multiplier digits[1].

The reduction of the number of summands will not be considered here. The case (v = n) will be therefore assumed, as the scheme proposed will work also for a reduced number of summands.

Consider now the case of two positive factors. To obtain the product, first represent the summands by the usual matrix as indicated in the upper portion of Fig. 1; (in the figure, n = 12). In the same figure, the significant bits are represented by dots; moreover, bits at the left and at the right of the significant ones are supposed to be zeros.

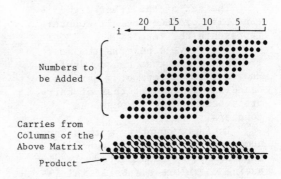

Fig. 1. Multiplication (12 x 12 bit) Through Addition, in a Single Stage, Using a Parallel Counter for Each Column. Carries are Propagated Through the Counters.

The process of multiplication is as follows. The single bit in column i = 1 represents the least significant bit of the product, so it does not require any transformation. The two bits in column i = 2 are applied to a (2,2) counter: the least significant of the two outputs represents the second least significant bit of the product, and is recorded in Fig. 1 on the last line, i = 2; the most significant output represents a carry, and it therefore recorded in i = 3.

In column 3 we have 4 bit: three of them belong to the original matrix, the fourth is the carry just mentioned. This four bits will be applied to a (4,3) counter, whose three outputs will be recorded: in column 3 (the least significant, representing the third least significant bit of the product) in column 4 and in column 5 (the most significant), respectively.

The following columns are treated in a similar way, using suitable counters.

The inputs of each counter are in part the bits of the corresponding column of the summands matrix, in part carry bits produced by the counters of the preceeding columns. In Fig. 1, carries produced by a given counter are connected by a diagonal segment.

The set of the least significant bits produced by all counters represents the result.

The above scheme is the most elementary one that can be devised. However, it suffers of a serious disadvantage, namely that of carry propagation delay through the counters.

In fact, counters with a large number of inputs are in general implemented by complicated circuits, having therefore a substantial inherent delay.

If one wishes to minimize the effects of such delay, a different scheme should be adopted. This scheme is based on the following remark. Consider the problem of

obtaining the product as divided in two steps. In the first step, obtain from the original set of addends a set of two numbers, whose sum equals the product. The second step obtains the product in a carry-propagating adder.

Carry propagation cannot be avoided; it is simply confined to this second step, where it can be accomplished by special, fast circuits.

Let us now describe the above process with reference to Fig. 2, that represents a 12 x 12 product.

The first step of the process consists of cascaded stages (in the example, 3 stages): the first stage transforms the matrix A into the matrix B; the second stage matrix B into C, and so on, until a matrix, composed of two rows only, is obtained: these two rows represent the numbers that, summed in a carry propagating adder, produce the result.

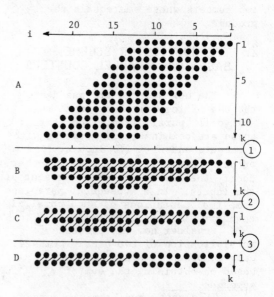

Fig. 2. A Multiplier Scheme, Obtaining Two Numbers, Whose Sum Equals the Product of 12 x 12 Bit, Through Three Stages, Using a Parallel Counter for Each Stage and for Each Column. Carries are not Propagated.

In the first stage, we begin by transcribing the single significant bit in column $i = 1$ (in the right upper corner) from matrix A into matrix B. The same is done for column $i = 2$, composed of two significant bits only.

The three bits of column $i = 3$, are applied to a (3,2) counter: the least significant, of the two output bits, is recorded in B, $i = 3$, the most significant bit is recorded in B, $i = 4$, in the second row. Which row is chosen for this second bit is inessential, provided it is recorded in column $i = 4$; the rule followed in Fig. 2 is convenient because it produces a compact matrix B.

The $i = 4$ column has 4 bit, and correspondingly, the parallel counter must have $m = 3$ outputs: the least significant bit will be recorded in B, $(i,k) = (3,1)$; the next bit in B, $(i,k) = (4,2)$; the third, most significant bit in B, $(i,k) = (5,3)$.

Note that in Fig. 2 matrix B, the diagonal segment, joining together the above three bits, signifies that these bits are the outputs of the parallel counter fed by the column just above the least significant bit $(k = 1)$. The rule is followed in all similar cases.

The process described above for column $i = 3$ and $i = 4$ is repeated for the subsequent columns, using each time an appropriate parallel counter.

The matrix B, thus obtained from A, has four rows; it is then transformed into matrix C by the same process.

Matrix C has 3 rows, so it is transformed into matrix D, a two-row matrix; the two rows represent the result of the process.

The above process can be justified as follows. With reference to the original matrix A, it can be said that the product is equivalent to the sum of all the bits $b_{i,k}$ in the same matrix, each multiplied by a weight, 2^{i-1}:

$$P = \sum_{k=1}^{n} \sum_{i=1}^{2n-1} b_{i,k} 2^{i-1}$$

The contribution to P of each column i is:

$$P_i = \sum_{k=1}^{n} b_{i,k} 2^{i-1} = 2^{i-1} \sum_{k=1}^{n} b_{i,k}$$

This same contribution is represented in matrix B by the output of the counter, $\sum_{k=1}^{k} b_{i,k}$, whose least significant bit is in column i, and therefore has weight 2^{i-1}.

The matrix B, therefore, is equivalent to matrix A as far as the evaluation of the product is concerned.

Matrices C and D are also equivalent to A, having been obtained from B and C respectively by the same transformation.

The procedure described can be applied to factors with arbitrary value of n, on the assumption that parallel counters having a suitable number of inputs are available.

The number of stages required is easily determined and appears as in Table 1.

Table 1.

Number of Stages Required for a Parallel Multiplier (vs. number n of bits of the multiplier) Using Parallel Counters Without Limitation on the Number of Inputs

Number of Bits in the Multiplier	Number of Stages
3	1
$3 < n \leq 7$	2
$7 < n \leq 127$	3
$127 < n \leq 2^{127} - 1$	4

3. THE USE OF COUNTERS WITH A LIMITED NUMBER OF INPUTS: (2,2) AND (3,2) COUNTERS

Counters with a large number of inputs are difficult to realize. It is therefore important to see how the method could be applied using counters with a limited number of inputs, n_1.

It is apparent that the method can be modified as follows. If the number of significant bits in a column of the matrix to be transformed (initially matrix A) is greater than the number n_1 of inputs to the available counters, divide the bits in groups, each having at most n_1 bits. Each group can then be applied to the counter's inputs, each counter providing thus for each group the number of ones coded in binary.

Such counts are placed in the B matrix, all with the least significant bit in column i, and using as many rows as necessary.

The same holds for the subsequent transformations, until a 2-row matrix is obtained.

The most important remark on the above procedure is that the number of stages necessary will in general be greater than that required with unrestricted counter inputs.

One might, in this connection-look for the minimum number of inputs, that can still be used for the implementation of the method.

This minimum number is of course two; (2,2) counters can be used as shown in the examples in Fig. 3, and Fig. 4, representing the cases n = 3 and n = 4 respectively.

The example n = 3 works as follows. Columns i = 1 and i = 2 are reproduced in B. Column i = 3 is composed of 3 bit: therefore 2 of them are applied to a (2,2) counter, whose outputs are reproduced in B, columns i = 3 and i = 4 respectively (in the figure, they are connected together by a segment); the 3rd bit is simply reproduced in B, i = 3.

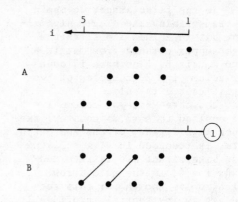

Fig. 3. A Multiplier Structure, Obtaining Two Numbers, Whose Sum Equals the Product of 3 x 3 Bit, Through the Use of 2 Input 2 Output Parallel Counters

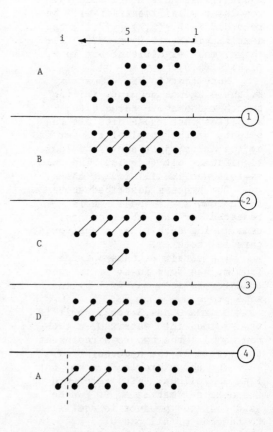

Fig. 4. Same as Fig. 3, for the Product of 4 x 4 Bit

Column 4 has 2 bit, as column 2: nevertheless it is transformed by a (2,2) counter, to produce the bits in columns 4 and 5 of B, because in B, column $i = 4$ there is already the carry from column 3. The single bit in column 5 is simply reproduced.

The case $n = 4$ is completely analogous. Considering cases with larger n, it can be found that the number of necessary stages, when using (2,2) counters, is 2^{n-2}. This means that, for practical values of n (e.g., n = 30), the number of stages would become very large and consequently the total delay would become too great.

As we will see in the following, the number of stages is drastically reduced if counters with n = 3 or more are used. On the other hand, it must be noted that counters with n larger than 2 are not difficult to implement. This is certainly the case for n = 3, that is a full adder network.

Figure 5 represents the multiplication process for the case n = 12 (like Fig. 2), using (3,2) counters and, when necessary, also some (2,2) counters. It can be seen that the total number of stages required is 5 (instead of 3, which represents the absolute minimum; see Fig. 2). The process is carried out in Fig. 5, with the following rules.

Columns 1 and 2, are simply reproduced in B (and in all following matrices).

Column 3, having 3 bit, is transformed in B into 2 bit: the least significant in column 3, the most significant in column 4 (second row). (They are connected by a diagonal segment, as used previously.)

Column 4 has 4 bit: three of them are transformed by a (3,2) counter, the fourth is simply reproduced in B, (4,3).

Column 5 has 5 bit: three of them are transformed by a (3,2) counter, the last two by a (2,2)

counter; the latter's outputs (in B, (5,3) and B, (6,4), respectively) are joined by a diagonal segment crossed by a bar to signify that they are outputs of a (2,2) counter.

Similar rules are applied to all the following columns, through the last column (23rd) which has a single bit.

The matrix B obtained by the application of the process, can be shown to be equivalent to A, as far as the evaluation of the product is concerned.

The same process can be used to obtain C from B, D from C, E from D and F from E. F has two rows, whose sum represents the product.

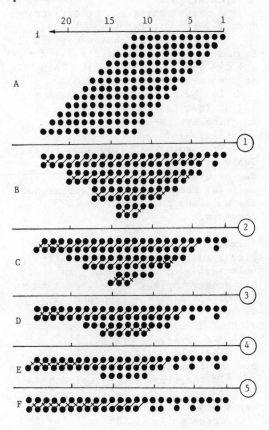

Fig. 5. Same as Fig. 2, Through the Use of 3 or 2 Input/2 Output Parallel Counters

Some remarks can be made about the described process, which was based on (3,2) counters.

(a) the number s of stages can be determined as follows.

It can be seen that the last 2-row matrix can be derived by a 3-row matrix. This is true regardless of the type of counters used.

A 3-row matrix can be derived from a 4-row matrix; in fact, three of the bits of each column can be reduced to two, by a (3,2) counter; the fourth bit is simply reproduced. This is obtained in the (s-1)th stage.

A 4-row matrix can be derived from a 6-row matrix, as can be easily verified. This is the (s-2)th stage.

A 6-row matrix can be derived from a 9-row matrix: (s-3th) stage.

A 9-row matrix can be derived from a 13-row matrix: $(2 + 2 + 2 + 2 + 1 \rightarrow 3 + 3 + 3 + 3 + 1)$. This is the (s-4)th stage.

In the example of Fig. 4, n = 12, so that the number of stages is given by: s-4 = 1; s = 5, as obtained.

Proceeding with the same rules, Table 2, valid for (3,2) counters, can be drawn up.

(b) The scheme of Fig. 5 is not the only one possible with (3,2) counters.

Fig. 6 represents a process, slightly different from that in Fig. 5 and leading to a considerable saving in components. In fact, the scheme in Fig. 5 requires a total of 136 counters (100 are (3,2) counters, 36 are (2,2)); the scheme of Fig. 6 requires 116 counters (104 are (3,2), 12 are (2,2)).

The rules applied in Fig. 6 are the following.

In the first stage, columns 1 to 13 are treated in the same way as in Fig. 5.

Columns 14, 15, 16 and 17 (having 10, 9, 8, 7 bit respectively in matrix A, are only partially reduced, so that in matrix B they are composed of 8 bit (taking into

Table 2.

Number of Stages Required for a Parallel Multiplier (vs. number of bits of the multiplier) Using (3,2) Counters Only

Number of Bits in the Multiplier	Number of Stages
3	1
4	2
4 < n ≤ 6	3
6 < n ≤ 9	4
9 < n ≤ 13	5
13 < n ≤ 19	6
19 < n ≤ 28	7
28 < n ≤ 42	8
42 < n ≤ 63	9

account the carries from the preceeding columns).

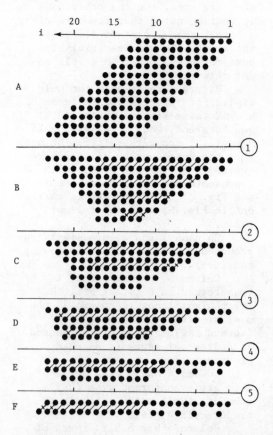

Fig. 6. Same as Fig. 5, With a Different Scheme Using Fewer Counters

All remaining columns are re-produced in matrix B without any reduction.

The reason of doing so is essentially the following. It is not convenient to try reduction of the number of bits in a given column, when it is preceeded by columns having a larger number of bits, because carries from the latter tend to increase the number of bits.

It should be remarked that in passing from matrix B to matrix C the last two rows of matrix B are reproduced in C without any trans-formation.

(c) A slightly different cri-terion is applied in Fig. 7, where a further reduction in the number of counters is achieved (113 in-stead of 116).

The scheme in Fig. 7 is the same as in Fig. 6 for columns 1 to 12.

Column 13 and the following, are only partially reduced to that in matrix B they have no more than 9 bit (while in Fig. 6, 8 is the maximum number of rows in matrix B.)

Although nothing can be said in general about the effect of such a rule, it can however be noted that both 9-bit columns and 8-bit columns are reduced successively to 6, 4, 3, and 2 bit in the succeeding matrices. The reduction of such columns from matrix A to matrix B requires less counters for 9 column than for 8. Moreover, although in the succeed-ing stages more counters are re-quired for a 9-row than for an 8-row B matrix, there is a net sav-

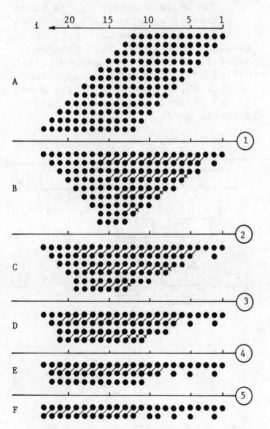

Fig. 7. Same as Fig. 6, With a Different Scheme, Using Fewer Counters

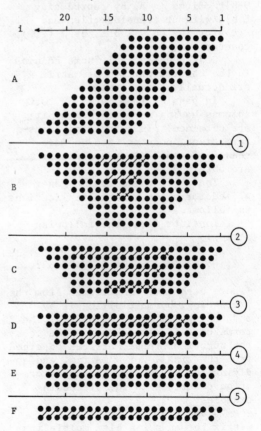

Fig. 8. Same as Fig. 7, With a Different Scheme, Using Fewer Counters

ing in the total number of counters.

(d) Another reduction scheme can finally be described, as the example in Fig. 8 shows. It requires the least number of component of all schemes considered: 110 counters (96 of (3,2) type; 14 of (2,2) type).

The rules applied in Fig. 8 can be described as follows. First, notice that in the original matrix A the middle column (12th) has 12 bit, and that proceeding from that columns to the right and to the left, columns have a decreasing number of bits.

In passing from matrix A to matrix B, columns are only partially reduced, so that no more than 9 rows are obtained. For example, column 10 (10 bit) is transformed in a 9-bit column in B, by reproducing 8 bit without transformation and transforming only 2 bit, by a (2,2) counter.

Consequently, only some columns in the central portion of matrix A are actually transformed.

In passing from matrix B to C, columns having no more than 6 bit are obtained. In succeeding transformations, columns with no more than 4, 3 and 2 bit respectively are obtained.

The above rules can be generalized for n x n bit multiplications as follows.

Consider first the following series:

2; 3; 6; 9; 13; 19; 28; 42; 63;...

(where each term is obtained from the preceeding, by multiplying it by 3/2 and taking the integral part). The terms of this series correspond to the number of those matrices obtained from the final, 2-row matrix, and applying the reverse of the transformation described in the preceeding examples.

Given then the original A matrix for an n x n bit multiplication, obtain through the first transformation a matrix B having a number of rows coinciding with the nearest term of the above series which is less than n.

All the following matrices will have a number of rows coincident with the terms of the series (in decreasing order of magnitude).

From the above examples it appears that the best rule is the last one described.

Although no proof is given here of the optimality of such rule, nevertheless all examples worked out for different values of n are in accordance with the results obtained for n = 12.

(e) It is interesting to compare the described schemes with the Wallace scheme. This can be considered as a parallel multiplier composed of (3,2) counters.

The Wallace multiplier is based on a tree of pseudo-adders, as shown in the block diagram of Fig. 9 (Wallace notation). Each pseudo-adder is effectively composed of a set of (3,2) counters, as appears in Fig. 10, where the notation used in the preceeding figures of this paper is used.

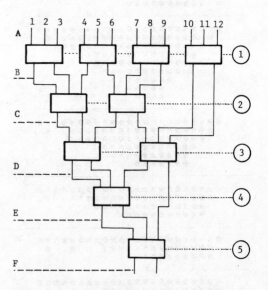

Fig. 9. Block Diagram for a Parallel (12 x 12) Multiplier Structure, According to Wallace

Fig. 10, concerning the case n = 12, requires a total of 136 counters (102 are (3,2), 34 are (2,2)), that is the same number of counters required in the Fig. 5 scheme. This coincidence is not valid in general. It can be shown that, for n > 12 the Wallace scheme requires less counters than the Fig. 5 scheme.

However, the schemes based on the rules illustrated in the preceeding paragraph d (see Fig. 8) requires less counters than Wallace's scheme.

For instance, for the case n = 24 one obtain:

Wallace scheme: 575 counters

Fig. 8 scheme: 506 counters

Fig. 5 scheme: 606 counters.

(f) The following remarks can be made about the described schemes. In all the examples (Fig. 5, 6, 7, 8) it can be seen that the bits in the least significant portion of the result are produced through a number of stages smaller than the total.

Examining, for instance, Fig. 5, it can be verified that:

the least significant bit (i=1) and the two bit in column i = 2 are produced without any stage.

the bit in column i = 3 is produced through the first stage;

the bit i = 4 is produced through the second stage; etc., etc.

This is very important if the speed of the circuit is considered, as each stage introduces a certain delay.

In fact, the above remark means that the least significant portion of the two final numbers is produced with a delay that increases progressively from the least significant bit (no delay) on.

Because the two final numbers must be added together, to obtain the product, in a carry-propagating adder, this means in turn that the carry propagation delay in the least significant half of the adder is overlapped by the progressively increasing delay through the multiplier structure. Whether the carry delay in the adder is greater than the multiplier delay or not, depends of course from the type of circuit used and also from the operands.

It can be seen also in the examples given (see e.g. Fig. 5) that the second final summand (second row in matrix F) has some zeros, regardless of the bits of the original operands. Such situation can be accounted for in the construction

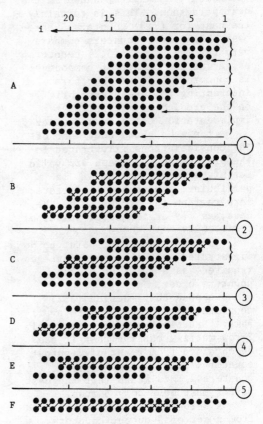

Fig. 10. The Wallace Scheme for a (12 x 12) Multiplier

of the adder, using half adders in
the stages corresponding to the
zeros of the second summand, thus
simplifying the adder.

4. THE USE OF HIGHER ORDER COUNTERS: (7,3) AND (15,4) COUNTERS

The (3,2) counter, i.e. the
full adder, is the commonest form
of implementation of the parallel
counters concept, and the use of
such counters in parallel multipliers has been discussed in the
preceeding point.

Higher order counters, i.e.
counters having a larger number of
inputs and outputs, although not
currently used, are nevertheless
entirely feasible with today's
technology, as will be shown in the
next paragraph. This is certainly
the case for (7,3) counters. Moreover, high order counters compare
very favorably with (3,2) counters
as far as the number of components
is concerned. It is therefore
interesting to investigate briefly
on the problem of multiplier's
implementation using such counters.

It can be shown that most of
the considerations illustrated in
the preceeding paragraph are valid
for higher order counters. In
particular, the scheme illustrated
in paragraph (d) proves to be the
best, as far as the total number of
counters is concerned.

The most important point to be
illustrated is the number of stages
required, as a function of the
counters order.

Suppose that, beside (3,2)
counters, (7,3) counters are available. Starting now from the final
2-row matrix, observe that it can
be obtained from a set of 2-output
counters, i.e. (2,2) or (3,2)
counters. This means that the next
matrix must have only 3 rows.

A 3-row matrix can be obtained
from a set of 3-output counters,
i.e. from counters having 7 inputs,
at most.

The next matrix must therefore
have 7 rows at most.

A 7 row matrix can be decom-
posed in two 3-row matrix and a 1-
row matrix. This means in turn that
it can be derived, through (7,3)
counters, from a matrix having 7 +
7 + 1 = 15 rows.

Proceeding with such rules, the
following series can be obtained:

$$2; \ 3; \ 7; \ 15; \ 35; \ 79; \ ...$$

that can be used as the series of the
preceeding paragraph (valid for (3,2)
counters).

For example, if a multiplier
is to be designed for numbers having 48 bit, it can be seen that 5
stages are required. The first
stage will obtain a 35-row matrix,
the second a 15-row matrix, etc.

If now we suppose that (15,4)
counters are available, beside (3,2)
and (7,3) counters, the following
series can be obtained, using rules
similar to those applied for the
preceeding case:

$$2; \ 3; \ 7; \ 21; \ 61; \ 226; \ ...$$

It can be seen therefore, that
for a 48 bit multiplier, 4 stages
will be required.

As was announced previously,
high order counters can afford an
important saving in components. For
example, if counters based on threshold devices are used (see next
paragraph), the total numbers of
transistors, required by the multiplier structure for 24 bit (ex-
cluding the carry propagating adder
and the network generating matrix A)
is as follows:

(3,2) counters:
    Wallace scheme: 1150 transistors
    scheme d):   1012 transistors
(7,3) counters:
    scheme d):   490 transistors

5. REMARKS ON PARALLEL COUNTERS

The schemes discussed in the
preceeding paragraphs are all based

on the use of parallel counters. It is therefore worthwhile to discuss briefly on their practical implementation.

Before describing some counters, let us discuss on some characteristics that prove useful in the peculiar application considered.

Among the different type of full adders, the most suitable for the application in parallel multipliers, from the point of view of economy and speed, are those which require input variables of one form only (natural or complemented), so that output variables of the same form only must be generated. If such condition is satisfied, outputs of one stage can be used directly as inputs to the next stages, without need of inverters, leading in general to a considerable saving in components and to a reduction of stage delay.

It must be noted that the above restriction can be partially released by allowing the use of counters producing outputs of only one form but different from the input's form "inverting counters." We will examine later some simple circuits, of this type.

The use of inverting counters does not modify substantially the described schemes. Consider the use of such counters in the scheme of Fig. 5 and suppose that all the bits of the final matrix F are to be obtained in true form. Assume then the preceeding matrix E to be in complemented form, the preceeding matrix D in true form, etc.; i.e., matrices are alternatively in true or complemented form. This situation can be obtained if when transforming from one matrix to the next, one use inverting counters or, when bits were simply to be reproduced, inverters.

All inverters can nevertheless be avoided, if single bits in the original matrix A are produced in a suitable form. Consider for example, columns 1 and 2; according to the

previous rule they should be in complemented form in matrix A; but they can be simply transferred from A to F is they are produced in A in true form. On the contrary, column 3 must be produced in A in complemented form, so that the single bit produced in matrix B (column 3) in true form, can be directly transferred to F, and so on.

It can thus be said that inverting counters can be used, provided that bits in the original matrix A are produced in a suitable form.

An interesting feature of all schemes of parallel multipliers is that each counter output is loaded by a single input of a counter in the next stage. This feature can be conveniently accounted for in the electrical design.

Some considerations will now be made on the implementation of parallel counters, with reference to some of the available logic circuitry and taking into account the above remarks.

(a) "And-or-Not" Logic. A full-adder, satisfying the above requirement, can be based on the following equations

$$R = AB + AC + BC$$

$$S = R(A + B + C) + ABC$$

where:

A,B,C, are input variables

R,S are the outputs.

A full adder of this type has been reported by Wallace[1]. It is an inverting counter, requiring 18 diodes and 3 transistors, and having a total delay of 60 ns.

It does not seem that the realization of counters of higher order, and satisfying the above requirement, has been investigated. Nevertheless it can be said that the number of components will increase

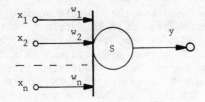

$$\ell = w_1 x_1 + w_2 x_2 + \ldots + w_n x_n$$

$\ell < S$	$\rightarrow$	$y = 1$	$y = 0$
$\ell \geq S$	$\rightarrow$	$y = 0$	$y = 1$
		$\underbrace{\qquad}_{\text{inverting}}$	$\underbrace{\qquad}_{\substack{\text{non}\\\text{inverting}}}$

Fig. 11. The Logical Definition of
Threshold Gates

rapidly along with n.

Similar conclusions can be accepted for "nor" (or "nand") logic, although cheaper circuits will be obtained.

(b) <u>Threshold Gates</u>. Counters using threshold gates can be the non-inverting type or of the inverting type according to the type of threshold gate used (see Fig. 11). An interesting scheme for inverting

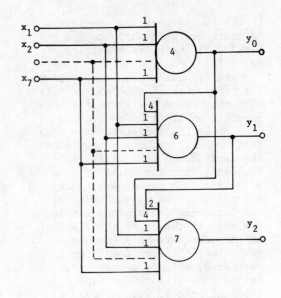

Fig. 13. A (7,3) Parallel Counter,
Using Inverting Threshold Gates

counters, is reported in Fig. 12 (for a (3,2) counter), and Fig. 13 (for (7,3) counter.)

A simple realization of an inverting (3,2) counter using resistor-transistor gates, is repre-

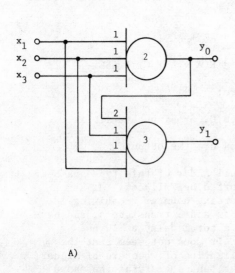

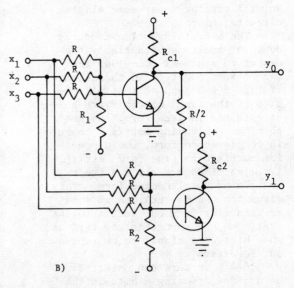

Fig. 12. A) (3,2) Parallel Counter, Using Inverting Threshold Gates
B) A Realization of an Inverting (3,2) Counter Using Resistor-
Transistor Threshold Circuits

sented in Fig. 12b.

It is probably the simplest circuit that can be devised for a full-adder, as it uses only 2 transistors (one for each output) and some resistors. Using available components, a delay of less than 100 ns can be obtained.

An investigation has been undertaken in our laboratory in order to explore the possibilities of threshold counters for parallel multipliers.

(c) <u>Current Switching</u>. Current switching circuits offer a means for implementing parallel counters. Current switching can be realized using transistors or criotrons. Transistor current switching circuits are the fastest logical circuits realizable with a given transistor type.[2]

Using available transistors, it should be possible to realize (3,2) counters having a delay of 10 - 20 ns. They are, however, less economical than all other circuits.

It should be noted that special circuits (i.e. not suitable for general purpose logic) could probably be devised in order to obtain fast and cheap counters. A similar situation is afforded by parallel adders, that can be realized using especially designed circuits (see reference 2).

6. CONCLUSIONS

Having established the possibility of a parallel digital multiplier, some considerations can now be made about the important aspects of speed and cost that can be encountered in a practical design.

It is worthwhile first to recall that if one assumes[1] that a third of all arithmetic operations in scientific computers are multiplications and that these at present take about four times as long as additions, the use of a fast multiplier allowing a multiplication in a memory cycle time, would approximately double the speed of computation.

There is therefore a chance that a parallel multiplier could become a convenient mean to improve the value of a computer, owing to the fact that its cost can be shown to be only a few percent of the total computer cost.

The following is an estimate about the type of multiplier circuits, based on actual memory cycle times.

Let us first note that the total multiplication time is composed of two parts: the first is the time elapsed from the application of the signals representing the two factors to the inputs of the multiplier, to the availability of the inputs to the carry-propagating adder; mainly consisting in the carry propagation delay.

In the design of a practical multiplier, one can assume as a goal to obtain a total delay equal or less that to the cycle time of the high-speed memory, so that the computer can work at its maximum speed, limited only by the memory speed. The choice of the type of circuits depends therefore from the memory cycle time.

If a core memory having a cycle of 4 μs or more is considered, threshold gates allow a very convenient solution. The fastest core memories have cycle time in the order of 1 μs. In this case, probably threshold gates could again be used, provided (3,2) counters having delays of the order of 50 ns are designed and carry propagating adders with less than 100 ns delay are employed.

In cases where fastest memories are considered (for instance, magnetic film memories, or tunnel diodes memories) having cycle times of 200 ns or less, fastest counters should be designed, for instance of the current switching type.

Although the problem is beyond the scope of this paper, it must also be noted that the realization of parallel multipliers should also influence computer organization. It is well known, indeed, that some important features of fast computers depend on the fact that during operations, that last longer than one memory cycle (typically, during multiplication or division), memory can be made available for other operations (e.g. input-output).

It appears therefore necessary to review the computer structure, as far as it depends from the duration of multiplications.

REFERENCES

1. C. S. Wallace, "A Suggestion for a Fast Multiplier," IEEE Trans. on Electronic Computers, Vol. EC-13, pp. 14-17, February, 1964.

2. D. H. Jarvis, L. P. Morgan, and J. A. Wearer, "Transistor Current Switching and Routing Techniques," IRE Trans. on Electronic Computers, Vol. EC-9, p. 302, September, 1960.

THE RESIDUE NUMBER SYSTEM

HARVEY L. GARNER

INTRODUCTION

In this paper we develop and investigate the properties of a novel system called the residue code or residue number system. The residue number system is of particular interest because the arithmetic operations of addition and multiplication may be executed in the same time as required for an addition operation. The main difficulty of the residue code relative to arithmetic operations is the determination of the relative magnitude of two numbers expressed in the residue code. The residue code is probably of little utility for general purpose computation, but the code has many characteristics which recommend its use for special purpose computations. The residue code is most easily developed in terms of linear congruences. A brief discussion of the pertinent properties of congruences is presented in the next section.

CONGRUENCES

The congruence relationship is expressed as

$$A \equiv \alpha \operatorname{Mod} b \qquad (1)$$

which is read, A is congruent to α Modulo b. The congruence states that the equation

$$A = \alpha + bt \qquad (2)$$

is valid for some value of t, where A, α, b and t are integers. α is called the residue and b the base or modulus of the number A.

As examples of congruences consider

$$10 \equiv 7 \operatorname{Mod} 3$$
$$10 \equiv 4 \operatorname{Mod} 3 \qquad (3)$$
$$10 \equiv 1 \operatorname{Mod} 3$$

In these examples the integers 7, 4, and 1 form a residue class of 10 Mod 3. Of particular importance is the least positive residue of the class which in this example is one. The least positive residue is that residue for which $0 \le \alpha < b$.

Consider the following set of congruences. Given

$$A_1 \equiv \alpha_1 \operatorname{Mod} b$$
$$\vdots$$
$$A_n \equiv \alpha_n \operatorname{Mod} b \qquad (4)$$

Then:
1. Congruences with respect to the same modulus may be added and the result is a valid congruence.

$$\sum_{i=1}^{n} A_i \equiv \left(\sum_{i=1}^{n} \alpha_i \right) \operatorname{Mod} b \qquad (5)$$

It follows that terms may be transferred from one side of a congruence to the other by a change of sign and also that congruences may be subtracted and the result is a valid congruence.
2. Congruences with respect to the same modulus may be multiplied and the result is a valid congruence.

Reprinted with permission from the IRE Transactions on Electronic Computers, Vol. EC-8, June 1959, pp. 140-147.

$$\prod_{i=1}^{n} A_i \equiv \left(\prod_{i=1}^{n} \alpha_i \right) \text{Mod } b \qquad (6)$$

It follows that both sides of the congruence may be raised to the same power or multiplied by a constant and the result is a valid congruence.

3. Congruences are transitive. If $A \equiv B$ and $B \equiv C$, then $A \equiv C$.

4. A valid congruence relationship is obtained if the number, the residue and the modulus are divided by a common factor.

5. A valid congruence relationship is obtained if the number and the residue are divided by some common factor relatively prime to the modulus.

The material of this section has presented briefly, without proof, the pertinent concepts of congruences. Additional material on the subject may be found in any standard text on number theory.[1]

DEVELOPMENT OF THE RESIDUE CODE

A residue code associated with a particular natural number is formed from the least positive residues of the particular number with respect to different bases. The first requirement for an efficient residue number system is that the bases of the difference digits of the representation must be relatively prime. If a pair of bases are not relatively prime, the effect is the introduction of redundancy. The following example will illustrate this fact. Contrast the residues associated with bases of magnitude 2 and 6 against the residues associated with bases of magnitude 3 and 4. In the first case, the bases are not relatively prime while in the second case the bases are relatively prime. The residues associated with the bases of magnitude 2 and 6 are unique for only 6 states while the residues associated with the bases of magnitude 3 and 4 provide a unique residue representation for 12 states. This is further clarified by Table 1.

Table 1.

Redundancy of a Nonrelatively-Primed Base Representation

Number	Least Positive Residue			
	Mod 2	Mod 6	Mod 3	Mod 4
0	0	0	0	0
1	1	1	1	1
2	0	2	2	2
3	1	3	0	3
4	0	4	1	0
5	1	5	2	1
6	0	0	0	2
7	1	1	1	3
8	0	2	2	0
9	1	3	0	1
10	0	4	1	2
11	1	5	2	3
12	0	0	0	0
13	1	1	1	1
14	0	2	2	2

An example of a residue number system is presented in Table 2. The number system shown in Table 2 uses the prime bases 2, 3, 5 and 7. The number system therefore contains 210 states. The 210 states may correspond to the positive integers 0 to 209. Table 2 shows the residue number representation corresponding to the positive integers 0 to 29. Additional integers

Table 2.

Natural Numbers and Corresponding Residue Numbers

N.N.	2357	N.N.	2357	N.N.	2357
0	0000	10	0103	20	0206
1	1111	11	1214	21	1010
2	0222	12	0025	22	0121
3	1033	13	1136	23	1232
4	0144	14	0240	24	0043
5	1205	15	1001	25	1104
6	0016	16	0112	26	0215
7	1120	17	1223	27	1026
8	0231	18	0034	28	0130
9	1042	19	1145	29	1241

of the number system may be found by congruence operations. Let a, b, c and d be the digits associated with the bases 2, 3, 5 and 7, respectively. The following congruences define a, b, c and d for the residue representation of the number N.

$$N \equiv a \bmod 2$$
$$N \equiv b \bmod 3$$
$$N \equiv c \bmod 5$$
$$N \equiv d \bmod 7 \qquad (7)$$

The residue number system is readily extended to include more states. For example, if a base 11 is added to the representation, it is then possible to represent 2310 states. **Table 3 shows the product and sum of** the first **nine** consecutive primes greater than or equal to 2. The product of the primes indicates the number of states of the number system, while the sum of the primes is a measure of the size of the representation in terms of digits. Table 3 also includes the number of bits required to represent each prime base in the binary number system.

Table 3.

Number of States and Digits Associated with a Residue Representation

i	p_i	$\sum_{i=1}^{n} p_i$	$\prod_{i=1}^{n} p_i$	p_i bits	$\sum p_i$ bits
1	2	2	2	1	1
2	3	5	6	2	3
3	5	10	30	3	6
4	7	17	210	3	9
5	11	28	2,310	4	13
6	13	41	30,030	4	17
7	17	58	510,510	5	22
8	19	77	9,699,690	5	27
9	23	100	223,092,670	5	32

RESIDUE ADDITION AND MULTIPLICATION

The residue number representation consists of several digits and is assumed to be in one to one correspondence with some positive integers of the real number system. The digits of the residue representation are the least positive residues of these real positive integers with respect to the different moduli which form the bases of the residue representation. It follows as a direct consequence of the structure of the residue number system and the properties of linear congruences that operations of addition and multiplication are valid in the residue number system subject to one proviso. The proviso is that the residue system must possess a number of states sufficient to represent the generated sum or product. If the residue number system does not have a sufficient number of states to represent the sums and the products generated by particular finite set of real integers then the residue system will overflow and more than one sum or product of the real number system may correspond to one residue representation. For a residue number with a sufficient number of states an isomorphic relation exists with respect to the operations of addition and multiplication in the residue system and a finite system of real positive integers.

Each digit of the residue number system is obtained with respect to a different base or modulus. It follows, therefore, that the rules of arithmetic associated with each digit will be different. For example, the addition and multiplication of the digits associated with moduli 2 and 3 follow rules specified in Table 4. No carry tables are necessary since the residue number system does not have a carry mechanism. Addition of two residue representations is effected by the modulo addition of corresponding digits of the two representations. Corresponding digits must have the same base or modulus. Modulo addition

Table 4.

Mod 2 and Mod 3 Sums and Products

$\oplus$	0	1
0	0	1
1	1	0

sum Mod 2

$\oplus$	0	1	2
0	0	1	2
1	1	2	0
2	2	0	1

sum Mod 3

$\odot$	0	1
0	0	0
1	0	1

product Mod 2

$\odot$	0	1	2
0	0	0	0
1	0	1	2
2	0	2	1

product Mod 3

of digits which have different bases is not defined. Multiplication in the residue system is effected by obtaining the modulo product of corresponding digits. The operations of addition and multiplication of two residue numbers are indicated by the following notation:

$$S = A \oplus B$$
$$p = A \odot B \tag{8}$$

Consider a residue number representation with bases 2, 3, 5 and 7. We assume an isomorphic relation between the residue number system and the real positive numbers 0 to 209. An isomorphic relation then exists for the operations of the multiplication and addition only if the product or sum is less than 210. The following examples employing residue numbers illustrate the addition and multiplication operations and the presence of an isomorphism or the lack of isomorphism in the case of overflow. Residue numbers will be distinguished by the use of parentheses.

$$29 + 27 = S = 56$$

$$29 \leftrightarrow (1\ 2\ 4\ 1)$$
$$27 \leftrightarrow (1\ 0\ 2\ 6)$$
$$56 \leftrightarrow (0\ 2\ 1\ 0)$$

$$\begin{array}{c}(1\ 2\ 4\ 1)\\ \oplus\\ \underline{(1\ 0\ 2\ 6)}\\ (0\ 2\ 1\ 0)\end{array} \tag{9}$$

The following operations are considered in performing the addition of the two residue representations.

$$1 + 1 \equiv 0 \text{ Mod } 2$$
$$2 + 0 \equiv 2 \text{ Mod } 3$$
$$4 + 2 \equiv 1 \text{ Mod } 5$$
$$1 + 6 \equiv 0 \text{ Mod } 7 \tag{10}$$

Consider the addition of two numbers which produce a sum greater than 209.

$$S = 100 + 200$$

$$\begin{array}{c}(0\ 1\ 0\ 2)\\ \oplus\\ \underline{(0\ 2\ 0\ 4)}\\ (0\ 0\ 0\ 6)\end{array} \tag{11}$$

The residue representation (0 0 0 6) corresponds to the real positive number 90. In this particular example, the sum has overflowed the residue representation. The resulting sum is the correct sum modulo 210.

$$300 \equiv 90 \text{ Modulo } 210$$

Finite real number systems and residue number systems have the same overflow characteristics. The sum which remains after the overflow is the correct sum with respect to a modulus numerically equal to the number of states in the finite number system.

The following is presented as an example of the process of residue multiplication.

$$p = 10 \times 17 = 170$$
$$10 \leftrightarrow (0\ 1\ 0\ 3)$$
$$17 \leftrightarrow (1\ 2\ 2\ 3)$$
$$170 \leftrightarrow (0\ 2\ 0\ 2)$$

(0 1 0 3)

$\odot$

(1 2 2 3)   (12)

(0 2 0 2)

The process of multiplication involved consideration of the following relations for each digit.

$1 \times 0 \equiv 0 \ \text{Mod} \ 2$

$1 \times 2 \equiv 2 \ \text{Mod} \ 3$

$0 \times 2 \equiv 0 \ \text{Mod} \ 5$

$3 \times 3 \equiv 2 \ \text{Mod} \ 7$ (13)

An overflow resulting from a multiplication is no different than the overflow resulting from an addition. Consider the product obtained from the residue multiplication of the numbers 10 and 100. The result in the modulo 210 number system is 160 since

$$1000 \equiv 160 \ \text{mod} \ 210$$ (14)

SUBTRACTION AND THE REPRESENTATION OF NEGATIVE NUMBERS

The process of subtraction is obtainable in the residue number system by employing a complement representation consisting of the additive inverses of the positive residue representation. The additive inverse always exists, since each of the elements of the residue representation is an element of a field. There is no basic problem associated with the subtraction operation. There is, however, a problem associated with the representation of negative numbers. In particular, some mechanism must be included in the number system which will permit the representation of positive and negative numbers. This problem is discussed in this and the following section.

The additive inverse of a residue number is defined by the following:

$$a \oplus a' = 0$$ (15)

The formula may be considered to apply to a digit of the residue system or equally well to the whole residue representation. Consider the following examples with reference to the modulo 210 residue number system.

$$a = (1 \ 2 \ 4 \ 1)$$ (16)

then

$$a' = (1 \ 1 \ 1 \ 6)$$

since

(1 2 4 1)

$\oplus$

(1 1 1 6)

(0 0 0 0)

The following examples have been chosen to illustrate the subtraction process and to some extent the difficulties associated with the sign of the difference.

$$D = A \ominus B = A \oplus B'$$ (17)

We consider first the case where the magnitude of A is greater than B.

Let

$A = 200 \qquad B = 100$

In residue representation

$$B' = (0 \ 2 \ 0 \ 5)$$ (18)

and

(0 2 0 4)

$\oplus$

(0 2 0 5).

(0 1 0 2)

The residue representation of the difference corresponds to positive 100 in the real number domain. We consider next the difference

$$D = B \ominus A = A' \oplus B \qquad (19)$$

where the magnitude of A is greater than B. Then

$$A' = (0\ 1\ 0\ 3) \qquad (20)$$

and

$$
\begin{array}{c}
(0\ 1\ 0\ 3) \\
\oplus \quad \underline{(0\ 1\ 0\ 2)} \\
(0\ 2\ 0\ 5)
\end{array}
$$

The difference (0 2 0 5) is the additive inverse of (0 1 0 2). Unless additional information is supplied, the correct interpretation of the representation (0 2 0 5) is in doubt. (0 2 0 5) may correspond to either +110 or –100.

The difficulties associated with whether a residue representation corresponds to a positive or negative integer can be partially removed by the division of the residue number range into two parts. This is exactly the scheme that is employed to obtain a machine representation of positive and negative natural numbers. For the system of natural numbers two different machine representations of the negative numbers may be obtained and are commonly designated the radix complement representation of negative numbers and the diminished radix complement representation of negative numbers.

The complement representation for a residue code is defined in terms of the additive inverse. Thus, the representation of negative A is A' where $A \oplus A' = 0$, and the range of A is restricted to approximately one-half of the total possible range of the residue representation. This can be illustrated by consideration of a specific residue code. This residue representation, employing bases of magnitude 2, 3, 5, and 7, is divided into two parts. The residue representations corresponding to the natural numbers 0 to 104 are considered positive. The residue repre-

sentations corresponding to the natural numbers 105 to 209 are considered inverse representations and associated with the negative integers from –1 to –105. The range of this particular number system is from –105 to +104. The arithmetic rules pertaining to sign and overflow conventions for this particular number system are the same rules normally associated with radix complement arithmetic.

The complement representation does eliminate in principle any ambiguity concerning the sign of the result of an arithmetic operation. However, there is a practical difficulty. The determination of the sign associated with a particular residue representation requires the establishment of the magnitude of the representation relative to the magnitude which separates the positive and negative representations. The determination of relative magnitude for a residue representation is discussed in the next section. It will be shown that the determination of relative magnitude is not a simple problem.

CONVERSION FROM A RESIDUE CODE TO A NORMAL NUMBER REPRESENTATION

It is frequently desirable to determine the natural number associated with a particular residue representation. The need for this conversion occurs frequently when investigating the properties of the residue system. The residue representation is constructed in such a manner that magnitude is not readily obtainable. The presence of digit weights in the normal polynomial type number representation greatly facilitates the determination of magnitude. However, it is possible to assign a weight to each digit of the residue representation in such a manner that the modulo m sum of the digit-weight products is the real natural number in a consistently weighted representation. m is the product of all the bases employed in the residue representation. The conversion technique is known as "The Chinese Remainder Theorem." The material which follows describes the conversion technique but omits the proof. A simple and straightforward proof is found in Dickson.[2] The proof does not refer specifically to residue number systems, but rather to a system of linear congruences. If so regarded, a system of congruences defines a component of a residue number system.

Consider a residue number system with bases $m_1 \ldots m_t$. The corresponding digits are labeled $a_1 \ldots a_t$. The following equations define the conversion process.

$$a_1 A_1 \frac{m}{m_1} + \ldots + a_t A_t \frac{m}{m_t} \equiv S \text{ Mod } m \tag{21}$$

where

$$A_i \frac{m}{m_i} \equiv 1 \text{ Mod } m_i$$

and

$$m = \prod_{j=1}^{t} m_j$$

The conversion formula for a particular residue number system is now obtained.

$$m_1 = 2 \qquad m_2 = 3 \qquad m_3 = 5 \qquad m_4 = 7$$

$$105 \, A_1 \equiv 1 \text{ Mod } 2 \quad \text{so } A_1 = 1$$

$$70 \, A_2 \equiv 1 \text{ Mod } 3 \quad \text{so } A_2 = 1$$

$$42 \, A_3 \equiv 1 \text{ Mod } 5$$

$$2 \, A_3 \equiv 1 \text{ Mod } 5 \quad \text{so } A_3 = 3$$

$$30 \, A_4 \equiv 1 \text{ Mod } 7$$

$$2 \, A_4 \equiv 1 \text{ Mod } 7 \quad \text{so } A_4 = 4$$

$$105 \, a_1 + 70 \, a_2 + 126 \, a_3 + 120 \, a_4$$
$$\equiv S \text{ Mod } 210 \tag{22}$$

The conversion formula is now used to determine the natural number corresponding to the residue representation (1 2 0 4).

$$105 \, (1) + 70 \, (2) + 126 \, (0) + 120 \, (4)$$
$$= 725$$

$$725 \equiv S \text{ Mod } 210$$

$$S = 95 \tag{23}$$

The above conversion formula may be obtained in a much more direct manner. The residue number representation may be regarded as a vector with the base vectors (1000), (0100), (0010) and (0001). The residue representation expressed in terms of the base vectors is:

$$(a_1 a_2 a_3 a_4) = a_1 (1000) \oplus a_2 (0100)$$
$$\oplus a_3 (0010) \oplus a_4 (0001) \tag{24}$$

The magnitude of the base vectors is

$$(1000) \leftrightarrow 105$$
$$(0100) \leftrightarrow 70$$
$$(0010) \leftrightarrow 126$$
$$(0001) \leftrightarrow 120 \tag{25}$$

Other conversion techniques exist. In particular it is possible by means of a deductive process to determine the magnitude of a particular residue representation. This requires both a knowledge of the nature of the residue system and the natural number representation associated with at least one residue representation.

Due to the deductive nature of the process, it is more suitable for human computation than for machine computation. The process is explained using the residue number of the previous example (1 2 0 4). The knowledge of the residue representation for unity which is (1 1 1 1) is assumed. Consider the effect of changing the second digit from one to two. The change adds the product $m_1 m_3 m_4 = 70$ to the number since 70 is congruent 1, modulo 3. The resulting residue representation (1 2 1 1) corresponds to 71. The effect of changing the third digit is to change the magnitude by some multiple of the product $m_1 m_2 m_4 = 42$. The correct change in magnitude is $42x$ where $42x \equiv 4$ Mod 5. So $42x = 84$ and the residue representation $(1\ 2\ 0\ 1)$ corresponds to 155. The fourth digit is modified by the addition of a three. The effect of this change is determined by $30x \equiv 3$ Mod 7. The magnitude change is 150. The sum of 150 and 155 modulo 210 yields the correct result 95, in correspondence with $(1\ 2\ 0\ 4)$.

Sign determination for the residue code is dependent on the determination of a greater than or less than relationship. A possible method might involve the conversion techniques described previously. Such a scheme would involve the standard comparison techniques associated with the determination of the relative magnitude of two numbers represented in a weighted representation. An alternate conversion procedure yields a conversion from the residue code to a non-consistently based polynomial number representation by means of residue arithmetic. Consider a residue code consisting of t digits. The t digits of the residue code are associated with t congruence relationships as follows:

$$S \equiv a_i \text{ Mod } m_i \quad 1 \le i \le t \quad (26)$$

S is the magnitude of the number expressed in normal representation. It is also possible to express the number S as

$$S = a_i + A_i m_i \quad (27)$$

A_i is the integer part of the quotient S divided by m_i. In regard to a greater or less than relationship, the determination of A_i divides the range of the residue representation into m/m_i parts. We proceed to calculate A_i from the set of t equations given above. Let

$$S = a_t + A_t m_t \quad A_t < \frac{m}{m_t} \quad (28)$$

This equation is then used to replace S in the remaining t - 1 equations,

yielding t - 1 equations of the form

$$A_t m_t \equiv (a_i + a_t') \text{ Mod } m_i \quad 1 \le i \le t - 1$$
$$\quad (29)$$

or

$$A_t \equiv (a_i + a_t')/m_t^i \text{ Mod } m_i$$

$$A_t \equiv d_t^i \text{ Mod } m_i$$

where $/m_t^i$ is the multiplicative inverse of m_t with respect to base m_i. The multiplicative inverse is defined as[*]

$$x_t/x_t^i \equiv 1 \text{ Mod } m_i \quad (30)$$

d_t^i is the least positive residue of $(a_i + a_t')/m_t$ with respect to base i. a_t' is the additive inverse of a_t. Let A_t be expressed as

$$A_t = d_t^{t-1} + A_{t-1} m_{t-1} \quad A_{t-1} < \frac{m}{m_t m_{t-1}}$$
$$\quad (31)$$

If this expression is substituted for A_t a set of t - 2 equations remain. The equations are of the form

$$A_{t-1} \equiv [d_t^i + (d_t^{t-1})']/m_{t-1} \text{ Mod } m_i$$
$$1 \le i \le t - 2$$

$$A_{t-1} \equiv d_{t-1}^i \text{ Mod } m_i \quad (32)$$

The system of equations shown below is generated by repetition of the above substitution process until no equations remain.

$$S = a_t + A_t m_t \quad (33)$$

$$A_t = d_t^{t-1} + A_{t-1} m_{t-1}$$

$$A_{t-1} = d_{t-1}^{t-2} + A_{t-2} m_{t-2}$$

$$\vdots$$

$$A_3 = d_3^2 + A_2 m_2$$

$$A_2 \equiv d_2^1 \text{ Mod } m_1 \quad (34)$$

---

[*]   The existence of the multiplicative inverse requires that x_t and m_i be relatively prime.

The equations are combined to yield:

$$S = a_t + m_t \{ d_t^{t-1} + m_{t-1}[d_{t-1}^{t-2}$$
$$+ m_{t-2}(d_{t-2}^{t-3} + \ldots \qquad (35)$$

$$= a_t + m_t d_t^{t-1} + m_t m_{t-1} d_{t-1}^{t-2}$$
$$+ m_t m_{t-1} m_{t-2} d_{t-2}^{t-3} + \ldots + \frac{m}{m_1} d_2^1 \quad (36)$$

where

$$A_t < m_t$$

$$d_{t-n}^{t-n-1} < m_{t-n-1}.$$

Therefore, S is never equal to or greater than m and d_2^1 divides the range into m_1 parts, d_3^2 divides each of the m_1 parts into m_2 parts, d_4^3 divides each of the m_2 parts into m_3 parts, etc.

The formulas which define the conversion process may be applied recursively to obtain a formula for a greater number of digits. The process has been extended to five variables and the results are shown in Fig. 1.

A somewhat simpler interpretation of the conversion process is obtained if (36) is considered from the vector viewpoint. Let the terms 1, m_t, $m_t m_{t-1}$, $\ldots$, m/m_1 be regarded as base vectors. The residue representation of the base vectors is readily obtainable and the following characteristics with respect to zero and nonzero digits of the base vectors are observed

$$1 \leftrightarrow (xxx \cdots xxx)$$
$$m_t \leftrightarrow (xxx \cdots xx0)$$
$$m_t m_{t-1} \leftrightarrow (xxx \cdots x00) \quad \text{x indicates a}$$
$$\vdots \qquad\qquad\qquad\qquad\quad \text{nonzero digit}$$
$$\qquad\qquad\qquad\qquad\qquad \text{0 indicates a}$$
$$\frac{m}{m_1} \leftrightarrow (x00 \ldots 000) \quad \text{zero digit}$$

$$(37)$$

The following equality exists between the vector representation of the residue code and the vector representation of the nonconsistently based code.

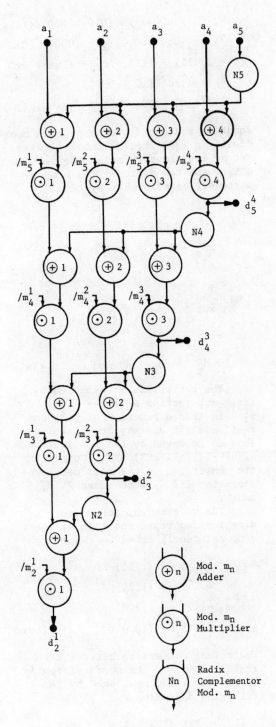

Fig. 1. Logic Required to Convert from the Residue Code to a Weighted Code

$$a_1(101\cdots000) \oplus a_2(010\cdots000) \oplus \cdots$$
$$\oplus\, a_{t-1}(000\cdots010) \oplus a_t(000\cdots001)$$
$$= a_t(111\cdots111) \oplus d_t^{t-1}(1xx\cdots xx0)$$
$$\oplus \cdots \oplus d_3^2(1x0\cdots000)$$
$$\oplus\, d_2^1(100\cdots000) \tag{38}$$

Equating the coefficients of each coordinate in (38) obtains the following set of equations relating the residue digits and the digit of the nonconsistently based number system.

$$a_t \equiv a_t \bmod m_t$$
$$xd_t^{t-1} + a_t \equiv a_{t-1} \bmod m_{t-1}$$
$$\vdots$$
$$xd_3^2 + \cdots$$
$$+\, xd_t^{t-1} + a_t \equiv a_2 \bmod m_2$$
$$d_2^1 + d_3^2 + \cdots$$
$$+\, d_t^{t-1} + a_t \equiv a_1 \bmod m_1 \tag{39}$$

The conversion is executed by first subtracting $a_t(111\cdots111)$; d_t^{t-1} is then a function of only one residue digit and may be determined. This is followed by the subtraction of $d_t^{t-1}(1xx\cdots xx0)$ etc. Consider the conversion of the residue representation (1204) with bases 2, 3, 5 and 7.

The weights and the corresponding residue representation of the nonconsistently based code are:

$$1 \leftrightarrow (1111)$$
$$m_4 = 7 \leftrightarrow (1120)$$
$$m_4 m_3 = 35 \leftrightarrow (1200)$$
$$m_4 m_3 m_2 = 105 \leftrightarrow (1000) \tag{40}$$

The actual conversion between the residue code and the nonconsistently based code is accomplished by the following operation:

```
 (120₄) 1st digit is a 4 since
⊕          4·1 ≡ 4 mod 7
 (0213) Subtract off 4(1111) = (0144)
```

```
    11₄0  2nd digit is a 3 since
⊕             3·2 ≡ 1 mod 5
    104   Subtract off 3(1120) = (1010)
```

```
    0₁00  3rd digit is a 2 since
⊕             2·2 ≡ 1 mod 3
    02    Subtract off 2(1200) = (0100)
```

```
    00    4th digit is 0.
```

Thus

$$S = 105\cdot0 + 35\cdot2 + 7\cdot3 + 1\cdot4$$
$$= 95 \tag{41}$$

Admittedly, the process required to obtain a magnitude leaves much to be desired though the conversion process is no more complicated than the standard change of base conversion process used for consistently based number systems. One presumed advantage of the residue number system was the absence of a carry process. The greater or less than process is essentially sequential and is in many ways similar to the carry process of ordinary arithmetic. The ultimate usefulness of the residue code for general purpose computation appears very much dependent on the development of simple techniques for the determination of the relative magnitude of two residue code digits.

DIVISION

The division process for residue codes is complicated by two factors. The first is the absence of a multiplicative inverse for the zero element. The second difficulty is the fact that residue division and the normal division process are in one to one correspondence only when the resulting quotient is an integer value. We shall consider first the problem of residue division of the elements of a single field and shall consider later the elements of several fields considered as a residue code. The division process represented in equation form as

$$\frac{a}{b} = q \tag{42}$$

implies the following equation:

$$a = bq \qquad (43)$$

The difference between normal arithmetic and residue arithmetic is that in residue arithmetic the product bq need not necessarily be equal to a, only the congruence of a and bq is required.

$$bq \equiv a \bmod m_n \qquad (44)$$

Multiplication by the multiplicative inverse of b designated $/b$ obtains

$$q \equiv a/b \bmod m_n \qquad (45)$$

The correct interpretation of q in the above equation is that the number a is obtained by forming the modulo sum consisting of b, q representations. The sum is carried out in a closed and finite modulo number system of base m_n. Thus, q corresponds to the quotient only when the quotient has an integer value. Examples may be obtained from the consideration of a modulo 5 number system

$$\frac{4}{2} = q \qquad (46)$$

$$2q \equiv 4 \bmod 5$$

$$q \equiv 2 \bmod 5$$

$$\frac{4}{3} = q \qquad (47)$$

$$3q \equiv 4 \bmod 5$$

$$q \equiv 3 \bmod 5$$

note $3 \times 3 \equiv 4 \bmod 5$

$$\frac{3}{4} = q \qquad (48)$$

$$4q \equiv 3 \bmod 5$$

$$q \equiv 2 \bmod 5.$$

In the above examples, q corresponds to the quotient only in the first example.

The residue code representation of a number consists of many digits, $A = (a_1, a_2, \cdots, a_n)$. Each digit of the representation is associated with a different prime base. The number system is a modulo m system where

$$m = \prod_{i=1}^{n} m_i$$

The division of two numbers in residue code may be expressed by a system of congruences. The solution $Q = (q_1, q_2, \cdots, q_n)$ must satisfy all the congruence relationships of the system. A zero digit in the divisor $B = (b_1, b_2, \cdots, b_n)$ means that B and m are not relatively prime hence the multiplicative inverse of B doesn't exist.

$$QB \not\equiv A \bmod m \qquad (49)$$

For the special case in which $b_i = 0$ and $a_i = 0$, a valid congruence relationship of the form

$$\frac{QB}{m_i} \equiv \frac{A}{m_i} \bmod \frac{m}{m_i} \qquad (50)$$

is obtainable.

The process of residue division has certain interesting properties and quite possibly has applications in respect to special problems. Unfortunately, the residue division process is not a substitute for normal division. It appears that the only way in which division can be effected in the residue code is by the utilization of techniques similar to those employed for division in a consistently weighted number system. The division process then requires trial and error subtraction or addition and the greater than or less than relationship. The division algorithm could also include trial multiplication since in the residue system addition and multiplication require the same period of time.

CONCLUSIONS

The material of this paper forms a preliminary investigation of the applicability of residue number systems to the arithmetic operations of digital computers. The residue system has been found attractive in terms of the operations of multiplication and addition. It is possible to realize practical logical circuitry to yield the product in the same operation time as for the sum since the product is not obtained by the usual procedure of repetitive addition. The main disadvantages of the residue number system are associated with the necessity of determining absolute magnitude. Thus, the division process, the detection of an overflow and the determination of the correct sign of a subtraction operation are processes which at this state of the investigation seem to involve considerable complexity. Nevertheless, there are certainly many special purpose applications well-suited to the residue code. In particular, there exists a class of control problems characterized by the absence of the need for division, the existence of a well-defined range for the variables and also by the fact that the sign of the variables is known. For the problems of this class, the use of the residue code should result in a reduction of the over-all computation period and give a computer with a higher bandwidth than obtainable with the conventional number system.

The ultimate usefulness of the residue code will probably be determined largely by the success of the circuit designer in perfecting circuitry ideally suited for residue code operations.

ACKNOWLEDGMENT

The material of this paper is essentially Chapter 5 of the author's Ph.D. dissertation[3]. At the time of the completion of the dissertation, the author was unaware of the work of Valach[4] and Svoboda[5,6] in Czechoslovakia, references of which were obtained from recent visitors to the Soviet Union. The author wishes to take this opportunity to acknowledge same.

REFERENCES

1. G. H. Hardy and E. M. Wright, An Introduction to the Theory of Numbers, Oxford University Press, London, England, 1956.
2. L. E. Dickson, Modern Elementary Theory of Numbers, University of Chicago Press, Chicago, Ill., 1939, p. 16.
3. H. L. Garner, "Error Checking and the Structure of Binary Addition," Ph.D. Dissertation, University of Michigan, Ann Arbor, Mich., 1958, pp. 105-140.
4. M. Valach, "Vznik Kodu a Ciselne Soustavy Zbykovych Trid," Stroje Na Zpracovany Informaci, Sbornik 3, 1955.
5. A. Svoboda and M. Valach, "Operatorove Obvody," Stroje Na Zpracovany Informaci, Sbornik 3, 1955.
6. A. Svoboda, "Rational Numerical System of Residual Classes," Stroje Na Zpracovany Informaci, Sbornik 5, 1957.

THE IBM SYSTEM/360 MODEL 91:
FLOATING-POINT EXECUTION UNIT

S. F. ANDERSON, J. G. EARLE, R. E. GOLDSCHMIDT,
AND D. M. POWERS

INTRODUCTION

The instruction unit of the IBM
System/360 Model 91 is designed
to issue instructions at a burst
rate of one instruction per cycle,
and the performance of floating-
point execution must support this
rate. However, conventional execution unit designs cannot support
this level of performance. The
Model 91 Floating-Point Execution
Unit departs from convention and
is instruction-oriented to provide
fast, concurrent instruction execution.

The objectives of this paper
are to describe the floating-point
execution unit. Particular attention is given to the design of
the instruction-oriented units
to reveal the techniques which
were employed to match the burst
instruction rate of one instruction per cycle. These objectives
can best be accomplished by dividing the paper into four sections-
General design considerations,
Floating-point terminology, Floating-point add unit, and Floating-
point multiply/divide unit.

The first section explains how
the desire for concurrent execution
of instructions has led to the design of multiple execution units
linked together by the floating-point
instruction unit. Then the concept

of instruction-oriented units is
discussed, and its impact on the
multiplicity of units is pointed
out. It is shown that, with the
instruction-oriented units as
building blocks and the floating-
point instruction unit as the
"cement", an execution unit
evolves which rises to the desired
performance level.

The section on floating-point
terminology briefly reviews the
System/360 data formats and floating-point definitions.

The next two sections describe
the design of the instruction-
oriented units. The first of these
is the floating-point add unit
description which is divided into
two sub-sections, Algorithm and
Implementation. In the algorithm
sub-section, the complete algorithm
for execution of a floating add/
subtract is considered with emphasis
on the difficulties inherent in the
implementation. Since the add unit
is instruction-oriented, (i.e., only
add-type instructions must be considered), it is possible to overcome the inherent difficulties by
merging the several steps of the
algorithm into three hardware areas.
The implementation section describes
these three areas, namely, characteristic comparison and pre-
shifting, fraction adder, and
postnormalization.

The last section describes the
floating-point multiply/divide unit.
This section describes the multiply
algorithm and its implementation
first, and then the divide algorithm
and its implementation. The emphasis

of the multiply algorithm sub-section is on recoding the multiplier and the usefulness of carry-save adders. In the implementation sub-section the emphasis is on the iterative hardware which is the heart of the multiply operation. An arrangement of carry-save adders is shown which, when pipelined by adding temporary storage platforms, has an iteration repetition rate of 50 Mc/sec. The divide algorithm is described next with emphasis on using multiplication, instead of subtraction, as the iterative operator. The discussion of divide implementation shows how the existing multiply hardware, plus a small amount of additional circuitry, is used to perform the divide operation.

GENERAL DESIGN CONSIDERATIONS

The programs considered "typical" by the users of high performance computers are floating-point oriented. Therefore, the prime concern in designing the floating-point execution unit is to develop an overall organization which will match the performance of the instruction unit. However, the execution time of floating-point instructions is slow compared with the issuing rate of these instructions by the instruction unit. The most obvious approach is to apply a faster technology and with special design techniques reduce the execution time for floating-point. But a study of many "typical" floating point programs revealed that the execution time per instruction would have to be 1 to 2 cycles in order to match the performance[3] of the instruction unit.* Conventional execution unit design, even with state-of-the-art algorithms, will not provide these execution times.

Another approach considered

was to provide execution concurrency among instructions; this obviously would require two complete floating-point execution units.† An attendant requirement would be a floating-point instruction unit. This unit is necessary to sequence the operands from storage to the proper execution unit; it must buffer the instructions and assign each instruction to a non-busy execution unit. Also, since the execution time is not the same for all instructions the possibility now exists for out-of-sequence execution, and the floating-point instruction must insure that executing out of sequence does not produce incorrect results.§ The organization for an execution unit capable of concurrent execution is shown in Fig. 1. Buffering and sequence control of all instructions, storage operands, and floating-point accumulators are the responsibility of the floating-point execution unit. Each of the execution units is capable of executing all floating-point instructions.

One might be led to believe that this organization is a suitable solution in itself. If multiply can be executed in seven cycles and two multiplies are executed simultaneously, then the effective execution time is 3.5 cycles. Similarly, for add the execution time would go from three cycles to 1.5 cycles. However, the operating delay of the floating-point instruction unit must be considered, and it is not always possible to execute concurrently because of the

---

* Even though the burst rate of the instruction unit is one instruction per cycle, it is not necessary to execute at the same rate.

† Since two complete execution units are necessary for concurrent execution, the cost-performance factor is important. Analysis showed that execution times of three cycles for add and seven cycles for multiply were reasonable expectations.
§ Dependence among instructions must be controlled. If instruction n + 1 is dependent on the result of instruction n, instruction n + 1 must not be allowed to start until instruction n is completed.

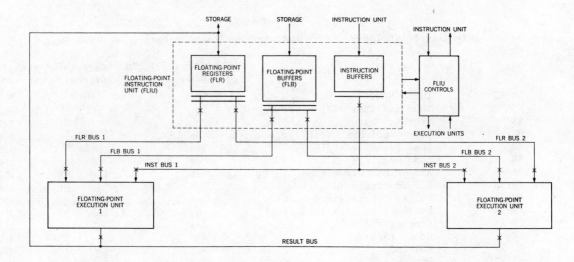

Fig. 1. Floating-point execution unit capable of concurrent execution.

dependence among instructions. When these problems are considered the effective execution time is close to three cycles per instruction, which is not sufficient. A third execution unit would not help because the complexity of the floating-point instruction unit increases, and the amount of hardware becomes prohibitive.

The next solution to be considered was to improve the execution time of each instruction by employing faster algorithms in the design of each execution unit. Obviously this would increase the hardware, but since the circuit delay is a function not only of the circuit speed but also of the number of loads on the input net and the length of the interconnection wiring, more hardware may not make the unit faster.[5] These two factors-the desire for faster execution of each instruction and the size sensitivity of the circuit delay, have produced a concept which is unique to the organization of floating-point execution units, and which was adopted for the Model 91: the concept of using separate execution units for different instruction types. Faster execution of each instruction can be achieved if the conventional execution unit is separated into arithmetic units designed to execute a subset of the floating-

point instructions instead of the entire set. This conclusion may not be obvious, but a unit designed exclusively for a class of similar instructions can execute those instructions faster than a unit designed to accommodate all floating-point instructions. The control sequences are shorter and less complex; the data flow path has fewer logic levels and requires less hardware because the designer has more freedom in combining serial operations to eliminate circuit levels; the circuit delay per level is faster because less hardware is required in the smaller, automomous units. To implement the concept in the Model 91, the floating-point instruction set was separated into two subsets: add and multiply/divide. Table 1 shows a list of the instructions and identifies the unit in which each instruction is executed. With this separation, an add unit which executed all add class instructions in two cycles, and a multiply/divide unit which executed multiply in six cycles and divide in eighteen cycles, were designed.

The use of this concept somewhat changes the character of concurrent execution. It is possible to have concurrent execution with one execution unit - i.e., two arithmetic units, add and multiply/divide.

Table 1.

Floating-Point Instructions Executed by Floating-Point Execution Unit

Type	Instruction	Condition code	Floating-point Arithmetic exceptions*	unit
RR-RX	Load (S/L)	No		FLIU
RR	Load and Test (S/L)	Yes		FLIU
RX	Store (S/L)	No		FLIU
RR	Load Complement (S/L)	Yes		ADD
RR	Load Positive (S/L)	Yes		ADD
RR	Load Negative (S/L)	Yes		ADD
RR-RX	Add Normalized (S/L)	Yes	U, E, LS	ADD
RR-RX	Add Unnormalized (S/L)	Yes	E, LS	ADD
RR-RX	Subtract Normalized (S/L)	Yes	U, E, LS	ADD
RR-RX	Subtract Unnormalized (S/L)	Yes	E, LS	ADD
RR-RX	Compare (S/L)	Yes		ADD
RR	Halve (S/L)	No		ADD
RR-RX	Multiply	No	U, E	M/D
RR-RX	Divide	No	U, E, FK	M/D

*Exceptions: U — Exponent-underflow exception
E — Exponent-overflow exception
LS — Significance exception
FK — Floating point divide exception

The performance is not quite as good as that attainable using two execution units, but less hardware is required for the implementation. Therefore, more arithmetic units can be added to improve the performance. First, two add units and two multiply/divide units were considered. But the floating-point instruction unit can assign only one instruction per cycle. Therefore, since an add operation is two cycles long, two add units could be replaced by one add unit if a new add class instruction could be started every cycle. This would introduce still another example of concurrent execution: concurrent execution within an arithmetic unit.

Such concurrency within a unit is facilitated by the technique of pipelining. If a section of combinatorial logic, such as the logic to execute an add, could be designed with equal delay in all parallel paths through the logic, the rate at which new inputs could enter this section of logic would be independent of the total delay through the logic. However, delay is never equal; skew is always present and the interval between input signals must be greater than the total skew of the logic section. But temporary storage platforms can be inserted which will separate the section of combinatorial logic into smaller synchronous stages. Now the total skew has been divided into smaller pieces; only the skew between stages has to be considered. The interval between inputs has decreased and now depends on the skew between temporary storage platforms. Essentially the temporary storage platform is used to separate one complete job, such as an add, into several pieces; then several jobs can be executed simultaneously. Thus, inputs can be applied at a predetermined rate and once the pipeline is full the outputs will match this rate.

The technique of pipelining does have practical limits, and these limits differ for each application. In general the rate at which new inputs can be applied is limited by the logic preceding the pipeline (e.g., add is limited to one instruction per cycle by the floating-point instruction unit) or by the rate at which outputs can be accepted. Also, both the rate of new inputs and the length of the pipeline are limited by dependencies among stages of the pipeline or between the output and successive inputs (e.g., the output of one add can become an input for the next).

The add unit requires two cycles for execution and is limited to one new input per cycle. Thus pipelining allows two instructions to be in execution concurrently, thereby increasing the efficiency with a small increase in hardware.

Further study of pipelining techniques would indicate that a three-cycle multiply and a twelve-cycle divide are possible. Here the technique of pipelining is used to speed up the iterative section of the multiply which is critical to multiply/divide execution. (This is discussed in detail in the section on the multiply/divide unit).

The execution unit would consist at this point of a floating-point instruction unit, an add unit which could start an instruction every cycle, and a multiply/divide unit which would execute multiply in three cycles and divide in twelve cycles. However the performance still would not match the instruction unit. The execution time would be adequate but the units would spend considerable time waiting for operands. Therefore, instead of duplicating the arithmetic unit (which is expensive) extra input buffer registers have been added to collect the operands and necessary instruction control information. When both operands are available, the control information is processed and a request made to use an arithmetic unit. These registers are referred to as "reservation stations". They can be and are treated as independent units.

The final organization is shown in Fig. 2. It consists of three parts: the floating-point instruction unit; the floating-point

add unit; and the floating-point multiply/divide unit. Another paper in this series[3] explains the floating-point instruction unit in detail. The problems involved and both the considered solutions and the implemented solutions are discussed. The floating-point add unit has three reservation stations and, as stated above, is treated as three separate add units, A1, A2 and A3. The floating-point multiply/divide unit has two reservation stations, M/D1 and M/D2. The last two sections of this paper describe the design of these two units in detail.

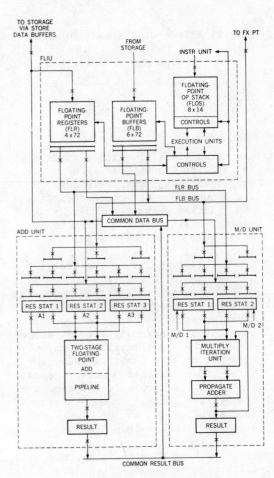

Fig. 2. Overall Organization of Floating-Point Unit

FLOATING-POINT TERMINOLOGY

The reader is assumed to be familiar
with System/360 architecture and
terminology.[2] However, the floating-
point data format and terminology
will be briefly reviewed here.

Floating-point data occupy a
fixed-length format, which may be
either a full-word short format or
a double-word format:

SHORT FLOATING-POINT BINARY FORMAT

Sign Characteristic

0 1 -- -- -- -- -- 7

Fraction

8 -- -- -- -- 31

LONG FLOATING-POINT BINARY FORMAT

Sign Characteristic

0 1 -- -- -- -- -- 7

Fraction

8 -- -- -- -- 63

The first bit(s) in either format
is (are the sign bit(s). The
subsequent seven bit positions
are occupied by the characteristic.
The fraction consists of six hexadecimal digits for the short format
or 14 hexadecimal digits for the
long.

The radix point of the fraction is
assumed to be immediately to the left
of the high-order fraction digit. To
provide the proper magnitude for the
floating-point number, the fraction is
considered to be multiplied by a power
of 16. The characteristic portion,
bits 1-7 of both floating-point formats, indicates this power. The characteristic is treated as an excess 64
number with a range from -64 through
+63 corresponding to the binary expression of the values 0-127.

Both positive and negative quantities have a true fraction, the
difference in sign being indicated
by the sign bit. The number is
positive or negative accordingly
as the sign bit is zero or one.

A normalized floating-point
number has a non-zero high-order
hexadecimal fraction digit. To
preserve maximum precision in subsequent operation, addition, subtraction, multiplication, and division are performed with normalized
results. (Addition and subtraction
may also be programmed to be performed with unnormalized results.
The operands for any floating-point
operation can be either normalized
or unnormalized).

FLOATING-POINT ADD UNIT

The challenge in the design of the
add unit was to minimize the number
of logical levels in the longest
delay path. However, the sequence
of operations necessary for the
execution of a floating-point add
impedes the design goal. Consider
the following operations:

a. Since the radix point must be
    aligned before an add can pro-
    ceed, the characteristics of
    the two operands must be com-
    pared and the difference be-
    tween them established.
b. This difference must be decoded
    into the shift amount, and the
    fraction with the smaller char-
    acteristic shifted right a
    sufficient number of positions
    to make the characteristics
    equal.
c. Since subtraction is to be
    performed by forming the two's
    complement of one of the frac-
    tions and then adding the two
    fractions in the fraction adder,
    one of the fractions must pass
    through true/complement logic.
d. The two operand fractions are
    added in a parallel adder. The
    carries must propagate from the
    low order end to the high order
    end.
e. Because of subtraction, the out-
    put must provide for both the

true sum and the complement
sum, depending on the high-
order carry.

f. If the system architecture
calls for left justification
or normalized operation, the
result out of the adder must
be checked for high-order
zeros and shifted left to
remove these zeros.

g. The characteristic must be
reduced by the amount of left
shift necessary to normalize
the resultant fraction.

h. The resultant operand must be
stored in the proper accumulator.

The above sequence of operations
implies a series of sequential execution stages, each of which is dependent on the output of the previous
stage. The problem then, is to arrange,
change and merge these operations to
provide fast, efficient execution for
a floating-point add.

None of the steps can be eliminated.
Each step is required in order to execute add; but the steps can be merged
so that the interface between them is

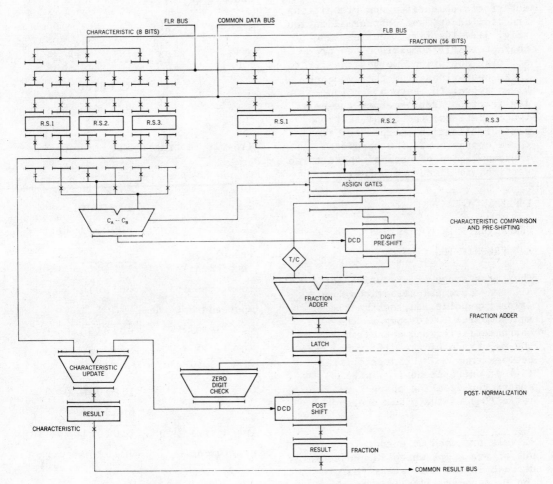

Fig. 3. Floating-Point Add Data Flow

eliminated,* and each step can be changed to provide only the necessary information to the next stage. For example, the long data format consists of 14 hexadecimal digits; therefore any difference between the two characteristics which is greater than 14 will result in an all zero fraction. This means that the characteristic difference adder need not generate a sum for the high-order three bits. Instead, if the difference is greater than 14, a shift of 15 is forced. As a result, the characteristic difference adder is faster and less expensive.

The add unit algorithm is separated into three parts: characteristic comparison and preshifting, fraction adder, and postnormalization (Fig. 3). The first section, the characteristic comparison and pre-shifting operation, merges the first three operations from the sequence given above; the second section— the fraction adder—merges the next two operations; the final section— postnormalization—merges the final three operations. The hardware implementation of each of these three sections is discussed below.

IMPLEMENTATION —

CHARACTERISTIC COMPARISON

AND PRESHIFTING

The first stage of execution for all two-operand instructions (floating-point add, subtract, and compare) is to compare the characteristics and establish the magnitude of the difference between them. The characteristic (C_B) of one operand is always subtracted from the characteristic (C_A) of the other operand

---

*Levels are used to encode the output of one step, which is subsequently decoded in the next step. Merging the two steps will eliminate these levels.

$(C_A - C_B)$. Characteristic B is always complemented as it is gated in at the reservation station.

If the output of the characteristic difference adder is the true sum or the complement of the true sum, the output can be decoded directly at the preshifter. But the adder always subtracts C_B from C_A and if $C_B > C_A$ the sum would be negative. Therefore, to eliminate the possibility of having to add a 1 in the low order position and complement when C_B is greater than C_A, an "end-around-carry" adder is used. This is shown by the example in Fig. 4.

$C_a > C_b$ $C_a = 1111100$ $C_b = 1101000$

$$1111100 \quad C_a$$
$$0010111 \quad \overline{C_b}$$
$$ 1 \text{ hot one}$$

(result is true) 1 $\overline{1101111}$ $C_a - C_b$

- - - - - - - - - - - - - - - -

$C_a < C_b$ $C_a = 1101000$ $C_b = 1111100$

$$1101000 \quad C_a$$
$$0000011 \quad \overline{C_b}$$
$$ 1 \text{ hot one}$$

(result is complement)   0 $\overline{1101100}$

comp. result   0010011

must add hot one   1

$$\overline{0010100} \quad C_a - C_b$$

- - - - - - - - - - - - - - - -

$C_a < C_b$ (end-around carry)

$$1101000 \quad C_a$$
$$0000011 \quad \overline{C_b}$$

(no carry)   0 $\overline{1101011}$

complement   0010100   correct result

Fig. 4. Examples of Exponent Arithmetic

The characteristic comparison can result in two states – $C_A \geq C_B$ or $C_B > C_A$. If $C_A \geq C_B$, there is a carry out of the high order position of the characteristic difference adder, and the carry is used to gate the fraction of operand B to the preshifter. The true sum output of the characteristic difference adder is the amount that the fraction must be shifted right to make the characteristics equal. If $C_B > C_A$, there is no carry out of the high order position of the characteristic difference adder, and the absence of a carry is used to gate the fraction of operand A to the preshifter. In this case the complement of the sum output of the characteristic difference adder is the amount that the fraction must be shifted right to make the characteristics equal. In both cases the second operand fraction (the one with the larger characteristic) is gated to the true-complement input of the fraction adder.

The characteristic of the unshifted fraction becomes the resultant characteristic. It is gated to the characteristic-update adder, and after updating, if necessary, it is gated to the accumulator specified by the instruction.

The output of the characteristic difference adder is decoded by the preshifter and the proper fraction shifted right the necessary number of positions. The preshifter is a parallel digit-shifter which shifts each of the 14 digits right any amount from zero to fifteen. The decode of the shift amount is designed into each level, thereby eliminating serial logic levels for decoding.

The preshifter consists of two circuit levels. The first level shifts a digit right by 0, 1, 2, or 3 digit positions. The second level shifts a digit right by 0, 4, 8, or 12 digit positions. Thus, by the proper combination of these amounts any right digit shift between and including 0 and 15 can be executed. Figure 5 shows an example of the preshifter.

The unshifted fraction is gated to the true/complement gates of the adder. Here the fraction is gated unchanged if the effective operation is ADD and complemented if the effective operation is SUBTRACT. The true/complement gating is overlapped with the preshifter on a time basis. The output of both the true/complement logic and the preshifter are the inputs to the fraction adder.

FRACTION ADDER

Most of the time required for binary adders is carry propagation time. Two operands must be combined and the carries allowed to ripple from right (low order) to left (high order). The usual method of finding the sum is to combine the half sum* of bit n (higher order) with the carry from bit $n - 1$ ($S_n = A_n \; \forall \; B_n \; \forall \; C_n$).[†]

The carry (C_n) into bit position n is also a three term expression which includes the carry into bit position $n - 1$

$$(C_n = A_{n-1} \cdot B_{n-1} \vee A_{n-1} \cdot C_{n-1} \vee B_{n-1} \cdot C_{n-1})$$

If the carry term is rearranged to read

$$C_n = A_{n-1} \cdot B_{n-1} \vee (A_{n-1} \vee B_{n-1}) C_{n-1},$$

---

*The half sum is the exclusive or of the two input bits, $(A_n \; \forall \; B_n)$.
†The two operand fractions are designated as A,B and the bits as $A_n, B_n, A_{n-1}, B_{n-1}$, etc. C_n is the carry into bit position n, which is the carry out from bit $n - 1$.

two new terms can be defined which separate the carry into two parts—generated carry, and propagated carry. The generated carry (G_{n-1}) is defined as $A_{n-1} \cdot B_{n-1}$, and the carry propagate function (often abbreviated to simply propagate or P_{n-1}) is defined as $A_{n-1} \vee B_{n-1}$. Now the carry expression can be rewritten as:

$$C_n = G_{n-1} \vee P_{n-1} C_{n-1}$$

$$C_n = G_{n-1} \vee P_{n-1} G_{n-1} \vee P_{n-1} P_{n-2} C_{n-2}$$

$$C_n = G_{n-1} \vee P_{n-1} G_{n-1} \vee P_{n-1} P_{n-2} G_{n-2}$$
$$\vee P_{n-1} P_{n-2} P_{n-3} C_{n-3}$$

.
.
.

The expansion can continue as far as one desires and one could conceive of C_n being generated by one large or block preceded by several and blocks (in fact n and blocks—one for each stage). But it is obvious that the limiting factor would be the circuit fan-in. Only a limited number of circuit stages can be connected together in this manner. This technique is defined as carry look-ahead, and by cascading different levels of look-ahead the technique can be made to fit the circuit fan-in, fan-out limitations.

For example, assume that four bits can be arranged in this manner, and that each four bits form a "group". The adder is now divided into groups and the carries and propagates can be arranged for carry look-ahead between groups just as they were for look-ahead between bits. It is possible to carry the concept even further and define a section as consisting of one or more groups. Now the adder has three levels of carry look-ahead: the bit level of look-ahead, the group level, and the section level.

The fraction adder of the floating-point add unit is a carry look-ahead adder. A group is made up of four bits (one digit) and two groups form a section. Since it must be capable of adding 56

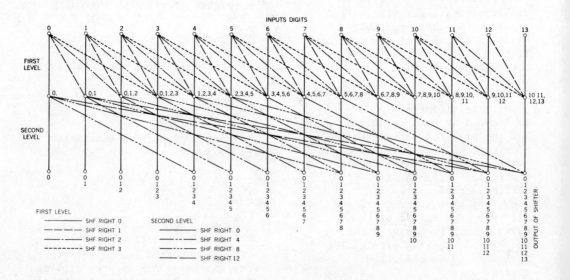

Fig. 5. Digit Pre-Shifter

bits, the fraction adder consists of seven sections and 14
groups. Each pair of input
bits generate the three bit
functions: half-sum (A ∀ B),
bit carry generate (A·B) and
bit propagate (A∨B). These
functions are combined to form
the group generate and propagate
which in turn are combined to

form the section generate and
propagate. A typical group is
shown in Fig. 6 and the group
and section look-ahead are
shown in Fig. 7.

The high-order sum consists
of nine bits to include the end-
around carry for subtraction and
the overflow bit for addition.
The end-around carry is needed

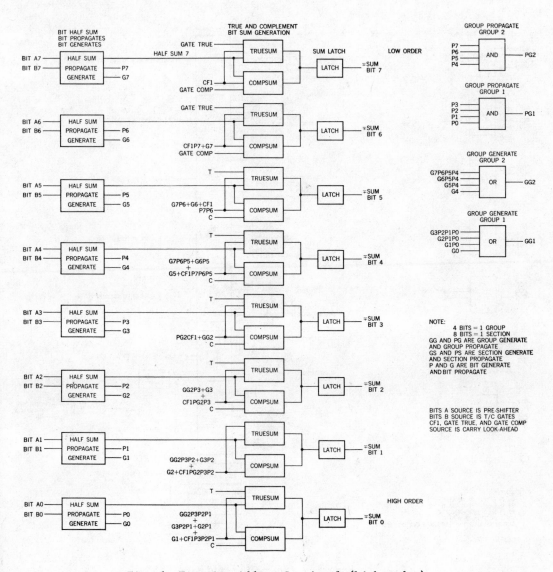

Fig. 6. Fraction Adder, Section 1 (high-order)

for subtraction because the fraction which is complemented may not be the subtrahend. This is illustrated by the example given in the description of the characteristic comparison. If the effective sign of the instruction is minus (the exclusive or of the sign of the two fractions and the instruction is the effective sign) the effective operation is subtract. Also, the high-order bit (ninth bit of the high-order section) is set to a one, thus conditioning it for an end-around-carry. If there is no end-around-carry when the effective sign is minus the adder output is complemented.

POST-NORMALIZATION

Normalization or postshifting takes place when the intermediate arith-

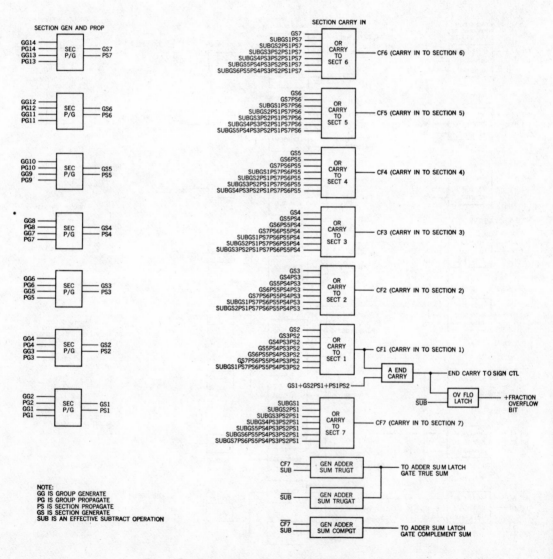

Fig. 7. Fraction Adder, Carry Look-Ahead

metic result out of the adder is
changed to the final result. The
output of the fraction adder is
checked for high-order zero digits
and the fraction is left-shifted
until the high-order digit is nonzero.

The output of the fraction adder
is gated to the zero-digit checker.
The zero-digit checker is simply a
large decoder, which detects the
number of leading zero digits, and
provides the shift amount to the
postshifter. Since this same amount
must be subtracted from the characteristic, the zero-digit checker also
must encode the shift amount for the
characteristic update adder.

The implementation of the digit
postshifter is the same as the digit
preshifter except for the fact that
the postshift is a leftshift.
The first level of the post-shifter
shifts each of the 14 digits left
0,1,2 or 3 and the second level
shifts each digit 0,4,8, or 12.
The output of the second level is
gated into the add unit fraction
result register, from which the
resultant fraction is routed to the
proper floating-point accumulator.

The characteristic update is
executed in parallel with the
fraction shift. The zero-digit
checker provides the characteristic
update adder with the two's complement of the amount by which the
characteristic must be reduced.
Since it is not possible to have a
post-shift greater than 13, the
high-order three bits of the
characteristic can only be changed
by carries which ripple from the
low order four bits. The update
adder makes use of this fact to
reduce the necessary hardware and
speed up the operation.

FLOATING-POINT MULTIPLY/ DIVIDE UNIT

Multiply and divide are complicated
operations. However, two of the
original design goals were to select
an algorithm for each operation
such that (1) both operations could
use common hardware, and (2) improvement in execution time could be
achieved which would be comparable
to that achieved in the floating-
point add unit. Several algorithms
exist for each instruction which
make the first design goal attainable.
Unfortunately, the best of the
algorithms generally used for divide
are not capable of providing an
improvement in execution comparable
to the improvement achievable by
those used for multiply. The
algorithm developed for divide in
the Model 91 uses multiplication
as the basic operator. Thus,
common hardware is used, and
comparable improvement in the
execution time is achieved.

In order to give a clear, consistent treatment to both instructions,
this section discusses the multiply
algorithm and hardware implementation first. Then the divide
algorithm is discussed separately.
Finally, it is shown how divide
utilizes the multiply execution
hardware and the hardware which
is unique to the execution of divide
is described.

MULTIPLY ALGORITHM

Computers usually execute multiply
by repetitive addition, and the
time required is dependent on
the number of additions required.[1,6]
A zero bit in the multiplier results
in adding a zero word to the partial
product. Therefore, because shifting
is a faster operation than add, the
execution time can be decreased
by shifting over a zero or a
string of zeros. Any improvement
in the multiply execution beyond
this point is not obvious. However,
certain properties of the binary
number system combined with complementing to allow subtraction
as well as addition can be used
to reduce the number of necessary
additions.

An integer in any number system
may be written in the following form:

$$a_n b^n + a_{n-1} b^{n-1} + \ldots + a_1 b^1 + a_0 b^0,$$

where

$0 \leq a \leq b - 1$, and b = base of the number system, one of the properties of numbering systems which is particularly interesting in multiply is that an integer can be rewritten as shown below.

$$a_n b^n + a_{n-1} b^{n-1} + \cdots + a_k b^k + \cdots + a_{n-x} b^{n-x},$$

where

$a_k = b - 1$ for any k.

In the binary number system a_k can take only the values 0 and 1. Thus, using the above property, a string of 1's can be skipped by subtracting at the start of the string and adding at the end of the string:

$$112_{10} = 2^6 + 2^5 + 2^4 = 2^7 - 2^4,$$

$$112_{10} = 111000_2 = 10000000_2 - 10000_2.$$

Therefore, a string of 1's in the multiplier can be reduced from an addition for each 1 in the string to a subtraction for the first 1 in the string, shift the partial product one position for each 1 in the string, and an addition for the last 1 in the string.

However, the method described above requires a variable shift and thus does not permit one to predict the exact number of cycles required to execute multiply. Furthermore, it does not permit the use of carry-save adders in the implementation. (Carry-save adders will be discussed later.)

A multiplier recoding-algorithm, which is based on the property described above, but which uses uniform shifts is used in the Model 91. The multiplier is divided into uniform groups of k bits each. These k bits are recoded to generate a multiple of the multiplicand, which is added to or subtracted from the partial product. The multiples are generated by shifting the position of the multiplicand in relation to the normal position at which it would enter the adder for a k equal to one. After adding the generated multiple to the partial product, the partial product is shifted k positions and the next group of k bits is considered.

The correct choice for k is important since an average of $1/2^k$ of the generated multiples will have a value of zero, and increasing k (over k equal to one) reduces the amount of operand reduction capability that is used inefficiently. However, if k is greater than two, carry propagate addition is necessary to generate the needed multiplicand multiples (shifting can only be used to generate multiples which are a power of two). In the context of a fast multiply, the carry-propagate adder increases the start-up time, which is undesirable. The Model 91 uses a k equal to two.

The technique used to scan the multiplier is shown in Fig. 8. Overlapping the high-order bit of one group and the low-order bit of the next group insures that the beginning and end of a string of 1's is detected once and only once. Table 2 shows which multiples are selected for all possible combinations of the two new bits and the overlapped bit.

Since the objective is fast

SCAN PATTERN

MULTIPLIER BIT   0 1 2 3 4 5 6 7 8 9 10 11 12 13 14 15 16 17 18 19 20 --- 47 48 49 50 51 52 53 54 55

TOTAL SCAN IS 29 PATTERNS OF THREE BITS EACH.
EACH PATTERN GENERATES ONE MULTIPLE

NOTE: BITS 0 AND 57
ARE ALWAYS ZERO

Fig. 8. Scanning Pattern for Multiplier

multiply execution, six groups of multiplier bits are recoded at one time, and the resultant six multiples are added to the partial product. Five iterations are sufficient to assimilate the full 56 bits of the multiplier fraction. Figure 9 shows how the multiplier fraction is separated for each iteration and how each iteration is separated for the six generated multiples.

A tree of carry-save adders is used to reduce the generated multiples from six to two. A carry-save adder, which can be used whenever successive addition of several operands is necessary, requires less hardware, has less data skew and has less delay than a carry-propagate adder.6 The individual carry-save adder takes three input operands and generates the resulting sum and carry. However, instead of connecting the carries to the next higher-order bits and allowing them to ripple, they are treated as independent outputs. In accordance with the customary rules for addition, the carries will be added to the next higher-order bits as separate inputs to the next carry-save adder down the tree.

Figure 10 illustrates a tree of carry-save adders which will reduce six input operands to two, thereby retiring 12 bits of the multiplier on each iteration. Note that the final output of the carry-save adder tree is two operands--sum and carry--which are shifted right 12 positions and loop back to become input operands. Thus, the partial product is accumulated as a partial sum and a partial carry. After the multiplier has been assimilated, these two operands, sum and carry, are added in a carry propagate adder to form the final product.

IMPLEMENTATION

A block diagram of the data flow

for the execution of a multiply is shown in Fig. 11. This data flow can be separated into two parts, the iterative hardware and the peripheral hardware (that hardware which is peripheral to the iterative hardware). The latter includes the input reservation stations, the pre-normalizer, the post-normalizer, the propagate adder, the result register, and the characteristic arithmetic.

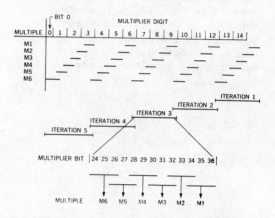

Fig. 9. Iterations and Multiple Generation for Multiply

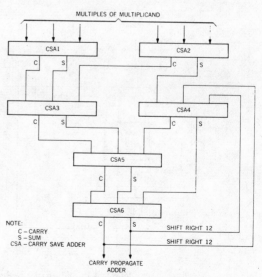

Fig. 10. Carry-Save Adder Tree

The peripheral hardware is described first, but since the iterative
hardware is the heart of multiply
execution, the major part of this
section is devoted to a discussion
of this hardware.

INPUT PERIPHERAL HARDWARE

The input hardware includes the
reservation stations, prenormalizer
and the characteristic arithmetic.
As was stated earlier, the multiply
unit has two reservation stations and
appears to the floating-point
instruction unit for assignment
purposes as two distinct multiply
units. If both units have been
selected for a multiply operation,
the first unit to receive both
operands is given priority to
begin execution. In the case where
both units receive their
second operand simultaneously,
the unit which was selected
by the floating-point execution
unit first is given priority
for execution.

The system architecture specifies
that multiply is a normalized
operation. Thus, if the input
operands are unnormalized, they
must be gated to the pre-normalizer,
normalized, and then returned
to the originating reservation
station. In some cases, one
additional machine cycle is added
to the execution time for each

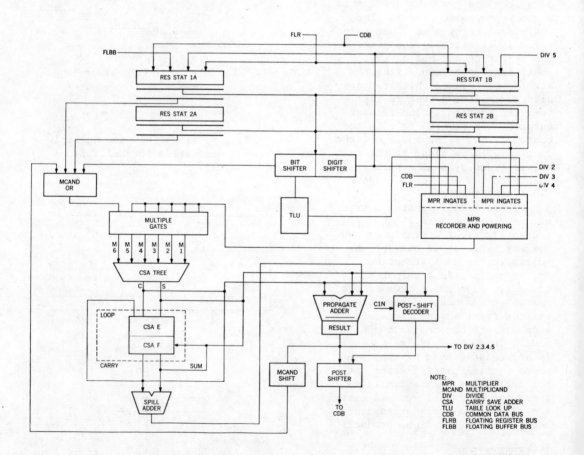

Fig. 11. Floating-Point Multiply/Divide Data Flow

unnormalized operand. However, normalization takes place as soon as the first operand enters the reservation station, provided there is not an operation in execution. Thus, normalizing can take place while the unit is waiting for the second operand.

The design of the zero digit detector and the left-shifter are similar to those described earlier for the add unit. If the zero digit detector, detects an all-zero fraction, the multiply is executed normally, but the outgate of the result to the floating-point accumulator is inhibited. Thus the required result, and all-zero-fraction, is stored.

The amount of left shifting necessary to normalize an operand is gated to the characteristic arithmetic logic, where the characteristic is updated for this shift. Characteristic arithmetic for multiply simply requires the two characteristics to be added but this operation can be overlapped with the execution of the multiply. Thus, the implementation is simple and straightforward.

It remains only to update the characteristic because of postnormalization. The post-shift can never be more than one digit because the input operands are normalized. Therefore, in order to eliminate logic levels at the end of multiply execution, two characteristics are generated: the normal resultant characteristic and the normal characteristic minus one. Subsequent to postnormalization the correct characteristic is outgated.

OUTPUT PERIPHERAL HARDWARE

The output peripheral hardware includes the carry-propagate adder, the result register and the postnormalizer. Since the product is accumulated as two operands (sum and carry) the output of the iterative hardware is gated to a carry-propagate adder to form the final

product. The design of the carry propagate adder is similar to the one used in the add unit with the exception that multiply does not require an end-around carry adder. A result register is created by latching the last level of the carry propagate adder. The output of the result register is gated to the common data bus via the postnormalizer. Detection of the need for postnormalization is done in parallel with the carry propagate adder and the result is gated to the common data bus, either shifted left one digit or unshifted.

ITERATIVE HARDWARE

The multiply execution area has conflicting design goals. The execution time must be short but the amount of hardware necessary for implementation has a practical upper limit. One could design a multiply unit which would take two cycles for execution. A large tree of twenty-eight carry-save adders could be interconnected so that the multiplicand and the multiplier would be the input to the tree and the output would be the product.[8] The performance of this multiply unit would be acceptable but the amount of hardware necessary for implementation is much too high.

The adopted alternative approach was to select a subset of the carry-save adder tree such that one iteration through the tree retires 12 bits of the multiplier. This iteration is repeated until the full 56 bits of the multiplier have been exhausted. If each iteration is fast enough, the multiply execution time for this method approaches that for the large tree of carry-save adders. In fact, if each iteration can be 20 nanoseconds the second method can execute a multiply in three cycles, and the iterative hardware can be reduced to 20 per cent of that required for the first method. Thus, with an iterative loop, the primary design problem is

to design the carry-save adder tree
so that the iteration period is
minimized. The faster the repetition rate of the iterative hardware,
the better the cost-performance ratio
of the multiply area.

There are several ways to arrange
the carry-save adders, and each method
affects the iteration period differently. For example, if they are arranged as shown in Fig. 12, the feedback loop (the partial product) is
from the output back to the input.
In this case, the iteration period
becomes the time required to make
one complete pass through the tree.
However, the adopted arrangement,
shown in Fig. 13, allows the iteration period to approach the delay
through the last carry-save adders
(these two carry-save adders are
accumulating the partial product).
But the delay through the path leading to the last two carry-save adders
(the multiplier recoding, multiple
generation and the first four carry-
save adders) is much longer than the
delay through the adders. If, however, temporary storage platforms
are inserted in the iterative loop
the concept of pipelining, explained earlier, can be put to use here.
Temporary storage platforms are inserted in the iterative hardware
for deskewing so that the rate of
inserting new inputs (twelve bits
of the multiplier) and the rate of
accumulating the partial product
may safely be made equal. Therefore, by pipelining the carry-save
adder tree, the second arrangement
can be used and the iteration period is equal to the delay through
the last two carry-save adders.

In order to explain the pipelined tree, the path is abstracted
in Fig. 14. Each block represents
the logic associated with the stages
of the pipeline and the first level
of each block represents the temporary storage platform. The period
of the clock is set by the logic delay of the accumulating loop. In
the abstract design the logic delay
of all paths between stages of the
pipeline is assumed to be the same

as the clock period.

Figure 15 is a timing diagram
for the abstracted iterative hardware. At clock time zero, the first
input, I_1, is gated into the temporary storage in stage one. At clock

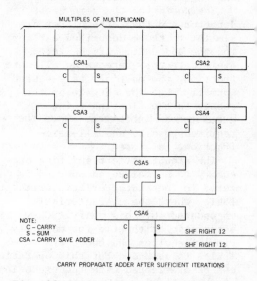

Fig. 12. CSA Tree with Feedback Loop
from Output

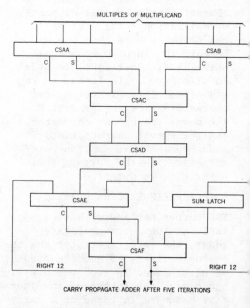

Fig. 13. CSA Tree with Accumulating
Loop at Output

time one, I_1, after being operated on by the logic in stage one, is gated in at stage two and I_2 is gated in at stage one. This process continues until at clock time three, the original input, I_1, is entering stage four. During this clock time, the pipeline is filled, i.e., each stage of the pipeline now contains data in various forms of completion. At clock time four, the last input, I_5, enters stage one, and the partial product starts to accumulate at stage four. The next three clock times are used to drain the pipeline and accumulate the full partial product. Thus the total iterative loop time is that necessary to fill up the carry-save adder tree plus five passes around the accumulating loop, or eight clock periods. If the feedback loop were from output to input, as shown in Fig. 12, the total iterative loop time would be twenty clock periods. Therefore the iterative loop time has been reduced by a factor of 2.5, with only a small increase in hardware. (This is described later.)

The actual implementation of the pipeline is not simple. First, the temporary storage platforms require extra hardware and add delay to the path. Second, the placement of the temporary storage platforms is important for two reasons: (1) The purpose of the temporary storage platform is to deskew the logic (difference between fast and slow logic paths) and the logic delay is not ideally distributed, and (2) the placement can affect the amount of hardware necessary for implementation.

The solution to the first problem led to a design in which the logic function was designed into the temporary platform; e.g., a latched carry-save adder or a latched multiple gate. The extra hardware is only that required for the feedback loop which latches the logic function; the added delay is eliminated because the logic function is designed into the temporary storage. The solution to the second problem was more complex. First, the clock used to control the temporary storage

platform ingate was designed as a series clock. All of the pulses of an iteration are initiated by a single oscillator pulse and then delayed to drive the ingates of the successive pipeline stages.

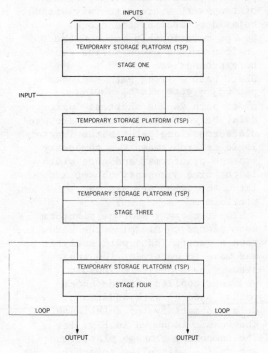

Fig. 14. Abstract Drawing of "Pipelined" Iteration

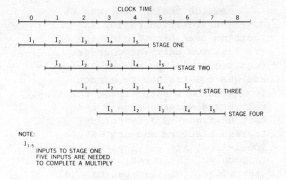

Fig. 15. Timing Diagram for Abstracted Iterative Hardware

The clock delay between successive temporary storage ingates is equal to the long path circuit and wiring delay of the logic between these ingates. The time between iterations (the oscillator period) is still the delay of the accumulating loop, but the time between pipeline stages is not equal to the clock period. This allows the placement of temporary storage to vary without being dependent on the clock.

The relationship between the logic skew and clock period can be expressed as
Short path > [long path – clock period] + gate width, where
short path is the shortest logic delay between two temporary storage platforms; long path is the longset logic delay between two temporary storage platforms; and gate width is the time necessary to set and latch the temporary storage platform.

The temporary storage platforms were placed to minimize the hardware; then a careful data path analysis was made to determine the logic skew. The above relationship was next applied and the short paths "padded" with additional delay to satisfy the relationship. The result is shown in Fig. 16. The temporary storage platforms are at the multiplier recorder, the multiple gates, carry-save adder C and the accumulating loop, and carry-save adders E and F.

Since the design goal was to make the iteration period as short as possible, the design of the last two carry-save adders required a minimum number of levels and was constrained to account for the "short path around the loop." Carry-save adders E and F are each designed as a temporary storage platform and are ortho-gonal-i.e., are not ingated simul-taneously. The first, carry-save adder E, is ingated on the first-half of the clock period and the second, carry-save adder F,

is ingated on the second half of the clock period.

The low order thirteen bits of the multiplier are gated into the latched multiplier recoder at clock time zero and recoded to six control lines. Every clock period—20 nano-seconds—a new set of bits is gated into the multipler recoder until the full word (56 bits) is exhausted. The next step in the pipeline is the latched multiple gates. Six multiples are generated by shifting the multi-plicand, under control of the out-put from the multiplier recoder. These six multiples are reduced to four (two sums and two carries) by carry-save adders (CSA) A and B.

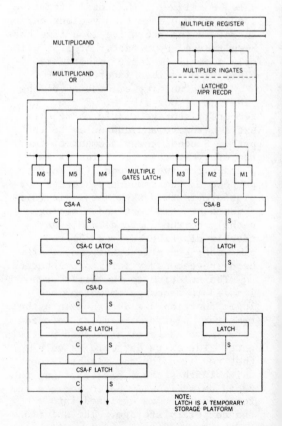

Fig. 16. Multiply Iterative Loop Showing Temporary Storage

Carry-save adder C takes three of these outputs and reduces them to two latched outputs. The sum from CSA-B is latched in parallel with CSA-C and combines with the two outputs from CSA-C to provide CSA-D with three inputs. At the output of CSA-D, the sum and carry are the result of multiplying twelve bits of the multiplier and the full multiplicand. The next two latched carry-save adders are used to accumulate the partial product. Each iteration adds the latest sum and carry from CSA-D to the previous results. After five iterations of the accumulating loop the output of CSA-F is the bit product in carry-save form. Now the sum and carry operands are gated to the carry progagate adder and the carries allowed to ripple to form the final product.

DIVIDE ALGORITHM

Several division algorithms exist,[1,6] of varying complexity, cost and performance, which could be used to execute the divide instruction in the Model 91. But because of the relatively complex and iterative nature of divide algorithms, the execution time is out of balance with other processor functions. Even the higher-performing conventional algorithms contain a shortcoming which requires the successive subtractions be separated by a performance-degrading decode interval.* The Model 91, how-

_____

*Conventional refers to previous division algorithms which use subtraction as the iterative operator. The faster algorithms generate more than one quotient bit in parallel through the use of pre-wired multiplies. However, the selection of the multiplies for the next iteration is dependent upon a decode of the partial remainder of the previous iteration.

ever, utilizes a unique divide algorithm which is based on quadratic convergence.[7,8,9,10] A major advantage is that the number of required iterations is reduced (proportional to $\log_2$ of the fraction length), which reduces the number of data-control interactions. Another important advantage is that MULTIPLY is the basic iterative operator. This both reduces the cost, by exploiting existing hardware, and enhances the execution time, because in the Model 91 MULTIPLY is extremely fast.

The divisor and dividend are considered to be the denominator and numerator of a fraction. On each interation a factor, R_k, multiplies both numerator and denominator so that the resultant denominator converges quadratically toward one (1) and the resultant numerator converges quadratically toward the desired quotient.

$$\frac{N}{D} \times \frac{R}{R} \times \frac{R_1}{R_1} \times \frac{R_2}{R_2} \times \ldots \times \frac{R_n}{R_n}$$

$$\implies NRR_1 \ldots R_n = \text{Quotient}$$

where N = numerator = dividend,
       D = denominator = divisor, and
       $DRR_1R_2 \ldots R_n \implies 1$.

The selection of the factor R_k is the essential part of the procedure and is based on the following: The divisor can be expressed as

$$D = 1 - x,$$

where $x \leq 1/2$ since D is a bit-normalized, binary floating-point fraction of the form

$$0.1 \, xxx\cdots.$$

Now, if the factor R is set equal to $1 + x$ and the denominator is multiplied by R

$$D_1 = DR = (1-x)(1+x) = 1 - x^2,$$

where $x^2 \leq 1/4$, since $x \leq 1/2$.
The new denominator is guaranteed

to have the form 0.11 xxxx $_2\cdots$. Likewise, selecting $R_1 = 1 + x^2$ will double the leading 1 on the next iteration to yield

$$D_2 = D_1 R_1 = (1 - x^2)(1 + x^2) = 1 - x^4$$
$$= 0.1111\text{xxxx}\cdots ,$$

where $x^4 \leq 1/16$ since $x \leq 1/2$.

In general, if $x_k < 1/2^n$ then $x_{k+1} < 1/2^{2n}$. Thus, by continuing the multiplication until x_k is less than the least significant bit of the denominator (divisor fraction), the desired result, namely a denominator equivalent to one $(0.1111111\cdots111)$, is obtained.

It is important to note that the multiplier for each iteration is the two's complement of the denominator,

$$R_{k+1} = 2 - D_k = 2 - (1 - x_n) = 1 + x_n.$$

Thus the multiplier for iteration k is formed by taking the two's complement of the result of iteration $(k - 1)$. However, in this form the algorithm is still not fast enough. For a 56-bit fraction, eleven multiples are required with a two's complement inserted between six of the multiples:

$$Q = NRR_1 R_2 R_3 R_4 R_5$$

$$R_5 = 2 - D_4 \text{ and } D_4 = DRR_1 R_2 R_3 R_4.$$

But if the number of bits in the multiplier could be reduced, the time for each multiply would be decreased. If in order to obtain n bits of convergence the multiplier is truncated to n bits $[1 + x_T$ where $(x_T - x) < 2^{-n}]$ it can be shown that the resultant denominator is equivalent to

$$(1 + x_T)(1 - x) = 1 - x^2 + |T| ,$$

where $0 < T$ (which is due to truncation) $< 2^{-n}$.

Because the additional term T is always positive, the resultant denominator can now have two forms:

$$D_k = \begin{cases} 0.11111\cdots\text{xxxxx}\cdots \\ 1.00000\cdots\text{xxxxx}\cdots \end{cases} .$$

The denominator can converge toward unity from above or below, but it will converge, so no additional problems are encountered.

Therefore, the number of bits in the multiplier can be reduced to the string bits (all 0 or all 1) and the number of bits of convergence desired. The string bits, since they are all 0 or all 1, can be skipped in the multiply. Thus the multiply time has been improved considerably and so, consequently, has the divide time. To improve the initial minimum string length, thus reducing the number of iterations, the first multiplier, R, is generated by a table-lookup which inspects the first seven bits of the divisor. The first multiply guarantees a result which has seven similar bits to the right of the binary point $(1 \pm x$ has form a.aaaaaaa $\cdots$etc.).

The following sequence outlines the operations which result in the execution of a divide.

1. Bit normalize the divisor and shift the dividend accordingly:

2. Determine the first multiplier, R, by a table-lookup.

3. Multiply D by R forming D_1.

4. Multiply N by R forming N_1.

5. Truncate D_k and complement to form R_k.

6. Multiply D_k by R_k forming D_{k+1}.

7. Multiply N_k by R_k forming N_{k+1}.

8. Iterate on 5, 6 and 7 until $D_{k+n} \implies 1$ and then $N_{k+n} = $ Quotient.

DIVIDE IMPLEMENTATION

Each iteration of divide execution consists of three operations as shown above. The problem in implementation is to accomplish these three operations utilizing the multiply hardware described previously and accomplish them in the minimum amount of time. But there are three points which create difficulty. First, the multiplier is a variable length operand, the length being different on each iteration. The first multiplier, determined by table-lookup, is ten bits and yields a minimum string length of seven; the second multiplier is fourteen bits; the third multiplier is twenty-eight bits, etc. In other words, the minimum string length can be doubled on each iteration after the first. Second, the result of one iteration is the multiplicand for the next iteration. Since the output of the multiply iterative hardware is two operands—carry and sum—the carry propagate adder must be included in the divide loop. Third, two multiplies are required in each iteration— one determines what to do on the next iteration (multiplier x denominator) and one converges the numerator towards the quotient (multiplier x numerator).

When all three of these points are considered simultaneously they present a dilemma. Since two multiplies are necessary it is desirable to overlap the two and save time, but any multiply for which the multiplier is greater than twelve bits requires that the carry-save adder loop be used. Also, the fact that the carry propagate adder must be included

in the loop lengthens the time for each iteration. Several design iterations were required before arriving at the correct solution.

First consider the entries in Table 2 and note that the leading string of 1's or 0's in the multiplier can be skipped since they result in a zero multiple out of the multiplier recoder. Also, if the input of the multiplier recoder is complemented the sign of the output changes but the magnitude remains the same. Thus, this property can be used to produce $\overset{+}{-}\, x_n$ at the output of the recoder.

Next consider a multiplier (complement of truncated denominator) such as the following:

$$1. \quad 0000\ 0000\ 000 \begin{bmatrix} 0\ 00xx\ xxxx\ xxx1 \\ 1\ 11xx\ xxxx\ xxx1 \end{bmatrix}$$
$$0. \quad 1111\ 1111\ 111$$

If all positions were recoded, a bit of value 1 would be recoded from the high-order end and a set of bits of value $\overset{+}{-}\, x_k$ from the right end ($1 \overset{+}{-} x_k$). However, if only the portion in brackets is gated to the recoder the output will have value $\overset{+}{-}\, 2^{12} x_k$.* The bits in the bracket are chosen such that the left-most three bits are identical. Thus, multiple six (refer to Fig. 9) is not used because a zero multiple is always recoded, and the product $\overset{+}{-}\, D_k x_k$ or $\overset{+}{-}\, N_k x_k$ is accomplished by the five operands gated to multiple gates one through five. If the un-shifted multiplicand is gated simultaneously into the sixth multiple gate the sum of all six operands is $D_k + (\overset{+}{-}\, D_k x_k)$ or $D_k(1 \overset{+}{-} x_k)$, which is the desired result. The result which is generated by adding the carry and sum out of the carry-save adder tree (refer to Fig. 11) is the following:

Table 2.

Multiplier Recoder Rules

Input			Output	Reason
n*	(n+1)	(n+2)	Multiple	
0	0	0	0	No String
0	0	1	+2	End of String
0	1	0	+2	Beginning & End
0	1	1	+4	End of String
1	0	0	-4	String Beginning
1	0	1	-2	Beginning & End
1	1	0	-2	String Beginning
1	1	1	0	Center of String

_____

* The multiplicand is shifted right twelve positions to compensate for the 2^{12} factor.

Table 3.

Formats of the Denominators and Their Multipliers

Digit	0	1	2	3	4	5	6	7	8	9	10	11	12	13	14	15	16
D	0	1xxx	xxxx	xxxx	xxxx	xxxx	xxxx	xxxx	xxxx	xxxx	xxxx	xxxx	xxxx	xxxx	xxxx	0000	0000
R	[01	xxxx	xxxx	xx0]	Determined by table lookup of denominator												
$D \times R = D_1$ {0		1111	111x	xxxx	xxxx	xxxx	xxxx	xxxx	xxxx	xxxx	xxxx	xxxx	xxxx	xxxx	xxxx	xxxx	xxxx
{1		0000	000x	xxxx	xxxx	xxxx	xxxx	xxxx	xxxx	xxxx	xxxx	xxxx	xxxx	xxxx	xxxx	xxxx	xxxx
R_1 {1		0000	$\overline{000x}$	$\overline{xxxx}$	$\overline{xx11}$	1] Determined by complementing denominator											
{0		1111	$\overline{111x}$	$\overline{xxxx}$	$\overline{xx11}$	1]											
$D_1 \times R_1 = D_2$ {0		1111	1111	1111	11xx	xxxx	xxxx	xxxx	xxxx	xxxx	xxxx	xxxx	xxxx	xxxx	xxxx	xxxx	xxxx
{1		0000	0000	0000	00xx	xxxx	xxxx	xxxx	xxxx	xxxx	xxxx	xxxx	xxxx	xxxx	xxxx	xxxx	xxxx
R_2 {1		0000	0000	0000	00xx	$\overline{xxxx}$	$\overline{xxx1}$										
{0		1111	1111	1111	11xx	$\overline{xxxx}$	$\overline{xxx1}$										
$D_2 \times R_2 = D_3$ {0		1111	1111	1111	1111	1111	111x	xxxx	xxxx	xxxx	xxxx	xxxx	xxxx	xxxx	xxxx	xxxx	xxxx
{1		0000	0000	0000	0000	0000	000x	xxxx	xxxx	xxxx	xxxx	xxxx	xxxx	xxxx	xxxx	xxxx	xxxx
R_3 {1		0000	0000	0000	0000	0000	$\overline{000x}$	$\overline{xxxx}$	$\overline{xxxx}$	1							
{0		1111	1111	1111	1111	1111	$\overline{111x}$	$\overline{xxxx}$	$\overline{xxxx}$	1							
$D_3 \times R_3 = D_4$ {0		1111	1111	1111	1111	1111	1111	1111	1111	xxxx	xxxx	xxxx	xxxx	xxxx	xxxx	xxxx	xxxx
{1		0000	0000	0000	0000	0000	0000	0000	0000	xxxx	xxxx	xxxx	xxxx	xxxx	xxxx	xxxx	xxxx
R_4 {1		0000	0000	0000	0000	0000	0000	0000	0000	$\overline{xxxx}$	$\overline{xxxx}$	$\overline{xxxx}$	$\overline{xxxx}$	$\overline{xxxx}$	$\overline{xxxx}$	$\overline{xxxx}$	11]
{0		1111	1111	1111	1111	1111	1111	1111	1111	xxxx	xxxx	$\overline{xxxx}$	xxxx	xxxx	$\overline{xxxx}$	xxxx	11]
D_5 {0 (not formed)		1111	1111	1111	1111	1111	1111	1111	1111	1111	1111	1111	1111	1111	1111	1111	1111
{1		0000	0000	0000	0000	0000	0000	0000	0000	0000	0000	0000	0000	0000	0000	0000	0000

Short precision divide result is $N_4 = NRR_1R_2R_3$
Long precision divide result is $N_5 = N_4R_4$

$$D_{k+1} = \begin{cases} 0.1111\ 1111\ 1111\ 1111\ 1111 \\ 1.0000\ 0000\ 0000\ 0000\ 0000 \end{cases}$$

111x xxxx →

000x xxxx →

Thus, without using the carry-save adder loop the leading string has been increased by nine bits.

Table 3 presents the format of the multipliers and their denominators. Notice that the first multiplier is ten bits and the second is seven. These are fixed and cannot be changed without making the table-lookup decoder larger. Thus the third multiplier is the first one capable of using more than nine bits. But if a multiplier of more than nine bits is used,

the carry-save adder loop must be included in the divide loop. Since this is undesirable (concurrency among multiplies is discussed below) the multiplier for the third and fourth iterations is chosen to be nine bits, thereby increasing the string length by nine each time. Thus, D_4 has 32 leading 1's or 0's. Now if D_4 is multiplied by multiplier four, R_4, the result will be 64 leading 1's or 0's, which is equivalent to unity within the desired accuracy. Therefore, since it is not necessary to calculate multiplier five, R_5, this multiply is not done and since only the numerator is going to be multiplied by multiplier four, the carry-save adder loop is used to speed up this last operation. (This is discussed more fully below).

The second difficulty, which was that the carry propagate adder must be included in the path, was used to solve the third difficulty. Consider Fig. 17, which is the divide loop. To begin the execution of a divide the divisor is multiplied by the first multiplier (R), and the first denominator (D_1) is generated at the output of the CSA tree. These two outputs are added in the carry propagate adder; the output loops back to the input and becomes the new multiplicand; the truncated and complemented output forms the new multiplier. Note that the complete loop contains two temporary storage platforms--one at CSA-C and one at the output of the propagate adder, the result latch. Thus as soon as R x D is gated into CSA-C, the next multiply, R x N, can be started. Now R x D advances to the result latch and loops back to start the next multiply R_1 x D_1. At this time R x N, which is latched in CSA-C, advances through the adder to the result latch. So the two multiplies follow each other around the divide loop. The first determines what the second should be multiplied by to converge eventually to the quotient.

This chain continues until multiplier four has been calculated. Since denominator five is equivalent to one, the multiply is not done. The 32-bit multiplier is gated into the reservation station and then gated to the multiplier twelve bits at a time as shown in Table 3. The result of this multiply, N_4, R_4, is the final quotient. The diagram in Fig. 18 shows the concurrency in the divide loop. The multiplier recoder latch is changed each time a denominator multiply is completed. Notice that two multiplies are always in execution, one in the first half of

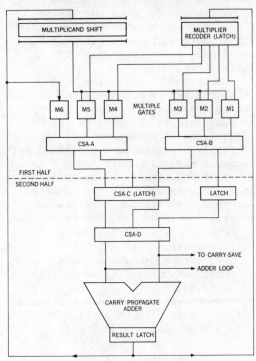

Fig. 17. Divide Loop

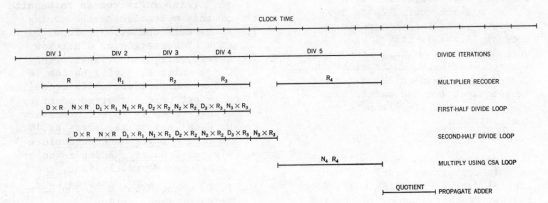

Fig. 18. Timing Diagram Showing Concurrency in Divide Loop

the divide loop (from input to CSA-C) and one in the second half of the divide loop from CSA-C to the result latch).

CONCLUSIONS

The prime effort during the design of the floating-point execution unit was to develop an organization which would achieve a balance between instruction execution and preparation. Early in the design phase it appeared that an organization which would achieve this result would have a poor cost-performance ratio.

Concurrency, obviously, had to be the key to high performance, but the connotation of concurrency in computers is parallel execution of different instructions. Thus the early organizations exhibited more than one execution unit and a high cost. In the final organization, concurrency is the key to the high performance, but this organization exhibits several levels of concurrency:

1. Concurrent execution among instruction classes.
2. Concurrent execution among instructions in the same class (add unit).
3. Concurrent execution within an instruction (multiply iterative hardware and divide loop).

The concepts of instruction-oriented units and reservation stations were used to keep the performance level sufficiently high but reduce the cost. These two concepts yield the same performance as several units without the cost of several units. The instruction-oriented units allow the design to be hand-tailored for faster execution and permit the use of a unique algorithm to execute divide.

ACKNOWLEDGMENTS

The design of a computer unit such as this—containing nearly as many logical decisions as IBM's previous largest central processor—requires a great deal of decision making.

The authors gratefully acknowledge the logical and engineering design contributions made by the following individuals: Mr. W. D. Silkman for the floating-point instruction unit; Messrs. J. J. DeMacedo, J. G. Gasparini, L. Grosman, R. C. Letteney and R. M. Wade for the multiply/divide unit; Messrs. M. Litwak, K. J. Pockett and K. G. Tan for the add unit; and Mr. E. C. Layden for the processor clock.

Acknowledgment is also made for the early planning efforts of Mr. R. J. Litwiller.

REFERENCES

1. W. Buchholtz, et. al, Planning a Computer System, McGraw-Hill, New York, 1962.
2. G. M. Amdahl, G. A. Blaauw, and F. P. Brooks, Jr. "Architecture of the IBM System/360," IBM Journal, Vol. 8, 1964, pp. 87-101.
3. D. W. Anderson, et. al., "Model 91 Machine Philosophy and Instruction Handling," IBM Journal, Vol. 11, 1967, pp. 8-24.
4. R. M. Tomasulo, "An Efficient Algorithm for Exploiting Multiple Arithmetic Units," IBM Journal, Vol. 11, 1967, pp. 25-33.
5. R. F. Sechler, A. K. Strube and J. R. Turnbull, "ASLT Circuit Design," IBM Journal, Vol. 11, 1967. pp. 74-85.
6. O. L. MacSorley, "High-Speed Arithmetic in Binary Computers," Proc. IRE, Vol. 49, 1961, pp. 67-91. (Also reprinted in this part of this volume.)
7. R. E. Goldschmidt, "Appl. of Division by Convergence," Master's Thesis, MIT, June, 1964.
8. C. S. Wallace, "A Suggestion for a Fast Multiplier," IEEE Trans. on Electronic Computers, Vol. EC-13, 1964, pp. 14-17.
9. M. V. Wilkes et al., Preparation of Programs for an Electronic Digital Computer, Addison-Wesley Cambridge, Mass., 1951.
10. T. C. Chen, "Fast Division Scheme," Private communication, November 4, 1963.

PART III COMPUTER ARCHITECTURE

This part treats the inter-connection of digital sub-systems (such as arithmetic units like those described in the previous part) to form general purpose computers. Clearly the sub-systems will be designed by methods such as those presented in Part I.

PRELIMINARY DISCUSSION OF THE LOGICAL DESIGN OF AN ELECTRONIC COMPUTING INSTRUMENT

ARTHUR W. BURKS, HERMAN H. GOLDSTINE, AND JOHN von NEUMANN

This paper is probably the single most significant paper in the field of computer design. It was the first widely distributed description of an electronic stored program computer; as such it profoundly influenced the "first generation" of computers. Because it was one of the first attempts to describe a computer, the paper is both rather basic and quite complete. It should be read and understood by those who design and develop computers. The authors carefully describe many alternatives before their solution for each of the major problem areas; although some of the tradeoffs are quite different now, the analysis presented here is a generally valid and certainly useful background for a computer designer.

SYMBOLIC SYNTHESIS OF DIGITAL COMPUTERS

IRVING S. REED

This paper effectively illustrates the "Western" approach to computer design. A mathematical description of the operation of a computer control unit is presented, which treats the control unit as a source of instructions to transfer and modify the contents of the machine's register. With an approach such as this it is possible to derive the control equations for the entire computer. These equations may be used to simulate the machine thus permitting its performance to be optimized for the ultimate application without requiring massive construction projects. In contrast the "Eastern" approach involved functional specification of the computer sub-systems, i.e., the arithmetic unit; generally only small portions of the machine were analysed in great detail or simulated.

THE BEST WAY TO DESIGN AN AUTOMATIC CALCULATING MACHINE

M. V. WILKES

This paper introduced the term Micro-Programming to describe a method intended to simplify the design and maintenance of computer control units. The essential idea of micro-programming is to use a memory to decode the instructions of the machine into a series of primitive operations (i.e., micro-orders) suitable for controlling various sub-systems (e.g., the arithmetic unit, memory, etc.) comprising the computer. When this paper was written in 1951, computers were so simple (i.e., with only a small and unsophisticated instruction set) that the main advantage of micro-programming was that highly repetitive diode matrices could be used to implement computer control units. As machines grew in complexity, the ease of design and subsequent redesign of micro-programmed control units have become the dominant feature. Another interesting aspect of micro-program-

219

ming is the possibility of developing a number of instruction sets for a given machine; these different instruction sets can be changed by replacing the control memory to permit a single machine to appear to have been custom-designed for each user's needs. This idea can be carried one step further as Wilkes notes by using a read and write memory which permits dynamic reconfiguration of the machine.

STRUCTURAL ASPECTS OF THE SYSTEM/360 MODEL 85 PART II: THE CACHE

J. S. LIPTAY

A cache memory is a relatively small fast memory inserted between the computer control unit and the main memory (which is large but slow). The cache is used to perform instruction look-ahead, permitting the processor to operate much faster on the average than it would otherwise. This paper describes what a cache memory is, how it is used, and how it is designed.

PARALLEL OPERATION IN THE CONTROL DATA 6600

JAMES E. THORNTON

The computer described by this paper is effective because it takes advantage of the parallelism inherent in a "sequential" computer. Multiple peripheral processors operate concurrently to perform input, output, and housekeeping operations without interrupting the central processor. The central processor is significant because it introduced the idea of using a number of specialized arithmetic sub-processors rather than a single general purpose arithmetic unit. The third novel feature is that operands are transferred between the central processor and the memory via eight operand registers which act somewhat like a small scratch-pad memory. This of course occurs under the programmer's control in

contrast to the cache memory of the previous paper which is transparent to the programmer.

Because photographs of the circuit modules in the final section of this paper are unavailable, the section has been deleted in this reprint.

THE SOLOMON COMPUTER

DANIEL L. SLOTNICK, W. CARL BORCK, AND ROBERT C. McREYNOLDS

The SOLOMON computer introduced the concept of parallel computation, where a single control unit dispatches instructions to an array of processing elements, each of which contains a memory and an arithmetic unit. For problems amenable to solution with an array processor, an n element processor solves the problems in 1/n of the time that a single processor system would require, with a complexity of somewhat less (because only one control unit is required) than n times the complexity of the single processor system. This appears to be one of the most attractive means for increasing computer performance in the future; especially since system speed with current single processor systems is nearing ultimate physical bounds (i.e., signals can propagate no faster than the speed of light, etc.). The major practical problem with SOLOMON and its successor ILLIAC IV is that it is difficult to construct programs that use the processors efficiently.

In a book such as this, size limitations make it impractical to survey the entire field of computer architecture. The interested reader is refered to the fine compilation edited by Bell and Newell*, for a broader and more comprehensive coverage of this important field.

---

* C. Gordon Bell and Allen Newell, Computer Structures: Readings and Examples, (New York: McGraw-Hill Book Company, 1971.)

PRELIMINARY DISCUSSION OF THE LOGICAL DESIGN OF
AN ELECTRONIC COMPUTING INSTRUMENT

ARTHUR W. BURKS, HERMAN H. GOLDSTINE, AND JOHN VON NEUMANN

PREFACE TO FIRST EDITION

This report has been prepared in accordance with the terms of Contract W-36-034-ORD-7481 between the Research and Development Service, Ordnance Department, U. S. Army and the Institute for Advanced Study. It is intended as the first of two papers dealing with some aspects of the overall logical considerations arising in connection with electronic computing machines. An attempt is made to give in this, the first half of the report, a general picture of the type of instrument now under consideration and in the second half a study of how actual mathematical problems can be coded, i.e., prepared in the language the machine can understand.

It is the present intention to issue from time to time reports covering the various phases of the project. These papers will appear whenever it is felt sufficient work has been done on a given aspect, either logical or experimental, to justify its being reported.

The authors also wish to express their thanks to Dr. John Turkey, of Princeton University, for many valuable discussions and suggestions.

ARTHUR W. BURKS
HERMAN H. GOLDSTINE
JOHN von NEUMANN

The Institute for Advanced Study
28 June 1946

Reprinted with permission from John von Neumann; Collected Works, vol. 5, ed. by A. H. Taub, Pergamon Press, Ltd. Oxford, 1961, pp. 34-79.

PREFACE TO SECOND EDITION

In this edition the sections dealing with the arithmetic organ have been considerably expanded and a more complete account of the arithmetic processes given. In addition, certain sections have been brought up to date in the light of engineering advances made in our laboratory.

ARTHUR W. BURKS
HERMAN H. GOLDSTINE
JOHN von NEUMANN

The Institute for Advanced Study
2 September 1947

1. PRINCIPAL COMPONENTS OF THE MACHINE

1.1. Inasmuch as the completed device will be a general-purpose computing machine it should contain certain main organs relating to arithmetic, memory-storage, control and connection with the human operator. It is intended that the machine be fully automatic in character, i.e., independent of the human operator after the computation starts. A fuller discussion of the implications of this remark will be given in Chapter 3 below.

1.2. It is evident that the machine must be capable of storing in some manner not only the digital information needed in a given computation such as boundary values, tables of functions (such as the equation of state of a fluid) and also the intermediate results of the computation (which may be wanted for varying lengths of time), but also the instructions which govern the actual

routine to be performed on the numerical data. In a special-purpose machine these instructions are an
integral part of the device and constitute a part of its design structure.
For an all-purpose machine it must be
possible to instruct the device to
carry out any computation that can be
formulated in numerical terms. Hence
there must be some organ capable of
storing these program orders. There
must, moreover, be a unit which can
understand these instructions and
order their execution.

1.3. Conceptually we have discussed above two different forms of
memory: storage of numbers and storage
of orders. If, however, the orders to
the machine are reduced to a numerical
code and if the machine can in some
fashion distinguish a number from an
order, the memory organ can be used to
store both numbers and orders. The
coding of orders into numeric form is
discussed in 6.3 below.

1.4. If the memory for orders is
merely a storage organ there must exist
an organ which can automatically execute the orders stored in the memory.
We shall call this organ the Control.

1.5. Inasmuch as the device is
to be a computing machine there must
be an arithmetic organ in it which can
perform certain of the elementary arithmetic operations. There will be,
therefore, a unit capable of adding,
subtracting, multiplying and dividing.
It will be seen in 6.6 below that it
can also perform additional operations
that occur quite frequently.

The operations that the machine
will view as elementary are clearly
those which are wired into the machine.
To illustrate, the operation of multiplication could be eliminated from the
device as an elementary process if one
were willing to view it as a properly
ordered series of additions. Similar
remarks apply to division. In general,
the inner economy of the arithmetic
unit is determined by a compromise between the desire for speed of opera-
tion--a nonelementary operation will
generally take a long time to perform
since it is constituted of a series of

orders given by the control--and the
desire for simplicity, or cheapness,
of the machine.

1.6. Lastly there must exist
devices, the input and output organ,
whereby the human operator and the machine can communicate with each other.
This organ will be seen below in 4.5,
where it is discussed, to constitute a
secondary form of automatic memory.

2. FIRST REMARKS ON THE MEMORY

2.1. It is clear that size of the
memory is a critical consideration in
the design of a satisfactory general-
purpose computing machine. We proceed
to discuss what quantities the memory
should store for various types of computations.

2.2. In the solution of partial
differential equations the storage requirements are likely to be quite
extensive. In general, one must remember not only the initial and boundary
conditions and any arbitrary functions
that enter the problem but also an extensive number of intermediate results.

a. For equations of parabolic or
hyperbolic type in two independent
variables the integration process is
essentially a double induction. To
find the values of the dependent variables at time $t + \Delta t$ one integrates
with respect to x from one boundary to
the other by utilizing the data at
time t as if they were coefficients
which contribute to defining the problem of this integration.

Not only must the memory have
sufficient room to store these intermediate data but there must be pro-
visions whereby these data can later
be removed, i.e., at the end of the
$(t + \Delta t)$ cycle, and replaced by the
corresponding data for the $(t + 2\Delta t)$
cycle. This process of removing data
from the memory and of replacing them
with new information must, of course,
be done quite automatically under the
direction of the control.

b. For total differential equations the memory requirements are
clearly similar to, but smaller than,

those discussed in (a) above.

c. Problems that are solved by iterative procedures such as systems of linear equations or elliptic partial differential equations, treated by relaxation techniques, may be expected to require quite extensive memory capacity. The memory requirement for such problems is apparently much greater than for those problems in (a) above in which one needs only to store information corresponding to the instantaneous values of one variable [t in (a) above], while now entire solutions (covering all values of all variables) must be stored. This apparent discrepancy in magnitudes can, however, be somewhat overcome by the use of techniques which permit the use of much coarser integration meshes in this case, than in the cases under (a).

2.3. It is reasonable at this time to build a machine that can conveniently handle problems several orders of magnitude more complex than are now handled by existing machines, electronic or electro-mechanical. We consequently plan on a fully automatic electronic storage facility of about 4,000 numbers of 40 binary digits each. This corresponds to a precision of 2^{-40} ~ 0.9×10^{-12}, i.e., of about 12 decimals. We believe that this memory capacity exceeds the capacities required for most problems that one deals with at present by a factor of about 10. The precision is also safely higher than what is required for the great majority of present day problems. In addition, we propose that we have a subsidiary memory of much larger capacity, which is also fully automatic, on some medium such as magnetic wire or tape.

3. FIRST REMARKS ON THE CONTROL AND CODE

3.1. It is easy to see by formal logical methods that there exist codes that are in abstracto adequate to control and cause the execution of any sequence of operations which are individually available in the machine and which are, in their entirety, conceivable by the problem planner. The really decisive considerations from the present point of view, in selecting a code, are more of a practical nature: simplicity of the equipment demanded by the code, and the clarity of its application to the actually important problems together with the speed of handling of those problems. It would take us much too far afield to discuss these questions at all generally or from first principles. We will therefore restrict ourselves to analyzing only the type of code which we now envisage for our machine.

3.2. There must certainly be instructions for performing the fundamental arithmetic operations. The specifications for these orders will not be completely given until the arithmetic unit is described in a little more detail.

3.3. It must be possible to transfer data from the memory to the arithmetic organ and back again. In transferring information from the arithmetic organ back into the memory there are two types we must distinguish: Transfers of numbers as such and transfers of numbers which are parts of orders. The first case is quite obvious and needs no further explication. The second case is more subtle and serves to illustrate the generality and simplicity of the system. Consider by way if illustration, the problem of interpolation in the system. Let us suppose that we have formulated the necessary instructions for performing an interpolation of order n in a sequence of data. The exact location in the memory of the (n + 1) quantities that bracket the desired functional value is, of course, a function of the argument. This argument probably is found as the result of a computation in the machine. We thus need an order which can substitute a number into a given order--in the case of interpolation the location of the argument or the group of arguments that is nearest in our table to the desired value. By means of such an order the results of a computation can be introduced into the instructions governing that or a different computation. This makes it possible for a sequence of instructions to be used with different sets of numbers located in different parts of the memory.

To summarize, transfers into the memory will be of two sorts: Total substitutions, whereby the quantity previously stored is cleared out and replaced by a new number. Partial substitutions in which that part of an order containing a memory location-number--we assume the various positions in the memory are enumerated serially by memory location-numbers--is replaced by a new memory location-number.

3.4. It is clear that one must be able to get numbers from any part of the memory at any time. The treatment in the case of orders can, however, be more methodical since one can at least partially arrange the control instructions in a linear sequence. Consequently the control will be so constructed that it will normally proceed from place n in the memory to place (n + 1) for its next instruction.

3.5. The utility of an automatic computer lies in the possibility of using a given sequence of instructions repeatedly, the number of times it is reiterated being either preassigned or dependent upon the results of the computation. When the iteration is completed a different sequence of orders is to be followed, so we must, in most cases, give two parallel trains of orders preceded by an instruction as to which routine is to be followed. This choice can be made to depend upon the sign of a number (zero being reckoned as plus for machine purposes). Consequently, we introduce an order (the conditional transfer order) which will, depending on the sign of a given number, cause the proper one of two routines to be executed.

Frequently two parallel trains of orders terminate in a common routine. It is desirable, therefore, to order the control in either case to proceed to the beginning point of the common routine. This unconditional transfer can be achieved either by the artificial use of a conditional transfer or by the introduction of an explicit order for such a transfer.

3.6. Finally we need orders which will integrate the input-output devices with the machine. These are discussed briefly in 6.8.

3.7. We proceed now to a more detailed discussion of the machine. Inasmuch as our experience has shown that the moment one chooses a given component as the elementary memory unit, one has also more or less determined upon much of the balance of the machine, we start by a consideration of the memory organ. In attempting an exposition of a highly integrated device like a computing machine we do not find it possible, however, to give an exhaustive discussion of each organ before completing its description. It is only in the final block diagrams that anything approaching a complete unit can be achieved.

The time units to be used in what follows will be:

$$1 \ \mu\text{sec} = 1 \ \text{microsecond}$$
$$= 10^{-6} \ \text{seconds},$$

$$1 \ \text{msec} = 1 \ \text{millisecond}$$
$$= 10^{-3} \ \text{seconds}.$$

4. THE MEMORY ORGAN

4.1. Ideally one would desire an indefintely large memory capacity such that any particular aggregate of 40 binary digits, or word (cf. 2.3), would be immediately available--i.e., in a time which is somewhat or considerably shorter than the operation time of a fast electronic multiplier. This may be assumed to be practical at the level of about 100 μsec. Hence the availability time for a word in the memory should be 5 to 50 μsec. It is equally desirable that words may be replaced with new words at about the same rate. It does not seem possible physically to achieve such a capacity. We are therefore forced to recognize the possibility of constructing a hierarchy of memories, each of which has greater capacity than the preceding but which is less quickly accessible.

The most common forms of storage in electrical circuits are the flip-flop or trigger circuit, the gas tube, and the electro-mechanical relay. To achieve a memory of n words would, of course, require about 40n such elements, exclusive of the switching elements. We saw earlier (cf. 2.2) that a fast memory of several thousand words is not at all unreasonable for an all-purpose instrument. Hence, about 10^5 flip-flops or analogous elements would be required! This would, of course, be entirely impractical.

We must therefore seek out some more fundamental method of storing electrical information than has been suggested above. One criterion for such a storage medium is that the individual storage organs, which accommodate only one binary digit each, should not be macroscopic components, but rather microscopic elements of some suitable organ. They would then, of course, not be identified and switched to by the usual macroscopic wire connections, but by some functional procedure in manipulating that organ.

One device which displays this property to a marked degree is the iconoscope tube. In its conventional form it possesses a linear resolution of about one part in 500. This would correspond to a (two-dimensional) memory capacity of 500 x 500 = 2.5 x 10^5. One is accordingly led to consider the possibility of storing electrical charges on a dielectric plate inside a cathode-ray tube. Effectively such a tube is nothing more than a myriad of electrical capacitors which can be connected into the circuit by means of an electron beam.

Actually the above mentioned high resolution and concomitant memory capacity are only realistic under the conditions of television-image storage, which are much less exigent in respect to the reliability of individual markings than what one can accept in the storage for a computer. In this latter case resolutions of one part in 20 to 100, i.e., memory capacities of 400 to 10,000, would seem to be more reasonable in terms of equipment built essentially along familiar lines.

At the present time the Princeton Laboratories of the Radio Corporation of America are engaged in the development of a storage tube, the Selectron, of the type we have mentioned above. This tube is also planned to have a non-amplitude-sensitive switching system whereby the electron beam can be directed to a given spot on the plate within a quite small fraction of a millisecond. Inasmuch as the storage tube is the key component of the machine envisaged in this report we are extremely fortunate in having secured the cooperation of the RCA group in this as well as in various other developments.

An alternate form of rapid memory organ is the acoustic feed-back relay line described in various reports on the EDVAC. (This is an electronic computing machine being developed for the Ordnance Department, U. S. Army, by the University of Pennsylvania, Moore School of Electrical Engineering.) Inasmuch as that device has been so clearly reported in those papers we give no further discussion. There are still other physical and chemical properties of matter in the presence of electrons or photons that might be considered, but since none is yet beyond the early discussion stage we shall not make further mention of them.

4.2. We shall accordingly assume throughout the balance of this report that the Selectron is the modus for storage of words at electronic speeds. As now planned, this tube will have a capacity of 2^{12} = 4,096 $\approx$ 4,000 binary digits. To achieve a total electronic storage of about 4,000 words we propose to use 40 Selectrons, thereby achieving a memory of 2^{12} words of 40 binary digits each. (Cf. again 2.3).

4.3. There are two possible means for storing a particular word in the Selectron memory--or, in fact, in either a delay line memory or in a storage tube with amplitude-sensitive deflection. One method is to store the entire word in a given tube and then to get the word out by picking out its respective digits in a serial fashion. The other method is to store in corresponding places in each of the 40 tubes one digit of the word. To get a word from the memory in this scheme requires, then, one switching mechanism to which all 40 tubes are connected in parallel. Such a switching scheme seems to us to be simpler than the technique needed in the serial system and is, of course, 40 times faster. We accordingly adopt the parallel procedure and thus are led to consider a so-called parallel machine, as contrasted with the serial principles being considered for the EDVAC. (In the EDVAC the peculiar characteristics of the acoustic delay line, as well as various other considerations, seem to justify a serial procedure. For more details, cf. the reports referred to in 4.1.) The essential difference between these two systems lies in the method of performing an addition; in a parallel machine all corresponding pairs of digits are added simultaneously, whereas in a serial one these pairs are added serially in time.

4.4. To summarize, we assume that the fast electronic memory consists of 40 Selectrons which are switched in parallel by a common switching arrangement. The inputs of the switch are controlled by the control.

4.5. Inasmuch as a great many highly important classes of problems require a far greater total memory than 2^{12} words, we now consider the next stage in our storage hierarchy. Although the solution of partial differential equations frequently involves the manipulation of many thousands of words, these data are generally required only in blocks which are well within the 2^{12} capacity of the electronic memory. Our second form of storage must therefore be a medium which feeds these blocks of words to the electronic memory. It should be controlled by the control of

the computer and is thus an integral part of the system, not requiring human intervention.

There are evidently two distinct problems raised above. One can choose a given medium for storage such as teletype tapes, magnetic wires or tapes, movie film or similar media. There still remains the problem of automatic integration of this storage medium with the machine. This integration is achieved logically by introducing appropriate orders into the code which can instruct the machine to read or write on the medium, or to move it by a given amount or to a place with given characteristics. We discuss this question a little more fully in 6.8.

Let us return now to the question of what properties the secondary storage medium should have. It clearly should be able to store information for periods of time long enough so that only a few per cent of the total computing time is spent in re-registering information that is "fading off." It is certainly desirable, although not imperative, that information can be erased and replaced by new data. The medium should be such that it can be controlled, i.e., moved forward and backward, automatically. This consideration makes certain media, such as punched cards, undesirable. While cards can, of course, be printed or read by appropriate orders from some machine, they are not well adapted to problems in which the output data are fed directly back into the machine, and are required in a sequence which is non-monotone with respect to the order of the cards. The medium should be capable of remembering very large numbers of data at a much smaller price than electronic devices. It must be fast enough so that, even when it has to be used frequently in a problem, a large percentage of the total solution time is not spent in getting data into and out of this medium and achieving the desired positioning on it. If this condition is not reasonably well met, the advantages of the high electronic speeds of the machine will be largely lost.

Both light-or electron-sensitive film and magnetic wires or tapes, whose motions are controlled by servomechanisms integrated with the control, would seem to fulfill our needs reasonably well. We have tentatively decided to use magnetic wires since we have achieved reliable performance with them at pulse rates of the order of 25,000/sec and beyond.

4.6. Lastly our memory hierarchy requires a vast quantity of dead storage, i.e., storage not integrated with the machine. This storage requirement may be satisfied by a library of wires that can be introduced into the machine when desired and at that time become automatically controlled. Thus our dead storage is really nothing but an extension of our secondary storage medium. It differs from the latter only in its availability to the machine.

4.7. We impose one additional requirement on our secondary memory. It must be possible for a human to put words on to the wire or other substance used and to read the words put on by the machine. In this manner the human can control the machine's functions. It is now clear that the secondary storage medium is really nothing other than a part of our input-output system, cf. 6.8.4 for a description of a mechanism for achieving this.

4.8. There is another highly important part of the input-output which we merely mention at this time, namely, some mechanism for viewing graphically the results of a given computation. This can, of course, be achieved by a Selectron-like tube which causes its screen to fluoresce when data are put on it by an electron beam.

4.9. For definiteness in the subsequent discussions we assume that associated with the output of each Selectron is a flip-flop. This assemblage of 40 flip-flops we term the Selectron Register.

5. THE ARITHMETIC ORGAN

5.1. In this chapter we discuss the features we now consider desirable for the arithmetic part of our machine. We give our tentative conclusions as to which of the arithmetic operations should be built into the machine and which should be programmed. Finally, a schematic of the arithmetic unit is described.

5.2. In a discussion of the arithmetical organs of a computing machine one is naturally led to a consideration of the number system to be adopted. In spite of the longstanding tradition of building digital machines in the decimal system, we feel strongly in favor of the binary system for our device. Our fundamental unit of memory is naturally adapted to the binary system since we do not attempt to measure gradations of charge at a particular point in the Selectron but are content to distinguish two states. The flip-flop again is truly a binary device. On magnetic wires or tapes and in acoustic delay line memories one is also content to recognize the presence or absence of a pulse or (if a carrier frequency is used) of a pulse train, or of the sign of a pulse. (We will not discuss here the ternary possibilities of a positive-or-negative-or-no-pulse system and their relationship to questions of reliability and checking, nor the very interesting possibilities of carrier frequency modulation.) Hence if one contemplates using a decimal system with either the iconoscope or delay-line memory one is forced into a binary coding of the decimal system—each decimal digit being represented by at least a tetrad of binary digits. Thus an accuracy of ten decimal digits requires at least 40 binary digits. In a true binary representation of numbers, however, about 33 digits suffice to achieve a precision of 10^{10}. The use of the binary system is therefore somewhat more economical of equipment than is the decimal.

The main virtue of the binary system as against the decimal is, however, the greater simplicity and speed with which the elementary operations can be performed. To illustrate,

consider multiplication by repeated
addition. In binary multiplication
the product of a particular digit of
the multiplier by the multiplicand is
either the multiplicand or null according as the multiplier digit is 1 or 0.
In the decimal system, however, this
product has ten possible values between
null and nine times the multiplicand,
inclusive. Of course, a decimal number
has only $\log_{10}2 \sim 0.3$ times as many
digits as a binary number of the same
accuracy, but even so multiplication
in the decimal system is considerably
longer than in the binary system. One
can accelerate decimal multiplication
by complicating the circuits, but this
fact is irrelevant to the point just
made since binary multiplication can
likewise be accelerated by adding to
the equipment. Similar remarks may be
made about the other operations.

An additional point that deserves
emphasis is this: An important part
of the machine is not arithmetical,
but logical in nature. Now logics,
being a yes-no system, is fundamentally
binary. Therefore a binary arrangement
of the arithmetical organs contributes
very significantly towards producing a
more homogenous machine, which can be
better integrated and is more
efficient.

The one disadvantage of the binary
system from the human point of view is
the conversion problem. Since, however, it is completely known how to
convert numbers from one base to another and since this conversion can be
effected solely by the use of the usual
arithmetic processes there is no reason
why the computer itself cannot carry
out this conversion. It might be
argued that this is a time consuming
operation. This, however, is not the
case. (Cf. 9.6 and 9.7 of Part II.
Part II is a report issued under the
title "Planning and Coding of Problems
for an Electronic Computing Instrument.") Indeed a general-purpose computer, used as a scientific research
tool, is called upon to do a very great
number of multiplications upon a relatively small amount of input data, and
hence the time consumed in the decimal

to binary conversion is only a trivial
percentage of the total computing time.
A similar remark is applicable to the
output data.

In the preceding discussion we
have tacitly assumed the desirability
of introducing and withdrawing data in
the decimal system. We feel, however,
that the base 10 may not even be a per-
manent feature in a scientific instrument and consequently will probably
attempt to train ourselves to use numbers base 2 or 8 or 16. The reason
for the bases 8 or 16 is this: Since
8 and 16 are powers of 2 the conversion to binary is trivial; since both
are about the size of 10, they violate
many of our habits less badly than
base 2. (Cf. Part II, 9.4.)

5.3. Several of the digital computers being built or planned in this
country and England are to contain a
so-called "floating decimal point."
This is a mechanism for expressing
each word as a characteristic and a
mantissa--e.g., 123.45 would be carried in the machine as (0.12345, 03),
where the 3 is the exponent of 10
associated with the number. There
appear to be two major purposes in a
"floating" decimal point system both
of which arise from the fact that the
number of digits in a word is constant,
fixed by design considerations for
each particular machine. The first of
these purposes is to retain in a sum
or product as many significant digits
as possible and the second of these is
to free the human operator from the
burden of estimating and inserting
into a problem "scale factors"--
multiplicative constants which serve
to keep numbers within the limits of
the machine.

There is, of course, no denying
the fact that human time is consumed in
arranging for the introduction of
suitable scale factors. We only argue
that the time so consumed is a very
small percentage of the total time we
will spend in preparing an interesting
problem for our machine. The first
advantage of the floating point is, we
feel, somewhat illusory. In order to
have such a floating point one must

waste memory capacity which could otherwise be used for carrying more digits per word. It would therefore seem to us not at all clear whether the modest advantages of a floating binary point offset the loss of memory capacity and the increased complexity of the arithmetic and control circuits.

There are certainly some problems within the scope of our device which really require more than 2^{-40} precision. To handle such problems we wish to plan in terms of words whose lengths are some fixed integral multiple of 40, and program the machine in such a manner as to give the corresponding aggregates of 40 digit words the proper treatment. We must then consider an addition or multiplication as a complex operation programmed from a number of primitive additions or multiplications (cf. § 9, Part II). There would seem to be considerably extra difficulties in the way of such a procedure in an instrument with a floating binary point.

The reader may remark upon our alternate spells of radicalism and conservatism in deciding upon various possible features for our mechanism. We hope, however, that he will agree, on closer inspection, that we are guided by a consistent and sound principle in judging the merits of any idea. We wish to incorporate into the machine—in the forms of circuits—only such logical concepts as are either necessary to have a complete system or highly convenient because of the frequency with which they occur and the influence they exert in the relevant mathematical situations.

5.4. On the basis of this criterion we definitely wish to build into the machine circuits which will enable it to form the binary sum of two 40 digit numbers. We make this decision not because addition is a logically basic notion but rather because it would slow the mechanism as well as the operator down enormously if each addition were programmed out of the more simple operations of "and," "or," and "not." The same is true for the subtraction. Similarly, we reject

the desire to form products by programming them out of additions, the detailed motivation being very much the same as in the case of addition and subtraction. The cases for division and square-rooting are much less clear.

It is well known that the reciprocal of a number a can be formed to any desired accuracy by iterative schemes. One such scheme consists of improving an estimate X by forming $X' = 2X - aX^2$. Thus the new error $1 - aX'$ is $(1 - aX)^2$, which is the square of the error in the preceding estimate. We notice that in the formation of X', there are two bona fide multiplications—we do not consider multiplication by 2 as a true product since we will have a facility for shifting right or left in one or two pulse times. If then we somehow could guess $1/a$ to a precision of 2^{-5}, 6 multiplications—3 iterations—would suffice to give a final result good to 2^{-40}. Accordingly a small table of 2^4 entries could be used to get the initial estimate of $1/a$. In this way a reciprocal $1/a$ could be formed in 6 multiplication times, and hence a quotient b/a in 7 multiplication times. Accordingly we see that the question of building a divider is really a function of how fast it can be made to operate compared to the iterative method sketched above: In order to justify its existence, a divider must perform a division in a good deal less than 7 multiplication times. We have, however, conceived a divider which is much faster than these 7 multiplication times and therefore feel justified in building it, especially since the amount of equipment needed above the requirements of the multiplier is not important.

It is, of course, also possible to handle square roots by iterative techniques. In fact, if X is our estimate of $a^{1/2}$, then $X' = \frac{1}{2}(X + a/X)$ is a better estimate. We see that this scheme involves one division per iteration. As will be seen below in our more detailed examination of the arithmetic organ we do not include a square-rooter in our plans because such a device would involve more equipment than we feel is desirable in a first model. (Concerning the iterative method of square-rooting, cf. 8.10 in Part II.)

5.5. The first part of our arithmetic organ requires little discussion at this point. It should be a parallel storage organ which can receive a number and add it to the one already in it, which is also able to clear its contents and which can transmit what it contains. We will call such an organ an Accumulator. It is quite conventional in principle in past and present computing machines of the most varied types, e.g., desk multipliers, standard IBM counters, more modern relay machines, the ENIAC. There are, of course, numerous ways to build such a binary accumulator. We distinguish two broad types of such devices: static, and dynamic or pulse-type accumulators. These will be discussed in 5.11, but it is first necessary to make a few remarks concerning the arithmetic of binary addition. In a parallel accumulator, the first step in an addition is to add each digit of the addend to the corresponding digit of the augend. The second step is to perform the carries, and this must be done in sequence since a carry may produce a carry. In the worst case, 39 carries will occur. Clearly it is inefficient to allow 39 times as much time for the second step (performing the carries) as for the first step (adding the digits). Hence either the carries must be accelerated, or use must be made of the average number of carries or both.

5.6. We shall show that for a sum of binary words, each of length n, the length of the largest carry sequence is on the average not in excess of $^2\log n$. Let $p_n(v)$ designate the probability that a carry sequence is of length v or greater in the sum of two binary words of length n. Then clearly $p_n(v) - p_n(v + 1)$ is the probability that the largest carry sequence is of length exactly v and the weighted average

$$a_n = \sum_{v=0}^{n} v[p_n(v) - p_n(v + 1)]$$

is the average length of such carry. Note that

$$\sum_{v=0}^{n} [p_n(v) - p_n(v + 1)] = 1$$

since $p_n(v) = 0$ if $v > n$. From these it is easily inferred that

$$a_n = \sum_{v=1}^{n} p_n(v)$$

We now proceed to show that $p_n(v) \leqq$ min $[1, (n - v + 1)/2^{v+1}]$.
     Observe first that

$$p_n(v) = p_{n-1}(v) + \frac{1 - p_{n-v}(v)}{2^{v+1}}$$

$$\text{if } v \leqq n$$

Indeed, $p_n(v)$ is the probability that the sum of two n-digit numbers contains a carry sequence of length $\geqq$ v. This probability obtains by adding the probabilities of two mutually exclusive alternatives: First: Either the n - 1 first digits of the two numbers by themselves contain a carry sequence of length $\geqq$ v. This has the probability $p_{n-1}(v)$. Second: The n - 1 first digits of the two numbers by themselves do not contain a carry sequence of length $\geqq$ v. In this case any carry sequence of length $\geqq$ v in the total numbers (of length n) must end with the last digits of the total sequence. Hence these must form the combination of 1, 1. The next v - 1 digits must propagate the carry, hence each of these must form the combination 1, 0 or 0, 1. (The combinations 1, 1 and 0, 0 do not propagate a carry.) The probability of the combination 1, 1 is 1/4, that one of the alternative combinations 1, 0 or 0, 1 is 1/2. The total probability of this sequence is therefore $1/4(1/2)^{v-1} = (1/2)^{v+1}$. The remaining n - v digits must not contain a carry sequence of length $\geqq$ v. This has the probability $1 - p_{n-v}(v)$. Thus the probability of the second case is $[1 - p_{n-v}(v)]/2^{v+1}$. Combining these two cases, the desired relation

$$p_n(v) = p_{n-1}(v) + \frac{1 - p_{n-v}(v)}{2^{v+1}}$$

obtains. The observation that $p_n(v)$ = 0 if $v > n$ is trivial.

We see with the help of the formulas proved above that $p_n(v) - p_{n-1}(v)$ is always $\leq 1/2^{v+1}$, and hence that the sum

$$\sum_{i=v}^{n} [p_i(v) - p_{i-1}(v)] = p_n(v)$$

is not in excess of $(n - v + 1)/2^{v+1}$ since there are $n - v + 1$ terms in the sum; since, moreover, each $p_n(v)$ is a probability, it is not greater than 1. Hence we have

$$p_n(v) \leq \min\left[1, \frac{n - v + 1}{2^{v+1}} \right]$$

Finally we turn to the question of getting an upper bound on $a_n = \sum_{v=1}^{n} p_n(v)$. Choose K so that $2^K \leq n \leq 2^{K+1}$. Then

$$a_n = \sum_{v=1}^{K-1} p_n(v) + \sum_{v=K}^{n} p_n(v) \leq \sum_{v=1}^{K-1} 1$$

$$+ \sum_{v=K}^{n} \frac{n}{2^{v+1}} = K - 1 + \frac{n}{2^K}$$

This last expression is clearly linear in n in the interval $2^K \leq n \leq 2^{K+1}$, and it is = K for $n = 2^K$ and = K+1 for $n = 2^{K+1}$, i.e., it is = $\log_2 n$ at both ends of this interval. Since the function $\log_2 n$ is everywhere concave from below, it follows that our expression is $\leq \log_2 n$ throughout this interval. Thus $a_n \leq \log_2 n$. This holds for all K, i.e., for all n, and it is the inequality which we wanted to prove.

For our case n = 40 we have $a_n \leq \log_2 40 \sim 5.3$, i.e., an average length of about 5 for the longest carry sequence. (The actual value of a_{40} is 4.62.)

5.7. Having discussed the addition, we can now go on to the subtraction. It is convenient to discuss at this point our treatment of negative numbers, and in order to do that right, it is desirable to make some observations about the treatment of numbers in general.

Our numbers are 40 digit aggregates, the left-most digit being the sign digit, and the other digits genuine binary digits, with positional values 2^{-1}, 2^{-2}, ..., 2^{-39} (going from left to right). Our accumulator will, however, treat the sign digit, too, as a binary digit with the positional value 2^0--at least when it functions as an adder. For numbers between 0 and 1 this is clearly all right: The left-most digit will then be 0, and if 0 at this place is taken to represent a + sign, then the number is correctly expressed with its sign and 39 binary digits.

Let us now consider one or more unrestricted 40 binary digit numbers. The accumulator will add them, with the digit-adding and the carrying mechanisms functioning normally and identically in all 40 positions. There is one reservation, however: If a carry originates in the left-most position, then it has nowhere to go from there (there being no further positions to the left) and is "lost." This means, of course, that the addend and the augend, both numbers between 0 and 2, produced a sum exceeding 2 and the accumulator, being unable to express a digit with a positional value 2^1, which would now be necessary, omitted 2. That is the sum was formed correctly, excepting a possible error 2. If several such additions are performed in succession, then the ultimate error may be any integer multiple of 2. That is the accumulator is an adder which allows errors that are integer multiples of 2--it is an adder modulo 2.

It should be noted that our convention of placing the binary point immediately to the right of the left-most digit has nothing to do with the structure of the adder. In order to make this point clearer we proceed to discuss the possibilities of positioning the binary point in somewhat more detail.

We begin by enumerating the 40 digits of our numbers (words) from left to right. In doing this we use an index $h = 1, ..., 40$. Now we might have placed the binary point just as well between digits j and $j + 1$, $j = 0, ..., 40$. Note, that $j = 0$ corresponds to the position at the extreme left (there is no digit $h = j = 0$); $j = 40$ corresponds to the position at the extreme right (there is no position $h = j + 1 = 41$); and $j = 1$ corresponds to our above choice. Whatever our choice of j, it does not affect the correctness of the accumulator's addition. (This is equally true for subtraction, cf. below, but not for multiplication and division, cf. 5.8.) Indeed, we have merely multiplied all numbers by 2^{j-1} (as against our previous convention), and such a "change of scale" has no effect on addition (and subtraction). However, now the accumulator is an adder which allows errors that are integer multiples of 2^j it is an adder modulo 2^j. We mention this because it is occasionally convenient to think in terms of a convention which places the binary point at the right end of the digital aggregate. Then $j = 40$, our numbers are integers, and the accumulator is an adder modulo 2^{40}. We must emphasize, however, that all of this, i.e., all attributions of values to j, are purely convention-- i.e., it is solely the mathematician's interpretation of the functioning of the machine and not a physical feature of the machine. This convention will necessitate measures that have to be made effective by actual physical features of the machine--i.e., the convention will become a physical and engineering reality only when we come to the organs of multiplication.

We will use the convention $j = 1$, i.e., our numbers lie in 0 and 2 and the accumulator adds modulo 2.

This being so, these numbers between 0 and 2 can be used to represent all numbers modulo 2. Any real number x agrees modulo 2 with one and only one number $\bar{x}$ between 0 and 2--or, to be quite precise: $0 \leq \bar{x} < 2$. Since our addition functions modulo 2, we see that the accumulator may be used to represent and to add numbers modulo 2.

This determines the representation of negative numbers: If $x < 0$, then we have to find the unique integer multiple of 2, $2s$ ($s = 1, 2, ...$) such that $0 \leq \bar{x} < 2$ for $\bar{x} = x + 2s$ (i.e., $-2s \leq x < 2(1 - s)$), and represent x by the digitalization of $\bar{x}$.

In this way, however, the sign digit character of the left-most digit is lost: It can be 0 or 1 for both $x \geq 0$ and $x < 0$, hence 0 in the left-most position can no longer be associated with the + sign of x. This may seem a bad deficiency of the system, but it is easy to remedy--at least to an extent which suffices for our purposes. This is done as follows:

We will usually work with numbers x between -1 and 1 and 1--or, to be quite precise: $-1 \leq x < 1$. Now the $\bar{x}$ with $0 \leq \bar{x} < 2$, which differs from x by an integer multiple of 2, behaves as follows: If $x \geq 0$, then $0 \leq x < 1$, hence $\bar{x} = x$, and so $0 \leq \bar{x} < 1$, the left-most digit of $\bar{x}$ is 0. If $x < 0$, then $-1 \leq x < 0$, hence $\bar{x} = x + 2$, and so $1 \leq \bar{x} < 2$, the left-most digit of $\bar{x}$ is 1. Thus the left-most digit (of $\bar{x}$) is now a precise equivalent of the sign (of x): 0 corresponds to + and 1 to -.

Summing up:

The accumulator may be taken to represent all real numbers modulo 2, and it adds them modulo 2. If x lies between - 1 and 1 (precisely: $-1 \leq x < 1$)--as it will in almost all of our uses of the machine--then the left-most digit represents the sign: 0 is + and 1 is -.

Consider now a negative number x with $-1 \leq x < 0$. Put $x = -y$, $0 < y \leq 1$. Then we digitalize x by representing it as $x + 2 = 2 - y = 1 + (1 - y)$. That is, the left-most (sign) digit of $x = -y$ is, as it should be, 1; and the remaining 39 digits are those of the complement of $y = -x = |x|$, i.e., those of $1 - y$.

Thus we have been led to the familiar representation of negative numbers by complementation.

The connection between the digits of x and those of $-x$ is now easily formulated, for any $x \gtreqless 0$. Indeed, $-x$ is equivalent to

$$2 - x = \{(2^1 - 2^{-39}) - x\} + 2^{-39}$$

$$= \left(\sum_{i=0}^{39} 2^{-i} - x\right) + 2^{-39}$$

(This digit index $i = 1, \ldots, 39$ is related to our previous digit index $h = 1$, $h = 1, \ldots, 40$ by $i = h - 1$. Actually it is best to treat i as if its domain included the additional value $i = 0$—indeed $i = 0$ then corresponds to $h = 1$, i.e., to the sign digit. In any case i expresses the positional value of the digit to which it refers more simply than h does: This positional value is $2^{-i} = 2^{-(h-1)}$. Note that if we had positioned the binary point more generally between j and $j + 1$, as discussed further above, this positional value would have been $2^{-(h-j)}$. We now have, as pointed out previously, $j = 1$.) Hence its digits obtain by subtracting every digit of x from 1—by complementing each digit, i.e., by replacing 0 by 1 and 1 by 0—and then adding 1 in the right-most position (and effecting all the carries that this may cause). (Note how the left-most digit, interpreted as a sign digit, gets inverted by this procedure, as it should be.)

A subtraction $x - y$ is therefore performed by the accumulator, Ac, as follows: Form $x + y'$, where y' has a digit 0 or 1 where y has a digit 1 or 0, respectively, and then add 1 in the right-most position. The last operation can be performed by injecting a carry into the right-most stage of Ac—since this stage can never receive a carry from any other source (there being no further positions to the right).

5.8. In the light of 5.7 multiplication requires special care, because here the entire modulo 2 procedure breaks down. Indeed, assume that we want to compute a product xy, and that we had to change one of the factors, say x, by an integer multiple of 2, say by 2. Then the product $(x + 2)y$ obtains, and this differs from the desired xy by 2y. 2y, however, will not in general be an integer multiple of 2, since y is not in general an integer.

We will therefore begin our discussion of the multiplication by eliminating all such difficulties, and assume that both factors x, y lie between 0 and 1. Or, to be quite precise: $0 \leq x < 1$, $0 \leq y < 1$.

To effect such a multiplication we first send the multiplier x into a register AR, the Arithmetic Register, which is essentially just a set of 40 flip-flops whose characteristics will be discussed below. We place the multiplicand y in the Selectron Register, SR (cf. 4.9) and use the accumulator, Ac, to form and store the partial products. We propose to multiply the entire multiplicand by the successive digits of the multiplier in a serial fashion. There are, of course, two possible ways this can be done: We can either start with the digit in the lowest position—position 2^{-39}— or in the highest position—position 2^{-1}—and proceed successively to the left or right, respectively. There are a few advantages from our point of view in starting with the right-most digit of the multiplier. We therefore describe that scheme.

The multiplication takes place in 39 steps, which correspond to the 39 (non-sign) digits of the multiplier $x = 0, \xi_1, \xi_2, \ldots, \xi_{39} = (0.\xi_1, \xi_2, \ldots, \xi_{39})$, enumerated backwards: $\xi_{39}, \ldots, \xi_2, \xi_1$. Assume that the $k - 1$ first steps $(k = 1, \ldots, 39)$ have already taken place, involving multiplication of the multiplicand y with the $k - 1$ last digits of the multiplier: $\xi_{39}, \ldots, \xi_{41-k}$; and that we are now at the kth step, involving multiplication with the kth last digit: ξ_{40-k}. Assume furthermore, that Ac now contains the quantity p_{k-1}, the result of the $k - 1$ first steps. [This is the (k - 1)st partial product. For k = 1 clearly $p_0 = 0$.] We now form

$$2p_k = p_{k-1} + \xi_{40-k}y,$$

i.e. $2p_k = p_{k-1} + y_k,$

$$y_k \begin{cases} = 0 \text{ for } \xi_{40-k} = 0 \\ = y \text{ for } \xi_{40-k} = 1 \end{cases} \quad (1)$$

That is, we do nothing or add y, according to whether $\xi_{40-k} = 0$ or 1. We can then form p_k by halving $2p_k$.

Note that the addition of (1) produces no carry beyond the 2^0 position, i.e., the sign digit: $0 \leq p_h < 1$ is true for h = 0, and if it is true for h = k - 1, then (1) extends it to h = k also, since $0 \leq y_k < 1$. Hence the sum in (1) is ≥ 0 and < 2, and no carries beyond the 2^0 position arise.

Hence p_k obtains from $2p_k$ by a simple right shift, which is combined with filling in the sign digit (that is freed by this shift) with a 0. This right shift is effected by an electronic shifter that is part of Ac.

Now

$$p_{39} = 2^{-1}[[\, 2^{-1}[2^{-1}\{\ldots(2^{-1}\xi_{39}y + \xi_{38}y)\ldots\} + \xi_2 y] + \xi_1 y]]$$

$$= \sum_{i=1}^{39} 2^{-i}\xi_i y = xy$$

Thus this process produces the product xy, as desired. Note that this xy is the exact product of x and y.

Since x and y are 39 digit binaries, their exact product xy is a 78 digit binary (we disregard the sign digit throughout). However, Ac will only hold 39 of these. These are clearly the left 39 digits of xy. The right 39 digits of xy are dropped from Ac one by one in the course of the 39 steps, or to be more specific, of the 39 right shifts. We will see later that these right 39 digits of xy should and will also be conserved (cf. the end of this section and the end of 5.12, as well as 6.6.3). The left 39 digits, which remain in Ac, should also be rounded off, but we will not discuss this matter here (cf. loc. cit. above and 9.9, Part II).

To complete the general picture of our multiplication technique we must consider how we sense the respective digits of our multiplier. There are two schemes which come to one's mind in this connection. One is to have a gate tube associated with each flip-flop of AR in such a fashion that this gate is open if a digit is 1 and closed if it is null. We would then need a 39-stage counter to act as a switch which would successively stimulate these gate tubes to react. A more efficient scheme is to build into AR a shifter circuit which enables AR to be shifted one stage to the right each time Ac is shifted and to sense the value of the digit in the rightmost flip-flop of AR. The shifter itself requires one gate tube per stage. We need in addition a counter to count out the 39 steps of the multiplication, but this can be achieved by a six stage binary counter. Thus the latter is more economical of tubes and has one additional virtue from our point of view which we discuss in the next paragraph.

The choice of 40 digits to a word (including the sign) is probably adequate for most computational problems but situations certainly might arise when we desire higher precision, i.e., words of greater length. A trivial illustration of this would be the computation of π to more places than are now known (about 700 decimals, i.e., about 2,300 binaries). More important instances are the solutions of N linear equations in N variables for large values of N. The extra precision becomes probably necessary when N exceeds a limit somewhere between 20 and 40. A justification of this estimate has to be based on a detailed theory of numerical matrix inversion which will be given in a subsequent report. It is therefore desirable to be able to handle numbers of 39k digits and signs

by means of program instructions. One
way to achieve this end is to use k
words to represent a 39k digit number
with signs. (In this way 39 digits in
each 40 digit word are used, but all
sign digits, excepting the first one,
are apparently wasted, cf. however,
the treatment of double precision numbers in Chapter 9, Part II.) It is,
of course, necessary in this case to
instruct the machine to perform the
elementary operations of arithmetic
in a manner that conforms with this
interpretation of k-word complexes as
single numbers. (Cf. 9.8-9.10, Part
II.) In order to be able to treat
numbers in this manner, it is desirable to keep not 39 digits in a product, but 78; this is discussed in
more detail in 6.6.3 below. To
accomplish this end (conserving 78 product digits) we connect, via our
shifter circuit, the right-most digit
of Ac with the left-most non-sign
digit of AR. Thus, when in the process of multiplication a shift is
ordered, the last digit of Ac is transferred into the place in AR made va-
cant when the multiplier was shifted.

5.9. To conclude our discussion
of the multiplication of positive numbers, we note this:

As described thus far, the multiplier forms the 78 digit product, xy,
for a 39 digit multiplier x and a 39
digit multiplicand y. We assumed
$x \geq 0$, $y \geq 0$ and therefore had $xy \geq 0$,
and we will only depart from these
assumptions in 5.10. In addition to
these, however, we also assumed $x < 1$,
$y < 1$, i.e., that x, y have their binary points both immediately right of
the sign digit, which implied the same
for xy. One might question the necessity of these additional assumptions.

Prima facie they may seem mere
conventions, which affect only the
mathematician's interpretation of the
functioning of the machine, and not a
physical feature of the machine. (Cf.
the corresponding situation in addition
and subtraction, in 5.7.) Indeed, if
x had its binary point between digits
j and j + 1 from the left (cf. the discussion of 5.7 dealing with this j; it

also applies to k below), and y between
k and k + 1, then our above method of
multiplication would still give the
correct result xy, provided that the
position of the binary point in xy is
appropriately assigned. Specifically:
Let the binary point of xy be between
digits ℓ and $\ell + 1$. x has the binary
point between digits j and j + 1, and
its sign digit is 0, hence its range
is $0 \leq x < 2^{j-1}$. Similarly y has the
range $0 \leq y < 2^{k-1}$, and xy has the
range $0 \leq xy < 2^{\ell-1}$. Now the ranges
of x and y imply that the range of xy
is necessarily $0 \leq xy < 2^{j-1} 2^{k-1} =
2^{j+k-2}$. Hence $\ell = j + k - 1$. Thus it
might seem that our actual positioning
of the binary point--immediately right
of the sign digit, i.e., j = k = 1--
is still a mere convention.

It is therefore important to
realize that this is not so: The
choices of j and k actually correspond
to very real, physical, engineering
decisions. The reason for this is as
follows: It is desirable to base the
running of the machine on a sole, consistent mathematical interpretation.
It is therefore desirable that all
arithmetical operations be performed
with an identically conceived
positioning of the binary point in Ac.
Applying this principle to x and y
gives j = k. Hence the position of
the binary point for xy is given by
$j + k - 1 = 2j - 1$. If this is to be
the same as for x, and y, then $2j - 1
= j$, i.e., j = 1 ensues--that is our
above positioning of the binary point
immediately right of the sign digit.

There is one possible escape: To
place into Ac not the left 39 digits of
xy (not counting the sign digit 0), but
the digits j to j + 38 from the left.
Indeed, in this way the position of
the binary point of xy will be $(2j - 1)
- (j - 1) = j$, the same as for x and y.

This procedure means that we drop
the left j - 1 and right 40 + j digits
of xy and hold the middle 39 in Ac.
Note that positioning of the binary
point means that $x < 2^{j-1}$, $y < 2^{j-1}$
and xy can only be used if $xy < 2^{j-1}$.
Now the assumptions secure only $xy <
2^{2j-2}$. Hence xy must be 2^{j-1} times

smaller than it might be. This is just the thing which would be secured by the vanishing of the left $j - 1$ digits that we had to drop from Ac, as shown above.

If we wanted to use such a procedure, with those dropped left $j - 1$ digits really existing, i.e., with $j \neq 1$, then we would have to make physical arrangements for their conservation elsewhere. Also the general mathematical planning for the machine would be definitely complicated, due to the physical fact that Ac now holds a rather arbitrarily picked middle stretch of 39 digits from among the 78 digits of xy. Alternatively, we might fail to make such arrangements, but this would necessitate to see to it in the mathematical planning of each problem, that all products turn out to be 2^{j-1} times smaller than their a priori maxima. Such an observance is not at all impossible; indeed similar things are unavoidable for the other operations. [For example, with the factor 2 in addition (of positives) or subtraction (of opposite sign quantities). Cf. also the remarks in the first part of 5.12, dealing with keeping "within range."] However, it involves a loss of significant digits, and the choice $j = 1$ makes it unnecessary in multiplication.

We will therefore make our choice $j = 1$, i.e., the positioning of the binary point immediately right of the sign digit, binding for all that follows.

5.10. We now pass to the case where the multiplier x and the multiplicand y may have either sign + or -, i.e., any combination of these signs.

It would not do simply to extend the method of 5.8 to include the sign digits of x and y also. Indeed, we assume $- 1 \leq x < 1, - 1 \leq y < 1$, and the multiplication procedure in question is definitely based on the ≥ 0 interpretations of x and y. Hence if $x < 0$, then it is really using $x + 2$, and if $y < 0$, then it is really using $y + 2$. Hence for $x < 0, y \geq 0$ it forms

$$(x + 2)y = xy + 2y;$$

for $x \geq 0, y < 0$ it forms

$$x(y + 2) = xy + 2x;$$

for $x < 0, y < 0$, it forms

$$(x + 2)(y + 2) = xy + 2x + 2y + 4,$$

or since things may be taken modulo 2, $xy + 2x + 2y$. Hence correction terms $- 2y, - 2x$ would be needed for $x < 0$, $y < 0$, respectively (either or both).

This would be a possible procedure, but there is one difficulty: As xy is formed, the 39 digits of the multiplier x are gradually lost from AR, to be replaced by the right 39 digits of xy. (Cf. the discussion at the end of 5.8.) Unless we are willing to build an additional 40 stage register to hold x, therefore, x will not be available at the end of the multiplication. Hence we cannot use it in the correction 2x of xy, which becomes necessary for $y < 0$.

Thus the case $x < 0$ can be handled along the above lines, but not the case $y < 0$.

It is nevertheless possible to develop an adequate procedure, and we now proceed to do this. Throughout this procedure we will maintain the assumptions $- 1 \leq x < 1, - 1 \leq y < 1$. We proceed in several successive steps.

First: Assume that the corrections necessitated by the possibility of $y < 0$ have been taken care of. We permit therefore $y \lesseqgtr 0$. We will consider the corrections necessitated by the possibility of $x < 0$.

Let us disregard the sign digit of x, which is 1, i.e., replace it by 0. Then x goes over into $x' = x - 1$ and as $- 1 \leq x < 0$, this x' will actually behave like $(x - 1) + 2 = x + 1$. Hence our multiplication procedure will produce $x'y = (x + 1)y = xy + y$, and therefore a correction $- y$ is needed at the end. (Note that we did not use the sign digit of x in the conventional way. Had we done so, then a correction $- 2y$ would have been necessary, as seen above.)

We see therefore: Consider $x \gtreqless 0$. Perform first all necessary steps for forming $x'y(y \gtreqless 0)$, without yet reaching the sign digit of x(i.e., treating x as if it were ≥ 0). When the time arrives at which the digit ξ_0 of x has to become effective--i.e., immediately after ξ_1 became effective, after 39 shifts (cf. the discussion near the end of 5.8)--at which time Ac contains, say, $\overline{p}$ (this corresponds to the p_{39} of 5.8), then form

$$\overline{p} \begin{cases} = \overline{p} & \text{if } \xi_0 = 0 \\ = \overline{p} - y & \text{if } \xi_0 = 1 \end{cases}$$

This $\overline{p}$ is xy. (Note the difference between this last step, forming $\overline{p}$, and the 39 preceding steps in 5.8, forming P_1, P_2, ..., P_{39}.)

Second: Having disposed of the possibility $x < 0$, we may now assume $x \geq 0$. With this assumption we have to treat all $y \gtreqless 0$. Since $y \geq 0$ brings back entirely to the familiar case of 5.8, we need to consider the case $y < 0$ only.

Let y' be the number that obtains by disregarding the sign digit of y' which is 1, i.e., by replacing it by 0. Again y' acts not like $y - 1$, but like $(y - 1) + 2 = y + 1$. Hence the multiplication procedure of 5.8 will produce $xy' = x(y + 1) = xy + x$, and therefore a correction x is needed. (Note that, quite similarly to what we saw in the first case above, the suppression of the sign digit of y replaced the previously recognized correction $- 2x$ by the present one $- x$.) As we observed earlier, this correction $- x$ cannot be applied at the end to the completed xy' since at that time x is no longer available. Hence we must apply the correction $- x$ digitwise, subtracting every digit at the time when it is last found in AR, and in a way that makes it effective with the proper positional value.

Third: Consider then $x = 0$, ξ_1, ξ_2, ..., $\xi_{39} = (\xi_1, \xi_2 \ldots \xi_{39})$. The 39 digits $\xi_1 \ldots \xi_{39}$ of x are lost in the course of the 39 shifts of the multiplication procedure of 5.8, going from right to left. Thus the opera-

tion No. $k + 1$ ($k = 0, 1, \ldots, 38$, cf. 5.8) finds ξ_{39-k} in the right-most stage of AR, uses it, and then loses it through its concluding right shift (of both Ac and AR). After this step $39 - (k + 1) = 38 - k$ further steps, i.e., shifts follow, hence before its own concluding shift there are still $39 - k$ shifts to come. Hence the positional values are 2^{39-k} times higher than they will be at the end. ξ_{39-k} should appear at the end, in the correcting term $- x$, with the sign $-$ and the positional value $2^{-(39-k)}$. Hence we may inject it during the step $k + 1$ (before its shift) with the sign $-$ and the positional value 1. That is to say, $-\xi_{39-k}$ in the sign digit.

This, however, is inadmissible. Indeed, ξ_{39-k} might cause carries (if $\xi_{39-k} = 1$), which would have nowhere to go from the sign digit (there being no further positions to the left). This error is at its origin an integer multiple of 2, but the $39 - k$ subsequent shifts reduce its positional value 2^{39-k} times. Hence it might contribute to the end result any integer multiple of $2^{-(38-k)}$--and this is a genuine error.

Let us therefore add $1 - \xi_{39-k}$ to the sign digit, i.e., 0 or 1 if ξ_{39-k} is 1 or 0 respectively. We will show further below, that with this procedure there arise no carries of the inadmissible kind. Taking this momentarily for granted, let us see what the total effect is. We are correcting not by $- x$ but by $\sum_{i=1}^{39} 2^{-i} - x = 1 - 2^{-39} - x$. Hence a final correction by $- 1 + 2^{-39}$ is needed. Since this is done at the end (after all shifts), it may be taken modulo 2. That is to say, we must add $1 + 2^{-39}$, i.e., 1 in each of the two extreme positions. Adding 1 in the right-most position has the same effect as in the discussion at the end of 5.7 (dealing with the subtraction). It is equivalent to injecting a carry into the right-most stage of Ac. Adding 1 in the left-most position, i.e., to the sign digit, produces a 1, since that digit was necessarily 0. (Indeed, the last operation ended in a shift, thus freeing the sign digit, cf. below.)

Fourth: Let us now consider the question of the carries that may arise in the 39 steps of the process described above. In order to do this, let us describe the kth step (k = 1, ..., 39), which is a variant of the kth step described for a positive multiplication in 5.8, in the same way in which we described the original kth step loc. cit. That is to say, let us see what the formula (1) of 5.8 has become. It is clearly $2p_k = p_{k-1} + (1 - \xi_{40-k}) + \xi_{40-k} y'$, i.e.

$$2p_k = p_{k-1} + y_k' ,$$

$$y_k' \begin{cases} = 1 \quad \text{for } \xi_{40-k} = 0 \\[2em] = y' \quad \text{for } \xi_{40-k} = 1 \end{cases} \qquad (2)$$

That is, we add 1 (y's sign digit) or y' (y without its sign digit), according to whether $\xi_{40-k} = 0$ or 1. Then p_k should obtain from $2p_k$ again by halving.

Now the addition of (2) produces no carries beyond the 2^0 position, as we asserted earlier, for the same reason as the addition of (1) in 5.8. We can argue in the same way as there: $0 \leq p_h < 1$ is true for h = 0, and if it is true for h = k - 1, then (1) extends it to h = k also, since $0 \leq y_k' \leq 1$. Hence the sum in (2) is ≥ 0 and < 2, and no carries beyond the 2^0 position arise.

Fifth: In the three last observations we assumed y < 0. Let us now restore the full generality of $y \gtreqless 0$. We can then describe the equations (1) of 5.8 (valid for $y \geq 0$) and (2) above (valid for y < 0) by a single formula,

$$2p_k = p_{k-1} + y_k''$$

$$y_k'' \begin{cases} = y\text{'s sign digit for } \xi_{40-k} = 0 \\[2em] = y \text{ without its sign digit} \\ \qquad\qquad \text{for } \xi_{40-k} = 1 \end{cases}$$

$$(3)$$

Thus our verbal formulation of (2) applies here, too: We add y's sign digit or y without its sign, according to whether $\xi_{40-k} = 0$ or 1. All p_k are ≥ 0 and < 1, and the addition of (3) never originates a carry beyond the 2^0 position. p_k obtains from $2p_k$ by a right shift, filling the sign digit with a 0. (Cf. however, Part II, Table 2 for another sort of right shift that is desirable in explicit form, i.e., as an order.)

For $y \geq 0$, xy is p_{39}, for y < 0, xy obtains from p_{39} by injecting a carry into the right-most stage of Ac and by placing a 1 into the sign digit in Ac.

Sixth: This procedure applies for $x \geq 0$. For x < 0 it should also be applied, since it makes use of x's non-sign digits only, but at the end y must be subtracted from the result.

This method of binary multiplication will be illustrated in some examples in 5.15.

5.11. To complete our discussion of the multiplicative organs of our machine we must return to a consideration of the types of accumulators mentioned in 5.5. The static accumulator operates as an adder by simultaneously applying static voltages to two inputs--one for each of the two numbers being added. When steady-state operation is reached the total sum is formed complete with all carries. For such an accumulator the above discussion is substantially complete, except that it should be remarked that such a circuit requires at most 39 rise times to complete a carry. Actually it is possible that the duration of these successive rises is proportional to a lower power of 39 than the first one.

Each stage of a dynamic accumulator consists of a binary counter for registering the digit and a flip-flop for temporary storage of the carry. The counter receives a pulse if a 1 is to be added in at that place; if this causes the counter to go from 1 to 0 a carry has occurred and hence the carry flip-flop will be set. It then remains to perform the carries. Each flip-flop has associated with it a gate, the output of which is connected to the next binary counter to the left. The carry is begun by pulsing all carry gates. Now a carry may produce a carry, so that the process needs to be repeated until all carry flip-flops register 0. This can be detected by means of a circuit involving a sensing tube connected to each carry flip-flop. It was shown in 5.6 that, on the average, five pulse times (flip-flop reaction times) are required for the complete carry. An alternative scheme is to connect a gate tube to each binary counter which will detect whether an incoming carry pulse would produce a carry and will, under this circumstance, pass the incoming carry pulse directly to the next stage. This circuit would require at most 39 rise times for the completion of the carry. (Actually less, cf. above.)

At the present time the development of a static accumulator is being concluded. From preliminary tests it seems that it will add two numbers in about 5 μsec and will shift right or left in about 1 μsec.

We return now to the multiplication operation. In a static accumulator we order simultaneously an addition of the multiplicand with sign deleted or the sign of the multiplicand (cf. 5.10) and a complete carry and then a shift for each of the 39 steps. In a dynamic accumulator of the second kind just described we order in succession an addition of the multiplicand with sign deleted or the sign of the multiplicand, a complete carry, and a shift for each of the 39 steps. In a dynamic accumulator of the first kind we can avoid losing the time required for completing the carry (in this case an average of 5 pulse times, cf. above) at each of the 39 steps. We order an addition by the multiplicand with sign deleted or the sign of the multiplicand then order one pulsing of the carry gates, and finally shift the contents of both the digit counters and the carry flip-flops. This process is repeated 39 times. A simple arithmetical analysis which may be carried out in a later report, shows that at each one of

these intermediate stages a single carry is adequate, and that a complete set of carries is needed at the end only. We then carry out the complement corrections, still without ever ordering a complete set of carry operations. When all these corrections are completed and after round-off, described below, we then order the complete carry mentioned above.

5.12. It is desirable at this point in the discussion to consider rules for rounding-off to n-digits. In order to assess the characteristics of alternative possibilities for such properly, and in particular the role of the concept of "unbiasedness," it is necessary to visualize the conditions under which rounding-off is needed.

Every number x that appears in the computing machine is an approximation of another number x´, which would have appeared if the calculation had been performed absolutely rigorously. The approximations to which we refer here are not those that are caused by the explicitly introduced approximations of the numerical-mathematical set-up, e.g., the replacement of a (continuous) differential equation by a (discrete) difference equation. The effect of such approximations should be evaluated mathematically by the person who plans the problem for the machine, and should not be a direct concern of the machine. Indeed, it has to be handled by a mathematician and cannot be handled by the machine, since its nature, complexity, and difficulty may be of any kind, depending upon the problem under consideration. The approximations which concern us here are these: Even the elementary operations of arithmetic, to which the mathematical approximation-formulation for the machine has to reduce the true (possibly transcendental) problem, are not rigorously executed by the machine. The machine deals with numbers of n digits, where n, no matter how large, has to be a fixed quantity. (We assumed for our machine 40 digits, including the sign, i.e., n = 39.) Now the sum and difference of two n-digit numbers are again n-digit numbers, but

their product and quotient (in general)
are not. (They have, in general, 2n
or ∞-digits, respectively.) Consequently, multiplication and division must
unavoidably be replaced by the machine
by two different operations which must
produce n-digits under all conditions,
and which, subject to this limitation,
should lie as close as possible to the
results of the true multiplication and
division. One might call then pseudo-
multiplication and pseudo-division;
however, the accepted nomenclature
terms them as multiplication and division with round-off. (We are now
creating the impression that addition
and subtraction are entirely free of
such shortcomings. This is only true
inasmuch as they do not create new
digits to the right, as multiplication
and division do. However, they can
create new digits to the left, i.e.,
cause the numbers to "grow out of
range." This complication, which is,
of course, well known, is normally met
by the planner, by mathematical arrangements and estimates to keep the numbers
"within range." Since we propose to
have our machine deal with numbers between - 1 and 1, multiplication can
never cause them to "grow out of
range." Division, of course, might
cause this complication, too. The
planner must therefore see to it that
in every division the absolute value
of the divisor exceeds that of the
dividend.)

Thus the round-off is intended to
produce satisfactory n-digit approximations for the product xy and the
quotient x/y of two n-digit numbers.
Two things are wanted of the round-
off: (1) The approximation should be
good, i.e., its variance from the
"true" xy or x/y should be as small as
practicable; (2) The approximation
should be unbiased, i.e., its mean
should be equal to the "true" xy or
x/y.

These desiderata must, however, be
considered in conjunction with some further comments. Specifically: (a) x
and y themselves are likely to be the
results of similar round-offs, directly
or indirectly inherent, i.e., x and y

themselves should be viewed as unbiased
n-digit approximations of "true" x' and
y' values; (b) by talking of "variances"
and "means" we are introducing statistical concepts. Now the approximations
which we are here considering are not
really of a statistical nature, but are
due to the peculiarities (from our
point of view, inadequacies) of arithmetic and of digital representation,
and are therefore actually rigorously
and uniquely determined. It seems,
however, in the present state of
mathematical science, rather hopeless
to try to deal with these matters
rigorously. Furthermore, a certain
statistical approach, while not truly
justified, has always given adequate
practical results. This consists of
treating those digits which one does
not wish to use individually in subsequent calculations as random variables
with equiprobable digital values, and
of treating any two such digits as
statistically independent (unless this
is patently false).

These things being understood, we
can now undertake to discuss round-off
procedures, realizing that we will have
to apply them to the multiplication and
to the division.

Let $x = (.\xi_1 \ldots \xi_n)$ and $y =
(.\eta_1, \ldots \eta_n)$ be unbiased approximations
of x' and y'. Then the "true" $xy =
(.\zeta_1 \ldots \zeta_n \zeta_{n+1} \ldots \zeta_{2n})$ and the "true"
$x/y = (.\omega_1 \ldots \omega_n \omega_{n+1} \omega_{n+2} \ldots)$ (this
goes on ad infinitum!) are approxima-
tions of $x'y'$ and x'/y'. Before we
discuss how to round them off, we must
know whether the "true" xy and x/y are
themselves unbiased approximations of
$x'y'$ and x'/y'. xy is indeed an unbiased approximation of $x'y'$, i.e.,
the mean of xy is the mean of $x(= x')$
times the mean of $y(= y')$, owing to the
independence assumption which we made
above. However, if x and y are closely
correlated, e.g., for x = y, i.e., for
squaring, there is a bias. It is of the
order of this mean square of $x - x'$,
i.e., of the variance of x. Since x has
n digits, this variance is about $1/2^{2n}$.
(If the digits of x', beyond n are entirely unknown, then our original assumptions give the variance of

$1/12.2^{2n}$.) Next, x/y can be written as $x.y^{-1}$, and since we have already discussed the bias of the product, it suffices now to consider the reciprocal y^{-1}. Now if y is an unbiased estimate of y', then y^{-1} is not an unbiased estimate of y'^{-1}, i.e., the mean of y's reciprocal is not the reciprocal of y's mean. The difference is $\sim y^{-3}$ times the variance of y, i.e., it is of essentially the same order as the bias found above in the case of squaring.

It follows from all this that it is futile to attempt to avoid biases of the order of magnitude $1/2^{2n}$ or less. (The factor $1/12$ above may seem to be changing the order of magnitude in question. However, it is really the square root of the variance which matters and $\sqrt{(1/12)} \sim 0.3$ is a moderate factor.) Since we propose to use $n = 39$, therefore $1/2^{78} (\sim 3 \times 10^{-24})$ is the critical case. Note that this possible bias level is $1/2^{39} (\sim 2 \times 10^{-12})$ times our last significant digit. Hence we will look for round-off rules to n digits for the "true" $xy = (.\zeta_1 \ldots \zeta_n \zeta_n \zeta_{n+1} \ldots \zeta_{2n})$ and $x/y = (.\omega_1 \ldots \omega_{n+1} \omega_{n+2} \ldots)$. The desideratum (1) which we formulated previously, that the variance should be small, is still valid. The desideratum (2), however, that the bias should be zero, need, according to the above, only be enforced up to terms of the order $1/2^{2n}$.

The round-off procedures, which we can use in this connection, fall into two broad classes. The first class is characterized by its ignoring all digits beyond the nth, and even the nth digit itself, which it replaces by a 1. The second class is characterized by the procedure of adding one unit in the (n + 1)st digit, performing the carries which this may induce, and then keeping only the n first digits.

When applied to a number of the form $(.\nu_1 \ldots \nu_n\nu_{n+1}\nu_{n+2} \ldots)$ (ad infinitum!), the effects of either procedure are easily estimated. In the first case we may say we are dealing with $(.\nu_1, \ldots, \nu_{n-1})$ plus a random number of the form $(.0, \ldots, 0\nu_n\nu_{n+1} \nu_{n+2} \ldots)$, i.e., random in the interval

$0, 1/2^{n-1}$. Comparing with the rounded off $(.\nu_1\nu_2 \ldots \nu_{n-1}1)$, we therefore have a difference random in the interval $-1/2^n, 1/2^n$. Hence its mean is 0 and its variance $1/3 \cdot 2^{2n}$. In the second case we are dealing with $(.\nu_1 \ldots \nu_n)$ plus a random number of the form $(.0 \ldots 00\nu_{n+1}\nu_{n+2} \ldots)$, i.e., random in the interval $0, 1/2^n$. The "rounded-off" value will be $(.\nu_1 \ldots \nu^n)$ increased by 0 or by $1/2^n$, according to whether the random number in question lies in the interval $0, 1/2^{n+1}$, or in the interval $1/2^{n+1}, 1/2^n$. Hence comparing with the "rounded-off" value, we have a difference random in the intervals, $0, 1/2^{n+1}$, and $0 - 1/2^{n+1}$, i.e., in the interval $- 1/2^{n+1}, 1/2^{n+1}$. Hence its mean is 0 and its variance $(1/12)2^{2n}$.

If the number to be rounded-off has the form $(.\nu_1 \ldots \nu_n\nu_{n+1}\nu_{n+2} \ldots \nu_{n+p})$ (p finite), then these results are somewhat affected. The order of magnitude of the variance remains the same; indeed for large p even its relative change is negligible. The mean difference may deviate from 0 by amounts which are easily estimated to be of the order $1/2^n \cdot 1/2^p = 1/2^{n+p}$.

In division we have the first situation, $x/y = (.\omega_1 \ldots \omega_n\omega_{n+1}\omega_{n+2} \ldots)$, i.e., p is infinite. In multiplication we have the second one, $xy = (.\zeta_1 \ldots \zeta_n\zeta_{n+1} \ldots \zeta_{2n})$, i.e., p = n. Hence for the division both methods are applicable without modification. In multiplication a bias of the order of $1/2^{2n}$ may be introduced. We have seen that it is pointless to insist on removing biases of this size. We will therefore use the unmodified methods in this case, too.

It should be noted that the bias in the case of multiplication can be removed in various ways. However, for the reasons set forth above, we shall not complicate the machine by introducing such corrections.

Thus we have two standard "round-off" methods, both unbiased to the extent to which we need this, and with the variances $1/3 \cdot 2^{2n}$, and $(1/12)2^{2n}$, that is, with the dispersions $(1/\sqrt{3})$ $(1/2^n) = 0.58$ times the last digit and $(1/2\sqrt{3})(1/2^n) = 0.29$ times the last digit. The first one requires no carry facilities, the second one requires them.

Inasmuch as we propose to form the product $x'y$ in the accumulator, which has carry facilities, there is no reason why we should not adopt the rounding scheme described above which has the smaller dispersion, i.e., the one which may induce carries. In the case, however, of division we wish to avoid schemes leading to carries since we expect to form the quotient in the arithmetic register, which does not permit of carry operations. The scheme which we accordingly adopt is the one in which ω_n is replaced by 1. This method has the decided advantage that it enables us to write down the approximate quotient as soon as we know its first $(n - 1)$ digits. It will be seen in 5.14 and 6.6.4 below that our procedure for forming the quotient of two numbers will always lead to a result that is correctly rounded in accordance with the decisions just made. We do not consider as serious the fact that our rounding scheme in the case of division has a dispersion twice as large as that in multiplication since division is a far less frequent operation.

A final remark should be made in connection with the possible, occasional need of carrying more than n = 39 digits. Our logical control is sufficiently flexible to permit treating $k(= 2, 3, \ldots)$ words as one number, and thus effecting n = 39k. In this case the round-off has to be handled differently, cf. Chapter 9, Part II. The multiplier produces all 78 digits of the basic 39 by 39 digit multiplication: The first 39 in the Ac, the last 39 in the AR. These must then be manipulated in an appropriate manner. (For details, cf. 6.6.3 and 9.9-9.10, Part II.) The divider works for 39 digits only: In forming x/y, it is necessary, even if x and y are available to 39k digits, to use only 39 digits of each, and a 39 digit result will appear. It seems most convenient to use this result as the first step of a series of successive approximations. The successive improvements can then be

obtained by various means. One way consists of using the well known iteration formula (cf. 5.4). For k = 2 one such step will be needed, for k = 3, 4, two steps, for k = 5, 6, 7, 8 three steps, etc. An alternative procedure is this: Calculate the remainder, using the approximate, 39 digit, quotient and the complete, 39k digit, divisor, thus obtaining essentially the next 39 digits of the quotient. Repeat this procedure until the full 39k desired digits of the quotient have been obtained.

5.13. We might mention at this time a complication which arises when a floating binary point is introduced into the machine. The operation of addition which usually takes at most 1/10 of a multiplication time becomes much longer in a machine with floating binary since one must perform shifts and round-offs as well as additions. It would seem reasonable in this case to place the time of an addition as about 1/3 to 1/2 of a multiplication. At this rate it is clear that the number of additions in a problem is as important a factor in the total solution time as are the number of multiplications. (For further details concerning the floating binary point cf. 6.6.7.)

5.14. We conclude our discussion of the arithmetic unit with a description of our method for handling the division operation. To perform a division we wish to store the dividend in SR, the partial remainder in Ac and the partial quotient in AR. Before proceeding further let us consider the so-called restoring and non-restoring methods of division. In order to be able to make certain comparisons, we will do this for a general base m = 2, 3, \ldots .

Assume for the moment that divisor and dividend are both positive. The ordinary process of division consists of subtracting from the partial remainder (at the very beginning of the process this is, of course, the dividend) the divisor, repeating this until the former becomes smaller than the latter. For any fixed positional value in the quotient in a well-conducted division this need be done at most m - 1 times. If, after precisely k = 0, 1, ..., m - 1 repetitions of this step, the partial remainder has indeed become less than the divisor, then the digit k is put in the quotient (at the position under consideration), the partial remainder is shifted one place to the left, and the whole process is repeated for the next position, etc. Note that the above comparison of sizes is only needed at k = 0, 1, ..., m - 2, i.e., before step 1 and after steps 1, ..., m - 2. If the value k = m - 1, i.e., the point after step m - 1, is at all reached in a well-conducted division, then it may be taken for granted without any test, that the partial remainder has become smaller than the divisor and the operations on the position under consideration can therefore be concluded. (In the binary system, m = 2, there is thus only one step and only one comparison of sizes, before this step.) In this way this scheme, known as the restoring scheme, requires a maximum of m - 1 comparisons and utilizes the digits 0, 1, ..., m - 1 in each place in the quotient. The difficulty of this scheme for machine purposes is that usually the only economical method for comparing two numbers as to size is to subtract one from the other. If the partial remainder r_n were less than the dividend d, one would then have to add d back into r_n - d in order to restore the remainder. Thus at every stage an unnecessary operation would be performed. A more symmetrical scheme is obtained by not restoring. In this method (from here on we need not assume the positivity of divisor and dividend) one compares the signs of r_n and d; if they are of the same sign, the dividend is repeatedly subtracted from the remainder until the signs become opposite; if they are opposite the dividend is repeatedly added to the remainder until the signs again become like. In this scheme the digits that may occur in a given place in the quotient are evidently ± 1, ± 2, ..., ±(m - 1), the positive digits corresponding to sub-

tractions and the negative ones to additions of the dividend to the remainder.

Thus we have 2(m - 1) digits instead of the usual m digits. In the decimal system this would mean 18 digits instead of 10. This is a redundant notation. The standard form of the quotient must therefore be restored by subtracting from the aggregate of its negative digits. This requires carry facilities in the place where the quotient is stored.

We propose to store the quotient in AR, which has no carry facilities. Hence we could not use this scheme if we were to operate in the decimal system.

The same objection applies to any base m for which the digital representation in question is redundant--i.e., when 2(m - 1) > m. Now 2(m - 1) > m whenever m > 2, but 2(m - 1) = m for m = 2. Hence, with the use of a register which we have so far contemplated, this division scheme is certainly excluded from the start unless the binary system is used.

Let us now investigate the situation in the binary system. We inquire if it is possible to obtain a quasi-quotient by using the non-restoring scheme and by using the digits 1, 0 instead of 1, - 1. Or rather we have to ask this question: does this quasi-quotient bear a simple relationship to the true quotient?

Let us momentarily assume this question can be answered affirmatively and describe the division procedure. We store the divisor initially in Ac, the dividend in SR and wish to form the quotient in AR. We now either add or subtract the contents of SR into Ac, according to whether the signs in Ac and SR are opposite or the same, and insert correspondingly a 0 or 1 in the right-hand place of AR. We then shift both Ac and AR one place left, with electronic shifters that are parts of these two aggregates.

At this point we interrupt the discussion to note this: multiplication required an ability to shift right in both Ac and AR (cf. 5.8). We have

now found that division similarly requires an ability to shift left in both
Ac and AR. Hence both organs must be
able to shift both ways electronically.
Since these abilities have to be present for the implicit needs of multiplication and division, it is just as
well to make use of them explicitly in
the form of explicit orders. These
are the orders 20, 21 of Table 1, and
of Table 2, Part II. It will, however,
turn out to be convenient to arrange
some details in the shifts, when they
occur explicitly under the control of
those orders, differently from when
they occur implicitly under the control of a multiplication or a division.
(For these things, c.f. the discussion
of the shifts near the end of 5.8 and
in the third remark below on one hand,
and in the third remark in 7.2, Part
II, on the other hand.)

Let us now resume the discussion
of the division. The process described
above will have to be repated as many
times as the number of quotient digits
that we consider appropriate to produce
in this way. This is likely to be 39
or 40; we will determine the exact number further below.

In this process we formed digits
$\zeta_i' = 0$ or 1 for the quotient, when the
digit should actually have been $\zeta_i = -1$
or 1, with $\zeta_i = 2\zeta_i' - 1$. Thus we have
a difference between the true quotient
z (based on the digits ζ_i) and the
quasi-quotient z' (based on the digits
ζ_i'), but at the same time a one-to-
one connection. It would be easy to
establish the algebraical expression
for this connection between z' and z
directly, but it seems better to do
this as part of a discussion which
clarifies all other questions connected
with the process of division at the
same time.

We first make some general remarks:
First: Let x be the dividend and
y the divisor. We assume, of course,
$-1 \leq x < 1, -1 \leq y < 1$. It will be
found that our present process of division is entirely unaffected by the
signs of x and y, hence no further restrictions on that score are required.

On the other hand, the quotient

z = x/y must also fulfill $-1 \leq z < 1$.
It seems somewhat simpler although this
is by no means necessary, to exclude
for the purposes of this discussion
z = - 1, and to demand $|z| < 1$. This
means in terms of the dividend x and
the divisor y that we exclude x = - y
and assume $|x| < y$.

Second: The division takes place
in n steps, which correspond to the n
digits $\zeta_1, \ldots, \zeta_n$ of the pseudo-quo-
tient z', n being yet to be determined
(presumably 39 or 40). Assume that
the k - 1 first steps (k = 1, ..., n)
have already taken place, having produced the k - 1 first digits: $\zeta_1, \ldots,$
ζ_{k-1}; and that we are now at the kth
step, involving production of the kth
digit; ζ_k. Assume furthermore, that
Ac now contains the quantity r_{k-1}, the
result of the k - 1 first steps. (This
is the (k - 1)st partial remainder.
For k = 1 clearly $r_0 = x$.) We then
form $r_k = 2r_{k-1} \mp y$, according to whether the signs of r_{k-1} and y do or do
not agree, i.e.

$$r_k = 2r_{k-1} \; \boxed{+} \; y$$

$$\boxed{+} \begin{cases} \text{is - if the signs of } r_{k-1} \text{ and y do} \\ \quad \text{agree} \\ \\ \text{is + if the signs of } r_{k-1} \text{ and y do} \\ \quad \text{not agree} \end{cases}$$

$$(4)$$

Let us now see what carries may
originate in this procedure. We can
argue as follows: $|r_h| < |y|$ is true
for h = 0 ($|r_0| = |x| < |y|$), and if
it is true for h = k - 1, then (4)
extends it to h = k also, since r_{k-1}
and $\boxed{+}$y have opposite signs. The
last point may be elaborated a little
further: because of the opposite signs

$$|r_h| = 2|r_{k-1}| - |y| < 2|y| - |y| = |y|$$

Hence we have always $|r_k| < |y|$, and
therefore a fortiori $|r_k| < 1$, i.e.,
$- 1 < r_k < 1$.

Consequently in equation (4) one
summand is necessarily $> - 2, < 2$,

the other is ≥ 1, < 1, and the sum is > -1, < 1. Hence we carry out the operations of (4) modulo 2, disregarding any possibilities of carries beyond the 2^0 position, and the resulting r_k will be automatically correct (in the range > -1, < 1).

Third: Note however that the sign of r_{k-1}, which plays an important role in (4) above, is only then correctly determinable from the sign digit, if the number from which it is derived is ≥ -1, < 1. (Cf. the discussion in 5.7.) This requirement however is met, as we saw above, by r_{k-1}, but not necessarily by $2r_{k-1}$. Hence the sign of r_{k-1} (i.e., its sign digit) as required by (4), must be sensed before r_{k-1} is doubled.

This being understood, the doubling of r_{k-1} may be performed as a simple left shift, in which the leftmost digit (the sign digit) is allowed to be lost--this corresponds to the disregarding of carries beyond the 2^0 position, which we recognized above as being permissible in (4). (Cf. however, Part II, Table 2, for another sort of left shift that is desirable in explicit form, i.e., as an order.)

Fourth: Consider now the precise implication of (4) above. $\zeta_1 = 1$ or 0 corresponds to $\boxed{+} = -$ or $+$, respectively. Hence (4) may be written

$$r_k = 2r_{k-1} + (1 - 2\zeta_k')y$$

i.e.

$$2^{-k}r_k = 2^{-(k-1)}r_{k-1} + (2^{-k} - 2^{-(k-1)}\zeta_k')y$$

Summing over $k = 1, \ldots, n$ gives

$$2^{-n}r_n = x + \left\{ (1 - 2^{-n}) - \sum_{k=1}^{n} 2^{-(k-1)} \zeta_k' \right\} y$$

i.e.

$$x = \left(-1 + \sum_{k=1}^{n} 2^{-(k-1)} \zeta_k' + 2^{-n} \right) y + 2^{-n} r_n$$

This makes it clear, that $\bar{z} = -1 + \sum_{k=1}^{n} 2^{-(k-1)} \zeta_k' + 2^{-n}$ corresponds to true quotient $z = x/y$ and $2^{-n}r_n$, with an absolute value $< 2^{-n} |y| \leq 2^{-n}$, to the remainder. Hence, if we disregard the term -1 for a moment $\zeta_1, \zeta_2, \ldots, \zeta_n, 1$ are the $n + 1$ first digits of what may be used as a true quotient, the sign digit being part of this sequence.

Fifth: If we do not wish to get involved in more complicated round-off procedures which exceed the immediate capacity of the only available adder Ac, then the above result suggests that we should put $n + 1 = 40$, $n = 39$. The $\zeta_1', \ldots, \zeta_{39}'$ are then 39 digits of the quotient, including the sign digit, but not including the right-most digit.

The right-most digit is taken care of by placing a 1 into the right-most stage of Ac.

At this point an additional argument in favor of the procedure that we have adopted here becomes apparent. The procedure coincides (without a need for any further corrections) with the second round-off procedure that we discussed in 5.12.

There remains the term -1. Since this applies to the final result, and no right shifts are to follow, carries which might go beyond the 2^0 position may be disregarded. Hence this amounts simply to changing the sign digit of the quotient $\bar{z}$: replacing 0 or 1 by 1 or 0 respectively.

This concludes our discussion of the division scheme. We wish, however, to re-emphasize two very distinctive features which it possesses:

First: This division scheme applies equally for any combinations of signs of divisor and dividend. This is a characteristic of the non-restoring division schemes, but it is not the

case for any simple known multiplication scheme. It will be remembered, in
particular, that our multiplication
procedure of 5.9 had to contain special
correcting steps for the cases where
either or both factors are negative.

    Second: This division scheme is
practicable in the binary system only;
it has no analog for any other base.

    This method of binary division will
be illustrated on some examples in 5.15.

    5.15. We give below some illus-
trative examples of the operations of
binary arithmetic which were discussed
in the preceding sections.

    Although it presented no difficul-
ties or ambiguities, it seems best to
begin with an example of addition.

	Decimal notation
Binary notation	(fractional form)
Augend . . 0.010110011	179/512
Addend . . 0.011010111	215/512
Sum . . 0.110001010	394/512
(Carries). 1111 111	

In what follows we will not show the
carries any more.
We form the negative of a number
(cf. 5.7):

	Decimal notation
Binary notation	(fractional form)
0.101110100	372/512
Comple- ment: . . 1.010001011	
1	
1.010001100 −1	+140/512

A subtraction (cf. 5.7):

	Decimal notation
Binary notation	(fractional form)
Subtrahend . 0.011010111	215/512
Minuend . . 0.110001010	394/512
Complement of subtrahend . 1.100101000	
1 −1	+297/512
Difference . 0.010110011	179/512

Some multiplications (cf. 5.8 and 5.9):

	Decimal notation
Binary notation	(fractional form)
Multiplicand 0.101	5/8
Multiplier . 0.011	3/8
0101	
0101	
0	
Product . . 0.001111	15/64

	Decimal notation
Binary notation	(fractional form)
Multiplicand 1.101	−3/8
Multiplier . 1.011	−5/8
0101	
0101	
1	
.101111	
Correction 1* 1 1	
1.110111	
Correction 2+ (Complement of the multiplicand)0.010	
1	
0.001111	15/64

A division (cf. 5.14):

	Decimal notation
Binary notation	(fractional form)
	Q.D.≠
Divisor . 1.011000	−5/8
Dividend 0.001111	15/64
0.011110	0
1.011000	
1.110110	
1.101100	1
0.100111	
1	
0.010100	
0.101000	0
1.011000	
0.000000	
0.000000	0

* For the sign of the multiplicand.
+ For the sign of the multiplier.
≠ Quotient digit.

```
      1.011000
      1.011000
      0.110000    1
      0.100111
              1
      1.011000
      .......     1
Quotient  0.10011
(uncorrected)
Quotient  1.100111
(corrected)            - 1 + 39/65
                     = - 25/64
```

Note that this deviates by 1/64, i.e., by one unit of the right-most position, from the correct result -3/8. This is a consequence of our round-off rule, which forces the right-most digit to be 1 under all conditions. This occasionally produces results with un-familiar and even annoying aspects (e.g., when quotients like 0 : y or y : y are formed), but it is neverthe-less unobjectionable and self-consis-tent on the basis of our general principles.

6. THE CONTROL

6.1. It has already been stated that the computer will contain an or-gan, called the control, which can automatically execute the orders stored in the Selectrons. Actually, for a reason stated in 6.3, the orders for this computer are less than half as long as a forty binary digit number, and hence the orders are stored in the Selectron memory in pairs.

Let us consider the routine that the control performs in directing a computation. The control must know the location in the Selectron memory of the pair of orders to be executed. It must direct the Selectrons to transmit this pair of orders to the Selectron regis-ter and then to itself. It must then direct the execution of the operation specified in the first of the two orders. Among these orders we can immediately describe two major types: An order of the first type begins by causing the transfer of the number, which is stored at a specified memory location, from the Selectrons to the Selectron register. Next, it causes the arithmetical unit to perform some arithmetical operations on this number (usually in conjunction with another number which is already in the arith-metical unit), and to retain the resul-ting number in the arithmetical unit. The second type order causes the trans-fer of the number, which is held in the arithmetical unit, into the Selectron register, and from there to a specified memory location in the Selectrons. (It may also be that this latter operation will permit a direct transfer from the arithmetical unit into the Selectrons.) An additional type of order consists of the transfer orders of 3.5. Further orders control the inputs and the out-puts of the machine. The process described at the beginning of this paragraph must then be repeated with the second order of the order pair. This entire routine is repeated until the end of the problem.

6.2. It is clear from what has just been stated that the control must have a means of switching to a speci-fied location in the Selectron memory, for withdrawing both numbers for the computation and pairs of orders. Since the Selectron memory (as tentatively planned) will hold 2^{12} = 4,096 forty-digit words (a word is either a number or a pair of orders), a twelve-digit binary number suffices to identify a memory location. Hence a switching mechanism is required which will, on receiving a twelve-digit binary number, select the corresponding memory loca-tion.

The type of circuit we propose to use for this purpose is known as a de-coding or many-one function table. It has been developed in various forms independently by J. Rajchman and P. Crawford.[*] It consists of n flip-

---

[*]Rajchman's table is described in an RCA Laboratories' report by Rajchman, Snyder and Rudnick issued in 1943 under the terms of an OSRD con-tract OEM-sr-591. Crawford's work is discussed in his thesis for the Master's degree at Massachusetts Institute of Technology.

flops which register an n digit binary
number. It also has a maximum of 2^n
output wires. The flip-flops activate
a matrix in which the interconnections
between input and output wires are
made in such a way that one and only
one of 2^n output wires is selected
(i.e., has a positive voltage applied
to it). These interconnections may be
established by means of resistors or by
by means of non-linear elements (such
as diodes or rectifiers); all these
various methods are under investigation. The Selectron is so designed
that four such function table switches
are required, each with a three digit
entry and eight (2^3) outputs. Four
sets of eight wires each are brought
out of the Selectron for switching
purposes, and a particular location is
selected by making one wire positive
with respect to the remainder. Since
all forty Selectrons are switched in
parallel, these four sets of wires may
be connected directly to the four
function table outputs.

   6.3. Since most computer operations involve at least one number
located in the Selectron memory, it is
reasonable to adopt a code in which
twelve binary digits of every order are
assigned to the specification of a
Selectron location. In those orders
which do not require a number to be
taken out of or into the Selectrons
these digit positions will not be used.

   Though it has not been definitely
decided how many operations will be
built into the computer (i.e., how many
different orders the control must be
able to understand), it will be seen
presently that there will probably be
more than 2^5 but certainly less than
2^6. For this reason it is feasible to
assign 6 binary digits for the order
code. It thus turns out that each order must contain eighteen binary digits,
the first twelve identifying a memory
location and the remaining six specifying an operation. It can now be explained why orders are stored in the
memory in pairs. Since the same memory
organ is to be used in this computer
for both orders and numbers, it is
efficient to make the length of each

about equivalent. But numbers of eighteen binary digits would not be sufficiently accurate for problems which
this machine will solve. Rather, an
accuracy of at least 10^{-10} or 2^{-33} is
required. Hence it is preferable to
make the numbers long enough to accommodate two orders.

   As we pointed out in 2.3, and
used in 4.2 et seq. and 5.7 et seq.,
our numbers will actually have 40 binary digits each. This allows 20
binary digits for each order, i.e., the
12 digits that specify a memory location, and 8 more digits specifying the
nature of the operation (instead of
the minimum of 6 referred to above).
It is convenient, as will be seen in
6.8.2. and Chapter 9, Part II, to group
these binary digits into tetrads,
groups of 4 binary digits. Hence a
whole word consists of 10 tetrads, a
half word or order of 5 tetrads, and
of these 3 specify a memory location
and the remaining 2 specify the nature
of the operation. Outside the machine
each tetrad can be expressed by a base
16 digit. (The base 16 digits are best
designated by symbols of the 10 decimal
digits 0 to 9, and 6 additional symbols,
e.g., the letters a to f. Cf. Chapter
9, Part II.) These 16 characters
should appear in the typing for and the
printing from the machine. (For further details of these arrangements, cf.
loc. cit. above.)

   The specification of the nature of
the operation that is involved in an
order occurs in binary form, so that
another many-one or decoding function
is required to decode the order. This
function table will have six input flip-
flops (the two remaining digits of the
order are not needed). Since there
will not be 64 different orders, not
all 64 outputs need be provided. However, it is perhaps worthwhile to connect the outputs corresponding to unused order possibilities to a checking
circuit which will give an indication
whenever a code word unintelligible to
the control is received in the input
flip-flops.

   The function table just described
energizes a different output wire for

each different code operation. As will be shown later, many of the steps involved in executing different orders overlap. (For example, addition, multiplication, division, and going from the Selectrons to the register all include transferring a number from the Selectrons to the Selectron register.) For this reason it is perhaps desirable to have an additional set of control wires, each of which is activated by any particular combination of different code digits. These may be obtained by taking the output wires of the many-one function table and using them to operate tubes which will in turn operate a one-many (or coding) function table. Such a function table consists of a matrix as before, but in this case only one of the input wires is activated at any one time, while various sets of one or more of the output wires are activated. This particular table may be referred to as the recoding function table.

The twelve flip-flops operating the four function tables used in selecting a Selectron position, and the six flip-flops operating the function table used for decoding the order, are referred to as the Function Table Register, FR.

6.4. Let us consider next the process of transferring a pair of orders from the Selectrons to the control. These orders first go into SR. The order which is to be used next may be transferred directly into FR. The second order of the pair must be removed from SR (since SR may be used when the first order is executed), but cannot as yet be placed in FR. Hence a temporary storage is provided for it. The storage means is called the Control Register, CR, and consists of 20 (or possibly 18) flip-flops, capable of receiving a number from SR and transmitting a number to FR.

As already stated (6.1), the control must know the location of the pair of orders it is to get from the Selectron memory. Normally this location will be the one following the location of the two orders just executed. That is, until it receives an order to do

otherwise, the control will take its orders from the Selectrons in sequence. Hence the order location may be remembered in a twelve stage binary counter (one capable of counting 2^{12}) to which one unit is added whenever a pair of orders is executed. This counter is called the Control Counter, CC.

The details of the process of obtaining a pair of orders from the Selectron are thus as follows: The contents of CC are copied into FR, the proper Selectron location is selected, and the contents of the Selectrons are transferred to SR. FR is then cleared, and the contents of SR are transferred to it and CR. CC is advanced by one unit so the control will be prepared to select the next pair of orders from the memory. (There is, however, an exception from this last rule for the so-called transfer orders, cf. 3.5. This may feed CC in a different manner, cf. the next paragraph below.) First the order in FR is executed and then the order in CR is transferred to FR and executed. It should be noted that all these operations are directed by the control itself--not only the operations specified in the control words sent to FR, but also the automatic operations required to get the correct orders there.

Since the method by means of which the control takes order pairs in sequence from the memory has been described, it only remains to consider how the control shifts itself from one sequence of control orders to another in accordance with the operations described in 3.5. The execution of these operations is relatively simple. An order calling for one of these operations contains the twelve digit specification of the position to which the control is to be switched, and these digits will appear in the left-hand twelve flip-flops of FR. All that is required to shift the control is to transfer the contents of these flip-flops to CC. When the control goes to the Selectrons for the next pair of orders it will then go to the location specified by the number so transferred. In the case of the unconditional trans-

fer, the transfer is made automatically;
in the case of the conditional transfer
it is made only if the sign counter of
the Accumulator registers zero.

      6.5. In this report we will dis-
cuss only the general method by means
of which the control will execute
specific orders, leaving the details
until later. It has already been explained (5.5) that when a circuit is
to be designed to accomplish a particular elementary operation (such as
addition), a choice must be made between a static type and a dynamic type
circuit. When the design of the control is considered, this same choice
arises. The function of the control
is to direct a sequence of operations
which take place in the various circuits of the computer (including the
circuits of the control itself). Consider what is involved in directing an
operation. The control must signal
for the operation to begin, it must
supply whatever signals are required
to specify that particular operation,
and it must in some way know when the
operation has been completed so that
it may start the succeeding operation. Hence the control circuits must
be capable of timing the operations.
It should be noted that timing is required whether the circuit performing
the operation is static or dynamic.
In the case of a static type circuit
the control must supply static control signals for a period of time sufficient to allow the output voltages
to reach the steady-state condition.
In the case of a dynamic type circuit
the control must send various pulses
at proper intervals to this circuit.

      If all circuits of a computer are
static in character, the control timing
circuits may likewise be static, and
no pulses are needed in the system.
However, though some of the circuits of
the computer we are planning will be
static, they will probably not all be
so, and hence pulses as well as static
signals must be supplied by the control to the rest of the computer.
There are many advantages in deriving
these pulses from a central source,
called the clock. The timing may then
be done either by means of counters
counting clock pulses or by means of
electrical delay lines (an RC circuit
is here regarded as a simple delay
line). Since the timing of the entire
computer is governed by a single pulse
source, the computer circuits will be
said to operate as a synchronized
system.

      The clock plays an important role
both in detecting and in localizing
the errors made by the computer. One
method of checking which is under consideration is that of having two identical computers which operate in parallel and automatically compare each
other's results. Both machines would
be controlled by the same clock, so
they would operate in absolute synchronism. It is not necessary to compare every flip-flop of one machine
with the corresponding flip-flop of
the other. Since all numbers and control words pass through either the
Selectron register or the accumulator
soon before or soon after they are
used, it suffices to check the flip-
flops of the Selectron register and
the flip-flops of the accumulator which
hold the number registered there; in
fact, it seems possible to check the
accumulator only (cf. the end of 6.6.2).
The checking circuit would stop the
clock whenever a difference appeared,
or stop the machine in a more direct
manner if an asynchronous system is
used. Every flip-flop of each computer
will be located at a convenient place.
In fact, all neons will be located on
one panel, the corresponding neons of
the two machines being placed in parallel rows so that one can tell at a
glance (after the machine has been
stopped) where the discrepancies are.

      The merits of any checking system
must be weighed against its cost.
Building two machines may appear to be
expensive, but since most of the cost
of a scientific computer lies in development rather than production, this
consideration is not so important as it
might seem. Experience may show that
for most problems the two machines need
not be operated in parallel. Indeed, in
most cases purely mathematical, exter-

nal checks are possible: Smoothness of the results, behavior of differences of various types, validity of suitable identities, redundant calculations, etc. All of these methods are usually adequate to disclose the presence or absence of error in toto; their drawback is only that they may not allow the detailed diagnosing and locating of errors at all or with ease. When a problem is run for the first time, so that it requires special care, or when an error is known to be present, and has to be located--only then will it be necessary as a rule, to use both machines in parallel. Thus they can be used as separate machines most of the time. The essential feature of such a method of checking lies in the fact that it checks the computation at every point (and hence detects transient errors as well as steady-state ones) and stops the machine when the error occurs so that the process of localizing the fault is greatly simplified. These advantages are only partially gained by duplicating the arithmetic part of the computer, or by following one operation with the complement operation (multiplication by division, etc.) since this fails to check either the memory or the control (which is the most complicated, though not the largest, part of the machine).

The method of localizing errors, either with or without a duplicate machine, needs further discussion. It is planned to design all the circuits (including those of the control) of the computer so that if the clock is stopped between pulses the computer will retain all its information in flip-flops so that the computation may proceed unaltered when the clock is started again. This principle has already demonstrated its usefulness in the ENIAC. This makes it possible for the machine to compute with the clock operating at any speed below a certain maximum, as long as the clock gives out pulses of constant shape regardless of the spacing between pulses. In particular, the spacing between pulses may be made indefinitely large. The clock will be provided with a mode of opera-

tion in which it will emit a single pulse whenever instructed to do so by the operator. By means of this, the operator can cause the machine to go through an operation step by step, checking the results by means of the indicating-lamps connected to the flip-flops. It will be noted that this design principle does not exclude the use of delay lines to obtain delays as long as these are only used to time the constituent operations of a single step, and have no part in determining the machine's operating repetition rate. Timing coincidences by means of delay lines is excluded since this requires a constant pulse rate.

6.6. The orders which the control understands may be divided into two groups: Those that specify operations which are performed within the computer and those that specify operations involved in getting data into and out of the computer. At the present time the internal operations are more completely planned than the input and output operations, and hence they will be discussed more in detail than the latter (which are treated briefly in 6.8). The internal operations which have been tentatively adopted are listed in Table 1. It has already been pointed out that not all of these operations are logically basic, but that many can be programmed by means of others. In the case of some of these operations the reasons for building them into the control have already been given. In this section we will give reasons for building the other operations into the control and will explain in the case of each operation what the control must do in order to execute it.

In order to have the precise mathematical meaning of the symbols which are introduced in what follows clearly in mind, the reader should consult the table at the end of the report for each new symbol, in addition to the explanations given in the text.

6.6.1. Throughout what follows $S(x)$ will denote the memory location No. x in the Selectron. Accordingly the x which appears in $S(x)$ is a 12-digit binary, in the sense of 6.2. The eight addition operations [S(x) → Ac +, S(x) → Ac - , S(x) → Ah +, S(x) → Ah -, S(x) → Ac + M, S(x) → Ac - M, S(x) → Ah + M, S(x) → Ah - M] involves the following possible four steps:

First: Clear SR and transfer into it the number at S(x).

Second: Clear Ac if the order contains the symbol c; do not clear Ac if the order contains the symbol h.

Third: Add the number in SR or its negative (i.e., in our present system its complement with respect to 2^1) into Ac. If the order does not contain the symbol M, use the number in SR or its negative according to whether the order contains the symbol + or -. If the order contains the symbol M, use the number in SR or its negative according to whether the sign of the number in SR and the symbol + or - in the order do or do not agree.

Fourth: Perform a complete carry. Building the last four addition operations (those containing the symbol M) into the control is fairly simple: It calls only for one extra comparison (of the sign in SR and the + or - in the order, cf. the third step above), and it requires, therefore, only a few tubes more than required for the first four addition operations (those not containing the symbol M). These facts would seem of themselves to justify adding the operations in question: plus and minus the absolute value. But it should be noted that these operations can be programmed out of the other operations of Table 1 with correspondingly few orders (three for absolute value and five for minus absolute value), so that some further justification for building them in is required. The absolute value order is frequently in connection with the orders L and R (see 6.6.7), while the minus absolute value order makes the detection of a zero very simple by merely detecting the sign of $- |N|$. (If $- |N| \geq 0$, then N = 0.)

6.6.2. The operation of S(x) → R involves the following two steps:

First: Clear SR, and transfer S(x) to it.

Second: Clear AR and add the number in the Selectron register into it.

The operation of R → Ac merits more detailed discussion, since there are alternative ways of removing numbers from AR. Such numbers could be taken directly to the Selectrons as well as into Ac, and they could be transferred to Ac in parallel, in sequence, or in sequence parallel. It should be recalled that while most of the numbers that go into AR have come from the Selectrons and thus need not be returned to them, the result of a division and the right-hand 39 digits of a product appear in AR. Hence while an operation for withdrawing a number from AR is required, it is relatively infrequent and therefore need not be particularly fast. We are therefore considering the possibility of transferring at least partially in sequence and of using the shifting properties of Ac and of AR for this. Transferring the number to the Selectron via the accumulator is also desirable if the dual machine method of checking is employed, for it means that even if numbers are only checked in their transit through the accumulator, nevertheless every number going into the Selectron is checked before being placed there.

6.6.3. The operation S(x) x R → Ac involves the following six steps:

First: Clear SR and transfer S(x) (the multiplicand) into it.

Second: Thirty-nine steps, each of which consist of the two following parts: (a) Add (or rather shift) the sign digit of SR into the partial product in Ac, or add all but the sign digit of SR into the partial product in Ac--depending upon whether the right-most digit in AR is 0 or 1--and effect the appropriate carries. (b) Shift Ac and AR to the right, fill the sign digit of Ac with a 0 and the digit of AR immediately right of the sign digit (positional value 2^{-1}) with the previously right-most digit of Ac. (There are ways to save time by merging these two operations when the right-most digit in AR is 0, but we will not discuss them here more fully.)

Third: If the sign digit in SR is 1 (i.e., -), then inject a carry into

Table 1.

	Symbolization		Operation
	Complete	Abbreviated	
1	$S(x) \rightarrow Ac+$	x	Clear accumulator and add number located at position x in the Selectrons into it
2	$S(x) \rightarrow Ac-$	x-	Clear accumulator and subtract number located at position x in the Selectrons into it
3	$S(x) \rightarrow AcM$	xM	Clear accumulator and add absolute value of number located at position x in the Selectrons into it
4	$S(x) \rightarrow Ac-M$	x-M	Clear accumulator and subtract absolute value of number located at position x in the Selectrons into it
5	$S(x) \rightarrow Ah+$	xh	Add number located at position x in the Selectrons into the accumulator
6	$S(x) \rightarrow Ah-$	xh-	Subtract number located at position x in the Selectrons into the accumulator
7	$S(x) \rightarrow AhM$	xhM	Add absolute value of number located at position x in the Selectrons into the accumulator
8	$S(x) \rightarrow Ah-M$	x-hM	Subtract absolute value of number located at position x in the Selectrons into the accumulator
9	$S(x) \rightarrow R$	xR	Clear register* and add number located at position x in the Selectrons into it
10	$R \rightarrow A$	A	Clear accumulator and shift number held in register into it
11	$S(x) \times R \rightarrow A$	xX	Clear accumulator and multiply the number located at position x in the Selectrons by the number in the register, placing the left-hand 39 digits of the answer in the accumulator and the right-hand 39 digits of the answer in the register
12	$A \div S(x) \rightarrow R$	x ÷	Clear register and divide the number in the accumulator by the number located in position x of the Selectrons, leaving the remainder in the accumulator and placing the quotient in the register
13	$Cu \rightarrow S(x)$	xC	Shift the control to the left-hand order of the order pair located at position x in the Selectrons
14	$Cu' \rightarrow S(x)$	xC'	Shift the control to the right-hand order of the order pair located at position x in the Selectrons
15	$Cc \rightarrow S(x)$	xCc	If the number in the accumulator is ≥ 0, shift the control as in $Cu \rightarrow S(x)$
16	$Cc' \rightarrow S(x)$	xCc'	If the number in the accumulator is ≥ 0, shift the control as in $Cu' \rightarrow S(x)$
17	$At \rightarrow S(x)$	xS	Transfer the number in the accumulator to position x in the Selectrons
18	$Ap \rightarrow S(x)$	xSp	Replace the left-hand 12 digits of the left-hand order located at position x in the Selectrons by the left-hand 12 digits in the accumulator
19	$Ap' \rightarrow S(x)$	xSp'	Replace the left-hand 12 digits of the right-hand order located at position x in the Selectrons by the left-hand 12 digits in the accumulator
20	L	L	Multiply the number in the accumulator by 2, leaving it there
21	R	R	Divide the number in the accumulator by 2, leaving it there

* Register means arithmetic register.

the right-most stage of Ac and place a 1 into the sign digit of Ac.

Fourth: If the original sign digit of AR is 1 (i.e., −), then subtract the contents of SR from Ac.

Fifth: If a partial carry system was employed in the main process, then a complete carry is necessary at the end.

Sixth: The appropriate round-off must be effected. (Cf. Chapter 9, Part II, for details, where it is also explained how the sign digit of the Arithmetic register is treated as part of the round-off process.)

It will be noted that since any number held in Ac at the beginning of the process is gradually shifted into AR, it is impossible to accumulate sums of products in Ac without storing the various products temporarily in the Selectrons. While this is undoubtedly a disadvantage, it cannot be eliminated without constructing an extra register, and this does not at this moment seem worthwhile.

On the other hand, saving the right-hand 39 digits of the answer is accomplished with very little extra equipment, since it means connecting the 2^{-39} stage of Ac to the 2^{-1} stage of AR during the shift operation. The advantage of saving these digits is that it simplifies the handling of numbers of any number of digits in the computer (cf. the last part of 5.12). Any number of 39k binary digits (where k is an integer) and sign can be divided into k parts, each part being placed in a separate Selectron position. Addition and subtraction of such numbers may be programmed out of a series of additions or subtractions of the 39-digit parts, the carry-over being programmed by means of $Cc \rightarrow S(x)$ and $Cc' \rightarrow S(x)$ operations. (If the 2^0 stage of Ac registers negative after the addition of two 39-digit parts, a carry-over has taken place and hence 2^{-39} must be added to the sum of the next parts.) A similar procedure may be followed in multiplication if all 78 digits of the product of the two 39-digit parts are kept, as is planned. (For the details, cf.

Chapter 9, Part II.) Since it would greatly complicate the computer to make provision for holding and using a 78 digit dividend, it is planned to program 39k digit division in one of the ways described at the end of 5.12.

6.6.4. The operation of division $Ac \div S(x) \rightarrow R$ involves the following four steps:

First: Clear SR and transfer $S(x)$ (the divisor) into it.

Second: Clear AR.

Third: Thirty-nine steps, each of which consists of the following three parts: (a) Sense the signs of the contents of Ac (the partial remainder) and of SR, and sense whether they agree or not. (b) Shift Ac and AR left. In this process the previous sign digit of Ac is lost. Fill the right-most digit of Ac (after the shift) with a 0, and the right-most digit of AR (before the shift) with 0 or 1, depending on whether there was disagreement or agreement in (a). (c) Add or subtract the contents of SR into Ac, depending on the same alternative as above.

Fourth: Fill the right-most digit of AR with a 1, and change its sign digit.

For the purpose of timing the 39 steps involved in division a six-stage counter (capable of counting to $2^6 = 64$) will be built into the control. This same counter will also be used for timing the 39 steps of multiplication, and possibly for controlling Ac when a number is being transferred between it and a tape in either direction (see 6.8.).

6.6.5. The three substitution operations [$At \rightarrow S(x)$, $Ap \rightarrow S(x)$, and $Ap' \rightarrow S(x)$] involve transferring all or part of the number held in Ac into the Selectrons. This will be done by means of gate tubes connected to the registering flip-flops of Ac. Forty such tubes are needed for the total substitutions, $At \rightarrow S(x)$. The partial substitution $Ap \rightarrow S(x)$ and $Ap' \rightarrow S(x)$ requires that the left-hand twelve digits of the number held in Ac be substituted in the proper places in the left-hand and right-hand orders respectively. This may be done by means of extra gate tubes, or by shifting the number in Ac and using the gate tubes required for At → S(x). (This scheme needs some additional elaboration, when the order directing and the order suffering the substitution are the two successive halves of the same word; i.e., when the latter is already in FR at the time when the former becomes operative in CR, so that the substitution effected in the Selectrons comes too late to alter the order which has already reached CR, to become operative at the next step in FR. There are various ways to take care of this complication, either by some additional equipment or by appropriate prescriptions in coding. We will not discuss them here in more detail, since the decisions in this respect are still open.)

The importance of the partial substitution operations can hardly be over-overestimated. It has already been pointed out (3.3) that they allow the computer to perform operations it could not otherwise conveniently perform, such as making use of a function table stored in the Selectron memory. Furthermore, these operations remove a very sizeable burden from the person coding problems, for they make possible the coding of classes of problems in contrast to coding each individual problem separately. Because Ap → S(x) and Ap' → S(x) are available, any program sequence may be stated in general form (that is, without Selectron location designations for the numbers being operated on) and the Selectron locations of the numbers to be operated on substituted whenever the sequence is used. As an example, consider a general code for the nth order integration of m total differential equations for p steps of independent variable t, formulated in advance. Whenever a problem requiring this rule is coded for the computer, the general integration sequence can be inserted into the statement of the problem along with coded instructions for telling the sequence where it will be located in the memory [so that the proper S(x) designations will be inserted into such orders as Cu → S(x), etc.]. Whenever this sequence is to be used by the computer it will automatically substitute the correct values of m, n, p and Δt, as well as the locations of the boundary conditions and the descriptions of the differential equations, into the general sequence. (For the details of this particular procedure, cf. Chapter 13, Part II.) A library of such general sequences will be built up, and facilities provided for convenient insertion of any of these into the coded statement of a problem (cf. 6.8.4). When such a scheme is used, only the distinctive features of a problem need be coded.

6.6.6. The manner in which the control shift operations [Cu → S(x), Cu' → S(x), Cc → S(x), and Cc' → S(x)] are realized has been discussed in 6.4 and needs no further comment.

6.6.7. One basic question must be decided before a computer is built is whether the machine is to have a so-called floating binary (or decimal) point. While a floating binary point is undoubtedly very convenient in coding problems, building it into the computer adds greatly to its complexity and hence a choice in this matter should receive very careful attention. However, it should first be noted that the alternatives ordinarily considered (building a machine with a floating binary point vs. doing all computation with a fixed binary point) are not exhaustive and hence that the arguments generally advanced for the floating binary point are only of limited validity. Such arguments overlook the fact that the choice with respect to any particular operation (except for certain basic ones) is not between building it into the computer and not using it at all, but rather between building it into the computer and programming it out of operations built into the computer. (One short reference to the floating binary point was made in 5.13.)

Building a floating binary point into the computer will not only complicate the control but will also increase the length of a number and hence increase the size of the memory and the arithmetic unit. Every number is effectively increased in size, even though the floating binary point is not needed in many instances. Furthermore, there is considerable redundancy in a floating binary point type of notation, for each number carries with it a scale factor, while generally speaking a single scale factor will suffice for a possibly extensive set of numbers. By means of the operations already described in the report a floating binary point can be programmed. While additional memory capacity is needed for this, it is probably less than that required by a built-in floating binary point since a different scale factor does not need to be remembered for each number.

To program a floating binary point involves detecting where the first zero occurs in a number in Ac. Since Ac has shifting facilities this can best be done by means of them. In terms of the operations previously described this would require taking the given number out of Ac and performing a suitable arithmetical operation on it: For a (multiple) right shift a multiplication, for a (multiple) left shift either one division, or as many doublings (i.e., additions) as the shift has stages. However, these operations are inconvenient and time-consuming, so we propose to introduce two operations (L and R) in order that this (i.e., the single left and right shift) can be accomplished directly. These operations make use of facilities already present in Ac and hence add very little equipment to the computer. It should be noted that in many instances a single use of L and possibly of R will suffice in programming a floating binary point. For if the two factors in a multiplication have no superfluous zeros, the product will have at most one superfluous zero (if $1/2 \leq X < 1$ and $1/2 \leq Y < 1$, then $1/4 \leq XY < 1$). This is similarly true in division (if $1/4 \leq X < 1/2$ and $1/2 \leq Y < 1$, then $1/4 < X/Y < 1$). In addition and subtraction any numbers growing out of range can be treated similarly. Numbers which decrease in these cases,

i.e., develop a sequence of zeros at the beginning, are really (mathematically) losing precision. Hence it is perfectly proper to omit formal readjustments in this event. (Indeed, such a true loss of precision cannot be obviated by any formal procedure, but, if at all, only by a different mathematical formulation of the problem.)

6.7. Table 1 shows that many of the operations which the control is to execute have common elements. Thus addition, subtraction, multiplication and division all involve transferring a number from the Selectrons to SR. Hence the control may be simplified by breaking some of the operations up into more basic ones. A timing circuit will be provided for each basic operation, and one or more such circuits will be involved in the execution of an order. The exact choice of basic operations will depend upon how the arithmetic unit is built.

In addition to the timing circuits needed for executing the orders of Table 1, two such circuits are needed for the automatic operations of transferring orders from the Selectron register to CR and FR, and for transferring an order from CR to FR. In normal computer operation these two circuits are used alternately, so a binary counter is needed to remember which is to be used next. In the operations $Cu \rightarrow S(x)$ and $Cc \rightarrow S(x)$ the first order of a pair is ignored, so the binary counter must be altered accordingly.

The execution of a sequence of orders involves using the various timing circuits in sequence. When a given timing circuit has completed its operation, it emits a pulse which should go to the timing circuit to be used next. Since this depends upon the particular operation being executed, these pulses are routed according to the signals received from the decoding and recoding function tables activated by the six binary digits specifying an order.

6.8. In this section we will consider what must be added to the control so that it can direct the mechanisms for getting data into and out of the computer and also describe the mechanisms themselves. Three different kinds of input-output mechanisms are planned.

First: Several magnetic wire storage units operated by servomechanisms controlled by the computer.

Second: Some viewing tubes for graphical portrayal of results.

Third: A typewriter for feeding data directly into the computer, not to be confused with the equipment used for preparing and printing from magnetic wires. As presently planned the latter will consist of modified Teletypewriter equipment, cf. 6.8.2 and 6.8.4.

6.8.1. Since there already exists a way of transferring numbers between the Selectrons and Ac, therefore Ac may be used for transferring numbers from and to a wire. The latter transfer will be done serially and will make use of the shifting facilities of Ac. Using Ac for this purpose eliminates the possibility of computing and reading from or writing on the wires simultaneously. However, simultaneous operation of the computer and the input-output organ requires additional temporary storage and introduces a synchronizing problem, and hence it is not being considered for the first model.

Since, at the beginning of the problem, the computer is empty, facilities must be built into the control for reading a set of numbers from a wire when the operator presses a manual switch. As each number is read from a wire into Ac, the control must transfer it to its proper location in the Selectrons. The CC may be used to count off these positions in sequence, since it is capable of transmitting its contents to FR. A detection circuit on CC will stop the process when the specified number of numbers has been placed in the memory, and the control will then be shifted to the orders located in the first position of the Selectron memory.

It has already been stated that the entire memory facilities of the wires should be available to the computer without human intervention. This means that the control must be able to select the proper set of numbers from those going by. Hence additional orders are required for the code. Here, as before, we are faced with two alternatives. We can make the control capable of executing an order of the form: Take numbers from positions p to $p + s$ on wire No. k and place them in Selectron locations v to $v + s$. Or we can make the control capable of executing some less complicated operations which, together with the already given control orders, are sufficient for programming the transfer operation of the first alternative. Since the latter scheme is simpler we adopt it tentatively.

The computer must have some way of finding a particular number on a wire. One method of arranging for this is to have each number carry with it its own location designation. A method more economical of wire memory capacity is to use the Selectron memory facilities to remember the position of each wire. For example, the computer would hold the number t_1 specifying which number on the wire is in position to be read. If the control is instructed to read the number at position p_1 on this wire, it will compare p_1 with t_1; and if they differ, cause the wire to move in the proper direction. As each number on the wire passes by, one unit is added or subtracted to t_1 and the comparison repeated. When $p_1 = t_1$ numbers will be transferred from the wire to the accumulator and then to the proper location in the memory. Then both t_1 and p_1 will be increased by 1, and the transfer from the wire to accumulator to memory repeated. This will be iterated, until $t_1 + s$ and $p_1 + s$ are reached, at which time the control will direct the wire to stop.

Under this system the control must be able to execute the following orders with regard to each wire: Start the wire forward, start the wire in reverse, stop the wire, transfer from wire to Ac, and transfer from Ac to wire. In addition, the wire must signal the control as each digit is read and when the end of a number has been reached. Conversely, when recording is done the control must have a means of timing the signals

sent from Ac to the wire, and of counting off the digits. The 2^6 counter
used for multiplication and division
may be used for the latter purpose, but
other timing circuits will be required
for the former.

If the method of checking by means
of two computers operating simultaneously is adopted, and each machine is
built so that it can operate independently of the other, then each will
have a separate input-output mechanism.
The process of making wires for the
computer must then be duplicated, and
in this way the work of the person
making a wire can be checked. Since
the wire servomechanisms cannot be
synchronized by the central clock, a
problem of synchronizing the two computers when the wires are being used
arises. It is probably not practical
to synchronize the wire feeds to within
a given digit, but this is unnecessary
since the numbers coming into the two
organs Ac need not be checked as the
individual digits arrive, but only
prior to being deposited in the Selectron memory.

6.8.2. Since the computer operates in the binary system, some means
of decimal-binary and binary-decimal
conversions is highly desirable.
Various alternative ways of handling
this problem have been considered. In
general we recognize two broad classes
of solutions to this problem.

First: The conversion problems
can be regarded as simple arithmetic
processes and programmed as sub-rou-
tines out of the orders already incorporated in the machine. The details of
these programs together with a more
complete discussion are given fully in
Chapter 9, Part II, where it is shown,
among other things, that the conversion of a word takes about 5 msec.
Thus the conversion time is comparable
to the reading or withdrawing time for
a word--about 2 msec--and is trivial
as compared to the solution time for
problems to be handled by the computer.
It should be noted that the treatment
proposed there presupposes only that
the decimal data presented to or received from the computer are in tetrads,

each tetrad being the binary coding of
a decimal digit--the information (precision) represented by a decimal digit
being actually equivalent to that represented by 3.3 binary digits. The
coding of decimal digits into tetrads
of binary digits and the printing of
decimal digits from such tetrads can
be accomplished quite simply and automatically by slightly modified Teletype
equipment, cf. 6.8.4 below.

Second: The conversion problems
can be regarded as unique problems and
handled by separate conversion equipment incorporated either in the computer proper or associated with the
mechanisms for preparing and printing
from magnetic wires. Such convertors
are really nothing other than special
purpose digital computers. They would
seem to be justified only for those
computers which are primarily intended
for solving problems in which the computation time is small compared to the
input-output time, to which class our
computer does not belong.

6.8.3. It is possible to use
various types of cathode ray tubes,
and in particular Selectrons for the
viewing tubes, in which case programming the viewing operation is quite
simple. The viewing Selectrons can
be switched by the same function tables
that switch the memory Selectrons. By
means of the substitution operation
$Ap \rightarrow S(x)$ and $Ap' \rightarrow S(x)$, six-digit
numbers specifying the abscissa and
ordinate of the point (six binary digits represent a precision of one part
in $2^6 = 64$, i.e., of about 1.5 per cent
which seems reasonable in such a component) can be substituted in this
order, which will specify that a particular one of the viewing Selectrons
is to be activated.

6.8.4. As was mentioned above,
the mechanisms used for preparing and
printing from wire for the first model,
at least, will be modified Teletype
equipment. We are quite fortunate in
having secured the full cooperation of
the Ordnance Development Division of
the National Bureau of Standards in
making these modifications and in designing and building some associated

equipment.

By means of this modified Teletype equipment an operator first prepares a checked paper tape and then directs the equipment to transfer the information from the paper tape to the magnetic wire. Similarly a magnetic wire can transfer its contents to a paper tape which can be used to operate a teletypewriter. (Studies are being undertaken to design equipment that will eliminate the necessity for using paper tapes.)

As was shown in 6.6.5, the statement of a new problem on a wire involves data unique to that problem interspersed with data found on previously prepared paper tapes or magnetic wires. The equipment discussed in the previous paragraph makes it possible for the operator to combine conveniently these data on to a single magnetic wire ready for insertion into the computer.

It is frequently very convenient to introduce data into a computation without producing a new wire. Hence it is planned to build one simple typewriter as an integral part of the computer. By means of this typewriter the operator can stop the computation, type in a memory location (which will go to the FR), type in a number (which will go to Ac and then be placed in the first mentioned location), and start the computation again.

6.8.5. There is one further order that the control needs to execute. There should be some means by which the computer can signal to the operator when a computation has been concluded, or when the computation has reached a previously determined point. Hence an order is needed which will tell the computer to stop and to flash a light or ring a bell.

SYMBOLIC SYNTHESIS OF DIGITAL COMPUTERS

IRVING S. REED

In an ideal sense a binary digital computer or what might be called more generally a Boolean* machine is an automatic operational filing system. It is a machine which accepts information automatically in the form of words constructed from an alphabet of only two symbols, say 0 and 1, the so-called binary coded words. For example a binary number is such a word. This information is stored or recorded in sets of elementary boxes or files, each containing one of the symbols 0 or 1. This information is either transformed or used to change other files or itself as a function of the past contents of all files within the system. If the contents of all files within the system are constrained to change only at discrete points of time, say the points n (n = 1,2,3, ...), then the machine may be termed a synchronous Boolean machine. The discussion in this paper will be restricted to the synchronous Boolean machine.

It is evident from the above discussion that the content of each elementary box or file within the system is a two valued function, say $A(t)$, of the real paramater time, t. Since the content of each file is constrained to change only at the discrete points of time $n\tau$, then a suitable definition for $A(t)$ is the following: Either $A(t) = 0$ or $A(t) = 1$ for $n\tau \leq t < (n + 1)\tau$ where (n = 0,1,2, ...). In this definition

the right continuity of $A(t)$ has been assumed for the sake of definiteness. Let the function $A(t)$ be called a file function.

Table 1 defines a unary and three binary operations of file functions, $F(t)$ and $G(t)$. From the definition of a file function and Table 1 the following theorem is now evident.

Theorem 1: The class of all file functions B is a Boolean algebra with respect to the operations $'$, $\cdot$, and +. B is an additive abelian group with respect to the operation $\oplus$ where the zero element is the file function, 0, which is 0 for all t, $t \geq 0$. More generally B is an algebraic or Stone[+] ring with respect to the operations $\cdot$ and $\oplus$ where the unit element of the ring is the file function, 1, which is 1 for all $t \geq 0$.

By Table 1, or otherwise, it is not difficult to establish the following useful identities, relating the operations $'$, $\cdot$, + and $\oplus$ between file functions F and G:

$$(1) \qquad F + G = F \oplus G \oplus FG,$$
$$F \oplus G = F' G + FG' \quad \text{and}$$
$$F' = F \oplus 1$$

Now to every file function $F(t)$ of the synchronous Boolean machine there corresponds the complementary file function $F'(t)$. Moreover, $F(t)$ uniquely determines $F'(t)$ and conversely. Thus it may be assumed that the complementary function of any file in a synchronous Boolean machine is always available within the machine for reference. In fact,

---

Reprinted with permission from the Proceedings of the ACM Meeting at Toronto, Ontario, Canada, September, 8-10, 1952, pp. 90-94.
* In honor of the great British mathematician, George Boole, who originally discovered the algebra needed to describe such machines.

+ Marshall Stone was the first to establish that every Boolean algebra is a ring.[1]

Table 1.

F(t)	G(t)	F'(t)	F(t) + G(t)	F(t)·G(t)	F(t) + G(t)
0	0	1	0	0	0
0	1	1	1	0	1
1	0	0	1	0	1
1	1	0	1	1	0

it may be assumed that there are 2 P files containing the functions $F_1(t)$, $F_2(t) \ldots, F_P(t); F_1'(t); F_2'(t), \ldots F_P'(t)$ where the first P files completely determine the contents of the remaining P files. From this fact and the description of the synchronous Boolean machine the following set of time difference equations characterize the behaviour of the synchronous Boolean machine as a function of time:

(2) $A_j(t + \tau) = f_j(A_1(t), A_2(t), \ldots,$
$A_N(t); W_1(t), W_2(t), \ldots, W_M(t)),$
$(j = 1, \ldots, N),$

where the initial condition is $A_1(0)$, $A_2(0), \ldots A_N(0)$, the functions $W_1(t)$, $W_2(t), \ldots, W_M(t)$ are the given input file functions or forcing functions, the functions $A_1(t), A_2(t), \ldots, A_N(t)$ are the dependent file functions of the system and P = N + M. The system of time difference Boolean equations (2) will be called the synchronous Boolean system. Within the particular class of Boolean functions of a real variable t, the Boolean algebra B of the file functions, there are 2^N possible solutions of (2), depending uniquely on the 2^N initial conditions (see references 2 and 3). If the forcing functions of (2) had been chosen from certain other subclasses of the class of all Boolean functions of a real parameter t it is possible to show that (2) has solutions in classes other than B. However, the present discussion will be restricted to the class B defined herein.

For brevity in notation let a function F(t) be denoted sometimes by F and in particular denote $G(t + \tau)$

by $G[\tau]$. This notation should not lead to any confusion since the subsequent arguments of this paper will be true for all $t \geq 0$. If $f_j = f_j(A_1, \ldots, A_{Nj} W_1, \ldots W_M)$ for $(j = 1, 2, \ldots N)$ of (2) is expanded in the disjunctive normal form it is evident that f_j may be expressed in the form

(3) $f_j = g_j A_j' + {}_0g_j' A_j'$

for $(j = 1, 2, \ldots N)$

where

$g_j = f_j(A_1, \ldots A_{j-1}, 0, A_{j+1}, \ldots A_{Nj} W_1 \ldots W_M)$ and

${}_0g_j' = f_j(A_1, \ldots, A_{j-1}, 1, A_{j+1} \ldots A_{Nj} W_1 \ldots W_M).$

Equation (3) with (1) obtains

(4) $f_j = g_j(1 \oplus A_j) \oplus {}_0g_j \oplus 1) A_j$
$= A_j \oplus [(g_j \oplus {}_0g_j) A_j \oplus g_j]$
$= A_j \oplus [g_j A_j' + {}_0g_j A_j]$

Equation (4) and the abelian group property of the operation $\oplus$ transforms (2) into

(5) $\Delta A_j = A_j[\tau] \oplus A_j = (g_1 \oplus {}_0g_j)$
$A_j \oplus g_j$
$= g_j A_j' + {}_0g_j A_j = a_j$ for
$(j = 1, 2, \ldots N)$

where Δ is called the change operator, defined by $\Delta F(t) = F(t + \tau) \oplus F(t)$ for all $t \geq 0$. The system of equations, given by (5) are the change equations of the synchronous Boolean system[2]. The word change is derived from the fact that for any file function $F(t)$, $\Delta F(t) = 1$ if, and only if, $F(t) = 0$ and $F(t + \tau) = 1$ or $F(t) = 1$ and $F(t + \tau) = 0$. That is, $\Delta F(t) = 1$ only when the symbol in the file with function $F(t)$ changes. Although system (5) is merely an algebraic transformation of system (2), it will be seen presently that a_j is precisely the Boolean function of file functions needed as the input function for a clocked one input electronic flip-flop, when considered as a possible dual file to store the functions A_j and A_j'.

When an Eccles-Jordan multivibrator has been designed to change only when triggered by a voltage pulse or spike of time duration ε, such that $\varepsilon \ll \tau$, this bistable device is called a flip-flop. The output of the flip-flop, which consists ordinarily of two triode vacuum tubes (valves) and associated circuits, is a voltage from each plate or anode of the tubes. There are essentially only two voltages which may appear on one of the anodes, except during the time of change. If the voltage of one anode is high, the voltage on the other is low and conversely. Let a high voltage on an anode represent the symbol 1 and the low voltage 0 and suppose the time for switching to be instantaneous in such a manner that the output voltage function is right continuous. Moreover, suppose the voltage pulse function $E(t)$, triggering the flip-flop is such that the flip-flop will change state at every point of time $n\tau (n = 1,2,3,4, \ldots)$ and at only these points. Then the output of one anode is a file function $F(t)$ and the voltage on the other anode is $F'(t)$, the complementary file function.

Now the file function $F(t)$, constructed above, is very specialized in that it is one of the two possible file functions which changes at every allowable point of time $n\tau (n = 1,2,3, \ldots)$. To allow the flip-flop to hold

any file function suppose $a(t)$ is a Boolean function of file functions such that $e(t)$ is a file function of the same physical nature as the output of the flip-flop, i.e., two voltage levels. Let $a(t)$ gate with the trigger or clock function $E(t)$ in such a manner that the condition $a(t) = 0$ will inhibit the next pulse of $E(t)$ from triggering the flip-flop and the condition $a(t) = 1$ will allow the next pulse of $E(t)$ to trigger or change the output of the flip-flop. Then the output function of the flip-flop which will now be denoted by $A(t)$, results clearly from Table 2. From Tables 2 and 1, one obtains

$$(6) \qquad A(t + \tau) = a'(t)\, A(t) + a(t)\, A'(t)$$
$$= A(t) \oplus a(t)$$

as the time difference equation for the output file function $A(t)$ of a clock gated flip-flop with file function input $a(t)$. By the group property of the binary operation $\oplus$ equation (6) may be solved for $a(t)$, obtaining,

$$(7) \qquad a(t) = A(t + \tau) \oplus A(t) = \Delta A(t) \quad .$$

Equations (6) and (7) with initial condition $A(0)$ are called the equations of the clocked one input flip-flop. It is interesting to note that (7) is a true linear operator equation in A for clearly the operator Δ is an automorphism of the ring B and any dependence of $a(t)$ on $A(t)$ is necessarily linear.

If equations (5) are compared with the change equation (7) of the

Table 2.

$a(t)$	$A(t)$	$A(t + \tau)$
0	0	0
0	1	1
1	0	1
1	1	0

clocked flip-flop, one observes the fact that if changes a_j have the right physical nature to act as inputs to flip-flops, that N flip-flops will act as files for $A_j(t)$ and at the same time analyze the synchronous Boolean system (7) for all $t > 0$. It is well known that Boolean function of functions with two voltage levels can be physically realized as a function with two voltage levels. For example, diode gating networks will realize such networks. The following theorem is now evident:

Theorem 2: Every synchronous Boolean system is representable by an electronic synchronous Boolean machine which consists only of clocked one input flip-flops and devices for producing sums and products of the outputs of the flip-flops and conversely.

Once a desired synchronous Boolean machine or automatic filing system has been conceived symbolically as a synchronous Boolean system in the form of (5), Theorem 2 assures one that a physical realization of the desired machine is possible. Therefore, in the initial synthesis of a digital computer it is desirable to concentrate one's attention on the abstract model of the digital computer. Except for certain electronic problems of synchronization, the synchronous Boolean system is sufficient to represent the abstract model of the desired binary digital computer or two symbol

automatic operational filing system. Thus, in this paper the symbolic synthesis of a digital computer may be regarded as equivalent to the synthesis of a synchronous Boolean system.

If one input clocked flip-flops are to be used to analyze a known or desired synchronous Boolean system, it is necessary by (5) and (7) that one obtain the change equations (5) of the system. The desired changes ΔA_j for $(j = 1,2, \ldots, N)$ of the file function A_j are functions of $A_1, A_2, \ldots A_N$; $W_1, \ldots W_M$. Thus, as it is well known, each ΔA_j may be obtained from either the disjunctive or conjunctive normal expansions or its equivalent valuation (truth) tables. A known or desired solution of this derived system of equations is entirely dependent on the initial condition imposed on the system.

In order to illustrate this procedure of synthesis, consider the desired operation of an unusual type of three stage counter, given in Table 3. The section of the table devoted to the changes, ΔA_1, ΔA_2, ΔA_3 is obtained directly from the first two sections of the table. For instance, 1 is placed in the third row of the column devoted to ΔA_1 since in that row $A_1 = 1$ and $A_1[\tau] = 0$. By using the valuation (truth) table approach and the rules of Boolean algebra this counter has the following set of change equations:

Table 3.

A_3	A_2	A_1	$A_3[\tau]$	$A_2[\tau]$	$A_1[\tau]$	ΔA_3	ΔA_2	ΔA_1	Classification of States
0	0	0	1	1	0	1	1	0	Periodic States of period 4
1	1	0	0	1	1	1	0	1	
0	1	1	1	0	0	1	1	1	
1	0	0	0	0	0	1	0	0	
0	1	0	1	0	1	1	1	1	Periodic States of period 2
1	0	1	0	1	0	1	1	1	
1	1	1	0	1	0	1	0	1	Transient State
0	0	1	0	0	1	0	0	0	Bound State

$$\Delta A_3 = (A_3' A_2' A_1)' = A_3 + A_2 + A_1'$$

$$\Delta A_2 = A_3' A_2' A_1' + A_3' A_2' A_1 + A_3 A_2' A_1'$$
$$+ A_3 A_2 A_1$$

$$= A_3' A_2' A_1' + A_3' A_2 + A_3 A_2' A_1$$

$$= A_3' (A_1' + A_2) + A_3 A_2' A_1$$

$$\Delta A_1 = (A_3' A_2' A_1 + A_3 A_2' A_1' + A_3' A_2' A_1)'$$

$$= (A_2' A_1 + A_3 A_2' A_1)'$$

$$= (A_2' [A_1' + A_3']) = A_2 + A_1 A_3$$

These equations are the input equations to three one input clocked-flip-flops, designated to hold the functions A_1, A_2 and A_3. It may be noted that this counter illustrates a classification of all possible types of states of a counter. By Table 1 if the initial condition of the system is any one of the states or configurations of period 4τ, the remaining three states follow in succession; then back to the initial state, forming a loop of period 4τ. From the table this counter has as well a loop of period 2τ, a transient state and a bound state.

If a more complex computing system is desired where at the outset very little is known about the end product, one must first hypothesize sets of files and possible operations between them. Then hypothetical combinatorial relationships may be established in such a manner that the desired input and output relationships of the system are to some degree satisfied. This procedure is aided conceputally by an understanding of the synchronous Boolean system and space-time charts of the various hypothesized files. If the first hypothetical system does not satisfy the desired notions for the system either the notions or the hypothesis or both must be modified and then the above procedure must be reiterated. If one assumes that the above iterative planning procedure arrives at a suitable compromised system, satisfying the desires of the planner, and if the planning has leaned heavily on the symbolization of the contents of

the files of the system, the planner will find usually that writing and reducing a set of change equations such as (5) will be accomplished already in many cases and almost mechanically in other cases. The minimization techniques of the Harvard group are sometimes of value in the algebraic reduction of the equations. However, care must be taken in not using these techniques too early in the game, for as it often happens, there may be large common parts to two or more change equations of the system which, in many cases, become lost when an individual function minimization technique is applied before noticing these common parts. To convert the change equations into electronic realizations is a fairly well discussed problem (see references 4, 5, and 6).

In conclusion, it should be mentioned that the use of two input clocked flip-flops as files is similar to the one input clocked flip-flop and, in fact, they are algebraically as well as electronically very intimately related. There are many topics concerning the subject of this paper which have been left out for the sake of brevity. More complete discussions are deferred to later papers.

The author wishes to express his deepest gratitude to his former teacher, Prof. E. T. Bell, who first taught Boolean algebra to the author, and encouraged these particular directions to the subject. Much acknowledgement goes to E. F. Steele who through long personal contact with the author did much by his keen physical insight to bring about the ideas contained in this paper. Finally, this paper probably would not have been written without the consecutive support of Northrop Aircraft, Computer Research Corp., and lastly the Lincoln Laboratory of the Massachusetts Institute of Technology.

REFERENCES

1. G. Birkhoff, Lattice Theory, Am. Math. Soc. Coll. Publications,

1948.
2. I. S. Reed, "Some Mathematical
    Remarks on the Boolean Machine,"
    Tech. Rep. No. 2, Project Lincoln,
    M.I.T., Dec. 19, 1951.
3. I. S. Reed, "Boolean Functions of
    a Real Variable and its Applica-
    tions to a Model of the Digital
    Computer and Discrete Probability,"
    Project Lincoln Rep., M.I.T.
4. R. E. Sprague, "Techniques in the
    Design of Digital Computers,"

Assoc. for Computing Machinery,
March 1951.
5. R. C. Jeffrey and I. S. Reed, "The
    Use of Boolean Algebra in Logical
    Design," Engineering Note E-458-1,
    Digital Computer Laboratory,
    M.I.T., Apr. 28, 1952.
6. R. C. Jeffrey and I. S. Reed,
    "Design of a Digital Computer by
    Boolean Algebra," Engineering Note
    E-462, Digital Computer Laboratory,
    M.I.T., May 20, 1952.

THE BEST WAY TO DESIGN AN AUTOMATIC
CALCULATING MACHINE

M. V. WILKES

I would like to begin by adding my congratulations to the many others which have been received by Professor Williams, Manchester University and Ferranti Ltd., on the construction of the machine which has just been inaugurated. In the face of this beautifully engineered machine, the title I have chosen for my opening remarks in this discussion may sound a little impertinent. But, as Dr. Kilburn remarked yesterday, the designer of an electronic calculating machine must continually take decisions, and he does not know when he takes them whether they are right or wrong. I might put it by saying that in a mathematical sense the solution to the problem of designing an electronic calculating machine is unstable. Two similar groups of engineers with similar backgrounds and assisted by similar groups of mathematicians will, if working independently, produce quite different machines. Moreover the machines finally built will depend on the scale on which the projects are conducted, the experience and background of the teams, and the state of technical developments at the time. The last item is important since new developments in electron tubes, or in non-linear devices of the germanium type, might well affect even so fundamental a decision as the choice between the serial or parallel modes of operation for the machine. It is desirable, therefore, to keep under review the considerations which underlie the de-

Reprinted with permission from the Report of the Manchester University Computer Inaugural Conference, Electrical Engineering Department of Manchester University, Manchester, England, July, 1951, pp. 16-18.

sign of calculating machines and to try to examine them in the light of general principles as well as of current technical developments. I am aware that in doing this one is in danger of saying things which are sufficiently obvious without being said, but I am in the fortunate position of having been asked to open a discussion rather than give a paper. I shall not, therefore, attempt to present a logical thesis but shall allow myself to raise issues rather than settle them.

I think that most people will agree that the first consideration for a designer at the present time is how he is to achieve the maximum degree of reliability in his machine. Amongst other things the reliability of the machine will depend on the following:

a. The amount of equipment it contains.

b. Its complexity.

c. The degree of repetition of units.

By the complexity of a machine I mean the extent to which cross-connections between the various units obscure their logical inter-relation. A machine is easier to repair if it consists of a number of units connected together in a simple way without cross-connections between them; it is also easier to construct since different people can work on the different units without getting in each other's way.

As regards repetition I think everyone would prefer to have in a particular part of the machine a group of five identical units rather than a group of five different units. Most people would prefer to have six identical units rather than five different units. How far one ought to be prepared to go in the direction of accepting a greater quantity of equipment in order to achieve repetition is a matter of opinion. The matter may be put as follows. Suppose that it is regarded as being equally desirable to have a particular part of the machine composed of a group of n different units, or composed of a group of kn identical units, all the units being of similar size. What is the value of k? My conjecture is that k > 2. I should say that I am thinking of a machine which has about 10 groups of units and that n is approximately equal to 10.

The remarks I have just made are of general application. I will now try to be more specific. If one builds a parallel machine one has a good example, in the arithmetical unit, of a piece of equipment consisting of identical units repeated many times. Such an arithmetical unit is, however, much larger than that in a serial machine. On the other hand I think it is true to say that the control in a parallel machine is simpler than in a serial machine. I am using the word control here in a very general sense to include everything that does not appertain to the store proper (i.e., it includes the access circuits) or to the registers and adders in the arithmetical unit. That the control can be simpler in a parallel machine may I think be seen by comparing the waveforms which must be produced in order to effect the transfer of a number from one register to another in a serial synchronous machine and in a parallel asynchronous machine. These are the two extreme cases. In the case of a serial synchronous machine the waveform must rise at some critical moment relative to the clock and must fall at another critical moment, and its edges must be sharp. In a parallel asynchronous machine all that is needed is a single pulse whose time of occurrence, length, and shape are all non-critical (see Fig. 1).

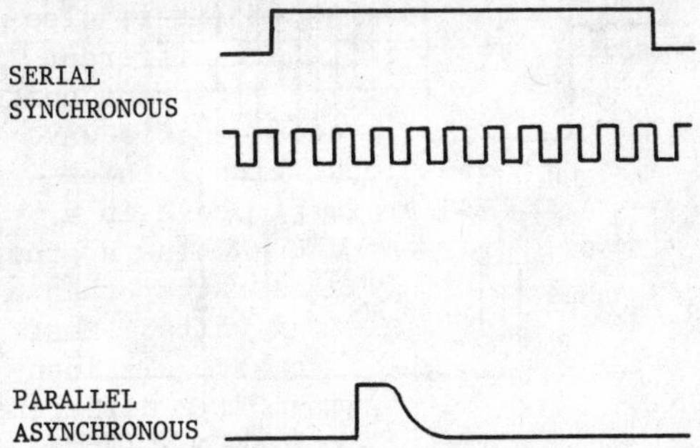

The arithmetical unit of a parallel machine is often shown diagrammatically as in Fig. 2.

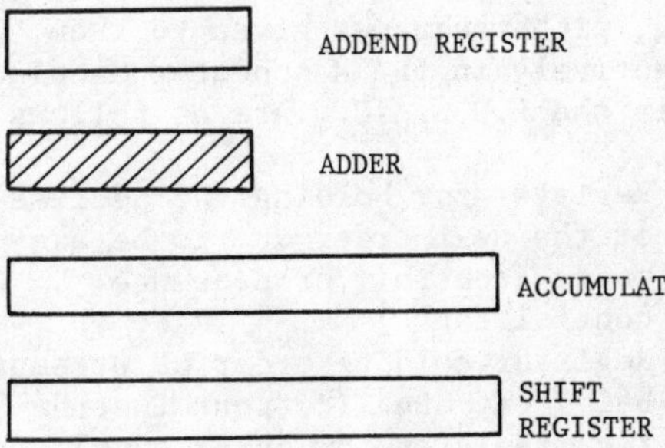

ADDEND REGISTER

ADDER

ACCUMULATOR

SHIFT REGISTER

Fig. 2.

At the beginning of a multiplication the multiplier is placed in the right-hand half of the accumulator register. The right-hand half of the shift register may be dispensed with if shifting is done in two stages. Showing the right-hand half of the accumulator as a separate register we then have the diagram of Fig. 3.

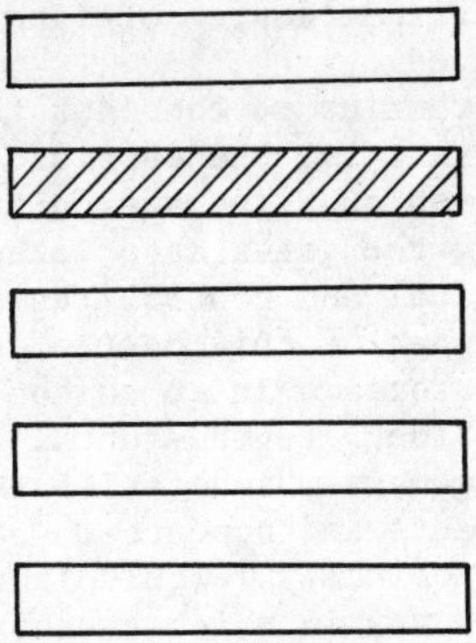

SERIAL SYNCHRONOUS

PARALLEL ASYNCHRONOUS

Fig. 1.

Fig. 3.

We are thus led to think of an arithmetical unit composed of a number of standard units each containing four flip-flops (one belonging to each of four registers) together with an adder. Gates would be provided to make possible the transfer of numbers from one register to another, through the adder when necessary. These transfers would be effected by pulsing one or more of a set of wires emerging from the arithmetical unit.

It is also necessary to have registers in the control of a machine. These, with the names given to them respectively in the Manchester machine and in the E.D.S.A.C., are as follows:

Register for holding the address of the next order due to be executed (control, or sequence control tank.)

Register holding order at present being executed (current instruction register, or order tank).

Register for counting the number of steps in a multiplication or shifting operation (not needed with the fast multiplier on the Manchester machine, timing control tank in the E.D.S.A.C.).

In addition the Manchester machine has a number of B registers.

If one B register is considered to be sufficient the parallel machine we are considering can use the same unit (containing 4 flip-flops and 1 adder) for the control registers as for arithmetical registers. In this way an extreme degree of repetition can be achieved.

It remains to consider the control proper, that is, the part of the machine which supplies the pulses for operating the gates associated with the arithmetical and control registers. The designer of this part of a machine usually proceeds in an ad hoc manner, drawing block diagrams until he sees an arrangement which satisfies his requirements and appears to be reasonably economical. I would like to suggest a way in which the control can be made systematic, and therefore less complex.

Each operation called for by an order in the order code of the machine involves a sequence of steps which may include transfers from the store to control or arithmetical registers, or vice versa, and transfers from one register to another. Each of these steps is achieved by pulsing certain of the wires associated with the control and arithmetical registers, and I will refer to it as a 'micro-operation.' Each true machine operation is thus made up of a sequence or 'micro-programme' of micro-operations.

Figure 4 shows the way in which pulses for performing the micro-operations may be generated. The timing pulse which initiates a micro-operation enters the decoding tree and is routed to one of the outputs according to the number set on the register R. It passes into the rectifier matrix A and gives rise to pulses on certain of the output wires of this matrix according to the arrangement of the rectifiers. These pulses operate the gates associated with the control and arithmetical registers, and cause the correct micro-operation to be performed. The pulse from the decoding tree also passes into matrix B and gives rise to pulses on certain of the output wires of this matrix. These pulses are conducted, via a short delay line, to the register R and cause the number set up

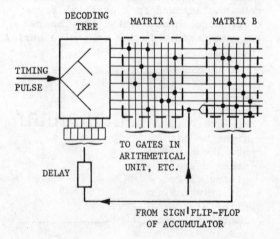

Fig. 4.

on it to be changed. The result is that the next initiating pulse to enter the decoding tree will emerge from a different outlet and will consequently cause a different micro-operation to be performed. It will thus be seen that each row of rectifiers in matrix A corresponds to one of the micro-orders in the sequence required to perform a machine operation.

The system as described would enable a fixed cycle of operations only to be performed. Its utility can be greatly extended by making some of the micro-orders conditional in the sense that they are followed by one of two alternative micro-orders according to the state of the machine. This can be done by making the output of the decoding tree branch before it enters matrix B. The direction the pulse takes at the branch is controlled by the potential on a wire coming from another part of the machine; for example, it might come from the sign flip-flop of the accumulator. The bottom row of matrix A in Fig. 4 corresponds to a conditional micro-order.

The matrix A contains sequences of micro-orders for performing all the basic operations in the order code of the machine. All that is necessary to perform a particular operation is that 'micro-control' shall be switched to the first micro-order in the appropriate sequence. This is done by causing the function digits of the order to be set up on the first four or five flip-flops of the register R, zero being set on the others.

A control system designed in this way is certainly very logical in structure but two comments, slightly contradictory in their implications, might be made. In the first place it might be said that there is nothing new about the arrangement since it makes use of flip-flops, gates, and mixing diodes which are the elements out of which any control is built. With this criticism I would agree. In fact, the controls of various machines now in existence or being constructed could no doubt be drawn in some way

closely resembling Fig. 4. The other objection is that the scheme appears to be rather extravagant in equipment. This I think is not true, particularly if some departures from the precise form of Fig. 4 are allowed. I think that by starting with a logical layout one is likely to arrive at a final arrangement which is both logical and economical. Moreover, one is able to see at each stage what one is sacrificing in the way of logical layout in order to achieve economy and vice versa.

In order to get some idea of the number of micro-orders required I have constructed a micro-programme for a simple machine with the following orders: add, subtract, multiply (two orders, one for the multiplier, one for the multiplicand), right and left shift (any number of places), transfer from the accumulator to the store, conditional operation depending on the sign of the number in the accumulator, conditional operation depending on the sign of the number in the B register (one B register is assumed), transfer from the store to the B register, input, and output. The micro-programme also provides for the preliminary extraction of the order from the store (Stage 1 in E.D.S.A.C. terminology). Only 40 micro-orders are required to perform all these operations.

The considerations involved in drawing-up a micro-programme resemble those involved in drawing-up an ordinary programme. The final details of the control are thus settled by a systematic process instead of by the usual ad hoc procedures based on the use of block diagrams. Of course, sound engineering would be necessary to produce designs for the decoding tree and the matrices which could be used for any desired micro-programme by arranging the rectifiers suitably in the matrices. One important advantage of this method of designing the control is that the order code need not be decided on finally until late stage in the construction of the machine; it would even be possible to change it after the machine had been put into operation simply by rewiring the matrices.

If desired some of the micro-orders can be made conditional in their action as well as (or instead of) conditional as regards the switching of micro-control. This can be done by making the output of the decoding tree branch before it enters matrix A. I doubt if much economy can be achieved this way and if it is done to any extent the advantage that micro-programming resembles ordinary pro-gramming is lost. Other variants of the scheme as I have described it will no doubt occur to you.

The matrices may be regarded as very high-speed stores holding fixed information. If they could be replaced by an erasable store to which informa-tion could be transferred from the main store of the machine when required we should have a machine with no fixed order code; the programmer would, in fact, be able to choose his order code to suit his own requirements and to change it during the course of the programme if he considered it desirable. Such a machine would have a number of fascinating possibilities but I doubt whether, in view of the amount of equipment it would doubtless involve, its construction could be justified.

STRUCTURAL ASPECTS OF THE SYSTEM/360 MODEL 85

II. THE CACHE

J. S. LIPTAY

Among the objectives of the Model 85 is that of providing a System/360 compatible processor with both high performance and high throughput. One of the important ingredients of high throughput is a large main storage capacity (see the accompanying article in Part I[1]). However, it is not feasible to provide a large main storage with an access time commensurate with the 80-nanosecond processor cycle of the Model 85. A longer access time can be partially compensated for by an increase in overlap, greater buffering, deeper storage interleaving, more sophistication in the handling of branches, and other improvements in the processor. All of these factors only partially compensate for the slower storage, and therefore, we decided to use a storage hierarchy instead.

The storage hierarchy consists of a 1.04-microsecond main storage and a small, fast store called a cache* which is integrated into the CPU. The cache is not addressable by a program, but rather is used to hold the contents of those portions of main storage that are currently being used. Most processor fetches can then be handled by referring to the cache, so that most of the time the processor has a short access time. When the program

Reprinted with permission from the IBM Systems Journal, Vol. 7, 1968, pp. 15-21.

* The term cache is synonymous with high-speed buffer, as used in other Model 85 documentation.

starts operating on data in a different portion of main storage, the data in that portion must be loaded into the cache and the data from some other portion removed. This activity must take place without program assistance, since the Model 85 must be compatible with the rest of the System/360 line.

This paper discusses organization of the cache and the studies that led to its use in the Model 85 and to selecting of values for its parameters.

CACHE ORGANIZATION

The main storage units that can be used on the Model 85 are the IBM 2365-5 and the 2385. They have a 1.04-microsecond cycle time and make available capacities from 512K bytes to 4096K bytes (K = 1024). The cache is a 16K-byte integrated storage, which is capable of operating every processor cycle. Optionally, it can be expanded to 24K bytes or 32K bytes.

Both the cache and main storage are logically divided into sectors, each consisting of 1K contiguous bytes starting on 1K-byte boundaries. During operation, a correspondence is set up between cache sectors and main storage sectors in which each cache sector is assigned to a single different main storage sector. However, because of the limited number of cache sectors, most main storage sectors do not have any cache sectors assigned to them (see Fig. 1). Each of the cache sectors has a 14-bit sector address register, which holds the address of the main storage sector to which it is assigned.

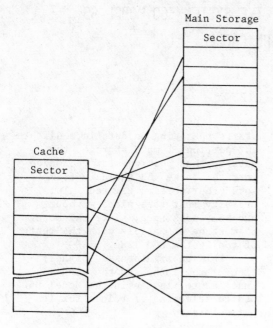

Main Storage

Sector

Cache

Sector

Fig. 1. Assignment of Cache Sectors to
Main Storage Sectors.

Assigning Cache Sectors

The assignment of cache
sectors is dynamically adjusted
during operation, so that they
are assigned to the main storage
sectors that are currently being
used by the program. If the
program causes a fetch from a
main storage sector that does
not have a cache sector assigned
to it, one of the cache sectors
is then reassigned to that main
storage sector. To make a good
selection of a cache sector to
reassign, enough information is
maintained to order the cache
sectors into an activity list.
The sector at the top of the list is
the one that was most recently referred to, the second one is the
next most recently referred to, and
so forth. When a cache sector is
referred to, it is moved to the top
of the list, and the intervening
ones are moved down one position.
This is not meant to imply an actual
movement of sectors within the
cache, but rather refers to a logical ordering of the sectors. When
it is necessary to reassign a sector, the one selected is the one
at the bottom of the activity list.
This cache sector is the one that
has gone the longest without being
referred to.

When a cache sector is assigned
to a different main storage sector,
the contents of all of the 1K bytes
located in that main storage sector
are not loaded into the cache at
once. Rather, each sector is
divided into 16 blocks of 64 bytes,
and the blocks are loaded on a demand basis. When a cache sector is
reassigned, the only block that is
loaded is the one that was referred
to. If they are required, the remaining blocks are loaded later, one
at a time. Each block in the cache
has a bit associated with it to record whether it has been loaded.
This "validity bit" is turned on
when the block is loaded and off
when the sector is reassigned.

Store Operations

Store operations always cause
main storage to be updated. If
the main storage sector being
changed has a cache sector assigned
to it, the cache is also updated;
otherwise, no activity related to
the cache takes place. Therefore,
store operations cannot cause a
cache sector to be reassigned, a
block to be loaded, or the activity
list to be revised. Since all of
the data in the cache is also in
main storage, it is not necessary
on a cache sector reassignment to
move any data from the cache to
main storage. All that is required
is to change the sector address
register, reset the validity bits,
and initiate loading of a block.
The processor is capable of buffering one instruction requesting the
storing of information in main
storage, so that it can proceed
with subsequent instructions even if
execution of the store instruction
cannot be initiated immediately.

Two processor cycles are required to fetch data that is in the cache. The first cycle is used to examine the sector address registers and the validity bits to determine if the data is in the cache. The second cycle is then used to read the data out of the cache. However, requests can normally be overlapped, so that one request can be processed every cycle. If the data is not present in the cache, additional cycles are required while the block is loaded into the cache from main storage.

The storage word size on which the Model 85 operates internally is 16 bytes. This is the width of the data paths to and from the storage units and is the amount the processor can store or fetch with a single request. Because a single 2365-5 storage unit operates on an 8-byte wide interface, two units are paired together and operated simultaneously. Except for the 512K configuration, main storage is interleaved four ways. Since a block is 64 bytes, four fetches to main storage are required to load one block into the cache. With four-way interleaving, this means one request to each basic storage module. To improve performance, the first basic storage module referred to during each block load is the one containing the 16 bytes wanted by the processor. In addition to being loaded into the cache, the data is sent directly to the processor, so that execution can proceed as soon as possible (see Fig. 2).

On the Model 85, channels store and fetch data by way of the processor. Channel fetches are processed by getting the required data from main storage without referring to the cache. Channel stores are handled the same way as processor stores. In this way, if a channel changes data that is in the cache, the cache is updated but the channels do not have any part of the cache devoted to them.

PERFORMANCE STUDIES

Among the questions that had to be answered to determine whether the cache approach should be taken were: (1) how effective is it, and (2)

Main Storage

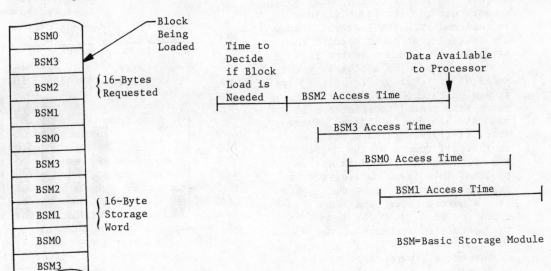

Fig. 2. Timing for a Block Load.

does its effectiveness vary substantially from one program to another? The principal tools used to
answer these questions are the tracing and timing techniques referred
to in Part I[1]. The tracing technique
produces an instruction-by-instruc-
tion trace of a program operating
under System/360 Operating System.
The output is a sequence of "trace
tapes," which contain every instruction executed, whether the problem
program or the operating system,
and the necessary information to
determine how long it takes to
be executed. These trace tapes
contain about 250,000 instructions
each and are used as input to a
timing program, which determines,
cycle-by-cycle, how the Model 85
would execute that sequence of
instructions. These techniques are
intended to determine internal performance and do not provide any information concerning throughput. An
intensive investigation preceded
selection of the programs used in
this study.

Cache Effectiveness

In order to measure the effectiveness of the cache, we postulated
a system identical to the Model 85
except that the storage hierarchy
is replaced by a single-level storage operating at cache speed. The
performance of such a system is
that which would be achieved by the
Model 85 if it always found the data
it wanted in the cache and if it
never encountered interference in
main storage due to stores. Therefore, it represents an upper limit
on the performance of the Model
85; how close the Model 85 approaches this ideal can serve as a
measure of how effective the cache
is. Nineteen trace tapes were
timed for both the Model 85 and
the postulated system, and the
performance of the Model 85 was
expressed as a percentage of the
performance of the ideal system.
Figure 3 shows the distribution

of performance data obtained. The
average was 81 percent of the
performance of the ideal system,
with a range between 66 and 94
percent.

An important statistic related to cache operation is the
probability of finding the data
wanted for a fetch in the cache.
Figure 4 shows the distribution
of this probability for the same 19

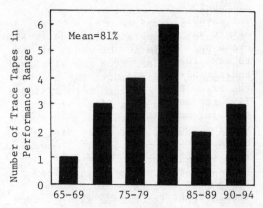

Fig. 3. Model 85 Performance Relative
to Single-Level Storage Operating at
Cache Speed.

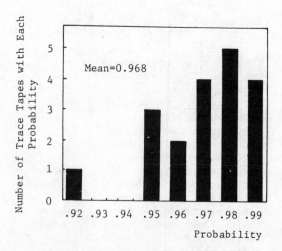

Fig. 4. Probability of Finding
Fetched Data in Cache.

trace tapes used for Fig. 3. The
average probability was 0.968. It
is worth noting that, if the addresses generated by a program were
random, the probability of finding
the data wanted in the cache would
be much less than 0.01. Therefore,
it can be said that what makes the
cache work is the fact that real
programs are not random in their
addressing patterns.

SELECTION OF CACHE PARAMETERS

Before the final cache design
was established, a great deal of
effort was expended on the choice of
cache parameters[2]. The tools used
to make the choice were the trace
and timing programs. From among
the trace tapes available, we picked
five representative ones and ran
them for many cache configurations,
varying cache size, sector size, and
block size. Tables 1 and 2 show the
results obtained. In Table 1, block
size is always 64 bytes; in Table 2,
the number of sectors is always sixteen. In both cases, performance is
compared with that of a single-level
storage operating at cache speed.
The selection of a 16K byte cache
with 16 sectors and 64 bytes per
block was made as the best balance
between cost and performance.

Replacement Algorithms

The choice of an algorithm for
the selection of a sector to reassign
was also the object of careful study.
From among the algorithms proposed,
two were selected as likely candi-
dates and incorporated into the timing program for study.

For one algorithm, the cache
sectors are partitioned with an
equal number of sectors in each
partition. An activity list is
maintained for each partition re-
flecting the use of the sectors within it. Each partition has a binary
address, and when a main storage
sector needs to be assigned a position in the cache, the low-order

bits of its sector address are used
to select one of the partitions.
The sector at the bottom of that
partition's activity list is the one
chosen for reassignment.

This algorithm was studied for
1, 2, 4, 8, and 16 partitions. When
there is only one partition, the algorithm becomes the Model 85 replacement algorithm. At the opposite
extreme, when there are sixteen partitions, there is only one sector in
each, and the idea of an activity
list for each partition is meaning-
less. In this case, the choice of
a cache sector to reassign depends
only on the low-order address bits
of the main storage sector for which
a place is being found in the cache,
and consequently each main storage
sector has only one possible place
where it can be put in the cache.

Table 1.

Average Performance Relative to an Ideal
System with Cache Size and Number of
Sectors Varied   Block Size = 64 Bytes

Number of Cache Bytes	Number of Sectors		
	8	16	32
8 K	0.693	0.744	0.793
16 K	0.765	0.825	0.861
32 K	0.857	0.891	0.902

Table 2.

Average Performance Relative to an Ideal
System with Cache Size and Number of
Bytes per Block Varied
Number of Sectors = 16

Number of Cache Bytes	Number of Bytes per Block		
	64	128	256
8 K	0.744		
16 K	0.825	0.810	0.781
32 K	0.891	0.885	0.870

The second algorithm involves a single usage bit for each cache sector. When a sector is referred to, its usage bit is turned on if it is not already on. When the last sector bit is turned on, all of the other bits are turned off and the process continues. If a sector has to be reassigned, it is selected randomly from among those with their usage bits off.

Table 3 summarizes the results obtained. The choice of the activity list was made because it provided the best balance between cost and performance.

Table 3.

Comparative Performance Using Different Cache Sector Replacement Algorithms

Algorithm	Performance
1 Partition*	1.000
2 Partitions	0.990
4 Partitions	0.987
8 Partitions	0.979
16 Partitions	0.933
Usage Bits	0.931

---

* Replacement algorithm chosen for the Model 85

SUMMARY COMMENT

The inclusion of a storage hierarchy represents one of the major advances in system organization present in the Model 85. Although the concept of a storage hierarchy is not new, the successful implementation of a nanosecond/microsecond level of hierarchy was inhibited until now by the lack of a suitable technology. As implemented in the Model 85, the fast monolithic storage physically integrated with the CPU logic yields the desired machine speed, while the large core storage yields storage capacity, the combination being transparent to the user. It is likely that with future progress in technology this nanosecond/microsecond hierarchy is not merely an innovation that worked out well for the Model 85, but rather it is a fundamental step forward that will be incorporated into most large systems of the future.

REFERENCES

1. C. J. Conti, D. H. Gibson, and S. H. Pitkowsky, "Structural Aspects of the System/360 Model 85, I. General Organization," IBM Systems Journal, Vol. 7, pp. 2-14, 1968.
2. D. H. Gibson, "Considerations in Block-Oriented Systems Design," Spring Joint Computer Conference, Vol. 30, pp. 75-80, 1967.

PARALLEL OPERATION IN THE CONTROL DATA 6600

JAMES E. THORNTON

HISTORY

About four years ago, in the summer of 1960, Control Data began a project which culminated last month in the delivery of the first 6600 Computer. In 1960 it was apparent that brute force circuit performance and parallel operation were the two main approaches to any advanced computer.

This paper presents some of the considerations having to do with the

Reprinted with permission from the Proceedings-Fall Joint Computer Conference, Vol.26, pt. 2, AFIPS Press, Montvale, N.J., 1964, pp. 33-40. A section of the paper which describes the physical construction of the machine has been deleted.

parallel operations in the 6600. A most important and fortunate event coincided with the beginning of the 6600 project. This was the appearance of the high-speed silicon transistor, which survived early difficulties to become the basis for a nice jump in circuit performance.

SYSTEM ORGANIZATION

The computing system envisioned in that project, and now called the 6600, paid special attention to two kinds of use, the very large scientific problem and the time sharing of smaller problems. For the large problem, a high-speed floating point central processor with access to a large central memory was obvious, Not so obvious, but important to the

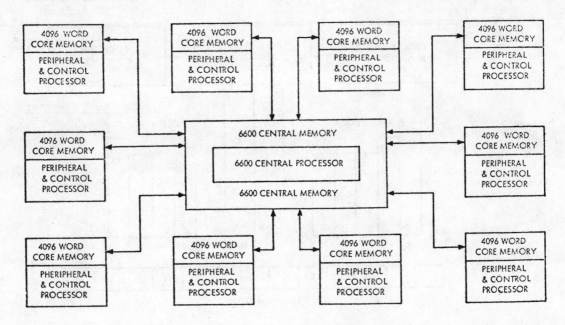

Fig. 1. Control Data 6600.

6600 system idea, was the isolation of this central arithmetic from any peripheral activity.

It was from this general line of reasoning that the idea of a multiplicity of peripheral processors was formed (Fig. 1). Ten such peripheral processors have access to the central memory on one side and the peripheral channels on the other. The executive control of the system is always in one of these peripheral processors, with the others operating on assigned peripheral or control tasks. All ten processors have access to twelve input-output channels and may "change hands," monitor channel activity, and perform other related jobs. These processors have access to central memory, and may pursue independent transfers to and from this memory.

Each of the ten peripheral processors contains its own memory for program and buffer areas, thereby isolating and protecting the more critical system control operations in the separate processors. The central processor operates from the central memory with relocating register and

file protection for each program in central memory.

PERIPHERAL AND CONTROL PROCESSORS

The peripheral and control processors are housed in one chassis of the main frame. Each processor contains 4096 memory words of 12 bits length. There are 12- and 24-bit instruction formats to provide for direct, indirect, and relative addressing. Instructions provide logical, addition, subtraction, shift, and conditional branching. Instructions also provide single word or block transfers to and from any of twelve peripheral channels, and single word or block transfers to and from central memory. Central memory words of 60 bits length are assembled from five consecutive peripheral words. Each processor has instructions to interrupt the central processor and to monitor the central program address.

To get this much processing power with reasonable economy and

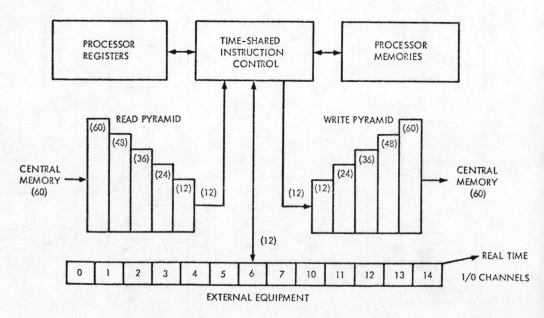

Fig. 2. 6600 Peripheral and Control Processors.

space, a time-sharing design was ad-opted (Fig. 2). This design contains a register "barrel" around which is moving the dynamic information for all ten processors. Such things as program address, accumulator con-tents, and other pieces of inform-ation totalling 52 bits are shifted around the barrel. Each complete trip around requires one major cycle or one thousand nanoseconds. A "slot" in the barrel contains adders, assembly networks, distribution net-work, and interconnections to per-form one step of any peripheral instruction. The time to perform this step or, in other words, the time through the slot, is one minor cycle or one hundred nanoseconds. Each of the ten processors, there-fore, is allowed one minor cycle of every ten to perform one of its steps. A peripheral instruction may require one or more of these steps, depending on the kind of instruction.

In effect, the single arith-metic and the single distribution and assembly network are made to appear as ten. Only the memories are kept truly independent. Inci-dentally, the memory read-write cycle time is equal to one complete trip around the barrel, or one thousand nonoseconds.

Input-output channels are bi-directional, 12-bit paths. One 12-bit word may move in one direction every major cycle, or 1000 nano-seconds, on each channel. Therefore, a maximum burst rate of 120 million bits per second is possible using all ten peripheral processors. A sustained rate of about 50 million bits per second can be maintained in a practical operating system. Each channel may service several peripheral devices and may inter-face to other systems, such as satellite computers.

Peripheral and control pro-cessors access central memory through an assembly network and a dis-assembly network. Since five

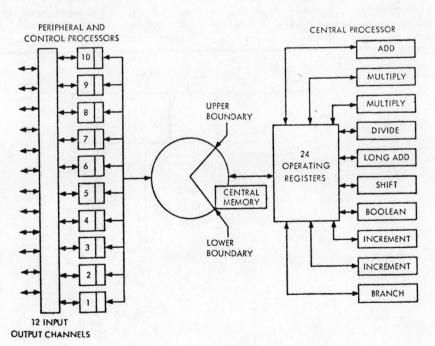

Fig. 3. Block Diagram of 6600.

peripheral memory references are
required to make up one central
memory word, a natural assembly network of five levels is used. This
allows five references to be "nested"
in each network during any major
cycle. The central memory is organized in independent banks with the
ability to transfer central words
every minor cycle. The peripheral
processors, therefore, introduce
at most about 2% interference at the
central memory address control.

A single real time clock,
continuously running, is available
to all peripheral processors.

CENTRAL PROCESSOR

The 6600 central processor may
be considered the high-speed arithmetic unit of the system (Fig. 3).
Its program, operands, and results
are held in the central memory. It
has no connection to the peripheral
processors except through memory and
except for two single controls. These
are the exchange jump, which starts
or interrupts the central processor
from a peripheral processor, and the
central program address which can be
monitored by a peripheral processor.

A key description of the 6600
central processor, as you will see in
later discussion, is "parallel by
function." This means that a number
of arithmetic functions may be performed concurrently. To this end,
there are ten functional units within
the central processor. These are the
two increment units, floating add
unit, fixed add unit, shift unit, two
multiply units, divide unit, boolean
unit, and branch unit. In a general
way, each of these units is a three
address unit. As an example, the
floating add unit obtains two 60-bit
operands from the central registers
and produces a 60-bit result which
is returned to a register. Information to and from these units is held
in the central registers, of which
there are twenty-four. Eight of these
are considered index registers, are of
18 bits length, and one of which always
contains zero. Eight are considered
address registers, are of 18 bits
length, and serve to address the five
read central memory trunks and the two
store central memory trunks. Eight are
considered floating point registers,
are of 60 bits length, and are the only
central registers to access central
memory during a central program.

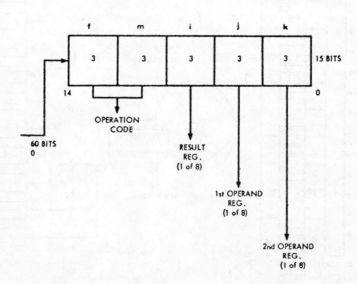

Fig. 4. 15-Bit Instruction Format.

In a sense, just as the whole central processor is hidden behind central memory from the peripheral processors, so, too, the ten functional units are hidden behind the central registers from central memory. As a consequence, a considerable instruction efficiency is obtained and an interesting form of concurrency is feasible and practical. The fact that a small number of bits can give meaningful definition to any function makes it possible to develop forms of operand and unit reservations needed for a general scheme of concurrent arithmetic.

Instructions are orgainzed in two formats, a 15-bit format and a 30-bit format, and may be mixed in an instruction word (Fig. 4). As an example, a 15-bit instruction may call for an ADD, designated by the f and m octal digits, from registers designated by the j and k octal digits, the result going to the register designated by the i octal digit. In this example, the addresses of the three-address, octal digit. In this example, the addresses of the three-address, floating add unit are only three bits in length, each address referring to one of the eight floating point registers. The 30-bit format follows this same form but substitutes for the k octal digit an 18-bit constant K which serves as one of the input operands. These two formats provide a highly efficient control of concurrent operations.

As a background, consider the essential difference between a general purpose device and a special device in which high speeds are required. The designer of the special device can generally improve on the traditional general purpose device by introducing some form of concurrency. For example, some activities of a housekeeping nature may be performed separate from the main sequence of operations in separate hardware. The total time to complete a job is then optimized to the main sequence and excludes the housekeeping. The two categories operate concurrently.

It would be, of course, most attractive to provide in a general purpose device some generalized scheme to do the same kind of thing. The organization of the 6600 central processor provides just this kind of scheme. With multiplicity of functional units, and of operand registers and with a simple and highly efficient addressing system, a generalized queue and reservation scheme is practical. This is called the scoreboard.

The scoreboard maintains a running file of each central register, of each functional unit, and of each of the three operand trunks to and from each unit. Typically, the scoreboard file is made up of two-, three-, and four-bit quantities identifying the nature of register and unit usage. As each new instruction is brought up, the conditions at the instant of issuance are set into the scoreboard. A snapshot is taken, so to speak, of the pertinent conditions. If no waiting is required, the execution of the instruction is begun immediately under control of the unit itself. If waiting is required (for example, an input operand may not yet be available in the central registers), the scoreboard controls the delay, and when released, allows the unit to begin its execution. Most important, this activity is accomplished in the scoreboard and the functional unit, and does not necessarily limit later instructions from being brought up and issued.

In this manner, it is possible to issue a series of instructions, some related, some not, until no functional units are left free or until a specific register is to be assigned more than one result. With just those two restrictions on issuing (unit free and no double result), several independent chains of instructions may proceed concurrently. Instructions may issue every minor cycle in the absence of the two restraints. The instruction executions, in comparison, range from three minor cycles for fixed add, 10 minor cycles for floating multiply, to 29 minor cycles for floating divide.

To provide a relatively continuous score of instructions, one buffer register of 60 bits is located at the bottom of an instruction stack capable of holding 32 instructions (Fig. 5). Instruction words from memory enter the bottom register of the stack pushing up the old instruction words. In straight line programs, only the bottom two registers are in use, the bottom being refilled as quickly as memory conflicts allow. In programs which branch back to an instruction in the upper stack registers, no refills are allowed after the branch, thereby holding the program loop completely in the stack. As a result, memory access or memory conflicts are no longer involved, and a considerable speed increase can be had.

Five memory trunks are provided from memory into the central processor to five of the floating point registers (Fig. 6). One address register is assigned to each trunk (and therefore to the floating point register). Any instruction calling for address register result implicity initiates a memory reference

on that trunk. These instructions are handled through the scoreboard and therefore tend to overlap memory access with arithmetic. For example, a new memory word to be loaded in a floating point register can be brought in from memory but may not enter the register until all previous uses of that register are completed. The central registers, therefore, provide all of the data to the ten functional units, and receive all of the unit results. No storage is maintained in any unit.

Central memory is organized in 32 banks of 4096 words. Consecutive addresses call for a different bank; therefore, adjacent addresses in one bank are in reality separated by 32. Addresses may be issued every 100 nanoseconds. A typical central memory information transfer rate is about 250 million bits per second.

As mentioned before, the functional units are hidden behind the registers. Although the units might appear to increase hardware duplication, a pleasant fact emerges from this design. Each unit may be trimmed to perform its function without regard to others. Speed in-

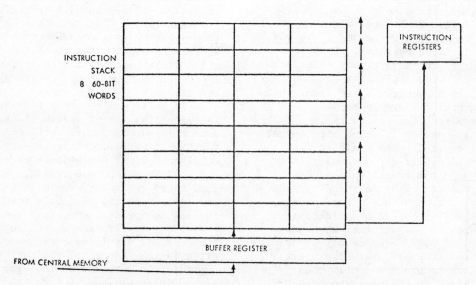

Fig. 5. 6600 Instruction Stack Operation.

creases are had from this simplified design.

As an example of special functional unit design, the floating multiply accomplishes the coefficient multiplication in nine minor cycles plus one minor cycle to put away the result for a total of 10 minor cycles, or 1000 nanoseconds. The multiply uses layers of carry save adders grouped in two halves. Each half concurrently forms a partial product, and the two partial products finally merge while the long carries propagate. Although this is a fairly large complex of circuits, the resulting device was sufficiently smaller than originally planned to allow two multiply units to be included in the final design.

To sum up the characteristics of the central processor, remember that the broad-brush description is "concurrent operation." In other words, any program operating within the central processor utilizes some of the available concurrency. The program need not be written in a particular way, although certainly some optimization can be done. The specific method of accomplishing this concurrency involves issuing as many instructions as possible while handling most of the conflicts during execution. Some of the essential requirements for such a scheme include:

1. Many functional units
2. Units with three address

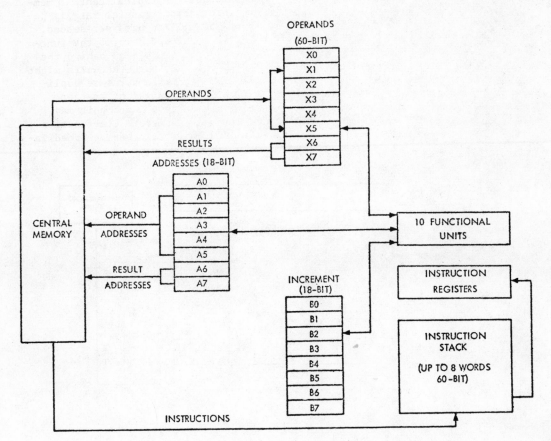

Fig. 6. Central Processor Operating Registers.

properties
3. Many transient registers
    with many trunks to and
    from the units
4. A simple and efficient
    instruction set

The 6600 Computer has taken advantage of certain technology advances, but more particularly, logic organization advances which now appear to be quite successful. Control Data is exploring advances in technology upward within the same compatible structure, and identical technology downward, also within the same compatible structure.

THE SOLOMON COMPUTER

DANIEL L. SLOTNICK, W. CARL BORCK, AND ROBERT C. McREYNOLDS

INTRODUCTION AND SUMMARY

The SOLOMON (Simultaneous Operation Linked Ordinal MOdular Network), a parallel network computer, is a new system involving the interconnections and programming, under the supervision of a central control unit, of many identical processing elements (as few or as many as a given problem requires), in an arrangement that can simulate directly the problem being solved.

The parallel network computer shows great promise in aiding progress in certain critically important areas limited by the capabilities of current computing systems. Many of these technical areas possess the common mathematical denominator of involving calculations with a matrix or mesh of numerical values, or more generally involving operations with sets of variables which permit simultaneous independent operation on each individual variable within the set. This group is typified by the solution of linear systems, the calculation of inverses and eigenvalues of matrices, correlation and autocorrelation, and numerical

solution of systems of ordinary and partial differential equations. Such calculations are encountered throughout the entire spectrum of problems in data reduction, communication, character recognition, optimization, guidance and control, orbit calculations, hydrodynamics, heat flow, diffusion, radar data processing, and numerical weather forecasting.

An example of the type of problem permitting the use of the parallelism is the numerical solution of partial differential equations. Assuming the value of a function, u, is known on the boundary, Γ, of a region, the solution of the Laplace equation[1] can be calculated at each mesh point, x, y in the region as illustrated in Fig. 1.

Since the iteration formula is identical for each mesh point in the region, the arithmetic capability provided by a processing element corresponding to each point will

The applied research reported in this document has been made possible through support and sponsorship extended by the U.S. Air Force Rome Air Development Center and the U.S. Army Signal Research and Development Laboratory under Contract Number AF30(602)2724: Task 730J. It is published for technical information only, and does not necessarily represent recommendations or conclusions of the sponsoring agency.

Reprinted with permission from the Proceedings of the Fall Joint Computer Conference, Vol. 22, 1962, pp. 97-107.

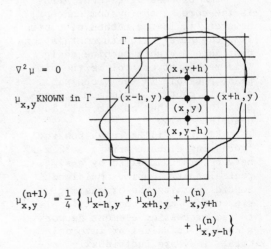

$$\nabla^2 \mu = 0$$

$$\mu_{x,y} \text{ KNOWN in } \Gamma$$

$$\mu_{x,y}^{(n+1)} = \frac{1}{4} \left\{ \mu_{x-h,y}^{(n)} + \mu_{x+h,y}^{(n)} + \mu_{x,y+h}^{(n)} + \mu_{x,y-h}^{(n)} \right\}$$

Fig. 1. Iterative Solution of Laplace's Equation

enable one calculation of the equation; i.e., a single program execution, to improve the approximation at each of the mesh points simultaneously.

Figure 2 illustrates a basic array of processing elements. Each of these elements possesses 4096 bits of core storage, and the arithmetic capabilities to perform serial-by-bit arithmetic and logic. An additional capability possessed by each processing element is that of communication with other processing elements. Processing element E can transmit and receive data serially from its four nearest neighbors: the processing elements immediately to right, A; left, C; above, B; and below, D.

A fifth source of input data is available to the processing element matrix through the "broadcast input" option. This option utilizes a register in the central control to supply constants when needed by an arbitrary number of the processing elements during the same operation cycle. This constant is treated as a normal operand by the processing elements and results in the central control unit becoming a "fifth" nearest neighbor to all processing elements.

The processing element array is the core of the system concept; however, it is the method of controlling the array which turns this concept into a viable machine design. This method of control is the simplist possible in the processing elements contain a minimum of control logic - the "multimodal" logic described below.

Figure 3 illustrates how the processing element array, a 32 x 32 network, is controlled by a single central control unit. Multimodal control permits the processing elements to alter control signals to the processing element network according to values of internal data. They are individually permitted to execute or ignore these central control signals.

Basically, the central control unit contains program storage (large capacity random-access memory), has the means to retrieve and interpret the stored instructions, and has the capability, subject to multimodal logic, to cause execution of these instructions within the array.

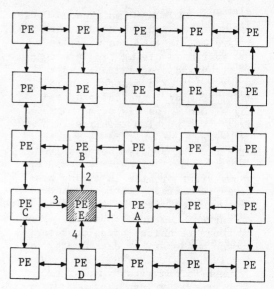

Fig. 2. Basic Array of Processing Elements

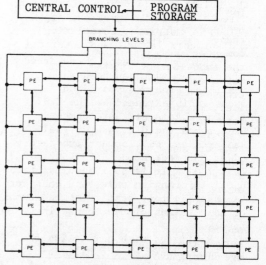

Fig. 3. PE Array Under Central Control

Thus, at any given instant, each processing element in the system is capable of performing the same operation on the operands stored in the same memory location of each processing element. These operands, however, may all be different. The flow of control information from the control unit to the processing elements is indicated in Fig. 3 by light lines. An instruction is retrieved from the program storage and transmitted to a register in central control. Within central control, the instruction is interpreted and the information contained is translated into a sequence of signals and transmitted from central control to the processing elements. Since this information must be provided to 1024 processing elements, it is necessary to branch this information and provide the necessary amplification and power. This is accomplished by transmission through branching levels, which provide the necessary power for transmission.

As described above, each processing element in the network possesses the capability of communicating with its four adjacent elements. The "edge" processing elements, however, do not possess a full complement of neighbors. The resulting free connections are used for input-output application. This makes possible very high data exchange rates between the central computer and external devices through the input-output subsystem. These rates could be still further increased by providing longer "edges"; i.e., by the use of a nonsquare network array.

Two input-output exchange systems are used by the input output equipment. The primary exchange system is a high speed system operating at a data rate near that of the processing element network. This system consists of magnetic tapes and rotating magnetic memories and serves the network with data storage during large net problems.

The secondary exchange system provides the user with communication with the primary exchange system through conventional high speed printers, and tape transports. The data at the output of this system is compatible with most conventional devices.

THE PROCESSING ELEMENT

The processing element (PE) logic, illustrated in Fig. 4, basically consists of two parts: the processing element memory, and the arithmetic and multimodal control logic.

The multimodal control within each processing element provides the capability for individual elements to alter the program flow as a function of the data which it is currently processing. This capability permits the processing element to classify data and make judgments on the course of programming which it should follow. Whenever individual elements are in a different mode of operation than specified by central control, they will not execute the specified command.

During each arithmetic operation, one word will be read serially from each of the two memory frames associated with a unique processing element. The operand in frame one will be transmitted by central control command, either to the internal adder or to that of one of the four adjacent elements which are its nearest neighbors in the network array. The five gates labeled A in Fig. 4 control the routing of information from frame one. Since only one of these may be activated during a single operation, a word in frame one can be entered in the operation select logic of only one of the five processing elements. The frame-two operand can be routed only into the unit's full adder.

Each PE in the system will communicate with a corresponding unit, thereby producing a flow of information between processing ele-

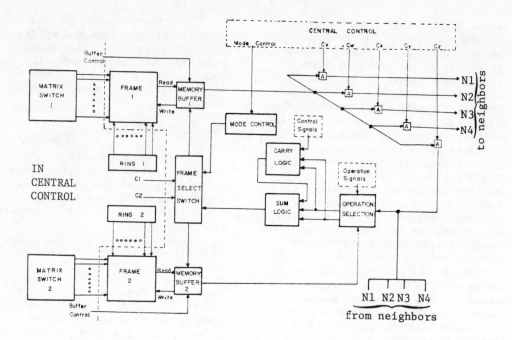

Fig. 4. Processing Element Block Diagram

ments during network operations.

Word addressing of the memory is performed by the matrix switches in the central control unit. These switches convert the address from the binary form of the instruction to one-of-n form required for addressing the memory frame. Provision is made for special addressing of specific memory locations for temporary storage of multiplier and quotient during multiplication and division. Successive bits are shifted into the PE logic by two digit counters in central control.

Three different types of storage are permitted: (1) the sum can be routed into frame one while the original word in frame two is rewritten; (2) the sum can be routed into frame two while the word in frame one is rewritten; and (3) information can be interchanged between frames. Note that in the first two operations, the word which was located in the memory frame into which the sum is routed is destroyed.

No information is altered during the third type operation.

Multimodal Operation: Multimodal operation gives the processing element the additional capability for altering program flow and tagging information on the basis of internal data. Any command given by the central control unit to the PE matrix is executed by the processing element only when the mode control signals from the control sequencer are identical with the coding of the processing element mode register. The central control unit may activate any combination of four states permitting a given command to be executed by individual elements in different multimodal states.

Upon comparison of a command field with the multimodal state, the execute signal is energized enabling the processing element to execute the command. When this signal is not energized, the command is not executed. If external routing is specified, the numbers in frame one are routed to the specified neighbors, regardless of mode state. The processing elements in a nonselected mode will not accept information; they will return bits of information read from memory to their respective frames unaltered.

Internally controlled mode advancement will take place as "condition met" signals are received from the arithmetic sum network. These signals transfer those processing elements which have satisfied the condition for transfer to a mode of operation specified by central control.

Modes can also be changed by the programmer by using special commands. The set mode command will automatically set all addressed processing elements into the directed mode state.

Commands for loading modes operate on the mode control flip-flops loading into or loading from two bits in memory specified by central control. The store mode command does not alter the contents of the mode control flip-flops. By programming, this capability can be used to tag information or results of calculations.

Row and Column Selection: In a number of matrix calculations, the use of a series of load and store mode commands to do row selection becomes quite cumbersome. Including the capability for commands to select particular rows or columns for the operations saves both time and processing element memory storage.

During row-column operations, the mode control logic is altered by the selection of control. Processing elements execute commands in a manner identical to the ordinary mode control operations. Nonselected rows will transmit required operands, but will not alter their memory contents. The selected processing elements operate in the conventional manner.

In combination with the multimodal operation, row-column selection is a useful programming tool. The hardware in central control consists of a holding register (switches) whose output is gated to either rows or columns. Two holding registers could permit simultaneous row and column selection.

Arithmetic Operation: Each of the two memory frames communicates with a two-bit memory buffer shown in Fig. 4. Each buffer holds the bit just read from memory, along with the result of the logical operation which is about to be written into memory.

The frame-one memory buffer includes a control flip-flop which can sense a bit set into the buffer during division or multiplication, as well as the condition of the summing network during a logical or arithmetic operation.

The frame-select switch controls the routing of the sum and memory bits according to the command from central control.

The arithmetic portion of the PE consists of two parts: operation selection logic and a modified full adder. Subtraction is performed by the addition of the complement of the subtrahend to the minuend. SOLOMON uses 2's complement arithmetic in the serial processing element to eliminate the endaround carry required when using 1's complement. The 2's complement is formed by an addition of 1 during the first bit cycle by initially setting the carry to a 1 and gating the complement of each bit. Therefore, a 1 is automatically added during a cycle when no carry is normally present. Negative numbers are stored in 2's complement form within the processing element memory.

Multiplication is accomplished by a series of shifts and additions. Prior to the start of the multiplication, the multiplier is stored in a specific memory location in frame one. The multiplicand is

also stored in frame one. When
the multiplication signal arrives,
the matrix switch is set so that
the first multiplier bit is read
out of memory into the flip-flop.
Gating then modifies the central
control signals according to the
value of the multiplier bit. They
will provide either a set of zeros,
or permit addition of the multiplicand to the partial product which
is stored in frame two. To maintain
the alignment of bits, the second
ring is started one bit time earlier
than ring one. Note that the
product need not be stored in the
same processing element as the
multiplicand and multiplier, since
the multiplication can be implemented in conjunction with any of
the four nearest neighbors.

Division is implemented
through a nonrestoring technique.
When a divisor is smaller than or
equal to the dividend, a test is
applied to determine if the quotient
will not possess any significant
bits. When this occurs, the processing element will enable the
overflow signal and not divide.
The central control unit can then
choose to ignore the overflow or
stop the computer for the operator
to make corrections.

Logical operations such as
"and," "or," and "exclusive or"
are included in the command rep-
ertoire. Other operations such
as comparisons are implemented by
varying combinations of the control
signals that permit flexibility
within the processing element logic.

Overflow (when addition or
subtraction results in a value
greater than the range of the computer) can be sensed and may initiate programmed corrective routines
in central control. The execute
signal is also transmitted to
central control for sensing to determine that some processing elements have met or have not met the
transfer conditions.

Processing Element Memory Organi-

zation: Each processing element
includes two memory frames each
with its own read and write circuitry. Each frame has a capacity
of sixty-four 32-bit words. These
frames are physically organized into
stacks as shown in Fig. 5. The
frame-one planes and frame-two
planes make up separate stacks
(stack I and stack II). These
stacks are driven in parallel from
central control.

Both sets of X-drivers are controlled from central control and
select one of 64 words in each
frame (see Fig. 6). The word selected from frame 1 can be different
from the word from frame 2. While
the selected X-drivers are turned
on (read-write), the Y-drivers will
sequence through the bit positions

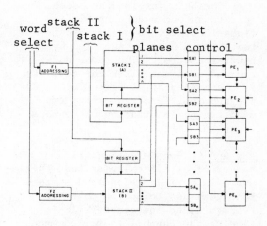

Fig. 5. Sharing of Memory Stacks

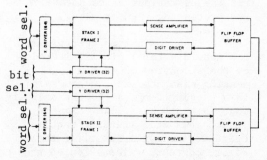

Fig. 6. Basic Operation of Memory Unit

with a series of read-write pulses, and thus cycle the bits of both selected words serially into the sense amplifiers. The Y-drivers of stack I can be offset by any number of bit positions from the Y-drivers of stack II. The outputs of the sense amplifiers are sent to the buffer flip-flop registers where they are gated by the processing element either into its own adder or to a designated nearest neighbor.

Writing the information back into the memory will be accomplished in a similar fashion, with the exception that the flip-flop buffer will control the digit driver, which, in turn, determines whether a one or a zero is written.

Drivers of convenient size and complexity can be built to drive up to 128 frame pairs. Therefore, a 1024-frame memory requires eight sets of X-and Y-drivers. When expanded systems are desired, an additional unit is provided with each module of 128 processing elements.

CENTRAL CONTROL

The Control Unit: The purpose of the Control Unit, Fig. 7, is to control the operations of the SOLOMON computer complex and to maintain the proper command distribution. This unit is the only one which addresses the program memory. All indexing, whether it is to be

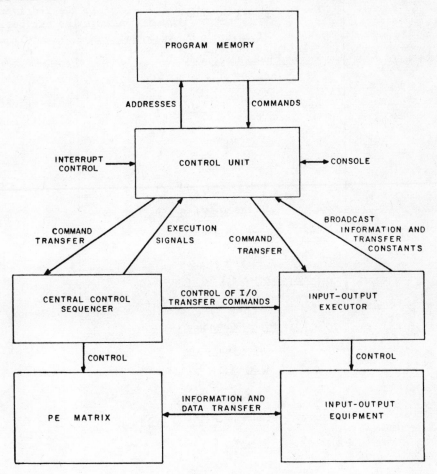

Fig. 7. Control Organization

performed on an input-output command or a processing element command is completed within this unit.
The unit has control over all broadcast and index registers. Loading,
transferring, and other operations
upon these registers are accomplished while processing element
matrix sequencing and input-output
control is taking place.

 The control unit has sufficient
command decoding logic to discrimi-

nate between four basic types of
commands: (1) processing element
commands, (2) input-output control
commands, (3) program control commands, and (4) commands which
transfer information between the
matrix and the input-output equipment.

 In processing element commands,
the control unit addresses the
program memory sequentially, and
receives the instruction. The

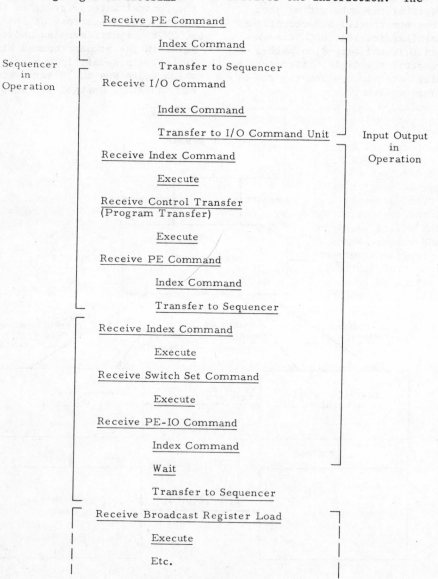

Fig. 8. Control Sequence

control unit ascertains that the instruction is intended for the sequencer, and then does the required indexing. When the sequencer has completed its previous instructions, the indexed command is transferred in parallel to the network sequencer. The control unit then addresses the program for the next instruction.

The input-output control commands are partially decoded and the addresses are indexed. When the input-output control has completed its previous instruction, the information from the program memory is transferred to the input-output executor.

The program control commands are completely executed within the control unit unless inputs are required from other control complexes. If the former is true, the control unit will complete the instruction and then return to the program memory for new instructions. When inputs from the other units are necessary, the control unit must wait until the device is not busy. Then the command will be executed. This class of instructions includes console control interrupt tests, switch test and control program, transfer instructions, and register controls.

The final class of instructions are those where both the input-output control and network sequencer are required to act together. With this type, both the sequencer and the input-output executor must have completed their previous instructions, then, with indexing completed, the command is transferred in parallel to the network sequencer, the control of the input-output executor is transferred to the sequencer, and the control unit is released to obtain the next instruction.

This organization of control will provide the programmer with the flexibility to maintain a maximum utilization of all control equipment (see Fig. 8). Interweaving instructions will provide a maximum amount of command overlap and results in the highest speed.

Network Sequencer: The sequencer, shown in Fig. 9, is the portion of the SOLOMON system whose major objective is to provide control signals for commands involving the processing element matrix. The device provides control signals to the input-output unit during information transfers.

The unit has two major functions, one to decode commands and

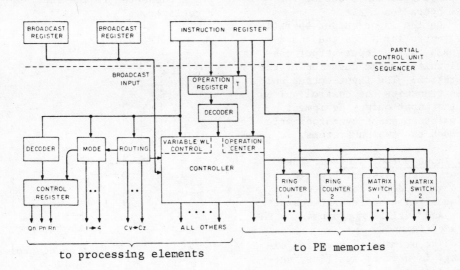

Fig. 9. Sequencer Block Diagram

provide control pulses and levels
to the processing element matrix,
and the second to control memory
addressing.

Memory address control is
provided by two digit counters
and two matrix switches. These
counters are loaded by the control unit and will advance or
decrement under control of the
operation register and controller.

While memory addressing is
mainly accomplished by counters,
the processing element controls
are more varied. After the operation register is loaded from the
control unit, it is decoded and
supplies command signals to the
controller. The controller supplies all the time-varying signals
to the processing element matrix
and transmits control pulses to
other sequencer registers.

The controller has the capability of selecting a broadcast
option which will enable the central control to act as a "fifth"
nearest neighbor to the network.
The frame one operand is replaced
by one of the broadcast registers
in the Control Unit. This option
will be selected by the programmer whenever a single constant is
required by a large number of
processing elements during the
same operation cycle.

During input-output operations,
the controller sends the coded
signals to the input-output control unit for the duration of the
operation. The input-output unit
then transmits the control pulses
to the input-output equipment
to maintain exact synchronization
between the two subsystems.

The Input Output System: The
input output system, Fig. 10,
is organized to facilitate
information transfer between network and auxiliary equipment with
high efficiency.

The primary information exchange is used as auxiliary network storage in large mesh problems. This exchange consists of

wide multi-channel magnetic tape
whose function is to keep a high
speed drum loaded. This drum
operating with parallel channels
can provide a bit rate comparable
with the network rate. Other
advanced storage devices are being
considered in this area.

This primary exchange system
communicates through the input
output buffer with the secondary
exchange system. This secondary
exchange system provides the user
with compatibility with existing
systems such as conventional
magnetic tape, card reader and
punch, high speed printers, paper
tape units and other devices. The
Format Converter provides conversions from the binary form required by the network to the format
required by the peripheral devices.

Both the primary exchange and
the core buffer can communicate
with the processing element network in two ways, the "edge" elements and geometric control.

In the first method, since
each element has the capability of
communication with its four adjacent
neighbors a processing element
located on the "edge" of the network has one or more free connections. These unused connections
are connected to the input-output
register.

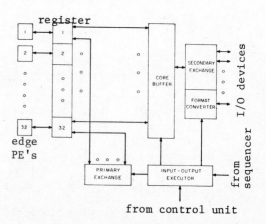

Fig. 10. Input Output Organization

Figure 11 shows the 32 x 32 matrix array with the capability to select the particular edge into which information is to be written. This flexibility increases the ease of loading the processing element network.

Additional flexibility is obtained through "geometric control." This technique employs special information transfer commands that enable the programmer to select specific rows or columns which are to communicate directly with the input output register. This eliminates the necessity of multiple transfers to obtain or load information directly into the interior of the matrix.

PROGRAMMING

In the overall evaluation of any computer system, consideration must be given both to the mathematical formulation of the problem to be solved and to the way in which this is reduced to a sequence of computer operations. Both of these aspects have a particular significance in the SOLOMON system. It is becoming increasingly apparent that the traditional methods of numerical analysis will be largely inapplicable to the new generation of computers represented by SOLOMON.

Present analytical and programming methods have evolved di-

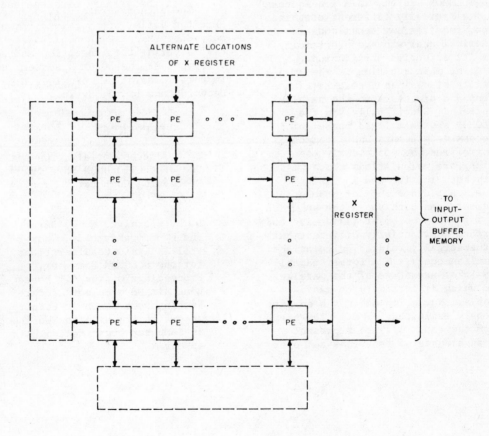

Fig. 11. Input Variations Possible With 32 x 32 Array

rectly and with little change from centuries of hand calculation and later from use of desk calculators. For this reason, such methods have been considered "natural," and the organization of present computing systems may be directly compared to the computing complex consisting of a human operator, an explicit computational algorithm, and mechanisms (or persons) capable of performing the required sequence of calculations. Heretofore, no serious attempt has been made to employ an approach to computer design which is based not on human capability and "natural" computation methods, but on potential computer capability and entirely new methods "natural" to the computer innovation.

Current developments demand an alteration of this state of affairs. The SOLOMON system, as a consequence of its radically different organization, requires new techniques in numerical analysis and programming for its effective utilization.

The main question is the amenability of basic mathematical functions and processes to the parallel approach. Specifically, in the SOLOMON system a fixed number of processing elements under common control must be efficiently used to perform calculations which will vary both in size and in basic type. A fixed number of processing elements can both speed the solution of a given problem of fixed size and perform substantially different but mathematically related calculations simultaneously. The former capability takes advantage of the parallelism which is intrinsic to many problems but which has not been previously exploited. The latter stems from the capability to represent broad classes of functions and oper-

ators mathematically in normal forms which distinguish between the represented quantities only by the values of constants that occur in their representations; examples of this are the representation of continuous functions by polynomials, of analytic functions by Taylor series, and of linear operators by matrices.

A previous paper[2] describes in detail the application of the SOLOMON system to problems in partial differential equations and certain matrix calculations. Results to date[1] establish a performance advantage between 60 and 200 for the SOLOMON Computer compared to currently available large scale digital systems.

ACKNOWLEDGEMENTS

The authors gratefully acknowledge the assistance received through many discussions with their associates during the conception and development of the SOLOMON system, and, in particular, E. R. Higgins, W. H. Leonard, and Dr. J. C. Tu.

REFERENCES

1. T. A. Jeeves, et.al., "On the Use of the SOLOMON Parallel-Processing Computer," Proc. EJCC, 1962.

2. D. L. Slotnick, W. C. Borck, and R. C. McReynolds, "Numerical Analysis Considerations for the SOLOMON Computer," Proceedings of the Air Force Rome Air Development Center-Westinghouse Electric Corporation Air Arm Division Workshop in Computer Organization. To appear.

APPENDIX

The papers which comprise the Appendix deviate somewhat from the topics treated previously.

A TRIGGER RELAY UTILIZING THREE-ELECTRODE THERMIONIC VACUUM TUBES

W. H. ECCLES AND F. W. JORDAN

This short paper introduced the idea of cross coupling two inverting amplifiers to create a bistable "relay." Although provision was made for switching in only one direction (i.e., to turn on the relay), a second input can be used to "reset" the relay.

This development of the bistable flip-flop was one of the crucial prerequisites necessary for the creation of the digital computer industry. Without the storage elements which have evolved from this trigger relay most of the electronic systems of today could never have been developed.

THE CORDIC TRIGONOMETRIC COMPUTING TECHNIQUE

JACK E. VOLDER

The concepts presented in this paper were initially developed to simplify special purpose airborne computers. Since that time, however, a number of general purpose computers have used CORDIC subprocessors in conjunction with conventional arithmetic units. It is widely used in the implementation of "scientific" calculators. This concept of a general purpose computer with a variety of special purpose processors is an attractive means to increase the utility of a given computer (with respect to that computer's job mix) without great expenditures.

The CORDIC processor operates in either of two modes: in the first mode the components of an arbitrary vector after undergoing a specified rotation are computed (clearly this can be useful in computing sin (X), cos (X), etc.); in the second mode the cartesian coordinates of an arbitrary vector are resolved into the length and angle of the vector (this can be used directly to determine inverse trigonometric functions, e.g., ARCSIN (X), ARCTAN (X), etc.).

The wide applicability and relative simplicity of the CORDIC concept encourage its use where the performance of a computer needs to be increased at nominal cost. It is of course only useful in those applications which require trigonometric computation.

A TRIGGER RELAY UTILISING THREE-ELECTRODE
THERMIONIC VACUUM TUBES

W. H. ECCLES AND F. W. JORDAN

In a well-known method of using a triode for the amplification of wireless signals an inductive coil is placed in the filament-to-anode circuit, and another coil magnetically coupled with this is introduced into the filament-to-grid circuit. This "back-coupling," as it is sometimes conveniently called, if it is arranged in the right sense, greatly exalts the magnification produced by the tube in any alternating E.M.F. applied to the grid; for the induced E.M.F. passed back to the grid is in correct phase relation to add directly to the original alternating E.M.F. applied there. If, instead of using inductive retroaction of this kind, we attempt to use resistance back-coupling, then the retroactive E.M.F. applied to the grid is exactly opposite in phase to the original alternating E.M.F., and the amplifying action of the triode is reduced. Since, however, one triode can produce opposition in phase the manner indicated, it is clear that two or any even number of similar triode-circuits arranged in cascade can produce agreement in phase. Hence we conclude that retroactive amplification can be obtained by effecting a back-coupling to the first grid from the second, fourth, and so on, anode circuit of a set of triodes arranged in an ohmically-coupled cascade.

It is possible to take advantage of the fact above stated for obtaining various types of continuously-acting relay, but the purpose of the present communication is to describe what may be called a one-stroke relay which, when operated by a small triggering electrical impulse, undergoes great changes in regard to its electrical equilibrium, and then remains in the new condition until re-set.

In what follows, the circuit comprising the space in the tube between anode and filament, the external conductors and the source of E.M.F., will be called the anode circuit, and the current flowing in it the anode current. The circuit comprising the space in the tube between the grid and the filament, external conductors and a source of E.M.F., will be called the grid circuit, and the current flowing in it the grid current.

The operation of the relay is most easily explained when two tubes, each with resistances and battery in its plate circuit, and with a resistance and battery in its grid circuit, are used and interconnected in the manner shown in Fig. 1.

Reprinted with permission from the
Radio Review, Vol. 1, Dec. 1919,
pp. 143-146.

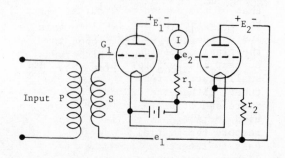

Fig. 1.

The electrical stimulus from outside which it is desired to detect and magnify is applied in the grid circuit in the first tube so as to make the grid transiently more positive in potential relative to the filament. This causes an increase of current in the plate circuit of the first tube, and consequently an increase of the potential difference between the terminals of the plate circuit resistance. This increased potential difference is transferred to the grid circuit of the second tube in such a manner that the grid becomes more negative than before relative to its filament. Consequently the plate current of the second tube decreases, and the potential difference between the terminals of its plate circuit resistance decreases also. This decrease of potential difference is now transferred to the grid circuit of the first tube in such a manner that it tends to make the grid more positive relative to the filament. The result of these processes is that a positive stimulus from outside given to the grid of the first tube initiates a chain of changes which results finally in the plate current of the first tube attaining the highest value possible under the E.M.F. of its battery, and the plate current of the second tube falling to its lowest possible value. This condition, therefore, persists after the disappearance of the initial stimulus. In the initial condition, with the two-tube arrangement just described, the plate current of the first tube is made very small, and that of the second tube large; after the reception of the outside stimulus on the grid of the first tube the final condition is a large plate current in the first tube and a small plate current in the second tube. Either the decreases or the increases of plate current can be used for indicating. In order to restore the initial conditions it is easy to interrupt for an instant the linkage between the tubes, or to stop the operation of one or both of the tubes, as, for instance, by dimming its filament.

The external stimulus is led into the primary P of transformer PS, of which the secondary is connected to grid G_1. The plate circuit of the first tube contains the indicating instrument I, such as an ammeter or a moving tongue relay. The resistance r_1 in the plate circuit of the first tube has its terminals connected to the filament and grid of the second tube. Similarly, the resistance r_2 in the plate circuit of the second tube has its terminals connected to the filament and the grid of the first tube. The plate circuits contain batteries E_1, E_2, and the grid circuits batteries e_1, e_2. The following values are typical, and show the performance of the relay:

E_1 = 78 volts E_2 = 74 volts

r_1 = 22,000 ohms r_2 = 12,000 ohms

e_1 = 31 volts e_2 = 17.5 volts

The change in the indication of an ammeter at I is from 0 - 2.5 microamperes.

The sensitiveness of the arrangement depends on the transformer PS to some extent. Using a telephone transformer of the kind made for Army C Mk. III. Amplifier with 20 ohms resistance in the primary, and with the primary connected to a Brown telephone of 60 ohms resistance, the relay is operated with certainty by snapping the thumb and finger at a distance of five feet from the telephone.

Figure 2 shows another mode of inter-connection of two tubes. The stimulus from outside is introduced to the grid of the first tube through a transformer, as before, and the indicating instrument is again placed in the plate circuit of the first tube. The two plate circuits are in parallel with a common battery E, and the connections are such that the changes of potential difference between the anode and

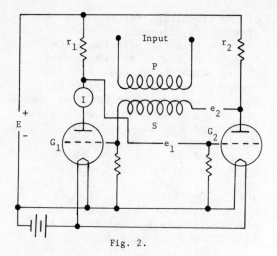

Fig. 2.

second tube are imposed between the filament and grid of the first. In order to help to maintain the grids' advantageous potentials, grid leak resistances are connected as indicated.

The following numerical values are typical dimensions:

E = 80 volts

$r_1 = r_2 = 100,000$ ohms

$e_1 = e_2 = 40$ volts

The sensitiveness of this relay could be made greater than that of Fig. 1, when these large resistances are used.

The devices just described were the subject of a patent numbered 10290/1918, taken out by the Admiralty, and the description is now published by permission.

the filament of the first tube are imposed between the filament and grid of the second tube, and the changes of potential difference between the anode and filament of the

THE CORDIC TRIGONOMETRIC COMPUTING TECHNIQUE

JACK E. VOLDER

INTRODUCTION

The CORDIC computing technique was developed especially for use in a real-time digital computer where the majority of the computation involved the discontinuous, programmed solution of the trigonometric relationships of navigation equations and a high solution rate for the trigonometric relationships of coordinate transformations. A prototype computer, CORDIC I, based on this computing technique, has been designed and constructed at Convair, Fort Worth. Although CORDIC I may be classified as an entire-transfer computer, its design is not based on the conventional "pencil and paper" computing technique of general-purpose computers.

FUNCTIONAL DESCRIPTION

For the sake of simplicity, the trigonometric operations in the CORDIC computer can be functionally described as the digital equivalent of an analog resolver. Similar to the operation of such a resolver, there are two computing modes, ROTATION and VECTORING. In the ROTATION mode, the coordinate components of a vector and an angle of rotation are given and the coordinate components of the original vector, after rotation through the given angle, are computed. In the

Presented at the Western Joint Computer Conf., San Francisco, Calif., March 3-5, 1959.

Reprinted with permission from the IRE Transactions on Electronic Computers, Vol. EC-8, Sept. 1959, pp. 330-334.

second mode, VECTORING, the coordinate components of a vector are given and the magnitude and angular argument of the original vector are computed. Similarly, as in the case of resolvers, the computing device of ROTATION plus feedback is employed in the VECTORING mode. The original coordinates are rotated until the angular argument is zero, so that the total amount of rotation required is the negative of the original argument, in which case the value of the X-component is equal to the magnitude of the original vector.

In essence, the basic computing technique used in both the ROTATION and VECTORING modes in CORDIC is a step-by-step sequence of pseudo rotations which result in an overall rotation through a given angle (ROTATION) or result in a final angular argument of zero (VECTORING).

It is necessary that the angular increments of rotation be computed in a decreasing order. There are several permissible values which may be chosen for the angular magnitude of the first rotation step. The magnitude actually chosen for the first increment is 90°. The expression for a set of coordinate components, Y_1 and X_1, rotated through plus or minus 90° is simply

$$Y_2 = \pm X_1 = R_1 \sin(\theta_1 \pm 90^\circ) \quad (1)$$

$$X_2 = \mp Y_1 = R_1 \cos(\theta_1 \pm 90^\circ). \quad (2)$$

The first step is unique in that a perfect rotation step is performed.

The rest of the computing steps can be clarified by examining the relationships, involved in a typical rotation step, which are shown in Fig. 1. Consider two given coordinate components, Y_i and X_i, in the plane coordinate system shown in the figure. In this discussion, the quantity i is equal to the number of the particular step under consideration. The components, Y_i and X_i, are associated with the ith step and describe a vector of magnitude R_i at an angle θ_i from the origin according to the relationship:

$$Y_i = R_i \sin \theta_i \qquad (3)$$

$$X_i = R_i \cos \theta_i \qquad (4)$$

In Fig. 1, the angle α_i is the special magnitude of rotation associated with each computing step. The general expression for α_i where $i > 1$ is

$$\alpha_i = \tan^{-1} 2^{-(i-2)} \qquad (5)$$

The peculiar magnitude of each α_i is such that a "rotation" of coordinate components through $\pm \alpha_i$ may be accomplished by the simple process of shifting and adding.

The two choices of positive or negative rotation are shown in Fig.1. The general expression for the rotated components is

$$Y_{i+1} = \sqrt{1 + 2^{-2(i-2)}} R_i \sin(\theta_i \pm \alpha_i)$$
$$= Y_i \pm 2^{-(i-2)} X_i \qquad (6)$$

$$X_{i+1} = \sqrt{1 + 2^{-2(i-2)}} R_i \cos(\theta_i \pm \alpha_i)$$
$$= X_i \mp 2^{-(i-2)} Y_i \qquad (7)$$

Note that, by restricting the angular rotation magnitude to (5), the right-hand terms of (6) and (7) may be obtained by two simultaneous shift-and-add operations. This is the fundamental relationship upon which this computing technique is based.

The computing action of adding (or subtracting) a shifted value of X_i to Y_i to obtain Y_{i+1}, while simultaneously subtracting (or adding) a shifted value of Y_i to X_i to obtain X_{i+1}, is termed "cross-addition."

While the expressions for Y_{i+1} and X_{i+1} are not perfect rotations because of the increase in magnitude by the terms under the radical, either of the two choices of direction produces the same change in magnitude. If, therefore, for each step, the coordinates are always rotated through either a positive or negative α_i, then the increase in magnitude may be considered as a constant. This requirement precludes the choice of zero rotation at any step. To identify the choice made in a particular step, the $\pm$ notation may be represented by the binary operator $+\xi_i$ where ξ_i can equal either $+1$ or -1. This substitution produces the general expressions

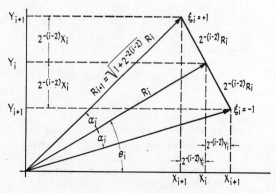

Fig. 1. Typical computing step.

$$Y_{i+1} = \sqrt{1 + 2^{-2(i-2)}} R_i \sin(\theta_i + \xi_i \alpha_i)$$
$$= Y_i + \xi_i 2^{-(i-2)} X_i \qquad (8)$$

$$X_{i+1} = \sqrt{1 + 2^{-2(i-2)}} R_i \cos(\theta_i + \xi_i \alpha_i)$$
$$= X_i - \xi_i 2^{-(i-2)} Y_i \qquad (9)$$

where

$$\xi_i = +1 \text{ or } -1 . \qquad (10)$$

Likewise, after the completion of the rotation step in which the i+1 terms are obtained, the i+2 terms may be computed from these terms with the results

$$Y_{i+2} = \sqrt{1 + 2^{-2(i-1)}}\sqrt{1 + 2^{-2(i-2)}}R_i$$

$$\cdot \sin(\theta_i + \xi_i\alpha_i + \xi_{i+1}\alpha_{i+1}) \quad (11)$$

$$X_{i+2} = \sqrt{1 + 2^{-2(i-1)}}\sqrt{1 + 2^{-2(i-2)}}R_i$$

$$\cdot \cos(\theta_i + \xi_i\alpha_i + \xi_{i+1}\alpha_{i+1}) \quad (12)$$

Similarly, the pseudo-rotation steps can be continued through any finite, pre-established number of steps without regard to the values assigned to ξ. Consider the initial coordinate components Y_1 and X_1 where

$$Y_1 = R_1 \sin \theta_1 \quad (13)$$

$$X_1 = R_1 \cos \theta_1 \quad (14)$$

By establishing the first and most significant step as a rotation through $\pm 90°$, and by establishing the number of steps as n, the expression for the final coordinate components will be

$$Y_{n+1} = \left[\sqrt{1+2^{-0}}\sqrt{1+2^{-2}}\ldots\sqrt{1+2^{-2(n-2)}} \right] R_1$$

$$\cdot \sin(\theta_1 + \xi_1\alpha_1 + \xi_2\alpha_2 + \ldots + \xi_n\alpha_n) \quad (15)$$

$$X_{n+1} = \left[\sqrt{1+2^{-0}}\sqrt{1+2^{-2}}\ldots\sqrt{1+2^{-2(n-2)}} \right] R_1$$

$$\cdot \cos(\theta_1 + \xi_1\alpha_1 + \xi_2\alpha_2 + \ldots + \xi_n\alpha_n) \quad (16)$$

The increase in magnitude of the components for a particular value of n is a constant and will be represented by the letter K. The value selected for n is a function of the desired computing accuracy and can be a constant for a particular computer. For example,

$$\text{if } n = 24$$

$$K = 1.646760255 \quad (17)$$

The necessary functional components and information flow for instrumenting the cross-addition are associated with the Y and X registers shown in Fig. 2.

It has not yet been shown how the prescribed sequence of rotation steps can be controlled to effect the desired over-all rotation. By examination of (15) and (16), it may

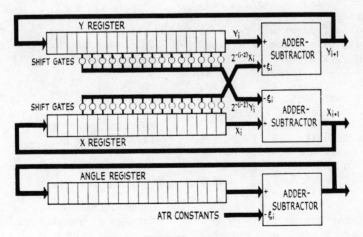

Fig. 2. CORDIC arithmetic unit

be shown that, for a rotation of a set of coordinate components Y_1 and X_1 through a given angle (as required in the ROTATION mode), it is necessary to obtain the expressions

$$Y_{n+1} = KR_1 \sin(\theta_1 + \lambda) \qquad (18)$$

$$X_{n+1} = KR_1 \cos(\theta_1 + \lambda) \qquad (19)$$

To obtain the relationships expressed in (18) and (19), it is required that

$$\lambda = \xi_1 \alpha_1 + \xi_2 \alpha_2 + \ldots + \xi_n \alpha_n \qquad (20)$$

and, as explained previously, for VECTORING it is required that

$$-\theta_1 = \xi_1 \alpha_1 + \xi_2 \alpha_2 + \ldots + \xi_n \alpha_n \qquad (21)$$

The sequences of (20) and (21) form a special radix representation equivalent to the desired angle, λ or θ where

$$\alpha_1 = 90^\circ \qquad (22)$$

$$\alpha_2 = \tan^{-1} 2^{-0} = 45^\circ \qquad (23)$$

$$\alpha_3 = \tan^{-1} 2^{-1} \quad 26.5^\circ \qquad (24)$$

$$\alpha_i = \tan^{-1} 2^{-(i-2)} \qquad (25)$$

The α terms are referred to as ATR (Arc Tangent Radix) constants, and are precomputed and stored in the computer. The ξ terms are referred to as ATR digits and are determined during each operation.

In the CORDIC computer, the ATR digits are determined sequentially, most significant digit first, and are used to control the conditional action of the adder-subtractors in the arithmetic unit. The following paragraphs contain a description of the manner in which the ATR code representation, $\xi_1 \xi_2 \xi_3 \ldots \xi_n$, can be determined for any given angle, λ or θ.

First, for any angle, λ or θ, there must be at least one set of values for the ξ operators that will

satisfy (20) or (21). Second, a simple technique must be available for determining the ATR code digits that satisfy these equations.

The following relationships are necessary and sufficient for any sequence of radix constants to meet the above requirements.

$$|\lambda \text{ or } \theta| \leq \alpha_1 + \alpha_2 + \alpha_3 + \ldots + \alpha_n + \alpha_n \qquad (26)$$

$$\alpha_i \leq \alpha_{i+1} + \alpha_{i+2} + \ldots + \alpha_n + \alpha_n \qquad (27)$$

For the satisfaction of the stipulative equations [(10) and (22)] it is required that λ or θ be represented

$$-180^\circ \leq \lambda \text{ or } \theta < +180^\circ \qquad (28)$$

Eq. (28) imposes no special consideration if the two's complement notation is used.

By employing an additional register and adder-subtractor (identified in Fig. 2 as the angle register) the relationship of (18) (ROTATION mode) can be instrumented by: (1) sensing the sign of the angle of ROTATION (or remainder if $i > 1$); and (2) either subtracting or adding to the angle the ATR constant corresponding to the particular step. In each step, the relationship instrumented is:

$$|\lambda_{i+1}| = ||\lambda_i| - \alpha_i| \qquad (29)$$

Execution of the first step of the nulling sequence to (26) results in

$$-\alpha_1 \leq |\lambda| - \alpha_1 \leq \alpha_2 + \alpha_3 + \ldots + \alpha_n + \alpha_n \qquad (30)$$

Application of the relationships of (27) results in

$$|\lambda_2| \equiv ||\lambda_1| - \alpha_1| \leq \alpha_2 + \alpha_3 + \ldots + \alpha_n + \alpha_n \qquad (31)$$

Continuation of the nulling sequence through α_n results in

$$|\lambda_{n+1}| \leq \alpha_n \qquad (32)$$

Eq. (32) can be used to prove that the remainder in the angle register converges to zero in the ROTATION mode.

The sequence of operation signs used to null λ to zero is the negative of the equivalent ATR code for the original angle λ_1. More simply, the ATR code digit of each step is equal to the sign of the quantity in the angle register before each step. Therefore, simultaneously with each nulling step in the angle register, the ATR code digit may be used to control the cross-addition step in the Y and X registers (shown in Fig. 2) to effect a rotation of components through an equal angular increment.

The proof of the convergence of the effective angular argument θ_{n+1} to zero, which is necessary in the VECTORING mode, may be obtained by replacing λ by θ in (29) through (32). In VECTORING, the sign of the angle θ_1 is obtained by sensing the sign of Y_1. The sequence of signs of Y_1 is the negative of the ATR code for the effective rotation performed on the components Y_1 and X_1. During each cross-addition operation in the Y and X register, the corresponding ATR constant can be conditionally added or subtracted, depending on ξ_1, to an accumulating sum in the angle register so that, at the end of the computing sequence, when $\theta_{n+1} = 0$, the quantity in the angle register will be equal to the original angular argument θ_1 of the coordinate components Y_1 and X_1.

The step-by-step results of a typical rotation computing sequence are shown in Table 1. The two's complement notation is used for all quantities, and for simplicity, shifted quantities are simply truncated without round-off.

The step-by-step results of a typical vectoring computing sequence are shown in Table 2.

Fig. 3 contains the solution flow for solving a typical navigation problem with the CORDIC computing technique. Specifically, this example shows the program sequence necessary for solving for the course angle and the distance-to-destination relationships in great circle steering.

Each operation of the computing sequence is represented by a box containing the X, Y and Angle registers. The particular operation performed is abbreviated as follows:

R_o = Rotation,

V_e = Vectoring,

M_u = Multiplication.

The explicit equations solved are

Table 1.

Typical ROTATION Computing Sequence

Y Register	X Register	Angle Register
0.0101110	1.1000101	$0.1100101 = \lambda$
+1.1000101	-0.0101110	$-0.1000000 \ \tan^{-1} \infty$
1.1000101	1.1010010	0.0100101
+1.1010010	-1.1000101	$-0.0100000 \ \tan^{-1} 1$
1.0010111	0.0001101	0.0000101
+0.0000110	-1.1001011	$-0.0010010 \ \tan^{-1} 2^{-1}$
1.0011101	0.1000010	1.1110011
-0.0010000	+1.1100111	$+0.0001001 \ \tan^{-1} 2^{-2}$
1.0001101	0.0101001	1.1111100
-0.0000101	+1.1110001	$+0.0000101 \ \tan^{-1} 2^{-3}$
1.0001000	0.0011010	0.0000001
+0.0000001	-1.1111000	$-0.0000010 \ \tan^{-1} 2^{-4}$
1.0001001	0.0100010	1.1111111
-0.0000001	+1.1111100	$+0.0000001 \ \tan^{-1} 2^{-5}$
1.0001000	0.0011110	0.0000000

$$C_A = \tan^{-1} \frac{\cos \lambda_D \sin(L_D - L_A)}{\sin \lambda_D \cos \lambda_A - \cos \lambda_D \sin \lambda_A \cos(L_D - L_A)} \qquad (33)$$

$$d = \tan^{-1} \frac{\cos \lambda_D \sin(L_D - L_A)}{\sin C_A [\sin \lambda_D \sin \lambda_A + \cos \lambda_D \cos \lambda_A \cos(L_D - L_A)]} \qquad (34)$$

where

C_A = course angle to destination

d = distance to destination

λ_A = present latitude

L_A = present longitude

λ_D = latitude destination

L_D = longitude of destination.

The form of (33) and (34) cannot be used for establishing the CORDIC solution-flow diagram. It is necessary to express the relationship with some form of rotation operators, such as rotation matrices; a similar change in form is also necessary for establishing analog resolver solution-flow diagrams. The only difference between Fig. 3 and an equivalent analog resolver solution flow diagram is the insertion of multiplication routines to compensate for the magnitude change factor K of each trigonometric operation. Note that, although five trigonometric operations are performed,

Table 2.

Typical VECTORING Computing Sequence

Y Register	X Register	Angle Register
0.0101110	1.1000101	0.0000000
-1.1000101	+0.0101110	+0.1000000 $\tan^{-1} \infty$
0.0111011	0.0101110	0.1000000
-0.0101110	+0.0111011	+0.0100000 $\tan^{-1} 1$
0.0001101	0.1101001	0.1100000
-0.0110100	+0.0000110	+0.0010010 $\tan^{-1} 2^{-1}$
1.1011001	0.1101111	0.1110010
+0.0011011	-1.1110110	-0.0001001 $\tan^{-1} 2^{-2}$
1.1110100	0.1111001	0.1101001
+0.0001111	-1.1111110	-0.0000101 $\tan^{-1} 2^{-3}$
0.0000011	0.1111011	0.1100100
-0.0000111	+0.0000000	+0.0000010 $\tan^{-1} 2^{-4}$
1.1111100	0.1111011	0.1100110
+0.0000011	-1.1111111	-0.0000001 $\tan^{-1} 2^{-5}$
1.1111111	0.1111100 = KR_1	0.1100101 = θ

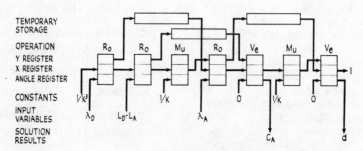

Fig. 3. Solution flow diagram

only two multiplication operations
are necessary.

CONCLUSION

The CORDIC computing technique
is especially suitable for use in a
special-purpose computer where the
majority of the computations involve
trigonometric relationships. In
general, the ROTATION and VECTORING
operations should be considered
constant-length routines in which
the number of word times per operation is euqal to the word length.

While not covered in this paper,
similar algorithms have been developed for multiplication, division,
conversion between binary and mixed
radix systems, extractions of square
root, hyperbolic coordinate transformations, exponentiation and generation of logarithms.

It is believed that similar
algorithms based on this fundamental concept of computation could be
developed for many other computing
requirements.

Amdahl, G. M., 218
Anderson, D. W., 218
Anderson, S. F., 193-218
Avizienis, A., 162
Bell, C. G., 220
Birkhoff, G., 264
Blaauw, G. A., 218
Block, E., 161
Booth, A. D., 163-166
Borck, W. C., 285-296
Britten, K. H. V., 166
Brooks, F. P., Jr., 218
Buckholtz, W., 218
Burks, A., 78, 161, 166, 221-259
Burtsey, V. S., 161
Caldwell, S. H., 100, 114
Campbell, S. J., 161
Cauturat, L., 24
Chen, T. C., 218
Conti, C. J., 276
Dadda, L., 167-180
Dickson, L. E., 192
Dolotta, T. A., 114
Earle, J. G., 193-218
Eccles, W. H., 299-301
Felker, J. H., 78
Frieman, C. V., 162
Garner, H. L., 181-192
Gibson, D. H., 276
Gilchrist, B., 161
Gimpel, J. F., 114
Goldschmidt, R. E., 193-218
Goldstine, H., 161, 166, 221-259
Hamming, R. W., 100
Hardy, G. H., 192
Huffman, D. A., 78, 100, 114
Huntington, E. V., 24
Jarvis, D. H., 180
Jeeves, T. A., 296
Jeffrey, R. C., 265
Jordan, F. W., 299-301
Karnaugh, M., 25-36, 56, 78
Keister, W., 36, 56, 78
Lehman, M., 161
Leiner, A. L., 78, 161
Liptay, J. S., 271, 276
Liu, C. N., 114

MacSorley, O. L., 118-162, 218
McCluskey, E. J., 37-57, 114
McReynolds, R. C., 285-296
Mealy, G. H., 58-78
Moore, E. F., 2, 78
Morgan, L. P., 180
Murray, F. J., 78
Nelson, E. C., 78
Newell, A., 220
Notz, W. A., 78
Paull, M. C., 114
Petrick, S. R., 114
Pitkowsky, S. H., 276
Pomerene, J. H., 161
Powers, D. M., 193-218
Quine, W. V., 57
Reed, I. S., 260-265
Rey, T. J., 166
Ritchie, A. E., 36, 56, 78
Robertson, J. E., 161
Rosser, G. H., Jr., 161
Sechler, R. F., 218
Shannon, C. E., 3-24, 56, 78
Slotnick, D. L., 285-296
Smith, J. L., 78, 161
Spencer, R. E., 166
Sprague, R. E., 265
Strube, A. K., 218
Svoboda, A., 192
Thornton, J. E., 277-284
Tomasulo, R. M., 218
Tracey, J. H., 101-114
Turnbull, J. R., 218
Unger, S. H., 79-100, 114
Valach, M., 192
Veitch, E. W., 36
Volder, J. E., 301-307
von Neumann, J., 161, 166, 221-259
Wallace, C. S., 180, 218
Washburn, S. H., 36, 56, 78
Wearer, J. A., 180
Weinberger, A., 78, 161
Whitehead, A. N., 24
Wilkes, M. V., 218, 266-270
Wong, S. Y., 161
Wright, E. M., 192
Wright, J. B., 78